THE ONE YEAR® SPORTS DEVOTIONS ~FOR~ KIDS

Jesse Florea

Jeremy Jones

Joshua Cooley

Tyndale House Publishers, Inc.
CAROL STREAM, ILLINOIS

Visit Tyndale's website for kids at www.tyndale.com/kids.

TYNDALE, Tyndale's quill logo, The One Year, and One Year are registered trademarks of Tyndale House Publishers, Inc.

The Tyndale Kids logo and the One Year logo are trademarks of Tyndale House Publishers, Inc.

The One Year Sports Devotions for Kids

For manufacturing information regarding this product, please call 1-800-323-9400.

ISBN 978-1-4143-4973-2

Printed in the United States of America

20	19	18	17	16	15
7	6	5	4	3	2

Who wants to go jump in a frozen lake? No takers. Okay, how about a quick dip in a freezing-cold ocean? Still nobody. Hmmm.

Well, about 1,000 people joined the Coney Island Polar Bear Club for its annual New Year's Day swim in the Atlantic Ocean in 2010. With so many human popsicles bobbing in 44-degree water, the club president said it was the biggest turnout ever for this New York City tradition!

The Coney Island Polar Bear Club is the oldest winter swimming organization in the United States. Every weekend from November through April, members gather at Coney Island to swim in the Atlantic. Water temperatures start in the low 60s at the beginning of the season, but they have been known to dip down into the mid-30s. The club was founded in 1903 by Bernarr Macfadden, who believed taking a dip in the chilly ocean could keep people healthy.

What's the Score?

The annual New Year's Day dip drew quite a crowd. Some came so they could wear a bathing suit and a Russian fur hat at the same time. But the real motivation was to raise money for children with life-threatening illnesses. The 2010 swim brought in about $25,000 to help kids.

Every year on New Year's Day people talk about making changes for the better. They plan to exercise more, eat healthier foods, and be nicer to their families. Some of these resolutions don't last long. This New Year's Day, come up with a plan of how you can make a difference with the talents and gifts God has given you. In Romans 12:7-8, the apostle Paul says everybody has a gift: "If your gift is serving others, serve them well. If you are a teacher, teach well. If your gift is to encourage others, be encouraging. If it is giving, give generously." With your God-given gifts, you can make a positive impact on the people in your life. And you don't have to jump into a freezing ocean to do it.

) On the Ball

What are your talents? List some here:

Now think of ways you can use those talents to help other people and to honor God.

) COACH'S COMMENT

If your gift is serving others, serve them well. If you are a teacher, teach well. If your gift is to encourage others, be encouraging. If it is giving, give generously. If God has given you leadership ability, take the responsibility seriously. And if you have a gift for showing kindness to others, do it gladly. ROMANS 12:7-8

The game shouldn't have been that close. When Nebraska faced Miami in the 1984 Orange Bowl for college football's national championship, the Cornhuskers entered the game as 10½-point favorites.

But with just seconds on the clock, Nebraska found itself trailing 31–30. The Cornhuskers had just scored with a fourth-and-eight play as quarterback Turner Gill pitched the ball to running back Jeff Smith for a 24-yard touchdown. All Nebraska had to do was kick an extra point to tie the game and end the season as undefeated national champions. (This game occurred before the NCAA played overtime in football.) Instead of going for the tie, Nebraska coach Tom Osborne chose to attempt a two-point conversion to win the game.

With the season on the line, Turner looked to again connect with Jeff. The quarterback rolled to his right and threw a pass into the end zone. But at the last instant, a Miami defensive back tipped the ball away to earn the Hurricanes the victory and the national championship!

⬜⬜ What's the Score?

The high-powered Nebraska offense had averaged 52 points a game en route to building a perfect 12–0 record. At one point during the season, the Cornhuskers managed to score seven touchdowns in just 12 minutes. Miami, on the other hand, had lost its season opener, but then stacked up a 10-game winning streak to make it into the Orange Bowl.

With three of the best football players in the country—Turner Gill, Mike Rozier, and Irving Fryar—Nebraska planned to defeat the Hurricanes with ease. But with Mike injured and Miami playing a great game, things didn't go as planned.

Has that ever happened to you? You thought you had a sure thing, but then the outcome you expected didn't happen at all. God wants us to plan and prepare for the future. But as we plan, we should also remember that God controls what happens in our lives. The book of Proverbs reminds us, "No human wisdom or understanding or plan can stand against the LORD." His plans are best. And his plans never fail!

⟩ On the Ball

As you make plans for this year, be sure to include God. Only God walks with you throughout your entire life. Always seek to do his will as you make your plans.

⟩ COACH'S COMMENT

No human wisdom or understanding or plan can stand against the LORD. **PROVERBS 21:30**

Maybe you've seen him in McDonald's commercials. A short, dark-haired boy with hands that move faster than your eyes can see. Steven Purugganan can stack cups in record speed. In fact, he set the world record in the individual cycle stack in sport stacking at the Greater Cleveland Ohio Sport Stacking Championships on January 3, 2009.

If you haven't seen this event, a competitor in the cycle stack must begin with 12 cups divided into three stacks. He starts by building pyramids of three, six, and three cups. Then he tears those down and creates two six-cup pyramids. Finally, he rips those apart and forms a 10-cup pyramid with one cup on each side. The last move has the athlete slide those cups down until he ends up the way he started with three stacks of cups.

It probably took you about 25 seconds to read that description of the cycle stack. Steven performed all those moves in 5.93 seconds! (You can see a video of speedy sport stackers like Steven on YouTube or by going to worldsportstackingassociation.org.)

Of course, Steven didn't always stack perfectly. Sometimes his cups fell down. A rule in sport stacking says an athlete must go back and fix his mistakes or his time doesn't count. Steven may have been young, but he knew to always fix his fumbles.

⬜ What's the Score?

Wouldn't it be cool if we could always go back and fix our mistakes? Maybe we'd study harder for that test. Maybe we'd remember to take out the trash like our parents asked. Maybe we wouldn't say the mean comment to the new kid.

The cool thing about the Christian life is that we can be forgiven for our past mistakes when we ask for God's forgiveness. That doesn't mean there won't be consequences for what we've done, but it does mean we don't have to walk around feeling guilty about our former fumbles. When we do something mean or don't follow through on a promise, we have the opportunity to go back to the person we wronged and say, "I'm sorry." The same thing is true about our relationship with Jesus Christ. When we sin, we need to ask him for forgiveness as well. First John 1:9 says, "If we confess our sins to him, he is faithful and just to forgive us our sins and to cleanse us from all wickedness." Isn't it cool that God promises to always forgive us when we fumble?

⟩ On the Ball

Is there a person you need to find to say, "I'm sorry"? Make a plan to ask for forgiveness.

⟩ COACH'S COMMENT

If we confess our sins to him, he is faithful and just to forgive us our sins and to cleanse us from all wickedness. 1 JOHN 1:9

Think of your most embarrassing moment. Maybe you accidentally called your teacher "Mom." Perhaps you laughed so hard at a friend's joke in the lunchroom that milk spurted out of your nose. Or maybe you tripped over your own feet as you were breaking away for the winning goal in a soccer game.

Those are all embarrassing (and the milk thing is a little gross), but probably not a lot of people witnessed your blunder. So can you imagine what it'd be like to be remembered for a mistake you made in front of an entire nation?

During the 1929 Rose Bowl, University of California star Roy Riegels picked up a fumble by Georgia Tech and ran 65 yards in the wrong direction. Instead of running 30 yards into the Golden Bears' end zone for a touchdown, Roy got turned around and ran the wrong way in front of tens of thousands of people in the stadium and hundreds of thousands listening on the radio. One radio announcer started shouting, "What am I seeing? What's wrong with me? Am I crazy? Am I crazy? Am I crazy?"

Roy nearly ran into his own end zone, but teammate Benny Lom caught up with Roy and screamed at him to stop. He did—on the three-yard line, where he was quickly tackled. For the rest of his life, he was known as Roy "Wrong Way" Riegels.

What's the Score?

So what does running the wrong way on a football field have to do with following Jesus Christ? A lot, actually. As you grow up, you might see some of your friends making bad decisions and going the wrong way in life. Maybe they'll use words they shouldn't. Maybe their actions will be harmful. As a Christian, you need to care enough to say, "Hey, you're heading in the wrong direction."

Benny cared enough for Roy to chase after him and tell him to turn around. That's exactly what God wants us to do. In the Bible, God commands, "Those who love God must also love their Christian brothers and sisters" (1 John 4:21). Sometimes showing love means standing up to a friend who's making a bad decision. Always try to be a good "teammate," and encourage your friends to go the right way.

) On the Ball

Do you know a friend who says he or she is a Christian but doesn't act like one? If so, you may want to tell your friend to get moving in the right direction.

) COACH'S COMMENT

He has given us this command: Those who love God must also love their Christian brothers and sisters. 1 JOHN 4:21

Can one player win a football game by himself? Probably not. But it certainly felt that way after Texas defeated the University of Southern California (USC) 41–38 in the 2006 BCS National Championship game. Texas quarterback Vince Young ran for 200 yards, passed for 267, and seemed to make every big play when the Longhorns needed it—including the biggest play of the game with 19 seconds on the clock.

Texas trailed the Trojans 38–33, and time was running out. It appeared as if USC would win its 35th game in a row and its third straight national championship when Texas was stuck on the nine-yard line and faced a fourth-and-five play. Vince took the ball and quickly looked for an open receiver. Almost immediately he got pressured from a USC defender on his left. Quickly tucking the ball, Vince sprinted to his right. His long strides took him past a diving defender and into the end zone for a 39–38 lead. Vince added a two-point conversion on the next play to make the final score 41–38.

⬜⬜ What's the Score?

Vince's heroics capped a stunning Texas comeback. Texas trailed 38–26 with 6:42 left in the fourth quarter. First, Vince ran in a touchdown from 17 yards away with four minutes left. Then he scored the winning touchdown—his third of the game. Justifiably, Vince was voted Most Valuable Player and given a crystal trophy. To many fans, it appeared as if Vince had won the game by himself.

But Vince knew better. He saw how the Texas defense had stopped the talented USC offense twice late in the game. He noticed how hard his offensive linemen and receivers had blocked for him. They deserved credit too.

Everybody can't be the quarterback. It's that way in the Christian life as well. Different people have different roles in God's body. Not everybody receives the same amount of attention and praise. But 1 Corinthians 12:22 tells us, "Some parts of the body that seem weakest and least important are actually the most necessary." No matter what you do for God's kingdom—even if you think it goes unnoticed—remember that you're a vital part of the body.

⟩ On the Ball

The Bible says every part of the body is important. If you end up serving behind the scenes, do your best, because you're a necessary part of God's body.

⟩ COACH'S COMMENT

There are many parts, but only one body. The eye can never say to the hand, "I don't need you." The head can't say to the feet, "I don't need you." In fact, some parts of the body that seem weakest and least important are actually the most necessary.

1 CORINTHIANS 12:20-22

How much time do you spend playing video games every day? Studies say the average kid spends 49 minutes a day video gaming. That's about the same amount of time that the average child spends reading each day.

Being balanced is a good thing. But in 2010, David Scherer of Clarksville, Tennessee, got a little out of whack. He spent 55 straight hours with a controller in his hand to set a world record for longest time spent playing a video game.

To David's credit, he normally wasn't a couch potato. He set a good example for kids as a swim coach and by staying busy at school and volunteering in his community. In fact, his reason for setting the world record was to raise money for his swim team to have a consistent place to practice. But still, 55 straight hours . . . yikes!

What's the Score?

Many kids spend too much time playing video games. And if it's not video games, a lot of other distractions can rob our time. Research shows that some kids spend about seven-and-a-half hours every day watching TV, playing video games, and being on the Internet. That's more than 52 hours a week, which is more than a full-time job!

It's important to make the most of your time. The Bible says, "Look carefully then how you walk, not as unwise but as wise, making the best use of the time, because the days are evil" (Ephesians 5:15-16, ESV). As you think about the things that you do, are there any changes you need to make to your schedule? Do you spend enough time with your friends? Do you help out enough around the house? Are you taking care of your pets? Or do you spend a lot of time by yourself in front of the TV or computer? The good habits you start now by managing your time will really help you as you grow.

) On the Ball

Do you need to change how you use your time? Create a plan to make the most of your time. Write down the top three things that you do with your time (don't count sleeping):

Now write down the top three things that you'd like to do with your time:

Time is a gift from God—use your gift wisely.

> COACH'S COMMENT

Look carefully then how you walk, not as unwise but as wise, making the best use of the time, because the days are evil. **EPHESIANS 5:15-16 (ESV)**

The Harlem Globetrotters are one of the most famous sports teams in the world. In fact, it was on this day in 1927 that the Globetrotters played their first game. The funny thing is, the Globetrotters began in Chicago, not the Harlem area of New York City. Plus, the team wasn't filled with globetrotters at all—they were athletes from Wendell Phillips High School on the south side of Chicago. Abe Saperstein, who founded the team, just wanted potential audiences to think his squad had traveled the globe.

The Globetrotters got paid $75 for playing their first game in Hinckley, Illinois. They didn't travel with their own opponent back then like they do today (oh, the poor Washington Generals, who have lost more than 10,000 straight games to the Globetrotters). Instead they drove around the United States and played anybody who'd pay them to come. During their first season, the Globetrotters amassed an impressive record of 101–16.

In 1939, the Harlem Globetrotters started adding silly antics to their games. They'd do fancy ball-handling skills and comedic routines. Fans loved it, but Abe warned the team only to be silly after it had built up a solid lead. Today, the Globetrotters have played in more than 115 countries in front of over 120 million fans.

⛹ What's the Score?

What's the first word that comes to mind when you think of the Harlem Globetrotters? If you've seen the team play, that word is probably *fun*. The Globetrotters make basketball fun. Sure, they show amazing skill, but their goal is to make everybody smile and have a good time.

Have you ever been to church or hung out with people who didn't smile? It's not much fun. It's okay for Christians to have fun. In fact, God wants us to enjoy life and have fun. Ecclesiastes 8:15 says, "I recommend having fun, because there is nothing better for people in this world than to eat, drink, and enjoy life." Of course, we also have to work hard and take care of our responsibilities. But with a little creativity, we can make our work fun—just like the Harlem Globetrotters do.

⟩ On the Ball

What's your least favorite thing to do? How can you make that thing more fun? Be creative. It's good to have fun, to be happy, and to work hard.

⟩ COACH'S COMMENT

I recommend having fun, because there is nothing better for people in this world than to eat, drink, and enjoy life. That way they will experience some happiness along with all the hard work God gives them under the sun. **ECCLESIASTES 8:15**

Hours before the 2009 BCS National Championship game, Florida Gators coaches had a problem: they couldn't find a bunch of their players. As the Florida coaches began to get worried and angry, they walked past star quarterback Tim Tebow's hotel room and heard something strange—singing.

Tim, who was born in the Philippines to a missionary family, was never shy about sharing his faith in Jesus Christ. He wore Bible verses on his eye black during college football games and always gave credit to God for his performances. Just hours before the biggest football game of his life, Tim had been reading his Bible and found a passage that he wanted to share with his teammates. He called about 15 players to his room, where he read them Matthew 11:28-29: "Then Jesus said, 'Come to me, all of you who are weary and carry heavy burdens, and I will give you rest. Take my yoke upon you. Let me teach you, because I am humble and gentle at heart, and you will find rest for your souls.'" Soon the room came alive with the players singing praises to God.

⛶ What's the Score?

The Florida Gators went on to win the national championship 24–14 over the Oklahoma Sooners. With the game tied 14–14 to begin the fourth quarter, Tim led the Gators on two scoring drives. First, Florida kicked a field goal with less than 11 minutes to play. Then with 3:07 left in the game, Tim threw a four-yard touchdown pass to David Nelson that wrapped up the victory. Tim ended with 231 passing yards, including two touchdowns and two interceptions. He also rushed for 109 yards.

Tim had an incredible amount of pressure on him to win the national championship. Instead of letting his nerves get the better of him, he gave his worries to God. Through years of trusting God and learning his Word, Tim knew God was big enough to handle anything that happened to him. By trusting in God's peace, Tim was able to come through with big plays during extremely stressful times.

⟩ On the Ball

What makes you worry? Is it schoolwork? tests? doing chores? a big game? Everybody runs into stressful situations. When you're feeling overwhelmed, be sure to turn to God. He has the strength and can give you the peace to make it through anything.

⟩ COACH'S COMMENT

Jesus said, "Come to me, all of you who are weary and carry heavy burdens, and I will give you rest. Take my yoke upon you. Let me teach you, because I am humble and gentle at heart, and you will find rest for your souls." MATTHEW 11:28-29

Nobody brings the saying "like a hot knife through butter" to life better than Ali Bahcetepe. If you've ever heated up a knife and cut into butter or warmed up a scoop and dipped it into ice cream, you know how easily the warm knife or scoop glides through.

Well, Ali wasn't interested in food. Instead of taking a knife through butter, he took his hands and sliced through concrete blocks.

On January 9, 2009, Ali smashed 888 concrete blocks in one minute. That means he broke nearly 15 of them every second! Fifteen a second! (That fact is so amazing, it's worth reading twice.)

People who witnessed this feat on a cold morning in Madrid, Spain, said that the Turkish martial-arts expert made it look easy. Dressed in simple white with a black belt around his waist, Ali stared at 1,020 blocks. They were lined up in stacks of 10 on either side of him. His hands were wrapped with tape, and a towel was draped over each stack to protect him from the rough concrete. When the timer began, Ali stepped forward, drove both hands down and crushed the first two stacks of blocks. His hands continued to work like two jackhammers, breaking 20 blocks with every "Hiya!" When one minute had expired, 888 blocks lay in pieces, and Ali had set a new world record.

⬜⬜ What's the Score?

Breaking nearly 900 blocks in one minute is an amazing feat of strength. The Bible contains many stories of people accomplishing phenomenal deeds. Judges 13–16 tells the story of Samson.

Samson ripped apart a lion with his bare hands, killed 1,000 men with the jawbone of a donkey, and carried massive city gates (that probably weighed 1,000 pounds) 38 miles up the side of a mountain. How was he able to do such awesome acts? The Bible is clear—the Spirit of the Lord.

God gave Samson the power to do things nobody had seen before. But when Samson disobeyed God by letting his hair be cut, God's power left him. However, after he was captured, Samson prayed to God to strengthen him one last time so he could bring down the temple of his enemy's false god (Judges 16:28). God gave him the strength to topple two huge stone pillars that supported the temple.

⟩ On the Ball

God's power can help you do amazing things. Pray and ask God to give you the power to accomplish things that will honor him.

⟩ COACH'S COMMENT

Samson prayed to the LORD, "Sovereign LORD, remember me again. O God, please strengthen me just one more time." JUDGES 16:28

In automotive sports, the relationship between man and machine is key to success. Bob Davis knew his machine—a 2005 Yamaha snowmobile—well. Bob and his snowmobile set a world record in 2008 when they traveled 12,163 grueling miles from January to March. That's like driving from Maine to San Diego, California, and back—twice! He started in Maine, went to Quebec and New Brunswick in Canada, and ended up back in Maine.

The former Marine helicopter pilot said the most difficult part of breaking the 60-day snowmobile record was being mentally tough. There were days when he just wanted to rest. But to achieve his goal, Bob knew he had to average 200 miles every single day. He was also aware of the dangers of the trip, so he packed plenty of food, clothing, emergency supplies, fuel, oil, and spare parts.

What's the Score?

Some of those parts came in handy. At one point, Bob drove through a slushy lake. The water froze and broke his driveshaft. On day 58, his rear suspension spring broke. But Bob said his snowmobile was super-reliable overall. He could trust it to perform every day.

Reliability. It means being trustworthy. Dependable. Think about those three words. Aren't those the exact characteristics you'd want in a friend? A friend who you can share your secrets with and know they won't be spread around. A friend who will always be there for you. A friend who sticks by you in good times and bad. Proverbs 20:6 says, "Many will say they are loyal friends, but who can find one who is truly reliable?"

As you look for reliable friends, don't forget to be a friend like that too. When you are reliable, trustworthy, and dependable, you're the kind of person people want for a friend.

) On the Ball

Do you have a reliable friend? If so, thank God for bringing that person into your life. And remember that Jesus is also that forever friend. He'll always be with you, and you can trust him with anything or with any problems that come your way.

) COACH'S COMMENT

Many will say they are loyal friends, but who can find one who is truly reliable?
PROVERBS 20:6

Some plays in sports become so famous that they're simply known by a couple of words. In the AFC Championship game on January 11, 1987, Denver Broncos quarterback John Elway led his team on what will forever be known as "The Drive."

Playing at Cleveland to decide who would go to the Super Bowl, the Broncos found themselves sitting on the two-yard line with five minutes left on the clock and trailing 20–13. In swirling winds and falling temperatures, John led the Broncos on a 15-play drive against the Browns' tough defense. The right side of John's uniform was caked with mud, but that didn't stop him from running for first downs or throwing pinpoint passes. John converted a third-and-18 play with less than two minutes in the game when he rifled a ball to Mark Jackson on Cleveland's 28-yard line. Then with 31 seconds left, John threw a low fastball to Mark in the end zone for a touchdown!

⬜⬜ What's the Score?

The Broncos continued the momentum from "The Drive" into overtime. They got the ball first and went 60 yards in nine plays to kick a field goal and win the game, 23–20. John Elway and his teammates' perseverance had paid off in a trip to the Super Bowl.

Perseverance is a big word. Simply put, it's the power of persistence in pursuit of an objective. (Try saying that 10 times fast!) It didn't take the Broncos one big play to reach their goal. It took 15 little ones. Perseverance is a process. Second Peter 1:5-7 says, "For this very reason, make every effort to add to your faith goodness; and to goodness, knowledge; and to knowledge, self-control; and to self-control, perseverance; and to perseverance, godliness; and to godliness, mutual affection; and to mutual affection, love" (NIV). When you persevere, you can win on the playing field and in your faith.

⟩ On the Ball

At the beginning of a new year, it's good to look at your goals for the next 12 months. What would you like to accomplish? Some goals aren't easy. You'll have to go step by step. Write down your goals for different areas of life:

At school, I want to _____ .

In my activities, I want to _____ .

In my personal life, I want to _____ .

In my relationship with God, I want to _____ .

⟩ COACH'S COMMENT

For this very reason, make every effort to add to your faith goodness; and to goodness, knowledge; and to knowledge, self-control; and to self-control, perseverance; and to perseverance, godliness; and to godliness, mutual affection; and to mutual affection, love. 2 PETER 1:5-7 (NIV)

"I guarantee it." People often guarantee that a candy bar will taste fresh or that a television will work a long time without breaking. But guaranteeing a victory in a game where you're a big underdog . . . nobody would be foolish enough to do that. Yet that's exactly what New York Jets quarterback Joe Namath did before Super Bowl III.

When the Super Bowl first started, the more experienced National Football League teams dominated the first two games against the new American Football League champions. (The leagues combined in 1970 as the NFL with two conferences—the NFC and the AFC.) But on January 12, 1969, the NFL's Baltimore Colts were heavily favored against the AFL's Jets. Before the game, the Colts were called "the greatest football team in history," while people joked that the Super Bowl would be the Jets' first professional football game. Joe got tired of the teasing. Three days before the game, a heckler yelled at Joe that the Jets didn't have a chance. Joe stopped and answered, "We're gonna win the game. I guarantee it."

What's the Score?

The Jets shocked the sporting world by defeating the Colts 16–7 in Super Bowl III. Joe completed 17 of 28 passes for 206 yards and was named the game's Most Valuable Player.

Although Joe backed up his boast, making promises you can't keep is dangerous. Had the Jets lost, Joe would've looked silly and been ridiculed for years. The Bible warns against making guarantees that you can't control. James 5:12 says, "Never take an oath, by heaven or earth or anything else. Just say a simple yes or no, so that you will not sin and be condemned." God wants you to always speak the truth. If you say yes, you need to come through. When you continually do what you say, you'll gain the trust and respect of the people around you.

) On the Ball

Words are powerful. As Christians, we need to watch what we say. Making a promise we can't keep or boasting about something that doesn't happen is the same as lying. Can you remember making a promise to someone that you didn't fulfill? If so, find that person, apologize, and fulfill your word.

) COACH'S COMMENT

Most of all, my brothers and sisters, never take an oath, by heaven or earth or anything else. Just say a simple yes or no, so that you will not sin and be condemned. JAMES 5:12

The yo-yo is the second oldest toy in the world. Experts believe only the doll was invented first. Before Jesus walked the earth as a child, kids had been playing with yo-yos. But perhaps in all of recorded history there has never been a more gifted "yo-yo-er" than Ben McPhee. In 2010, this talented Australian set a Guinness World Record by keeping 16 yo-yos spinning at the same time!

Ben managed this amazing feat at the London Annual Toy Fair. The old record was nine yo-yos, so Ben nearly doubled the mark. He had yo-yos hanging from hooks, spinning from his fingers, even dangling from his ears and teeth. One of the yo-yo strings actually got caught between his teeth and flossed out an old piece of meat. Just kidding.

☐☐ What's the Score?

The yo-yo may be an old toy, but some things haven't changed. You must still learn the fundamentals to make it work. Yo-yoing takes discipline to master. You have to flick your wrist just right and release the yo-yo at the correct angle. The string must be wound properly. Each twitch of a finger can cause it to do something different. Like any skill, to be a yo-yo master, you have to be disciplined.

Just as Ben practiced for countless hours before setting a yo-yo record, we have to put in a lot of time to be leaders in our Christian faith. The book of Titus describes what a leader in the church should look like. It says he shouldn't get angry easily and that he should share what he has with others. The apostle Paul also writes that a Christian leader should "live wisely and be just. He must live a devout and disciplined life" (Titus 1:8). Being disciplined is important to God.

⟩ On the Ball

What do you think it means to live a disciplined life? Basically, it means you think before you act and don't let any bad habits control you. Do you have any bad habits? Everybody does. The key is controlling them and not letting them rule your life. Pray to God to help you be disciplined and overcome your bad habits.

⟩ COACH'S COMMENT

He must love what is good. He must live wisely and be just. He must live a devout and disciplined life. TITUS 1:8

Who's the best professional football team of all time? If you want to start an argument, ask that question at a big family get-together and watch your uncles, cousins, or grandpa go at it.

There have been many excellent football teams over the years, but only one has gone undefeated for an entire season—the 1972 Miami Dolphins. The Dolphins went through the regular season with a perfect 14–0 record. Then they beat the Cleveland Browns and Pittsburgh Steelers in the play-offs. Finally, the Dolphins defeated the Washington Redskins 14–7 in Super Bowl VII to make their record 17–0.

Surprisingly, Miami entered the Super Bowl a three-point underdog to Washington. However, a stingy Redskin defense and an aggressive Dolphin running game helped the Dolphins build a 14–0 lead at halftime. The Redskins' only touchdown came with 2:07 left in the game when a botched Miami field goal was run back for a score. But 14–7 was as close as Washington would get as the underdog Dolphins completed their perfect season.

⬜⬜ What's the Score?

Having a perfect season is the dream of every NFL team. But it's not easy to be perfect. You probably feel that way too. You can try to be perfect, but it doesn't work out. Somebody may do something that causes you to get angry. You lie to your parents to avoid getting in trouble. You think nasty thoughts about a friend who has hurt you.

In the history of the world, only one person has lived perfectly: Jesus Christ. Jesus' thoughts and actions always reflected God. He knew the right way to handle every situation. When people mistreated him, he had the perfect response. Even though there's no way we can be perfect, our goal should be to follow Jesus' example. The apostle Paul, who wrote roughly half of the New Testament, said that he hadn't reached perfection, but he was going to try really hard to be perfect (Philippians 3:12). That's a good mind-set to have.

❯ On the Ball

Nobody can be perfect. But that doesn't mean we shouldn't try to follow the high standard that Jesus Christ set for us. With Jesus' help, we can live a life that will be celebrated for years to come.

❯ COACH'S COMMENT

I don't mean to say that I have already achieved these things or that I have already reached perfection. But I press on to possess that perfection for which Christ Jesus first possessed me. PHILIPPIANS 3:12

Trivia question: What popular children's toy inspired the name of the biggest single-day sporting event in the United States? Answer: the Super Ball.

It's true. When the NFL was trying to decide the name of its championship game, Kansas City Chiefs owner Lamar Hunt said the game should be called the "Super Bowl." He'd recently seen his kids playing with a Super Ball, and he liked the name. Until that point, NFL experts say the game was going to be called "The Big One." But when Lamar said "Super Bowl," the name stuck. And it's a good thing. Can you imagine saying, "Who won the Big One XLV?" That would sound weird. It's much cooler to say, "Who won Super Bowl 45?" The answer to either question is the Green Bay Packers.

Do you know who won the first Super Bowl? The answer is again . . . the Green Bay Packers. The Packers beat Lamar's Kansas City Chiefs 35–10. The game was close at halftime as Green Bay entered intermission ahead 14–10. But the Packers scored 21 second-half points to run away with the game.

⬜⬜ What's the Score?

Green Bay easily won the first Super Bowl thanks to the unlikely efforts of Max McGee. Max had caught only four passes all season, yet he caught seven passes for two touchdowns in the Super Bowl. Packers quarterback Bart Starr completed 16 of 23 passes for 250 yards (138 yards just to Max) to be named Most Valuable Player.

Max was an unlikely hero, just like the Super Bowl name came from an unlikely source. The Bible says that God uses things that seem foolish at first: "God chose things the world considers foolish in order to shame those who think they are wise. And he chose things that are powerless to shame those who are powerful" (1 Corinthians 1:27). Just because you have an idea that you think is silly, don't be afraid to share it. God can use you to make a difference. Just imagine what would've happened if Lamar didn't share his foolish idea about the Super Bowl. (By the way, Lamar's kids' Super Ball was put on display at the Pro Football Hall of Fame.)

) On the Ball

Don't be afraid to say something you believe just because other people may think it's foolish. God can use a seemingly silly idea to change the world. And he uses people of all ages to do his work.

) COACH'S COMMENT

God chose things the world considers foolish in order to shame those who think they are wise. And he chose things that are powerless to shame those who are powerful.

1 CORINTHIANS 1:27

Hockey's penalty shot is one of the most exciting plays in sports. It's just shooter versus goalie. The puck sits at center ice until the offensive player skates up to control it. Then the goalie comes out from the net to gain a better blocking angle. The skater must continually move toward the net, faking and dekeing as he approaches. Finally, a shot is taken. With the quality of NHL goalies, it's hard to score on a penalty shot. But at the 2009 All-Star Game, Phoenix Coyotes forward Shane Doan made it look easy as he won the Elimination Shootout competition.

Shane won the competition in the seventh round after displaying a dizzying array of shots and moves. A player was eliminated if the goalie blocked the goal. The finals came down to Shane, Marc Savard of the Boston Bruins, and Colorado Avalanche's Milan Hejduk. In the last round, Shane scored on a nifty bang-bang move as he slipped the puck between the goalie's legs. Marc and Milan were both turned away in their attempts.

What's the Score?

Shane grew up playing hockey in Halkirk, Alberta. Whether it was on a frozen pond, icy field, or community rink, Shane always had a pair of skates on his feet and a hockey stick in his hands. The only thing Shane was more passionate about than hockey was his relationship with Jesus Christ. While Shane was growing up, his parents were the directors of Circle Square Ranch, a Christian summer camp. Shane helped out as a counselor and even as a horsemanship instructor.

When Shane saw some of his friends get into things that went against his beliefs, he stayed close to Jesus. "The thing that it comes down to for me is Jesus loves you," Shane said. "Jesus loves you exactly the way you are, and he'll continue to love you no matter what."

The disciple John put it this way: "This is real love—not that we loved God, but that he loved us and sent his Son as a sacrifice to take away our sins" (1 John 4:10). When Shane thought about God's amazing love and sacrifice, he couldn't help but love God back and follow him with his life.

) On the Ball

Take a moment to think about God's love for you. "Jesus loves you" sounds like a simple statement, but there's so much meaning packed into it. Pray and thank God for his love and for the great sacrifice he made for you.

) COACH'S COMMENT

This is real love—not that we loved God, but that he loved us and sent his Son as a sacrifice to take away our sins. 1 JOHN 4:10

Are you ready for some octopush? Okay, that doesn't have the same ring as "Are you ready for some football?" Maybe that's why underwater hockey has never caught on big.

When Alan Blake invented underwater hockey in 1954 in Great Britain, he called the sport octopush because eight players worked together on a team to push the puck toward the goal. Of course, the puck was called a squid, and the goal was known as a gulley. Seriously. And you didn't use a stick; you played with a pusher.

To play underwater hockey, a player needs a mask, a snorkel, flippers, and a glove to protect his or her playing hand from the bottom of the pool. Participants must hold their breaths, dive under the water, and attempt to knock the squid toward their opponent's gully. Stop laughing; it's a real sport. In 1976, the British Octopush Association was founded to govern the sport. Today, underwater hockey is played in more than 40 countries and is especially popular in Australia, New Zealand, South Africa, the United States, and Canada.

What's the Score?

Underwater hockey may sound a bit strange, but it takes a lot of strategy and skill to do well. The modern game has six players from each team in the water at a time, and it's important that somebody's always underwater battling for the puck. The problem is that most players can hold their breaths for only 15 to 20 seconds at a time, so athletes are always going up to the surface.

Being able to breathe is important in underwater hockey and in life. The Bible talks a lot about breath, especially about the power of God's breath. When Moses led the Israelites out of captivity in Egypt, they got stuck at the Red Sea. Instead of telling his people to jump in and try to hold their breaths to swim across, God used his breath to part the waters. After Moses and the Israelites passed through the Red Sea, they sang a praise song to God that said, "At the blast of your breath, the waters piled up" (Exodus 15:8).

) On the Ball

Read Moses' song to God in Exodus 15:1-18. Now write your own praise song to God about what he's done in your life. Maybe you can even write about how God gave you breath.

) COACH'S COMMENT

At the blast of your breath, the waters piled up! The surging waters stood straight like a wall; in the heart of the sea the deep waters became hard. EXODUS 15:8

Most kids learn about Jackie Robinson in school. They know that Jackie was the first African American to sign a major league contract and that he suffered threats and racial taunts. But few people know the story of Willie O'Ree.

Eleven years after Jackie broke the color barrier in baseball, Willie became the first African American to play in the National Hockey League. On this day in 1958, Willie laced up his skates and took the ice for the Boston Bruins in a game against Montreal.

Boston had suffered a number of injuries to its team so they called up Willie from the Quebec Aces to play left wing. Willie, who was known for his fast skating, did his job well filling in for the Bruins. Later, Willie admitted that some fans and opposing players called him names, but he said his Boston teammates always supported him.

⬚⬚ What's the Score?

There wasn't a lot of fanfare when Willie broke the color barrier in hockey. He was the best player in the Boston farm system, so he got called up to do a job. Interestingly, Willie only had one eye, but he never complained or mentioned it to anybody. Even Boston coach Milt Schmidt didn't know Willie was partially blind.

Willie was a great example that race and physical limitations shouldn't determine how a person is viewed. When Jesus looks at all of us, he sees every part of us, including our skin color, as part of his perfect creation. When God's Son came to earth and died on a cross, he shed his blood for all people. Romans 10:12 tells us, "Jew and Gentile are the same in this respect. They have the same Lord, who gives generously to all who call on him." Everyone has an equal opportunity to pray and accept Jesus as Savior. He generously gives his love and grace to all people—and we should do the same.

⟩ On the Ball

Have you ever seen another child be put down for the color of his or her skin or a physical limitation? Maybe it's even happened to you. Pray and thank God that he sees all of us as his perfect creation. Then try to be a friend to all kinds of people.

⟩ COACH'S COMMENT

Jew and Gentile are the same in this respect. They have the same Lord, who gives generously to all who call on him. ROMANS 10:12

To play on an undefeated team is a dream for many athletes. But can you imagine playing for a team that didn't lose a game for nearly three years? That's what the University of California Los Angeles (UCLA) men's basketball team did. From January 23, 1971, until January 19, 1974, the team won 88 straight games! The Bruins were so dominant in those days that they won the NCAA championship seven years in a row, from 1967 to 1973. That's seven consecutive national championships!

UCLA's 88-game winning streak came to an end against Notre Dame in a contest the Bruins should have won. UCLA built a 17-point lead in the first half and was ahead 70–59 with 3:30 remaining on the clock. However, the Fighting Irish scored the last 12 points of the game to win 71–70. Dwight Clay nailed a jump shot from the corner to give Notre Dame a one-point lead with 28 seconds left. UCLA got six shots at the basket in the last 21 seconds, but every shot was missed as the Bruins' amazing winning streak came to an end.

What's the Score?

Leading by 11 points with less than four minutes in the game, UCLA didn't expect to lose. But the Bruins got sloppy. They turned over the ball several times and missed their shots. The Bruins didn't remain diligent until the final buzzer.

As believers in Jesus Christ, we need to stay diligent in following him until the end of our lives. The Bible warns about losing our focus. The apostle John says to be diligent to get the reward that we worked hard to achieve (2 John 1:8). Sometimes, standing up for God and following him will be hard. Being a Christian isn't always a popular choice. But when we remain diligent in following God, our reward is way better than a championship trophy—it's living with him forever in heaven.

On the Ball

Don't get lazy in your Christian faith. Be diligent in following Jesus. Your reward in heaven will be worth it!

COACH'S COMMENT

Watch out that you do not lose what we have worked so hard to achieve. Be diligent so that you receive your full reward. 2 JOHN 1:8

Figure skaters make jumping and spinning on a quarter-inch-thick metal blade look effortless. And nobody did it better than Michelle Kwan. Michelle has won more figure-skating titles than anybody in US history. But her first title came on this day in 1996 as she claimed the US Figure Skating Championship in San Jose, California.

Just 15 years old at the time, Michelle skated a nearly flawless long program to win the title. She started the routine with a triple lutz, double toe-loop jump combination. Michelle landed all her triple jumps and showed her artistry with beautiful spiral sequences and blurring spins. Her only mistake came at the end of the program as she did a single axel instead of a double. When the music ended, Michelle laughed at her error and bowed to the adoring crowd. Her scores of mainly 5.8 in the technical areas and 5.9 in presentation easily earned her the championship.

⬜⬜ What's the Score?

During her skating career, Michelle won 42 championships, including nine US titles and five world championships. Her smile, work ethic, and athleticism were characteristics that young skaters around the world wanted to emulate. But the attribute that most came to mind when people talked about Michelle was grace. She was graceful on the ice and demonstrated grace off the ice as well.

Grace is a key word when it comes to our Christian faith. Instead of giving us what we deserve for all our sins, God showed us grace by sending Jesus to earth to pay the penalty. Titus 3:7 reminds us, "Because of his grace he declared us righteous and gave us confidence that we will inherit eternal life."

Some people remember what grace means by using this acronym: God's Riches At Christ's Expense. We get to experience the kingdom of heaven even though we deserve hell. There's nothing we could ever do to earn God's grace, but he gives it to us freely. We can be confident that we'll live forever with him.

❭ On the Ball

Memorize this acronym for grace: God's Riches At Christ's Expense. Remember to thank God for the grace he shows us every day even though we sin. Grace really is an amazing gift.

❭ COACH'S COMMENT

Because of his grace he declared us righteous and gave us confidence that we will inherit eternal life. TITUS 3:7

Usually tennis is thought of as a gentlemen's sport, but not when John McEnroe took the court. For 15 years, John was known as the bad boy of professional tennis. He'd complain about calls, yell at fans in the stands, and throw his racket when he made a bad shot. The only thing that could keep up with John's mouth was his amazing talent. From 1981 to 1984, he finished as the top-ranked player in the world, according to the Association of Tennis Professionals (ATP).

Sometimes John's bad attitude was a problem that even his talent couldn't overcome. At the 1990 Australian Open, John was disqualified from the tournament for his poor behavior. John was ahead of Mikael Pernfors when the umpire ended the match after citing John for his third unsportsmanlike conduct infraction.

John's first warning came in the third set when he stared at a lineswoman who made a call in Mikael's favor. Then in the fourth set, he missed a shot and slammed his racket to the ground. The umpire called him for "racket abuse." The final straw came when John argued against the racket abuse penalty and then called a tournament official a bad name. According to ATP rules, three infractions demanded an immediate disqualification. The match was given to Mikael.

□□ What's the Score?

Rarely do you see a professional athlete lose his cool with an official. From a young age, athletes are taught to respect the umpires. But John rarely finished a match without yelling at an umpire. Sometimes John was right. He knew the ball was in when it was called out, and he let his anger about the bad call explode. John won seven Grand Slam tournaments and 104 career singles titles. Yet some experts wonder how good John could've been had he been able to control his temper.

The Bible is clear. In Ecclesiastes 7:9, King Solomon (who's considered one of the wisest people in history) wrote, "Control your temper, for anger labels you a fool." John's anger often made him look foolish. Fans would boo his tantrums. Newspapers in Great Britain called him "SuperBrat." When you play sports or deal with people at school or church or home, do your best to keep your anger under control.

) On the Ball

Do you have a problem with anger? Write down a situation that made you angry:

Now pray and ask God to forgive you and to give you the strength and wisdom to handle the situation differently next time.

) COACH'S COMMENT

Control your temper, for anger labels you a fool. ECCLESIASTES 7:9

You wouldn't think an 11-time Winter X Games medalist would be nervous before a competition. But Tanner Hall admitted to reporters that he was a little nervous heading into the 2009 men's SuperPipe Finals in Aspen, Colorado.

Tanner, who had won a gold medal in the three previous years, knew that year's event would be a little different because the pipe was bigger. At the 2009 Winter X Games, the SuperPipe was 540 feet long, 22 feet deep, and 75 feet across, with a pitch of 18 degrees. In other words, it was longer, steeper, and more dangerous than the pipe had been in other competitions.

With the athletes going faster and higher, France's Xavier Bertoni shocked everybody by winning the gold with a score of 93.66. Tanner settled for silver with 92 points. Xavier's final run clinched the gold as he nailed an alley-oop flat spin 360, a switch 720, and a 1260 in which he spun around three-and-a-half times!

What's the Score?

Whether it was nerves or just the fact that another skier turned in an amazing performance, Tanner didn't end up winning a gold medal. He tried his hardest, but maybe his worries kept him from doing his best.

You've probably felt nervous before a big game or performance. It's natural to get butterflies in your stomach every once in a while. But the Bible encourages Christians not to worry. Philippians 4:6 says, "Don't worry about anything; instead, pray about everything. Tell God what you need, and thank him for all he has done."

When we worry, we tend to focus on our problems and not on God's power. But through God's power, we can overcome anything. It's okay to tell God what we need. Sometimes we need confidence. Sometimes it's strength or concentration. Whenever you start to worry, remember to turn to God and ask him to help calm your nerves.

) On the Ball

The next time you start to feel nervous, remember to pray to God and ask him to help you through the situation. And while you're praying, praise God for all he's done for you in the past.

) COACH'S COMMENT

Don't worry about anything; instead, pray about everything. Tell God what you need, and thank him for all he has done. PHILIPPIANS 4:6

By working together, families at St. Mary's Diocesan School for Girls in South Africa proved they could accomplish anything—including setting a new world record! Beginning on January 23, 2009, St. Mary's started a 24-hour swim-a-thon to raise money for the school. By the end of those 24 hours, 3,941 people had participated in the relay by swimming one length of the pool.

All those kicks and strokes set a new Guinness World Record for "most people swimming one length in a 24-hour relay." You didn't even know there was a world record for that, did you? Not only did St. Mary's accomplish a huge goal, but they also raised more than 400,000 rand (South African currency). Most of that money went to install heating equipment in the pool, while the rest was saved for other pool-related expenses.

What's the Score?

Which is harder: five people trading off laps and swimming for 24 hours or nearly 4,000 people swimming one lap each in the same time? The answer is obvious. St. Mary's came together as a community to easily set a record and to raise a lot of money.

As Christians, we need to have that same "team" attitude. God gives us the strength to make the right decisions and to accomplish big things on earth. When we work together with other believers, we can create a tidal wave of goodness. By speaking with one voice and coming together with one mind, we work as one body. The apostle Paul wrote, "May the God who gives endurance and encouragement give you the same attitude of mind toward each other that Christ Jesus had, so that with one mind and one voice you may glorify the God and Father of our Lord Jesus Christ" (Romans 15:5-6, NIV).

God gave us his Word so we can know him, understand how we should live, and stand up for the truth. When believers all stand up for the same thing, it creates a lot of teamwork. And in God's eyes, teamwork is a good thing.

) On the Ball

Do you see other kids at school or at church accomplishing big things? Is there something that needs to be improved in your neighborhood or school? Whether you're leading a movement or joining in the process, always look to work as a team.

) COACH'S COMMENT

May the God who gives endurance and encouragement give you the same attitude of mind toward each other that Christ Jesus had, so that with one mind and one voice you may glorify the God and Father of our Lord Jesus Christ. ROMANS 15:5-6 (NIV)

Scoring in some sports is easier than in others. A final score of 5–3 in a basketball game would be ridiculous because scoring is so simple. But a 2–1 hockey game is normal because getting the puck past a goalie and into the net is difficult. But in 1981, Mike Bossy of the New York Islanders made scoring goals look easy.

On this day in 1981, Mike entered a game against the Quebec Nordiques with 48 goals in the first 49 games of the season. He needed just two goals to notch 50 goals in 50 games—a feat that had only been accomplished by hockey great Maurice "Rocket" Richard during the 1944–45 season. Of course, the Nordiques knew Mike was close to tying the record, so they covered him like a blanket. For the first two periods, Mike rarely saw the puck and never got a shot on goal.

It looked like Mike's dream of tying the record would end, until he scored a power-play goal with just over four minutes remaining in the game. Minutes later, Mike got a perfect pass from Bryan Trottier and tallied his fiftieth goal of the year, setting off a huge celebration in the Nassau Coliseum.

⬚⬚ What's the Score?

When a lot of players would've thought the game was over, Mike Bossy worked extra hard to reach his goal of scoring 50 goals in the first 50 games. Have you ever been in a game when nothing was going right for you? Maybe your team wasn't passing the ball to you or a really good defender was guarding you. Did you give up or try harder? Mike tried harder. For more than 55 minutes of the hockey game, he didn't have a chance to score. Then bang-boom, he found the back of the net twice and made history.

The apostle Paul writes in Philippians 3:14, "I press on to reach the end of the race and receive the heavenly prize for which God, through Christ Jesus, is calling us." Whether it's a class at school or playing for a team, you need to try your hardest until the end of the race.

⟩ On the Ball

When you always try your best, you honor God. And when you give your best effort to follow Jesus and to live for him, you can accomplish great things. Reaching your goal in living for Jesus might not cause a celebration at the Nassau Coliseum, but it will create a huge party in heaven.

⟩ COACH'S COMMENT

I press on to reach the end of the race and receive the heavenly prize for which God, through Christ Jesus, is calling us. PHILIPPIANS 3:14

The first Winter Olympics looked a lot different from the Games today. There were no TV cameras. No elaborate productions. On this day in 1924, nearly 260 athletes from 16 nations took part in the opening ceremonies in Chamonix, France, for the first Winter Olympics. Those athletes (247 men and 11 women) competed in 18 different events. Finland and Norway dominated the first Winter Olympics by claiming 28 of the 43 medals awarded.

Compare those numbers to the 2010 Winter Games in Vancouver, British Columbia, where more than 5,500 athletes and officials represented 80 countries. While the numbers have gotten bigger, some things haven't changed. For example, the United States has always been good in speed skating. In the 1924 Games, American Charlie Jewtraw won the first event by earning top honors in 500-meter speed skating. His gold medal can now be found at the Smithsonian Institution in Washington, DC.

What's the Score?

Some sporting events just seem to get bigger and bigger. The Winter Olympics had a very humble beginning. In fact, it wasn't even originally called the "Olympics." Instead, this event was referred to as "International Winter Sports Week." Not many people even knew about the competition. Today, millions of people around the world watch the Winter Games.

Jesus Christ had a humble beginning. He was born in a manger and welcomed to the world by shepherds. But the Bible says, "Jesus grew in wisdom and in stature and in favor with God and all the people" (Luke 2:52). God's Son grew bigger and smarter, and his actions pleased God and the people around him.

You may know what it's like to have a humble beginning. But don't think for an instant that you can't grow into something (or somebody) who will be recognized around the world. Follow Jesus' example by working to improve your mind and body. When you concentrate on the things that are important to God, people will notice.

) On the Ball

God often grows something small into something amazing. When you stay humble and follow God, you'll blossom into something big—for his glory and in his timing.

) COACH'S COMMENT

Jesus grew in wisdom and in stature and in favor with God and all the people. LUKE 2:52

Have you ever heard of a flying fish? Well, the people of Port Lincoln, Australia, have taken the idea of a "flying fish" to a ridiculous level. Every year nearly 50,000 people gather in this small fishing town to celebrate the Tunarama Festival. And the highlight? A tuna-tossing competition, of course. To be more specific, it's the World Champion Tuna Toss.

But don't think competitors grab a can of StarKist tuna and chuck it into the sea. That would be too easy. Instead these athletes grab slimy fish that weigh between 17 and 22 pounds and see how far they can throw them through the air. The record in this unusual competition was set in 1998 when former Olympic hammer thrower Sean Carlin threw a massive tuna more than 122 feet! Now that's a flying fish. And this is no fishy fable.

The Tunarama Festival started in 1962 as a way to promote the newly started fishing industry. Today, Australia's largest tuna cannery is located in Port Lincoln.

☐☐ What's the Score?

Throwing a ginormous tuna takes a lot of strength. It also requires a lot of soap, because there's no way these competitors can smell good after launching a stinky fish into the air. Sean developed his strength by training for the Olympics. He even placed eighth in the hammer throw in the 1992 Summer Olympics in Barcelona.

As Christians, we find our strength in God. First Chronicles 16:11 reminds us to "search for the LORD and for his strength; continually seek him." God's strength helps us do the right thing, even if our friends are making poor choices. His strength helps us tell others about Jesus Christ. His strength gives us an inner joy, even when things don't go perfectly for us. But for most of us, his strength will probably show up in different ways from tuna throwing.

⟩ On the Ball

What kind of strength do you need from God? List some areas in which you need help. Maybe it's to do better in your schoolwork. Perhaps you want to treat people with more kindness. Write down a couple of things, and then pray for God to give you strength in these areas:

⟩ COACH'S COMMENT

Search for the LORD and for his strength; continually seek him. 1 CHRONICLES 16:11

Fans can do some pretty crazy stuff to support their favorite athlete or team. Maybe you've seen shirtless football fans with painted bodies cheering on their team in freezing weather. Those guys seem ridiculous. But those fans' actions are nothing compared to a German fan who stabbed a professional tennis player in the back during a match in Germany in 1993.

At the time, Monica Seles was the No. 1–ranked player in the world. She had beaten Germany's Steffi Graf to take over the top spot. The fan wanted Steffi to be first again, so he rushed from the crowd and stabbed Monica's back while she was sitting down between games. Monica's physical injuries didn't take long to heal, but mentally it took her years to come back. Finally, on January 27, 1996, Monica won the Australian Open— her ninth Grand Slam victory—showing that she had returned to her old form. Monica used pinpoint ground strokes and focused concentration to defeat Anke Huber 6–4, 6–1 in the finals.

What's the Score?

When Monica claimed the 1996 title, it marked the fourth time that she'd won the Australian Open. But this victory was one of the most memorable because of what she had to overcome.

Overcoming obstacles is nothing new to athletes. All athletes have had to deal with injuries, bumps, and bruises. But Monica had to overcome both physical and mental scars. Sometimes when she sat down between games, she couldn't help but think about somebody charging her from behind. Tournament organizers even stationed extra people behind her chair to protect her.

Maybe you've run into a few bumps or bruises in your life. God doesn't promise us that everything will go smoothly when we become Christians. But he does promise to walk with us and strengthen us in hard times. First Peter 5:10 says, "After you have suffered a little while, he will restore, support, and strengthen you, and he will place you on a firm foundation." No matter what has happened in your past, you can trust God to help support you. When you stay close to Jesus in difficult times, he will raise you up again.

⟩ On the Ball

Bad things can happen in our lives. But even when they do, we need to trust God and let him help us to heal. By God's strength and with his help, we can be confident that we'll again walk on a firm foundation.

⟩ COACH'S COMMENT

After you have suffered a little while, he will restore, support, and strengthen you, and he will place you on a firm foundation. 1 PETER 5:10

The high-flying tricks of the Winter X Games snowmobile freestyle competition take years to master. Without the proper training and practice, a rider could easily end up with a broken bone—or in a wheelchair. Even the names of the tricks sound dangerous. Who's up for trying a "superman flip," "backflip no-hander," or "kiss-of-death"? When you're riding a 500-pound snowmobile and jumping over 100-foot gaps, you want to know what you're doing.

Yet Texas native Caleb Moore had only ridden a snowmobile for about a month when he went out and claimed the bronze medal in snowmobile freestyle at the 2010 Winter X Games. And, yes, there were more than three riders in the competition. In fact, 12 of the best riders in the world converged in Aspen, Colorado, for the event. Justin Hoyer won the gold, beating out the 2009 champ, Joe Parsons. Caleb shocked everybody by earning the bronze medal after practicing for just 33 days.

⬜⬜ What's the Score?

Although Caleb was new to riding a snowmobile, he was no stranger to extreme sports. He and his brother Colten were experienced ATV riders. A friend of theirs, veteran snowmobile freestyler Sam Rogers, told the brothers to try snowmobiling. They did.

First, they jumped on fake snow into a pit near their home in Krum, Texas. Then they drove up to Michigan's Upper Peninsula to train at Evolution Sled Park. The brothers took to the sport like a polar bear to a snow cone. In just over a month, they were ready to compete against the world's best.

But the truth is, if Sam had never encouraged the Moore brothers to try the sport, their toes may have never touched the snow. Sometimes all it takes is an encouraging word to change a person's life. God wants us to encourage each other. First Thessalonians 5:11 tells us to "encourage each other and build each other up." Who knows? Maybe your words will inspire somebody close to you to become a champion.

〉 On the Ball

Do you have a friend with a lot of talent who's not doing the most she can with it? Maybe you can see an ability in a friend that he hasn't discovered yet. Write down one friend you want to encourage to try something new: _____.

Be an encourager in your friends' lives.

〉 COACH'S COMMENT

Encourage each other and build each other up, just as you are already doing.
1 THESSALONIANS 5:11

Baseball and January go together like hotdogs and chocolate sauce. Yuck! In many parts of the world, it's way too cold to grab a bat and swing away. Yet on this day in 1936, baseball was on everybody's mind as the first players in baseball's Hall of Fame were announced. And what an amazing class it was!

Ty Cobb batted .367 in his career, hit over .400 in three seasons, and won 12 batting titles. Babe Ruth smashed an amazing 714 home runs. His New York Yankees won four World Series. Honus Wagner won eight batting titles and stole 722 bases in his career. Christy Mathewson won 373 games as a pitcher. "Matty," as his teammates called him, won 37 games during the 1908 season. Walter Johnson was a power pitcher who won 417 games. He amassed 3,508 strikeouts and 110 career shutouts.

What's the Score?

Although these five athletes were elected to the Hall of Fame in 1936, the actual Baseball Hall of Fame didn't open in Cooperstown, New York, until 1939. Today, more than 350,000 people visit the National Baseball Hall of Fame every year.

Cooperstown showcases a who's who of baseball greats. Just look at the statistics for Ty Cobb, Babe Ruth, Honus Wagner, Christy Mathewson, and Walter Johnson. They're staggering! No modern-day pitcher would ever dream of winning 37 games in a season. And Babe not only could crush a ball with his bat, but he also won nearly a hundred games as a pitcher.

Baseball players are judged by what they do on the field. Similarly, we're judged for what we do with our lives. Jesus said, "The Son of Man will come with his angels in the glory of his Father and will judge all people according to their deeds" (Matthew 16:27). Try to build up some impressive statistics for Jesus Christ. Tell others about Jesus. Show kindness to the people around you. Be a friend to someone who's lonely. Pick up trash around your school or town. Give some of your money to help the poor. Good works don't save us, but they do show whose team we're on.

) On the Ball

God doesn't want us to just sit around. To be a Hall of Famer for Jesus Christ, you need to get in the game. Swing for the fences to help people with the talents you've been given. Your actions can make a difference for Christ.

) COACH'S COMMENT

The Son of Man will come with his angels in the glory of his Father and will judge all people according to their deeds. MATTHEW 16:27

The Flying Tomato got bruised—fortunately not juiced—at the 2010 Winter X Games. Shaun White, nicknamed "The Flying Tomato" for his red hair and high-flying tricks, took a scary fall in the half-pipe as he tried to land a Double McTwist 1260.

While that may sound like a delicious fast food sandwich, the Double McTwist 1260 was actually one of the most dangerous tricks in snowboarding. Just imagine shooting off the lip of the half-pipe and traveling 20 feet into the air. Then you have to complete two head-over-heels flips and three and a half twists. Oh yeah, don't forget to land upright, because gravity will be pulling you back to earth.

When Shaun came back to earth in a practice run before the snowboarding finals, he misjudged where he was in the air, slipped, and smacked his head on the icy edge of the pipe. His helmet popped off and flew 15 feet. Fortunately, his head stayed squarely attached to his neck. Just minutes after the wreck, Shaun was back taking another practice run.

What's the Score?

When Shaun White's head hit the side of the cement-hard half-pipe, fans wondered if he'd be able to get up. Some thought his chances of competing in the Olympics in a couple of weeks would be dashed. Not only did he walk away from the scary fall, but he also won the Winter X Games gold medal an hour later—his third-straight half-pipe title.

Competing in snowboarding is risky. God doesn't want us to take unnecessary risks in our lives. We need to use our brains and not put ourselves in danger. But sometimes even when we're careful, we can find ourselves in scary situations. God promises to never leave us. Isaiah 43:2 says, "When you go through deep waters, I will be with you. When you go through rivers of difficulty, you will not drown." God is there to protect us and walk us through difficult times. Turn to God when you're injured or nervous about what's going on around you. He can protect you.

) On the Ball

When you find yourself in a slippery situation, don't forget to pray to God. He's always close to you and can help direct your steps. Even when you fall down, God can pick you up and give you the strength to keep going.

) COACH'S COMMENT

When you go through deep waters, I will be with you. When you go through rivers of difficulty, you will not drown. When you walk through the fire of oppression, you will not be burned up; the flames will not consume you. ISAIAH 43:2

New sports seem to pop up all the time. At Winter X Games 14 in 2010, a new event was introduced that sounded sort of simple. The Skiing SuperPipe High Air had one goal—jump very, very high. It was sort of like the high jump. But instead of jumping over a bar in running shoes, competitors strapped skis on their feet, zoomed down the half-pipe, and soared as high as they could into the air.

The new event brought a lot of excitement to the superpipe, but nobody was more excited than Peter Olenick. The Aspen, Colorado, native flew 24 feet, 11 inches above the lip of the pipe to win the gold medal. That's like jumping over a two-story house! Peter's jump was more than a foot higher than the jump of Canada's Justin Dorey, who placed second. Kevin Rolland from France earned the bronze medal with a jump of 23 feet, 4 inches.

⬜⬜ What's the Score?

Peter had never won a gold medal at the Winter X Games, even though for seven years the competition took place in his hometown. By concentrating on doing well in an event near his home, Peter was able to share his victory with family and friends.

Before ascending into heaven, Jesus gave his followers some very important instructions. He said the Holy Spirit would come upon them and give them power to be his witnesses "in Jerusalem, throughout Judea, in Samaria, and to the ends of the earth" (Acts 1:8). God's Son said these words in Jerusalem. And if you look at a map, you'll see that Jesus' directions encourage his followers to tell others about him close to home and then to spread out.

By focusing on being a light for Jesus in your hometown, you'll be able to impact the people closest to you. Begin by showing God's love in your house. Then expand to your neighborhood and school. Finally, what can you do to tell people in your town about Jesus? By following God's plan for being a witness, you can make a difference for him.

❯ On the Ball

Think of a person close to you who has never prayed to accept Jesus Christ as his or her Savior. Write down that person's name:_____ . Start praying for that person and ask God to give you the opportunity to share God's love with him or her. When it comes to being a witness for Jesus, it's good to start close to home.

❯ COACH'S COMMENT

You will receive power when the Holy Spirit comes upon you. And you will be my witnesses, telling people about me everywhere—in Jerusalem, throughout Judea, in Samaria, and to the ends of the earth. ACTS 1:8

Officials at the 2009 Asian Open in Japan told pro snowboarder Janna Meyen-Weatherby that she would automatically be placed in the finals. So during early rounds of the competition, she took it easy and waited out bad weather at the bottom of the mountain. But there must have been some confusion. Another rider ran over and told Janna that they were calling her name at the starting gate. She was about to be disqualified. Instead of freaking out, Janna laughed. She quickly gathered her gear and rushed up the lift. She took her run with no practice and reached the finals. A longtime friend marveled at Janna's calm. Janna admitted that she may have flipped out a few years earlier, but since then Jesus had totally changed her on the inside.

Janna was one of the best female snowboarders. She became a pro as a teenager. Janna was the first woman to win four Winter X gold medals in a row. But no matter how much she won in snowboarding, Janna was always depressed, angry, and bitter—until she gave her life to Jesus. Some of the biggest changes God brought to her life were peace, contentment, and joy. Her friends and fellow pros noticed. Snowboarding magazines even wrote articles about how much Janna had changed, thanks to God.

What's the Score?

Sometimes it's easier to understand peace when you look at its opposites. Peace is the quiet when an explosive war ends. Peace is the calm after a raging thunderstorm. Peace is the eye of the hurricane when the ferocious winds rage all around.

That's the kind of peace God brings us. His peace "exceeds anything we can understand. His peace will guard your hearts and minds as you live in Christ Jesus" (Philippians 4:7). We just need to remember to look for it. Take your eyes off your storms. Don't focus on the size of your big test or enemy. Don't look down at potential failure. Instead, read God's words, and let his peace fill you up.

) On the Ball

Trade your troubles for God's peace. Write down your problems, and put the paper in an envelope. Write Philippians 4:7 and other verses about peace on another piece of paper. Throw away your problem envelope, and keep God's encouragement instead.

) COACH'S COMMENT

You will experience God's peace, which exceeds anything we can understand. His peace will guard your hearts and minds as you live in Christ Jesus. PHILIPPIANS 4:7

C. J. and Damien Hobgood kicked off the 2006 season surfing head-to-head in the finals of the Globe Sebastian Inlet Pro. The twin brothers traded waves and launched airs. In the end, Damien came out on top, beating his brother for the first time in a pro heat. The difference was $5,000. But even more valuable were the family bragging rights.

C. J. and Damien grew up competing—and fighting—about everything, even the clothes they wore to school. They tried so hard to be different and to establish their own identities. But that wasn't easy to do because they were identical twins. Early in their surfing careers, magazines mixed up their pictures, and sponsors tried to contract both of them for the price of one.

For a while the brothers tried to keep their distance from each other. But as they secured their spots on the pro tour, they grew closer together and realized how valuable it was to have a brother so near. They also grew in their faith in God and realized that being a twin was a big part of the identities God gave them.

What's the Score?

We all want to establish our own identities, just like Damien and C.J. did. That might become even more important to you in the next few years. But no matter who you are and what you like to do, your most important identity is found in being God's child.

The Bible tells us in Galatians 4:6, "Because we are his children, God has sent the Spirit of his Son into our hearts, prompting us to call out, 'Abba, Father.'" *Abba* is a word like *Daddy*. It means we're tight with God. And it means we're royalty because God is the King. Let that shape who you are and how you see yourself. No matter what anyone else says, you belong to God and are in line to inherit all his treasures.

⟩ On the Ball

Make a list of all the things that make you *you*. Include everything from unusual freckles and scars to family relations to talents and abilities. Put "God's son or daughter" right on top of the list.

_____   _____

_____   _____

_____   _____

_____   _____

_____   _____

⟩ COACH'S COMMENT

Because we are his children, God has sent the Spirit of his Son into our hearts, prompting us to call out, "Abba, Father." Now you are no longer a slave but God's own child. And since you are his child, God has made you his heir. GALATIANS 4:6-7

The New York Giants needed somebody to make a play. On this day in 2008, the Giants trailed the New England Patriots 14–10, with only 2:42 left in Super Bowl LXII. New England had entered the game with a perfect 18–0 record and was trying to make history as the second undefeated team in NFL history. Could the Giants make a comeback?

Giants quarterback Eli Manning started marching his team down the field. With just over a minute left, the Giants faced third-and-five. New England's defensive line collapsed the pocket quickly, and a Patriot defender grabbed Eli's jersey. But Eli somehow broke free and flung the ball downfield. Wide receiver David Tyree leaped and grabbed the hanging pass. Patriots safety Rodney Harrison hit David in the air and tried to knock the ball out. But David fell and somehow pinned the ball to the top of his helmet for a first down! It was an unbelievable completion.

Three plays later the Giants scored a touchdown and won the Super Bowl 17–14. Many people called David's catch the greatest play ever.

⛶ What's the Score?

In Romans 12:9, the Bible tells us to "hold tightly to what is good"—just like David held on to that ball. There was no way he was letting go of that football even when he was hit and battered in the air.

Sometimes it feels like the devil's tacklers are slamming you to the ground. They do all they can to get you to let go of your grip on God. Your enemy would like nothing more than for you to treat other people badly or to compromise your faith. Sometimes wrong behaviors look tempting. God doesn't want you to even entertain ideas of sinning; God wants you to hate what is wrong and to hold on to him. Grab on to God like your hands are made of glue. Hold on to your faith like a Super Bowl victory depends on it. That's your greatest play.

⟩ On the Ball

Dive into your playbook, the Bible. Choose and read one whole book of the Bible today.

⟩ COACH'S COMMENT

Don't just pretend to love others. Really love them. Hate what is wrong. Hold tightly to what is good. ROMANS 12:9

Right before Super Bowl XLI, the two opposing coaches took out a full-page ad in *USA Today* that proclaimed their love for Jesus. Indianapolis Colts coach Tony Dungy and Chicago Bears coach Lovie Smith wanted everybody to know their lives were dedicated to Jesus Christ. Both men were respected for living out their faith on the sidelines. Tony and Lovie both coached with calm, respectful styles. They didn't scream and swear like many other NFL coaches.

Not only were both men Christians, but they were two of only a handful of African American coaches in the NFL. When Tony's Colts controlled the game and won 29–17, he became the first African American coach to win a Super Bowl. During the trophy ceremony, Tony told the world, "I'm proud to be the first African American coach to win this. But again, more than anything, Lovie Smith and I are not only African American but also Christian coaches, showing you can do it the Lord's way. We're more proud of that."

⬜⬜ What's the Score?

Should the color of the coaches' skin have been any big deal at all? No, but it was, because it had taken decades for African Americans to even get the chance to be head coaches in the NFL. The Bible teaches us that God's love is equal for every person, no matter his or her race or social status. In Jesus, "we have all been baptized into one body by one Spirit, and we all share the same Spirit" (1 Corinthians 12:13). That means we should treat and love all people equally.

Sadly, it wasn't until about 50 years ago that laws in the United States called for African Americans to be treated equally. Tony and Lovie proved that things are much better now. But there are still many ways that different races don't trust each other. Look around your church. Is everyone one color? Or are all of God's children represented? Sometimes we need to make a special effort to reach out and build bridges with different races. When we do, we learn to value each other for what's inside—like God does.

⟩ On the Ball

Look up and read Martin Luther King Jr.'s "I Have a Dream" speech. And look for someone of a different race to talk to or introduce yourself to today.

⟩ COACH'S COMMENT

Some of us are Jews, some are Gentiles, some are slaves, and some are free. But we have all been baptized into one body by one Spirit, and we all share the same Spirit.

1 CORINTHIANS 12:13

From above it looked more like a military battle than a sporting event. With 600 combatants taking on 600 foes, it was a battle . . . and a game. It was dodgeball. On this day in 2010 at the University of Alberta in Edmonton, Canada, 1,200 students, faculty, and staff gathered for the world's biggest dodgeball game. Dodgeball was popular at the college, and student groups thought it would be a fun way to bring the community together.

The game pitted Team Green against Team Gold—school colors. When the whistle blew, the bravest players ran full-speed ahead to grab the 400 squishy, red balls in the middle of the court. Other players hung back, just trying to dodge the round, red missiles. After hundreds of throws, catches, dodges, and misses, Matt Flemmer was the only Team Green player left. Then he was nailed, and Gold claimed victory. Everybody won, though. The game blew away San Diego State University's old world record of 450 people.

What's the Score?

The great thing about dodgeball is that anybody can play. You just have to avoid getting hit by one of those bouncy, red balls. If you've ever taken one to the face, you know you want to do whatever it takes to get out of the way.

In the Bible, the Israelites boasted that they had figured out how to make the ultimate dodge—avoiding death and destruction. But they were wrong. God's response through Isaiah was that the only way to dodge death was through Jesus, the "precious cornerstone that is safe to build on" (Isaiah 28:16). He is the only foundation worth building our lives on. He is the only way we can dodge spiritual death and find eternal life with God that will never be shaken.

) On the Ball

What are you trying to dodge in life? Write those things down on little pieces of paper. Then wad them into balls, and throw them across your room. Commit to building your life only on Jesus.

) COACH'S COMMENT

You boast, "We have struck a bargain to cheat death and have made a deal to dodge the grave. The coming destruction can never touch us, for we have built a strong refuge made of lies and deception." Therefore, this is what the Sovereign LORD says: "Look! I am placing a foundation stone in Jerusalem, a firm and tested stone. It is a precious cornerstone that is safe to build on. Whoever believes need never be shaken."

ISAIAH 28:15-16

For decades, when people pictured a hockey player, an image of a man's scarred face and mouth with missing teeth would come to mind. That all changed in 1998 when the Nagano Winter Olympics became the first one to feature women's ice hockey. Not many women in the world played hockey at the time. There were no pro leagues. This was the biggest competition on the biggest stage for the sport.

And the games lived up to the excitement. In the gold-medal contest, the two best teams and biggest rivals—the United States and Canada—played. In the first period, the goalies kept things scoreless. The Americans broke through with two goals in the second period as Shelley Looney tallied on a power play and Sandra Whyte found the back of the net. The Canadians cut the lead to 2–1 with about four minutes left. But in the end the United States won 3–1. The Americans made it all the way through the Olympics undefeated.

What's the Score?

The American women were overjoyed. The Canadians were devastated—they'd won every world championship since 1987. But both teams felt good because it was a victory for the sport they loved. The 1998 American and Canadian women's hockey teams opened doors for girls around the world to play hockey. The sport became much more accessible and accepted after that Olympics.

Jesus opened a door for us in a similar way. Before his death and resurrection, only the high priests could come close to meeting directly with God. The Israelites had to follow lots of strict laws and to make animal sacrifices for their sins. There were many barriers between God and the people. But Jesus did away with all those things. He made a door for us to go directly to God. That's why the Bible calls him our High Priest (Hebrews 4:14). Because of him, we can "come boldly to the throne of our gracious God" (Hebrews 4:16) and relate to him directly. That's the most important victory ever!

) On the Ball

Go boldly to God's throne by praying. Thank him that Jesus opened the door for you, and ask him who you can open the door for.

) COACH'S COMMENT

Let us come boldly to the throne of our gracious God. There we will receive his mercy, and we will find grace to help us when we need it most. HEBREWS 4:16

No one would have blamed you for turning off the TV after the third quarter of Super Bowl XXXVI in 2002. The New England Patriots had a 17–3 lead over the St. Louis Rams. The outcome of the game was decided—or was it?

The favored Rams came to life in the fourth quarter. They scored a touchdown about five minutes into the quarter to cut the Patriots' lead to a touchdown. Late in the game, Rams quarterback Kurt Warner put together an amazing drive that ended in another Rams touchdown. Suddenly the game was tied 17–17 with only 1:30 on the clock.

Would the Patriots play it safe by running out the clock and going for overtime? Nope, they went for the win. With second-year quarterback Tom Brady behind center, New England moved the ball downfield. With six seconds left, Patriots kicker Adam Vinatieri came on for a 48-yard field goal attempt. Patriots fans held their breath as the ball was snapped. Adam sent the ball sailing. He raised his arms immediately. The kick was good! The Patriots were Super Bowl champions.

⬜⬜ What's the Score?

Adam faced a high-pressure kick. His skills were put to the test in that one moment of fame or failure. It's what he had practiced for his whole life. He was ready to make it count.

Your faith will be tested in similar big moments when success or failure is on the line. Maybe it will be an opportunity to go on a mission trip or to change a life by making friends with someone who really needs one. Maybe it will be resisting a temptation to do drugs or to get into a relationship that pulls you away from God. First Peter 1:7 says, "These trials will show that your faith is genuine." These challenges are like fire to gold— it makes it more pure. Whenever you feel the heat in life, remember that God is using these circumstances to refine your character and to make you more like him. Be ready, and make the most of your big moments.

) On the Ball

Practice now for tests that will come later. What will you do when

+ someone offers you drugs?
+ a friend tries to show you pornography?
+ friends pressure you to lie to your parents?

- -

) COACH'S COMMENT

These trials will show that your faith is genuine. It is being tested as fire tests and purifies gold—though your faith is far more precious than mere gold. So when your faith remains strong through many trials, it will bring you much praise and glory and honor on the day when Jesus Christ is revealed to the whole world. 1 PETER 1:7

- -

This wasn't how it was supposed to be. Lindsey Vonn was the American poster girl for the 2010 Winter Olympics. No American had ever won the women's downhill race. Lindsey was expected to do that and more. She carried the nation's hopes for multiple gold medals in several races. But two weeks before the Vancouver Games, Lindsey crashed and badly injured her right shin. She couldn't even put her ski boot on, so how could she recover in time to compete?

Lindsey tried to rest and heal, but the hype was huge. Her face appeared all over the news. The media swarmed. All of it tested Lindsey's patience and endurance. Bad weather worked in her favor as the women's downhill was postponed several times. Every day counted toward healing and improved her chances of competing.

On race day, Lindsey stood ready in the starting gate. American Julia Mancuso had just posted an excellent run, and Lindsey knew she had to go all out to win. She skied aggressively. Her leg hurt, and she came close to losing control on the last big jump. But Lindsey crossed the finish line more than a half-second faster than anyone else. She won the gold and burst into tears of relief and joy! It was an epic Olympic accomplishment.

⬜⬜ What's the Score?

Skiing in pain was not how Lindsey had planned her Olympics. Her injury was a big, unexpected obstacle. But she pressed through, and reaching her goal made it all worthwhile.

God doesn't promise that we will always win the gold in life, but he does promise that if we "patiently endure testing and temptation," we will "receive the crown of life" (James 1:12). It's an excellent reminder that God works in the middle of our struggles. He uses those struggles to teach us and help us grow stronger. God doesn't promise to take away all our problems or pain while we're here on earth. But he does promise an eternal reward that makes it all worthwhile in the end. Hang on to that hope when you feel beat up by life.

⟩ On the Ball

Draw a picture of your struggles in life as a ski race. Put yourself on skis speeding over them with God's help.

⟩ COACH'S COMMENT

God blesses those who patiently endure testing and temptation. Afterward they will receive the crown of life that God has promised to those who love him. JAMES 1:12

The two British teens wanted a challenge. For Rob Gauntlett and James Hooper, that meant something extreme. After graduating from high school, the two set out on a 26,000-mile journey from the North Pole to the South Pole. They planned to start north of Greenland, then ski and dogsled on thin ice. They wanted to bike through North and South America and finish by sailing into Antarctica.

What experience did Rob and James have? Not much. They had climbed Mount Everest before—with little experience, preparation, or funding. So they went into this trek the same way: little preparation or funding and no experience with dogsledding or sailing. But they had each other. And whether it was stupid or adventurous, that's all they seemed to need.

Rob and James came near death a couple of times. Rob fell through the ice once. The whole journey was tough, but the two made it to the South Pole. After reaching the South Pole, they arrived in Sydney, Australia, 409 days after they started. They had looked death in the face and explored a huge portion of the earth. Plus, they inspired millions who watched along the way.

▢▢ What's the Score?

Rob and James didn't back down from a challenge. Long ago in Old Testament times, two other friends wanted to go for a seemingly impossible challenge. The Israelites were close to the Promised Land, so they sent spies to scope it out. Most of the spies came back and reported that it was too scary, too wild, and too hard to go there. But that's not the way Joshua and Caleb saw it. They said, "The land we traveled through and explored is a wonderful land!" Joshua and Caleb knew that if the people trusted God, they would experience a more amazing life than they could imagine. The Israelites' faith was adventurous. They knew God would deliver what he promised. And they knew any risks in obeying him would pay off with blessings.

⟩ On the Ball

What do you feel God is calling you to do? Where have you been scared to follow him? Complete this list.

Risks/Hard Parts: Rewards/Good Parts:

_____   _____

_____   _____

_____   _____

_____   _____

⟩ COACH'S COMMENT

They said to all the people of Israel, "The land we traveled through and explored is a wonderful land! And if the LORD is pleased with us, he will bring us safely into that land and give it to us. It is a rich land flowing with milk and honey." NUMBERS 14:7-8

Think of some of your favorite things to do in the snow. Maybe you thought of skiing, sledding, or making a snow fort. Snow is most fun when you can play in it. That's what students at Michigan Tech thought, so they used snow for the ultimate group project—with a twist. On this day in 2006, college students, faculty, kids, and others from Houghton, Michigan, got together to break some snow records.

The winter warriors—3,745 of them—waged the world's biggest snowball fight. Talk about a blizzard of snowballs! And if anyone needed any ammunition inspiration, all that person had to do was look over at the world's largest snowball, which was 21 feet high and three inches around! Once everybody was good and tired of throwing snowballs, 3,784 people flopped down to make snow angels at one time—also the most ever.

Students organized everything at Michigan Tech's Sherman Field, but they pulled in the whole community as well. They all had to work together to make these chilly records happen, and every person counted—literally.

What's the Score?

Do you sit on the sidelines at school, church, or home? Or are you willing to jump in and be part of making something good happen? Don't just sit back and watch. Get involved. Really live. Be unified with others.

The Bible tells us that we need to be "agreeing wholeheartedly with each other, loving one another, and working together with one mind and purpose" (Philippians 2:2). That's true of God's work and of doing good around us. It takes everyone, and that includes you. So go for it. Raise your hand. Sign up. Volunteer. You'll be surprised how much fun it can be. After all, lots of things in life are more fun together, including snowball fights.

) On the Ball

Get involved. Sign up to serve others at church or school. Or do you have your own idea? Ask some friends to help, and then get going. Fill in this sentence with an idea. "Now is the time for me to _____."

) COACH'S COMMENT

Make me truly happy by agreeing wholeheartedly with each other, loving one another, and working together with one mind and purpose. PHILIPPIANS 2:2

The idea seemed ridiculous. A bobsled team from Jamaica? It's a tropical island! People laughed. No snow ever fell on the small Caribbean nation. But that didn't stop Jamaica from sending a bobsled team to the 1988 Winter Olympics in Calgary, Canada.

The team started training in Jamaica and began practicing on ice tracks a few months before the Olympics. They were strong athletes, and their fast starts were impressive. By the time they reached Calgary, the Jamaicans were steadily improving. They were a crowd favorite because they were the ultimate underdogs and had such positive attitudes. The Olympics ended for the Jamaican four-man sled team when they crashed—going 75 miles per hour. All of the men were okay, and they eventually got up and walked the rest of the track to the finish line.

The Jamaicans were serious about wanting to win. They returned to the Olympics in 1992 but didn't do well. Then in the 1994 Games, Jamaica finished a respectable 14th—ahead of teams from the United States, Russia, and France. The Jamaicans may not have won any medals, but they won over the world.

☐☐ What's the Score?

How do you handle criticism? What's your response when people laugh at you? It's natural to want to run away, retaliate, and throw insults back, but 1 Peter 3:9 tells us not to. Instead, God wants us to "pay them back with a blessing." That's exactly what the Jamaican bobsled team ended up doing. Their positive attitudes and hard work brought joy to sports fans and won over their critics.

It is hard not to "retaliate with insults when people insult you." But God has promised that he will bless you for it. Ask him for his strength to bless back with kind words or respectful actions. And stay focused on your goal . . . no matter what critics may say.

⟩ On the Ball

Write down an insult or criticism you feel like giving someone who has put you down. Then turn the paper over and write words or actions that can bless that person instead.

⟩ COACH'S COMMENT

Don't repay evil for evil. Don't retaliate with insults when people insult you. Instead, pay them back with a blessing. That is what God has called you to do, and he will bless you for it. 1 PETER 3:9

Canadian ice skaters and Australian sailors make sense. People living around all that ice or water have the opportunity to get good at those sports. But how do you explain a luger from India or cross-country skiers from Algeria and Ethiopia? They make you say, "Huh? Where did those guys come from?"

The Winter Olympics can be filled with dreamers who defy the odds. They're committed and brave. And they get the coolest nicknames. Eddie the Eagle (real name Eddie Edwards) was Great Britain's first-ever ski jumper in 1988. Kwame Nkrumah-Acheampong was called "The Snow Leopard" in 2010. This slalom skier was Ghana's first-ever winter Olympian. No, there is no snow in the African nation of Ghana. And there are hardly any swimming pools in Equatorial Guinea where Eric the Eel was from. You can read about him on August 28.

Athletes like these might have been total underdogs from underdog countries, but they were serious about their sports. They came to compete—even if they knew they wouldn't win. They gave their all to represent their countries and to open doors for others to go through. And these athletes have often endeared themselves to the crowd, because they tried—hard. Their faith in what could happen inspires us all.

⏸ What's the Score?

Psalm 37:4 tells us, "Take delight in the LORD, and he will give you your heart's desires." That's one cool verse. But it doesn't mean we'll always get anything we want. The key is to first delight in the Lord. When we pursue him and commit ourselves to him, God shapes our hearts and desires. He brings them in line with his desires for us. As we follow God's purposes and plans for our lives, our hearts' desires become unstoppable.

Don't be afraid to dream big. Love and live for God with all your strength. Put your faith in what can happen through him.

❭ On the Ball

Dream big. List a few large accomplishments you want to achieve in life.

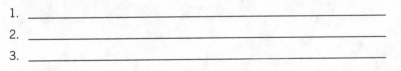

1. _____

2. _____

3. _____

❭ COACH'S COMMENT

Take delight in the LORD, and he will give you your heart's desires. PSALM 37:4

Canadians Jamie Salé and David Pelletier entered the pairs figure-skating finals of the 2002 Winter Olympics in second place. The leaders were Russia's Elena Berezhnaya and Anton Sikharulidze, but Anton stumbled during the performance. When Jamie and David skated a beautiful, flawless routine, the crowd in Salt Lake City, Utah, roared. The commentators proclaimed victory for the Canadians. They had clearly outskated the competition.

But when the judges' scores were announced, nobody could believe their ears. The Russians had won. The crowd booed. The commentators were horrified. David and Jamie were heartbroken. The next day, newspapers proclaimed, "Robbed!" And skating officials launched an investigation.

It didn't take long to uncover the truth. A French judge confessed that she had been ordered to give the victory to the Russians. The competition was fixed. So the decision was made to give the Canadian pair gold medals, too.

⬜⬜ What's the Score?

God was not happy about judges cheating in the Olympics. How can we tell? The Bible is clear about God's view of injustice. "I, the LORD, love justice; I hate robbery and wrong-doing," he says. Justice is righting a wrong, often for those who can't do it themselves. Many Bible verses tell us to work for justice, especially for people who are weak or who are being taken advantage of. Zechariah 7:9-10 tells us, "Judge fairly, and show mercy and kindness to one another. Do not oppress widows, orphans, foreigners, and the poor."

That applies to the Olympics and to our everyday lives. We should try to help other people when we see them being mistreated or cheated. What if no one would have called for a closer look into the ice-skating competition? What if no one stands up against that bully in your class or helps the single mother on your block? Join God in making things right.

⟩ On the Ball

Fill in the blanks in this statement. "I know _____ is being mistreated. I can _____ to help." Talk to your parents about helping too.

⟩ COACH'S COMMENT

I, the LORD, love justice; I hate robbery and wrongdoing. In my faithfulness I will reward my people and make an everlasting covenant with them. ISAIAH 61:8 (NIV)

John Wooden is remembered as one of the best college basketball coaches of all time. But his family remembers him for something else. For years, John wrote a special letter once a month. He tied it with a ribbon and placed it on a stack. He had nowhere to send these letters because they were to his wife, Nell, who had died in 1985. Coach, as everyone called him, said he missed telling her things. The letters were an expression of the undying love they had shared while Nell was alive.

John was a basketball icon, mostly for his coaching success at the University of California, Los Angeles (UCLA). His record there was 627 wins and only 147 losses. He led UCLA to 10 NCAA championships in 12 years during the 1960s and '70s. But John was also a hero and an inspiration off the court. He loved God deeply, and he taught his players integrity and values as well as ball-handling skills. He passed along his famous Pyramid of Success, which was built on virtues such as skill, enthusiasm, industriousness, patience, and faith.

John's favorite Bible passage was 1 Corinthians 13, also known as the love chapter. "Faith, hope, and love" guided his relationships with his wife and with his players. When John died in 2010 at the age of 99, everyone knew he was excited to be reunited with his true loves in heaven: Jesus and his wife, Nell.

⬜⬜ What's the Score?

John's unending love for his wife proved that "love never gives up, never loses faith, is always hopeful, and endures through every circumstance" (1 Corinthians 13:7). It's sad, but love doesn't always last in our world. Too many marriages and relationships break apart too often.

John and Nell's love was a great example of committed love. It's also a beautiful reflection of God's love for us. The Woodens didn't let anything tear apart their love. God won't let anything change his love for us. He wants that nonstop, unconditional love of his to flow through us to other people, too. Marriage is still off in the future for you, but you're never too young to commit to receiving and sharing God's perfect love.

⟩ On the Ball

Write a letter to a parent, a brother or sister, or a longtime good friend. Let that person know you love him or her and appreciate who he or she is in your life.

⟩ COACH'S COMMENT

Love never gives up, never loses faith, is always hopeful, and endures through every circumstance. **1 CORINTHIANS 13:7**

The third time wasn't a charm. The twentieth time was—at least it was for Dale Earnhardt at the Daytona 500. Dale was considered by many to be the best NASCAR driver of all time. But NASCAR's great prize kept eluding him during his amazing career.

The Daytona 500 is kind of like the Super Bowl of NASCAR. It's called "The Great American Race," and it is the biggest, richest, and most prestigious event in car racing. When Dale pulled up to the starting line in 1998, the Daytona 500 was the only race he had never won. He'd tried for 19 years! He'd come close. He had dominated many Daytonas but had lost in lots of different ways, including a flipped car, a blown tire on the last lap, and a final-lap pass.

Finally, 1998 was Dale's year. His No. 3 car ran in the lead for 107 of the 200 laps and was in first for the last 60 laps. He even held off a furious charge by Bobby Labonte and Jeremy Mayfield at the end. Finally, Dale had made it into the winner's circle at the Daytona 500.

What's the Score?

What have you been working on for a long time but can't seem to accomplish? What hangs over your head and won't go away? What makes you cry out to God, "How long must I struggle with anguish in my soul, with sorrow in my heart every day?" (Okay, maybe you wouldn't say it exactly like that.)

It can be easy to give up when we struggle for a long time. But when we stay patient and persistent, we give God a chance to work. Waiting is tough. But it doesn't mean being lazy; we need to stay active. Keep working toward your goal. Keep trying. Instead of sitting around thinking about quitting, try these ideas from Psalm 13:5-6: Trust in God's unfailing love; celebrate because God has saved you; and sing to the Lord because he is good.

) On the Ball

Sing your favorite worship song to God and pray, "Lord, it's been so long that _____ _____ just won't seem to happen. Please help me to trust you with it."

) COACH'S COMMENT

How long must I struggle with anguish in my soul, with sorrow in my heart every day? How long will my enemy have the upper hand? PSALM 13:2

If you're looking for real horsepower, try the sport of skijoring. It's like cross-country skiing, but you get pulled by a horse. In 1928, skijoring made it into the Winter Olympics in St. Moritz, Switzerland, as a demonstration sport. It never made it back into the Games, but it's still pretty cool.

The word *skijoring* literally means "ski driving." But you can think of it as water skiing behind a horse on snow. You attach yourself to a harness, and a horse pulls you through the snow on skis. The sport started in Scandinavia using reindeer, then spread to Europe as an easy way for farmers to get around their land in winter.

People still skijor in Europe, and some want to bring it back to the Olympics. If you live in a cold, snowy climate, don't be surprised if you see someone speeding by behind a horse or a dog. You can impress your friends by saying, "Hey, check it out—skijoring."

What's the Score?

In Bible times and even in more recent history, horses meant power. If your king had an army of horses, you could conquer and rule other nations. So the psalmist was making a big statement when he said God wasn't impressed with the strength of horses or humans. Instead, "the LORD's delight is in those who fear him, those who put their hope in his unfailing love" (Psalm 147:11).

God's priority is on his love, and he wants that to be No. 1 for us, too. Where is your trust? Is it in your stuff: your money, toys, or gadgets? Could you give up all those things? There's nothing necessarily wrong with having cool stuff (horses included), but it is wrong to rely on things instead of on God. Make sure the harness of your priorities is connected to the one and only true God.

) On the Ball

What's your most favorite game, gadget, or thing? Go without it for a day or—even better—a week. Talk to God when you feel like picking it up.

> COACH'S COMMENT

He takes no pleasure in the strength of a horse or in human might. No, the LORD's delight is in those who fear him, those who put their hope in his unfailing love. PSALM 147:10-11

Nothing felt right as Dan Jansen started the 500-meter speed-skating competition at the 1988 Calgary Olympics. His legs were weak. His mind was numb. His heart was broken. His closest sister, Jane, had died just a few hours earlier of leukemia.

Dan's sister loved speed skating and loved watching him compete. For Jane, he tried to clear his brain and skate for gold. Dan exploded out of the starting blocks but lost his balance on the first turn. He fell, slid, and crashed into the wall. He buried his face in his hands.

The Olympics seemed cursed for Dan. Although he had won numerous championships and set world records, he crashed again in the 1992 Winter Games and again in his first race in the 1994 Olympics. He had one race left: the 1,000 meters. On the last lap, he slipped but kept his balance. Dan crossed the finish line with a new world record and a gold medal—finally! It would never erase the grief of losing his sister, but he had finally fulfilled his dream. Dan skated a victory lap with his baby daughter in his arms. He had named her Jane . . . after his sister.

▢▢ What's the Score?

Dan discovered that grief can overwhelm our hearts, minds, and bodies. Losing someone we love is sad, and it can make us feel helpless and even hopeless. There's a normal process of missing our loved ones that we have to go through to heal. God understands that. He knows the pain of death and loss—he watched his own Son die on a cross for the sins of the world.

Staying close to God during times of grief won't magically make our pain go away, but God will bring us comfort and hope. King David knew that. He wrote, "Even though I walk through the valley of the shadow of death, I fear no evil, for You are with me; Your rod and Your staff, they comfort me" (Psalm 23:4, NASB). No matter how badly you hurt, keep turning to God and to the people around you for help.

⟩ On the Ball

Write to God about someone you love who has died or moved far away. Be totally honest and tell God how you miss that person. If you have a friend who lost a loved one, hang out with him or her. Say you're sorry and ask if he or she wants to talk about it. You don't have to know what to say; just listen.

⟩ COACH'S COMMENT

Even though I walk through the valley of the shadow of death, I fear no evil, for You are with me; Your rod and Your staff, they comfort me. **PSALM 23:4 (NASB)**

Kelly Clark boosted higher out of the half-pipe than any other woman at the 2002 Winter Olympics, and she grabbed the United States' first women's snowboarding gold medal ever. It was the highlight of a year in which Kelly won every competition she entered, including the Winter X Games. She was 18 and had reached all her life goals. Not long after that . . . she was totally empty and unhappy. She was ready to quit snowboarding. She didn't even know if she wanted to live. That's when Kelly met Jesus Christ.

Kelly returned to the Olympics in Torino in 2006 and in Vancouver in 2010. Both times she rocked praise music over the loudspeakers during her runs. And there was that sticker, right on the nose of her board for the whole world to see. It said, "Jesus, I cannot hide my love."

There were no gold repeats for Kelly. She finished fourth in 2006 and claimed a bronze medal in 2010. Was she disappointed? Sure. Kelly was a tough competitor and one of the best in the world. But she was much more satisfied with life because of her relationship with God, no matter what color medal she won.

What's the Score?

A professional snowboard is prime real estate. It's where pros put stickers of their sponsors who pay them big bucks. The stickers are marks of their identities and loyalties. That's why Kelly's board was the perfect place for her to announce her love and devotion to Jesus.

The apostle Paul might have done that if he snowboarded. He said, "I am not ashamed of this Good News about Christ" (Romans 1:16). He couldn't help but tell people about all Jesus had done for him and what Jesus could do for them, too. How about you? You might have a different way to reach out to others than Paul or Kelly. That's the way talking about Jesus should be—you don't have to memorize somebody else's speech. Just be natural, talking about how Jesus works in your life.

) On the Ball

What's your thing: sports, music, art, debate, Scouts? Think of three ways you can show and share your love for Jesus in natural ways.

1. _____
2. _____
3. _____

) COACH'S COMMENT

I am not ashamed of this Good News about Christ. It is the power of God at work, saving everyone who believes—the Jew first and also the Gentile. ROMANS 1:16

NASCAR drivers often fight bumper to bumper for position in a race. But at the 1979 Daytona 500, they ended up fighting with their fists. As Cale Yarborough dropped inside to try to pass Donnie Allison on the final lap, Donnie wasn't going to let Cale through. The cars bumped, and Cale's wheels ran off the track. He swung out of control, and both cars swerved into the wall, crashed, and slid into the infield. Donnie's brother, Bobby, drove up to check on the two, and that's when a fight broke out.

These three racers had already been involved in a spinout earlier in the day. This one cost Cale and Donnie the race. Tempers flared. Cale blamed the Allison brothers for double-teaming him. They denied it. Cale hit Bobby with his helmet, and the three started wrestling and punching in the mud.

Meanwhile, Richard Petty was a half-lap behind when the crash happened. He hadn't won anything for 45 races, and his doctors had told him not to drive in this race because he had recently had surgery. But Richard ended up coming away with a victory.

☐☐ What's the Score?

The big Daytona fight got a lot of attention, but it didn't get any of the racers involved what they wanted—first place. No matter whose fault it truly was, the fight showed what was in the racers' hearts. James's words fit well: "You are jealous of what others have, but you can't get it, so you fight and wage war to take it away from them" (James 4:2).

If we let our jealousy and pride drive us, we're scheming and waging war in our hearts. It's the same as fighting even if we don't throw punches. How can we avoid it? Ask God for what you want instead of getting jealous. You can trust his good plans for you. When we ask God for something and trust him to know what's best for us, we can relax and not fight others for it. That helps us avoid crashing. After all, even second place is better than not finishing at all—Cale would surely agree.

) On the Ball

What or who are you jealous of? Write it down. Tape it on a toy car. And drive it off your deck. Pray as you do, and consider it a symbol of your getting rid of your jealousy.

) COACH'S COMMENT

You want what you don't have, so you scheme and kill to get it. You are jealous of what others have, but you can't get it, so you fight and wage war to take it away from them. Yet you don't have what you want because you don't ask God for it. JAMES 4:2

Short-track speed skating is known for its fast crashes. But no crash is more famous than the one that occurred in the 1,000-meter finals at the 2002 Winter Olympics. Australia's Steven Bradbury knew he didn't have much of a chance for the gold medal against Apolo Ohno, Ahn Hyn-Soo, Li Jiajun, and Mathieu Turcotte. Australia had never won a gold medal in the Winter Olympics, and it didn't look like that would change.

Steven was in last place coming into the final turn—not last place by a hair, but last place by a lot. Apolo and the other three racers powered into the sharp turn. One of them lost control. Suddenly, all four racers in front of Steven skidded across the ice like bowling pins. The Aussie cruised through the wreckage and crossed the finish line first. He threw his arms up, half in celebration and half in disbelief. Steven's strategy had paid off. He knew he wasn't the fastest skater. This was his third Olympics, but he had never given up on his golden dreams. His hard work paid off with a big surprise.

What's the Score?

When God said, "The silver is mine, and the gold is mine" (Haggai 2:8), he was talking about his power over the whole world, not Olympic medals. But the statement still fits. God has control over the whole world. He can see everything that will happen; we can't. That's why we need to trust God and to keep pursuing him no matter how bad things look in front of us.

Just as in Steven's race, sometimes the unexpected happens. No one expected him to win—Steven didn't expect himself to win! But his faithfulness put him in a position to claim the gold. Don't give up. Keep going after God and obeying his commands. Be ready to seize the victory whenever it opens up in front of you.

) On the Ball

What do you get tired of doing for God? Obeying your parents? Being kind to your brother or sister? Not listening to raunchy popular songs? Don't give up! Stay committed to living for God and serving him.

) COACH'S COMMENT

The silver is mine, and the gold is mine, says the LORD of Heaven's Armies. HAGGAI 2:8

What do you call an expo center in Sofia, Bulgaria, lined with 360 identical tables and chess games? A world record! But not for the most people playing chess at once (you can read about that on October 21). On this day in 2009, Kiril Georgiev played 360 people at once! This Bulgarian chess master earned a spot in the Guinness World Records for playing the most simultaneous games of chess by one individual.

How did he do it? All of Kiril's opponents sat at tables. It was slow going, but Kiril walked from game to game. He played for more than 14 hours and walked more than 12 miles in the process! Who says chess isn't good exercise? Kiril averaged three moves an hour.

Before you think you can gather 361 of your closest friends and beat the record, there are a lot of official requirements. Maybe the hardest is that a record breaker must win at least 80 percent of the games. Kiril's final score was 284 wins, 6 losses, and 70 ties. The guy had serious brain power!

What's the Score?

Do you get bored with a game of chess after half an hour? Kiril must have been tempted to hurry up and get the record finished. But he remained patient and made sure all 360 games counted.

We live much of our lives in the fast lane, quickly going from one thing to another. But we can learn a lesson from chess. It's a slow game. You have to think about what you're doing and look several moves ahead. One wrong move and you're done. "Haste makes mistakes," Proverbs 19:2 says. So chess players are careful not to make hasty moves.

The Bible tells us we also make mistakes in life when we get in too big a hurry without seeking knowledge first. Have you ever rushed in and made a mess of a situation because you didn't know everything you needed to? Stay patient. Learn from people who know more than you. And trust God to guide you with his perfect timing.

) On the Ball

Practice slowing down. Try working a 1,000-piece jigsaw puzzle. Maybe your family can set it up on a table and solve it together slowly. It's good practice to focus on taking things one step at a time.

) COACH'S COMMENT

Enthusiasm without knowledge is no good; haste makes mistakes. **PROVERBS 19:2**

Do you like squash? No, not the vegetable—the sport. Never heard of it? It's similar to racquetball. The main differences are a smaller court, a longer racquet, and a less bouncy ball. The name *squash* is a reference to the squashable ball.

Did you know the longest winning streak in the history of college sports comes from squash? In February 2010, Trinity College won its 12th straight national championship. That's impressive, but this is even more impressive: The win was the Trinity Bantams' 224th team victory in a row. The last time Trinity lost was February 22, 1998—that's more than 12 years without feeling the sting of defeat.

It all started when the college president asked the coach what it would take to compete with the bigger Ivy League schools. Coach Paul Assaiante said he would need to recruit players from other countries where squash was more popular. So he did. Trinity has had players from every continent except Antarctica. The teams looked like a miniature United Nations, with players from Pakistan, India, Sweden, England, Colombia, and more. Paul helped his guys from all over the world unite to form strong teams—strong enough that no one seemed to be able to beat them.

What's the Score?

The Trinity College teams are a good example of what God's Kingdom will be like one day when "the LORD will be king over all the earth" (Zechariah 14:9). There will be people from every nation, speaking every language, and getting along with everyone else. In fact, the church around the world should already be like that. Even though we have different customs, languages, and ways of worshiping God, we should respect and help each other as much as we can. After all, we are all on the same team.

At the same time, we need to remember that there are also people all around us from different cultures and countries who need to know Jesus. How can we tell them about Christ if we don't know them? Start today to make friends with kids from different races and nationalities in your community.

) On the Ball

Talk to your parents or pastor about ways you can connect with and help international families in your area.

) COACH'S COMMENT

The LORD will be king over all the earth. On that day there will be one LORD—his name alone will be worshiped. ZECHARIAH 14:9

Dean Potter wanted to fly. For years, he had been one of the best and most respected rock climbers in the world. Heights didn't scare him. But he had also been fascinated by flying. So in 2009, Dean climbed up the Eiger, a famous mountain in Switzerland. He put on a special suit and walked to the edge of a rock that stuck out like a diving board. Then he jumped.

Dean fell about 600 feet. Then his special wingsuit caught the air, and Dean started flying. To get an idea of what the wingsuit looked like, picture a flying squirrel. The suit had extra fabric wings under the arms and between the legs. Almost three minutes later, Dean pulled a parachute and landed near a small Swiss town. He was 9,000 feet lower and four miles away from where he started! It was the longest human free-fall flight ever made.

What's the Score?

Was Dean crazy? Some would say so. Other people in the world had tried using wingsuits. Some had died trying. It was an incredibly risky activity. But Dean believed in following his passions. And seeing him fly is an amazing picture of how God's strength can fill us and keep us soaring.

Have you ever watched an eagle fly? It's an effortless glide through the sky. Isaiah told us that's how God's strength is. He wrote, "Those who trust in the LORD will find new strength. They will soar high on wings like eagles. They will run and not grow weary. They will walk and not faint" (Isaiah 40:31). Are you weary? Do you feel like fainting in your spiritual life? Turn your heart to God and let him lift you back up.

) On the Ball

Watch for some big birds soaring. You might have hawks or pelicans living near you. Worship God with prayer and singing as you see them glide gracefully through the skies. Picture God filling your spiritual wings the same way.

) COACH'S COMMENT

Those who trust in the LORD will find new strength. They will soar high on wings like eagles. They will run and not grow weary. They will walk and not faint. ISAIAH 40:31

Tim Howard knew it was time. He had earned the job as the starting goalkeeper for the New York/New Jersey MetroStars going into the 2001 MLS season. But before the season began, he had to get something out. At the preseason media day, Tim announced that he had Tourette's syndrome. Tourette's is a disorder of the nervous system that causes the body to twitch or tic on its own.

Tim had dealt with Tourette's since he was a kid, but he had never gone public with his physical struggles. He knew there would be more attention on him as a starter. Plus, Tim had grown a lot in his relationship with Christ. He saw how both soccer and Tourette's were gifts. They gave him chances to glorify God and to help kids and other people. Getting his secret out was a relief.

What's the Score?

Tourette's never held Tim back in soccer. His career proved it. He went on to play in the powerful English Premier League, first with Manchester United, then with Everton. Tim also became the starting keeper for the US National Team. He was a strong leader and one of the top goalies in the world. And he never quit telling people about his Tourette's or his God.

Tim didn't know how people would respond when he first opened up about Tourette's. Most were supportive. But some members of the media made fun of him. No matter what reactions he received, Tim lived out the words of the apostle Paul: "That's why I take pleasure in my weaknesses, and in the insults, hardships, persecutions, and troubles that I suffer for Christ. For when I am weak, then I am strong" (2 Corinthians 12:10).

What frustrates you? Does something hold you back? Maybe it has fancy medical letters, such as ADD. Or maybe you're small or big for your age. It might take some work, but God can help you overcome any challenge you face.

) On the Ball

Don't run away from your problem. Pick a hard challenge, and attack it. Make a plan to accomplish it with your parents' help. Don't count it a failure if you struggle. Keep going for it and repeating 2 Corinthians 12:10.

) COACH'S COMMENT

That's why I take pleasure in my weaknesses, and in the insults, hardships, persecutions, and troubles that I suffer for Christ. For when I am weak, then I am strong. 2 CORINTHIANS 12:10

Michael Kettman was 13 when he found out that the record for spinning basketballs at one time was seven. *Seven?* he thought. *I can beat that.* A year later he set a new record by spinning 10. And he was only getting started. In 1999, Michael raised the world record to 28 basketballs spun at one time!

That's so many balls that Michael had to be creative about where to spin them. He held on his lap a special rack made of plastic pipe. Michael slapped one ball at a time to get it spinning on the tip of a ballpoint pen. Then he placed it on a nail head on the plastic rack. His biggest challenge was getting all the balls spinning before the first ones slowed down and fell off. He had about 90 seconds to get all 28 balls spinning. The last ones spun on Michael's fingertips. The balls didn't spin long—but long enough to make the record official.

What's the Score?

Michael was a master basketball spinner, but he could only keep everything going for a short time. Sometimes our lives can feel like we're trying to keep a whole collection of balls spinning—and it all quickly gets out of control. When that happens, we need to let the balls fall and recognize that God is in control. Getting worried and upset will only stress us out. God gives us a better way to deal with life. He says, "Be still, and know that I am God" (Psalm 46:10).

That means we need to be quiet and trust him. We should set aside our problems and projects for a little while and rest in him. Reading the Bible can remind us of who God is. So can going for a walk through his creation as you talk or sing to him. Try it, and remember that God can keep your world from spinning out of control.

) On the Ball

Take some time to be still with God. Find a special place where you won't be distracted, maybe a park or a tree fort. You might even set down a basketball outside to remind you to put aside whatever's bothering you. Then breathe deeply, and read God's Word.

) COACH'S COMMENT

Be still, and know that I am God! I will be honored by every nation. I will be honored throughout the world. PSALM 46:10

Diane Van Deren had been running for 12 days when she crossed the finish line of the Yukon Arctic Ultramarathon on this day in 2009. She had run 430 miles in the dead of winter. Temperatures were negative 30 degrees. But that wasn't the worst part. On the 11th day, Diane broke through the ice and fell shoulder deep into icy water. Her boots froze to her feet. Still, Diane was the first and only woman to complete the race.

Had Diane lost her mind to want to run races like the Yukon Ultramarathon? Well, only a part of it. Doctors removed a racquetball-size part of Diane's brain to help her terrible epileptic seizures. The surgery got rid of the seizures, but Diane also lost a lot of her memory and organization skills. But for some reason, Diane could also run for hours without stopping. Her lack of memory helped, too, because she literally couldn't remember how long or how far she had gone. Running was Diane's therapy. In a race like the Yukon, she got plenty of it.

What's the Score?

Diane's lack of memory helped her run, but it was a big challenge in life. She chose to put her limitations behind her and make the most of what they enabled her to do.

Most of us won't have part of our brain removed, but a bigger part of us has been removed by Christ—our sin. Paul told us to forget the past and look forward to what lies ahead (Philippians 3:13). Why? "To reach the end of the race and receive the heavenly prize for which God, through Christ Jesus, is calling us" (Philippians 3:14). We all have something we need to overcome. Sometimes challenges in one part of our lives can be strengths in another part of it. Look ahead to God's finish line, and keep running for it.

) On the Ball

Run 430 miles, and see how you feel. Just kidding. But take a short run around your neighborhood. Pray as you go, and let God clear your head of any troubles that are bothering you.

) COACH'S COMMENT

I have not achieved [perfection], but I focus on this one thing: Forgetting the past and looking forward to what lies ahead. PHILIPPIANS 3:13

Lhakpa Ri may be the easiest 23,000-foot mountain in the world to climb. But that's like saying tigers are the gentlest of the big cats to wrestle. You can still easily get bitten.

Yet in 2004, Erik Weihenmayer thought Lhakpa Ri was the perfect place to lead a group of six blind Tibetan teenagers on their first mountain-climbing expedition. Oh, and you've heard the expression "the blind leading the blind"? Erik was blind too. But that hadn't stopped him from climbing some of the world's tallest mountains, including Mount Everest, which is Lhakpa Ri's neighbor. Blind people were treated as outcasts in Tibet. One of the young climbers had been sold as a slave by his parents. He later escaped and lived on the streets. Erik's goal was to give these kids an opportunity to build their confidence and achieve something great.

Each blind climber had a sighted escort and would hold on to his or her guide's trekking pole or backpack or listen to a bell. Each guide gave lots of verbal instructions, too, to help the teens avoid rocks or holes on the rugged terrain. The climbers could tell they were extremely high by the sound of falling rock. The negative 30-degree temperatures reminded them, too. The group didn't reach the top of Lhakpa Ri, but they did make it to Everest's Advanced Base Camp. At 21,000 feet, it was the highest altitude ever reached by blind teens or kids.

⬜⬜ What's the Score?

Talk about faith. The Tibetan teens trusted their lives to their guides and leaders in a hostile environment that was tough climbing even for people who could see. That's the kind of faith God wants us to have. The Bible describes it this way: "Faith is the confidence that what we hope for will actually happen; it gives us assurance about things we cannot see" (Hebrews 11:1).

We can't see God, but we can trust him. We can't tell what will happen in the future, but we can trust that what God promised will be true. Until then, we can listen for God's guidance and keep climbing even when we can't see the way. One day we'll see it all clearly. For now we need to trust like our lives depend on it . . . which they do.

⟩ On the Ball

Make a list of things you know are real even though you can't see them. Here's a freebie to get you started: gravity.

_____   _____

_____   _____

_____   _____

_____   _____

⟩ COACH'S COMMENT

Faith is the confidence that what we hope for will actually happen; it gives us assurance about things we cannot see. HEBREWS 11:1

If Canada's road to Olympic hockey gold were paved with ice, it needed a Zamboni—because it was anything but smooth. The Canadian men were the favorites at the 2010 Vancouver Games on their home turf. But they lost to the United States and placed sixth in the early rounds. That meant Canada would have to get past tough teams from Germany, Slovakia, and Russia to reach the gold-medal game.

The Canadians were discouraged. Other Canadian athletes had lost in events they were favored to win. It felt like the honor of the entire country rested on the men's hockey team. But there was hope. The Canadians won three straight games to reach the gold-medal contest.

The American team wasn't supposed to be that good, but they remained undefeated all the way to the finals. With 24.4 seconds left in regulation, the Americans showed their grit by tying the score 2–2 and forcing overtime. Canada had given up a 2–0 lead, and it seemed that the United States had the momentum. Suddenly the failures, doubts, and mistakes all came rushing in. But seven minutes into overtime, Sidney Crosby whipped a quick shot past the American goalie. The hockey-crazy nation of Canada had its gold medal—the nation's first hockey gold medal won on its home soil. One act erased all the disappointments, frustrations, and questions.

What's the Score?

With one act, Sidney Crosby brought hockey redemption for Canada. All that mattered were the gold medals around the Canadian heroes' necks.

The death and resurrection of Jesus gives us our miracle moment, and it's far, far greater than a sports medal. The apostle Paul wrote, "Christ's one act of righteousness brings a right relationship with God and new life for everyone" (Romans 5:18). All our mistakes and sins are forgotten when we accept his forgiveness. Our sins are removed forever as far as the east is from the west (Psalm 103:12). A gold medal can be lost, stolen, or melted. Nothing can ever take away the gift of new life that Jesus gives.

⟩ On the Ball

Build a pile of rocks or marshmallows outside. With one big swing, knock it down. Thank God that Jesus destroyed all your sin in his one act of righteousness on the cross.

⟩ COACH'S COMMENT

Adam's one sin brings condemnation for everyone, but Christ's one act of righteousness brings a right relationship with God and new life for everyone. **ROMANS 5:18**

For baseball fans, few days are as sweet as March 1. It marks the mandatory date for all Major League Baseball players to report to spring training. Pitchers and catchers typically arrive in the second week of February, but it isn't until March when spring training gets fully under way in Arizona and Florida. As palm trees sway in the breeze, spring training provides a chance for all 30 major league teams to start fresh.

It's a time of anticipation and renewal. Whether a team's record was 100–62 or 62–100 the previous season, there are great possibilities with a 0–0 record. In March, pitchers seem to have some extra zip on their fastballs and bite on their curveballs. Young players who are trying to make the big leagues play with boundless zeal. Even veterans seem to have a little more bounce in their step. Hall of Famer Rogers Hornsby once said, "People ask me what I do in winter when there's no baseball. I'll tell you what I do. I stare out the window and wait for spring."

What's the Score?

Fresh starts are a good thing. But it's not just baseball teams that need them. We all do. According to the Bible, we were all born with a terrible sin problem that separates us from a holy God. In fact, before we put our faith in Christ, Ephesians 2:1 describes us as "dead because of [our] disobedience and [our] many sins." Being dead? Whoa! Talk about needing a fresh start!

That's exactly what God gives us when we put our faith in Jesus and believe that his death paid the penalty for our sins. Ephesians 2 continues by saying that, through Christ, we can be raised "from the dead" and seated "with him in the heavenly realms" (verse 6). No matter how many times you've sinned or how bad your sins are, God wants to give you a fresh start through faith in his Son. Spring training has nothing on that fresh start!

) On the Ball

List as many sins as you can think of on a chalkboard or a dry-erase board. When finished, wipe the board clean to signify the fresh start God gives us through Christ.

) COACH'S COMMENT

He raised us from the dead along with Christ and seated us with him in the heavenly realms because we are united with Christ Jesus. EPHESIANS 2:6

Did you catch any of the skeleton competition at the 2010 Winter Olympics in Vancouver, where Amy Williams of Great Britain and Canada's Jon Montgomery took home Olympic gold? No, skeleton isn't an X-ray contest between Olympic athletes to see who has the healthiest bones! That would be silly. The sport of skeleton requires athletes to run down a bobsled track, jump headfirst onto a lunch tray (at least that's what it looks like), and race down a mountain at breakneck speed.

Skeleton is not for the faint of heart. Riders, who wear little protection other than a helmet, reach speeds up to 85 miles per hour! On some courses, they can experience g-force ratings of plus five. That means the fastest riders feel like they weigh more than five times their actual weight as they're barreling down the track. Skeleton racers can only steer by using slight body movements, and they don't have brakes. Only getting to the bottom slows them down. Gulp.

What's the Score?

All this talk about skeletons brings to mind a cool Bible story about bones. In Genesis 50:25, Joseph made an interesting request. You remember Joseph, right? His father, Jacob, gave him a coat of many colors, which made his brothers jealous. So they sold Joseph into slavery, and he wound up in Egypt, where he eventually became second in command to Pharaoh and was happily reunited with his family.

Just before dying, Joseph made his brothers promise that one day the Israelites would transport his dead bones out of Egypt. It might sound like an odd request, but actually it showed great faith.

Joseph remembered God's promise to his great-grandfather, Abraham—that God would make a great nation of Abraham's descendants and bring them into the Promised Land. Sure enough, more than 400 years later when God freed Israel from Egyptian slavery, Moses honored Joseph's request (Exodus 13:19), and Joseph's bones were buried in the Promised Land (Joshua 24:32).

Joseph had great faith, which the Bible defines as belief in something we can't see. We can't see God, but we must have faith in him. In fact, Hebrews 11:6 says no one can please God without faith. We can't get to heaven without it. That's the truth—make no bones about it.

) On the Ball

Faith can be hard to understand. To learn more, read all of Hebrews 11. Write down a couple of your favorite lines:

) COACH'S COMMENT

It is impossible to please God without faith. Anyone who wants to come to him must believe that God exists and that he rewards those who sincerely seek him. HEBREWS 11:6

Other than the magazine's name and date, there were no words on the cover of the March 3, 1980, edition of *Sports Illustrated*. No headlines were needed. The simple, full-page photograph of Team USA ice-hockey players celebrating wildly said it all: the United States, vast underdogs, had defeated the mighty Soviet Union in the Winter Olympics. It was the "Miracle on Ice."

In 1980, the United States and the Soviet Union (now known as Russia) were embroiled in the Cold War, a standoff of world superpowers. The United States and the Soviet Union were bitter enemies—in politics, sports, and anything else possible. So anticipation was sky high when the two nations met in the 1980 Olympic semifinals in Lake Placid, New York. At the time, the Soviets were the world's premier hockey power, having won the 1976 Olympic gold medal. The Americans, meanwhile, were a bunch of unknown college and amateur players.

Yet somehow, the Americans stunned the Soviets, winning 4–3. The Americans completed their improbable march to the gold medal with a 4–2 win over Finland.

Team USA's win over the Soviets continues to resonate to this day. In fact, the International Ice Hockey Federation chose that game as the top international hockey story of the century. It wasn't just a hockey win for the Americans. It was a Cold War victory over a bitter enemy.

☐☐ What's the Score?

There's no doubt about it: beating your enemy feels great. The US team's gold medal performance in 1980 wouldn't have held the same charm had it beaten, say, Luxembourg. As humans, we love watching our enemies fail, especially if we can help the cause. But the Bible says this attitude is wrong.

In Matthew 5, Jesus readjusts our thinking by commanding us to love our enemies and to actually pray for them. This is because all people, even those we don't like, are created in God's image. If our heavenly Father loves them, we must also. There is no room for hate or bitterness toward others among true followers of Jesus. We must show Christlike love to all people, even those who are hard to love. This, after all, is what Jesus did, even when his enemies hung him on the cross.

⟩ On the Ball

Invite someone you haven't really gotten along with to your house or include that person on your sports team.

⟩ COACH'S COMMENT

You have heard the law that says, "Love your neighbor" and hate your enemy. But I say, love your enemies! Pray for those who persecute you! MATTHEW 5:43-44

A lot of athletes seem to be getting into trouble these days. Sometimes a local newspaper's sports section reads more like a criminal-court docket. Some of the highest-profile players have been convicted of crimes. In 2010, NBA star Gilbert Arenas was given a hefty fine and sentenced to a halfway house and community service for bringing guns into the Washington Wizards' locker room. In 2009, Plaxico Burress, a Super Bowl champion wide receiver from the New York Giants, was sentenced to two years in prison for carrying a gun into a New York club, where he accidentally shot himself. And from 2007 to 2009, NFL quarterback Michael Vick served a 19-month sentence in federal prison and a two-month home confinement for running a brutal dogfighting operation in Virginia.

Sadly, the list goes on and on. More than ever, it seems, prominent athletes all over the sports world are making negative headlines for gambling, drunk driving, drugs, illegal steroids, assault, and more.

⬜⬜ What's the Score?

Imagine this scene: Every person who has ever committed a crime, not just athletes, stands in an enormous courtroom, awaiting his or her final verdict. The judge reviews each case and looks at the countless defendants. "Each one of you is guilty as charged," he says, solemnly. "You all deserve the full punishment, which is the death penalty."

A silence falls over the room. Then the judge looks at his son, who stands in the courtroom, although he is completely innocent. "But my son has agreed to pay all your punishment himself," the judge continues. "You may go free if you repent and accept this gift of mercy."

Wow! How amazing would it be if that actually happened? Actually, it has! That's what God (the Judge of the universe) has done for us (guilty sinners) through his Son, Jesus Christ. By Jesus' death, he has justified us in God's eyes. *Justification* is a legal term found in the Bible that describes how God removes our guilt. By trusting in Christ, we are justified, or made right, with a holy God. Through justification, which we can read about in Romans 5, God credits Jesus' righteousness to us and forgives our sins. God does not justify everyone—only those who repent and trust in Christ. But for those who do, it's the greatest acquittal we'll ever know!

⟩ On the Ball

Ask your parents to take you to a local courthouse to watch a public trial, or watch a courtroom scene on TV. While watching it, thank God for providing justification through Christ.

⟩ COACH'S COMMENT

Since we have been justified through faith, we have peace with God through our Lord Jesus Christ. ROMANS 5:1 (NIV)

Mush! No, not a sloppy bowl of oatmeal or the lima beans your baby brother just smeared on the kitchen wall. *Mush* is the common command given to sled dogs to get them running. And the best place to hear this term shouted is at the famous Iditarod Trail Sled Dog Race. The Iditarod is not your everyday race. It's an extreme adventure in Alaska where competitors race on dogsleds from Anchorage to Nome. The trail is 1,150 miles long, which is like traveling from Washington, DC, to Omaha, Nebraska—except it's not on smooth, government-maintained highways. It's on Arctic tundra! Temperatures on the trail often dip below zero. Brrrr!

The Iditarod, which is held each March, has been run every year since 1973 and typically takes between 10 to 17 days. In 2002, Martin Buser set the fastest-finish record by completing the race in eight days, 22 hours, 46 minutes, and two seconds. That's still more than a week in the freezing-cold wilderness. Brrrr again!

What's the Score?

Iditarod competitors endure many dangers and great personal discomfort to achieve a remarkable goal. Christians, too, are called to a similar life. In 2 Corinthians 1, the apostle Paul gives a vivid description of what he endured while spreading the gospel of Jesus Christ across the ancient world. At various times during his ministry, Paul was hungry, thirsty, cold, imprisoned, beaten, whipped, stoned, and shipwrecked. He suffered greatly for the sake of Christ.

Even today, many Christians around the world suffer greatly for their faith, especially in places like Africa, the Middle East, and Asia, where certain countries outlaw Christianity. If you are a Christian in America, chances are you won't have to endure what Paul did because of the many religious freedoms we enjoy. But the Bible clearly says that all Christians will suffer in some way for their faith. That's because we live in a sinful world opposed to God and all who follow him. It may not be physical suffering, but all Christians eventually feel ridiculed or left out because of their faith. The good news is "the more we suffer for Christ, the more God will shower us with his comfort through Christ" (2 Corinthians 1:5). How much difficulty are you willing to endure for God?

) On the Ball

Commit to praying at least once a week for the missionaries your church supports. They are no strangers to suffering. Also pray for God to give you strength and boldness when you endure difficulties because of your faith.

) COACH'S COMMENT

The more we suffer for Christ, the more God will shower us with his comfort through Christ. 2 CORINTHIANS 1:5

In 2010, a basketball player named Jeremy Lin created headlines for two reasons: he made it to the NBA after playing college ball at Harvard University, and he was Asian American. That may not seem like that big of a deal, right? But Jeremy became the first former Ivy Leaguer to play in the NBA in eight years and the first Asian American NBA player since Wataru Misaka played three games for the New York Knicks in 1947. The six-foot-three-inch guard didn't get drafted, but he made the roster with the Golden State Warriors as a free agent. Jeremy's parents were from China and emigrated from Taiwan to California, where he was born and raised.

Perhaps the most famous Asian player ever is Yao Ming, the seven-foot-six-inch center whom the Houston Rockets selected No. 1 overall in the 2002 NBA draft. In 2007, seven-foot center Yi Jianlian was drafted sixth overall by the Milwaukee Bucks. Both Yao and Yi were born in China.

⏸ **What's the Score?**

Jeremy's family background received a lot of attention when he made it to the NBA. But race or ethnicity shouldn't receive any attention when it comes to how we treat others. The gospel—the Good News of forgiveness of sins through Jesus Christ—is color blind. It crosses all racial boundaries and any ethnic lines. God doesn't favor one race of people any more than another. All people, the Bible says, are created in God's image.

We see a great example of this in Jesus' parable in Luke 10 about a Samaritan traveler who helps a Jewish man who was beaten by robbers. Jesus told his Jewish audience to treat others in the same way. The story would have shocked Jesus' listeners, because Jews and Samaritans in first-century Palestine hated each other. In fact, they often wouldn't even travel through each other's countries. But true followers of Jesus have no excuse for any type of racial prejudice. We should not make jokes about another race or exclude someone from an activity because of his or her skin color. Any unkind remark against another race is really like telling God, "You messed up when you created those people." And that's not what Jesus taught.

⟩ **On the Ball**

Make friends with someone from a different race and learn about that person's culture. You'll be surprised at what you can learn!

⟩ **COACH'S COMMENT**

A despised Samaritan came along, and when he saw the man, he felt compassion for him. LUKE 10:33

"I bet on baseball." Those words shook the sports world when Pete Rose said them in 2004. In an illustrious 24-year Major League Baseball career, Pete made a name for himself as "Charlie Hustle"—the player who never quit. By the time he retired in 1986, he was baseball's all-time hit king, having surpassed the legendary Ty Cobb, with 4,256 career base hits. In his final three seasons, Pete was a player-manager for the Cincinnati Reds and then took over as full-time manager in 1987 for another three seasons.

But in 1989, he was banned from baseball for life after an investigation revealed that he had wagered money on the sport—a serious breach of baseball's rule book—while managing the Reds. Pete denied the charges for nearly 15 years before finally admitting in 2004 to betting on baseball as the Reds' manager in 1987 and 1988. In other words, he spent about 15 years lying.

What's the Score?

Before we shake our heads in disgust at Pete, let's be honest: all of us have lied. It comes naturally to us because of our sinful nature. This is a serious problem. God specifically forbids lying in the Ten Commandments (Exodus 20:16) and throughout Scripture. Lying, in fact, started with Satan himself in the Garden of Eden. God had created a perfect world for the first humans, Adam and Eve. He gave them only one rule: they were not allowed to eat fruit from the tree of the knowledge of good and evil. God said they would die if they did. But Satan, disguised as a serpent, lied to Eve: "You won't die!" he said. Adam and Eve believed Satan's lie, ate the fruit, and brought sin and death into the world.

Lying is a terrible sin in God's sight. It is deceitful and has its origins with God's enemy. In John 8:44, Jesus called Satan the "father of lies." Jesus, on the other hand, is described as "the way, the truth, and the life" (John 14:6). Our lives must be marked by truth, both in our actions and our words. There is no such thing as a "little white lie" or a "half-truth." A half-truth is really a whole lie. As Zechariah 8:16 commands us, "Tell the truth to each other."

> On the Ball

Identify any areas in your life in which you are tempted to lie, and ask your parents to help you tell the truth.

> COACH'S COMMENT

This is what you must do: Tell the truth to each other. ZECHARIAH 8:16

Three's a crowd, or so the saying goes. But after a flurry of major roster moves in 2010, the Miami Heat hoped its "Big Three" would fill the team's trophy case with championship hardware for years to come. Regardless of whether the team flopped or flew, the 2010–2011 NBA season was all about Miami's collection of superstars—LeBron James, Dwyane Wade, and Chris Bosh. In the prior off-season, the Heat had

+ re-signed Dwyane, its franchise star who had helped bring an NBA title to South Beach in 2006;
+ traded for LeBron, Cleveland's No. 1 overall draft pick in 2003; and
+ signed Chris as a free agent.

Never before in NBA history had such a talented trio agreed to join forces on one team. At the time of the talent merger, LeBron and Dwyane were six-time All-Stars, while Chris was a five-time All-Star. LeBron was also the two-time reigning league MVP. With all three players at age 28 or younger when they combined their talents, the future looked awfully bright for Miami and its Big Three.

☐☐ What's the Score?

By basketball standards, the Heat's Big Three were pretty impressive. But the Bible talks about three persons who are infinitely greater: the Holy Trinity. The triune God of Scripture is God the Father, God the Son (Jesus), and God the Holy Spirit. They are all mentioned in a number of Scripture passages, including today's verse, 2 Corinthians 13:14.

While understanding the Trinity can be difficult, this teaching is vitally important for every Christian. Perhaps the best way to define the Trinity is this way:

1. God is three persons.
2. Each person is fully God.
3. There is one God.

Each person of the Godhead has distinct and separate functions. God the Father spoke the words of creation and planned our salvation by sending Jesus into the world. Jesus' primary role was to be our sin bearer. And the Spirit gives us new spiritual life and helps us to grow in godliness. Despite their unique roles, all three persons of the Trinity are fully God. Any attempt to say that Jesus or the Spirit is not fully God is a serious error. Although there is much more to understand and learn about the Trinity, we should acknowledge that we serve one God, in three persons, and that he is awesome!

⟩ On the Ball

To learn more about the Trinity, read Bible passages such as Matthew 3:16-17, Matthew 28:19, Ephesians 4:4-6, 1 Peter 1:2, and Jude 1:20-21.

⟩ COACH'S COMMENT

May the grace of the Lord Jesus Christ, the love of God, and the fellowship of the Holy Spirit be with you all. 2 CORINTHIANS 13:14

Tiger Williams spent much of his impressive NHL career on his backside. Then again, what did you expect from the league's all-time leader in penalty minutes? At only 5 feet 11 inches and 190 pounds, Tiger certainly didn't possess the typical build of a brawling enforcer. But that didn't stop the Saskatchewan native from getting into countless on-ice fights. Tiger paid the price for his angry brawls. In his 14-year NHL career from 1974 to 1988, he led the league in penalty minutes three different seasons and finished his career with 3,966 penalty minutes, setting the league record. As of the 2010–2011 season, no active player was remotely close to his dubious mark.

Lost in all the hostility was the fact that Tiger was a pretty good left wing. He tallied 241 goals and 272 assists in his career and made the NHL All-Star Game in 1981, the same season he scored a career-high 35 goals. The following season, he helped lead the Vancouver Canucks on a surprising run to the Stanley Cup finals. But Tiger will always be most remembered as the player who was quite familiar with the "sin bin."

⬜⬜ What's the Score?

Hockey fans can't argue that Tiger didn't deserve to spend all that time in the penalty box. His actions had consequences. But there was one man who paid a terrible penalty for countless sins that he never committed. That man is Jesus Christ.

According to the Bible, since the fall of man in Genesis, every human who has ever lived, including you, was born with a sin problem that deserves death and separation from God forever. God's holiness and justice demands that someone must pay the penalty for our sins. It should have been us. But in his mercy, God sent his own Son, Jesus Christ, to die in our place. Jesus, who was without sin, endured God's holy wrath on the cross for our sake. Jesus freely gave his life to pay the penalty for our sin. Now, through faith in him, we can receive forgiveness of sins and eternal life with God.

⟩ On the Ball

Memorize today's verse below about Jesus paying the penalty we deserved with his perfect life. Thank you, Jesus!

⟩ COACH'S COMMENT

He himself is the sacrifice that atones for our sins—and not only our sins but the sins of all the world. 1 JOHN 2:2

He was simply known as "The Answer." Of course, he was also known for having possibly the best crossover dribble in NBA history. Allen Iverson, the former Georgetown University star, was much more than just a great ball handler. As the NBA's No. 1 overall draft pick in 1996, Iverson enjoyed a 14-year NBA career in which he won rookie of the year, was the league's Most Valuable Player, and finished with 24,368 points.

But Allen will always be known for his crossover move. At a spindly six-feet, 165 pounds (a waif by the NBA's outsized standards), he masterfully switched directions so fast while dribbling that his defenders often had no time to react. Michael Jordan, Kobe Bryant, you name it—Allen "broke the ankles," as the basketball expression goes, of some of the game's all-time greats. Really, Allen's crossover was all about creating space. Using his blink-of-an-eye reflexes, he created open areas on the court where he could shoot, pass, or drive to the basket.

What's the Score?

When it came to creating space on NBA courts, Allen took a backseat to no one. But when it comes to creating space—as in "outer space" and everything else in the universe—that unique act belongs to God alone. As Genesis 1:1 says, God created everything we see (and can't see) from nothing. He spoke powerful words, and everything came into being in six days—light, galaxies, planets, stars, earth, water, mountains, trees, plants, animals, birds, fish, humans. Everything.

Evolution, or any other theory that takes God out of the equation and attempts to explain the universe's origin, is simply not true. We are created beings. That means we owe our very existence to an all-powerful creator. It also means we are not in charge. We have to answer to a higher authority. We can't just do whatever pleases us. Knowing that a holy, sovereign God created us should completely change our outlook on life. It should prompt us to consider why our creator made us. God created everything for his glory, so we are meant to worship him!

) On the Ball

Hold out your hand and try to create something from nothing—a bird, a tree, a rock, or something else. Say a special word or phrase like "Poof" or "Rock-em-Sock-em Rock" if you'd like. After many failed attempts, it should be clear that

1. we can't create anything out of nothing, and
2. our God is an awesome creator!

) COACH'S COMMENT

In the beginning God created the heavens and the earth. GENESIS 1:1

Injury? What injury? In locker rooms all over the world, that's the stance many professional athletes take with boo-boos big and small. Whether it's the pitching ace working through elbow pain, the NFL tailback running on a tender knee, or the hockey player staying mum about the ringing in his head, athletes hide their injuries all the time.

Sometimes it's driven by pride—the notion that "I can't get hurt." Sometimes athletes ignore injuries for fear of losing a starting role to a healthy teammate. Sometimes it's just complete denial. Here are three examples:

1. In January 2010, the Boston Red Sox learned that high-priced starting pitcher Daisuke Matsuzaka apparently hid a leg injury from them for about a year.
2. In February 2010, an ESPN.com article on US Olympic skier Lindsey Vonn and her painful shin injury claimed fellow American Julia Mancuso "and a host of foreign athletes . . . hid their injuries, not wanting to make excuses for potentially poor performances."
3. In November 2009, the Associated Press reported that 30 of 160 NFL players surveyed that season admitted to hiding or downplaying the effects of a concussion they had suffered.

⬜⬜ What's the Score?

While athletes often minimize or flat-out hide their injuries, we sometimes try to do the same with our sin. We like to conceal our wrongdoings, and when we do admit to them, we tend to downplay them, like they aren't that serious. But sin is deadly serious. Sinning, according to the Bible, is disobeying God's laws. And it's an insult to his holiness.

We would be wise to view our sin as God does. The Bible describes sin in the harshest language possible. Verses such as Psalm 45:7, Proverbs 6:16-19, and Hosea 9:15 use the word *hate* to explain God's attitude toward sin and evil.

The book of Hosea is all about God's judgment on ancient Israel because of the nation's sins. Our disobedience deserves punishment and death. That's a sobering thought. But here's the good news: Even though God hates our sins and has every right to punish us, he mercifully chose to offer us the gift of salvation through his Son, Jesus Christ. God doesn't minimize our sins, but he is also a God of love, not hate, who wants to forgive us.

⟩ On the Ball

Work on not hiding or minimizing your sins. Rather, take your sins seriously by confessing them specifically and asking for forgiveness from those you have offended and from God.

⟩ COACH'S COMMENT

The LORD says, "All their wickedness began at Gilgal; there I began to hate them. I will drive them from my land because of their evil actions." **HOSEA 9:15**

If you play sports, you probably have a rival. Somewhere out there, there's a team or individual who beats you as much as, or more than, you beat them. They always seem to muddle your plans for a championship. Sound familiar? You are not alone. Throughout sports history, rivalries have existed.

One of Major League Baseball's greatest rivalries is between the New York Yankees and the Boston Red Sox. The NFL has the Washington Redskins and the Dallas Cowboys, the Chicago Bears versus the Green Bay Packers, and other longtime rivalries. In the NBA, no rivalry may go back as far as the Los Angeles Lakers and the Boston Celtics. College football has great traditional rivalries such as Harvard versus Yale, Michigan versus Ohio State, Alabama versus Auburn, and Oregon versus Oregon State. College basketball's greatest rivalry may be Duke and North Carolina.

Sports rivalries exist at the individual level too. In the 1960s, Jack Nicklaus and Arnold Palmer consistently battled on the PGA Tour. Boxing gave us Muhammad Ali and Joe Frazier. Tennis has produced great theater whenever Rafael Nadal and Roger Federer play. Rivalries certainly add excitement to sports, but sadly, they also produce plenty of unkindness. Rivalries often bring out the worst of our sinful natures and create a wall of hostility between players, fans, and entire cities.

☐☐ What's the Score?
In Ephesians 2, the Bible talks about another wall of hostility. For centuries, God's chosen people, the Jews, thought they were better than Gentiles, or non-Jews, because God had given the Jews the sacred Old Testament Law and writings. First-century Jews often scoffed at Gentiles and assumed they couldn't go to heaven. It was, in a sense, a rivalry between the two people groups.

But God didn't want them to bicker and compete. Age, gender, and race don't matter to him. Jesus' sacrificial death and resurrection breaks down all barriers. He wants people of all ages, countries, and ethnicities to place their faith in him. The amazing truth of the gospel is that anyone can be saved! God's love is bigger than any rivalry.

⟩ On the Ball
The next time you play your rival or see your rival around town, do something nice. Tell your rival you respect how hard he or she competes or what a good shot he or she has. Say you like playing against him or her. By striking up a friendship, you may one day be able to share your faith in Jesus with your rival.

⟩ COACH'S COMMENT
Christ himself has brought peace to us. He united Jews and Gentiles into one people when, in his own body on the cross, he broke down the wall of hostility that separated us.
EPHESIANS 2:14

When it comes to the ability to dish out mockery, college students have no equal. Okay, middle-school, high-school, and elementary-aged kids are pretty good at making fun of others too. But college students get to mock people on TV. Have you ever watched a Duke University basketball game? If you have, you've probably seen the Cameron Crazies.

"Cameron Crazies" is the nickname for the rowdy, passionate student cheering section that fills the lower seating section at Cameron Indoor Stadium. No one is exactly sure when, where, or how the group got its name, but the Crazies are clearly some of the best in college basketball—and maybe all sports—at teasing and intimidating opposing players. If you've ever seen a basketball game where a visiting player's shot missed the basket entirely, you probably heard the crowd chant, "Air ball!" Guess who invented the phrase—that's right, the Cameron Crazies. They are masters of making fun. They thrive on ridicule. They've teased short players, large players, bald coaches, and players with long arms. They've mercilessly taunted players who had run afoul of the law. They even once mocked a player who had recently suffered a punctured lung.

What's the Score?

The Cameron Crazies do some funny antics, but there's nothing funny about teasing somebody. According to the Bible, slandering someone is no laughing matter. Slander is speaking falsely about someone in a way that attacks his or her character. In other words, it's spreading cruel lies. Any time we joke about someone, we are in danger of slipping into slander. God hates slander. In fact, the important laws God gave to Moses in the book of Leviticus included a ban on slander (19:16).

But we should not just avoid slander. We should also steer clear of any unkind speech. God calls his children to show Christlike love in their words. That means any name-calling, mean-spirited teasing, or swearing is prohibited. When we speak about others, people should notice that our speech is different from the world's. The Cameron Crazies might be passionate fans, but they are not the example we want to follow.

) On the Ball

Think of five people whom, honestly, you'd like to slander or ridicule. Now commit to telling them something kind the next time you see them.

) COACH'S COMMENT

Do not go about spreading slander among your people. LEVITICUS 19:16 (NIV)

Lots of kids swim. Others dance. Still others perform gymnastics. But not many plug their noses, jump into a pool, and do all three at once. Welcome to the wonderful world of synchronized swimming. March is a big month for this unique aquatic sport. This time each year, USA Synchro, America's governing body for synchronized swimming, hosts the US Collegiate Championships and the US Junior Championships. Many of these swimmers are aspiring Olympians.

This unique sport, which made its Olympic debut in 1984, combines elements of swimming, dancing, and gymnastics in a pool. Female competitors perform two routines—a technical program filled with required moves and an artistic program where swimmers are free to perform moves of their own choice. As in gymnastics and figure skating, a panel of judges scores the routines to determine a winner. Synchronized swimming differs from other team sports, though, by featuring two or more teammates who are trying to perfectly imitate each other's movements. The most graceful swimmer in the world won't score well in synchro if she isn't imitating her teammate well.

🏊 What's the Score?

Imitating your team in synchronized swimming is very important. But it might not be a good idea in other situations. In 3 John 1:11, the Bible commands us to "not imitate what is evil but what is good" (NIV). We live in a world where people fight, lie, cheat, steal, curse, take the Lord's name in vain, speak unkind words, disobey their parents, dishonor God, etc.

Maybe you know some people who do these things. We are not to follow their example. Rather, we should be very careful whom we hang out with because we are to imitate what is good. God calls us to follow his laws, imitate Christ's example of how to treat others, and surround ourselves with those who love him. The more we do these things, the easier it is to obey God and imitate what is good.

⟩ On the Ball

Make friends with a strong Christian who loves God and obeys his Word.

⟩ COACH'S COMMENT

Dear friend, do not imitate what is evil but what is good. Anyone who does what is good is from God. Anyone who does what is evil has not seen God. **3 JOHN 1:11 (NIV)**

Let's hear it for underdogs! No, not the people who push you high on a swing by running underneath you. Underdogs are the teams that nobody expects to win. The 2010 NCAA men's basketball tournament witnessed perhaps the greatest collection of underdog stories in the history of the sport.

Think about these games from a wild March Madness: of the 32 first-round games, lower seeds won 10 times—the most shocking of which was 14th-seeded Ohio crushing third-ranked Georgetown, 97–83. Northern Iowa made a strong showing by stunning UNLV and top-ranked Kansas to reach the Sweet Sixteen. Cornell, not exactly a perennial basketball power, did the same by upsetting Temple and Wisconsin. And who figured St. Mary's would bounce Richmond and second-ranked Villanova? Of course, the greatest underdog story that year was fifth-seeded Butler University, a small program from basketball-crazy Indiana. The Bulldogs crashed the party big-time and nearly upset mighty Duke in the NCAA final. Yes, in the 2010 NCAA tournament, underdogs certainly had a lot to bark about!

What's the Score?

Did you know the Bible is full of underdogs too? Consider Nehemiah. He lived during the fifth century BC, when God's people were returning to their homeland after Babylon's King Nebuchadnezzar had conquered Jerusalem and exiled the people a century earlier. Jerusalem was in ruins. Its once-great wall was destroyed, its gates were burned, and its inhabitants were sad and afraid. Without a wall, the exiles returning to Jerusalem could have been attacked at any time.

Nehemiah knew the odds were stacked against him. The task of rebuilding the wall was not easy. The labor was grueling, and there were plenty of hostile neighbors who threatened Nehemiah with violence. But Nehemiah trusted God, and God protected him. Working from dawn until dusk every day, Nehemiah's construction crews defeated their enemies (Nehemiah 6:16) and finished rebuilding the wall in only 52 days! Nehemiah's inspiring victory is a great example for us when we feel like the underdogs. You see, the odds don't matter to God. He is all-powerful and can do whatever pleases him. He simply wants people, like Nehemiah did, to fully trust in him. God loves using underdogs like us to show his power and glory.

) On the Ball

Read the book of Nehemiah to learn more about a true underdog tale!

- -

) COACH'S COMMENT

When our enemies and the surrounding nations heard about it, they were frightened and humiliated. They realized this work had been done with the help of our God.
NEHEMIAH 6:16

- -

Women's figure skating has always been a beautiful, elegant sport. But in the weeks leading up to the 1994 Winter Olympics in Lillehammer, Norway, it got ugly. Really ugly. Two days before the US National Championships in Detroit, Michigan, skater Nancy Kerrigan was attacked backstage by a man with a metal baton. The attacker clubbed Nancy's right leg, forcing her to miss the competition, which her rival, Tonya Harding, won.

The next month Tonya's ex-husband, Jeff Gillooly, and several other men pled guilty for their roles in the attack. On March 16, 1994, Tonya pled guilty to a felony charge of conspiracy, although she denied having full knowledge of the attack before it occurred. Both Nancy and Tonya competed in the Lillehammer Olympics. Nancy overcame her injury to win the silver medal, while Tonya finished eighth. That March, to avoid jail time, Tonya agreed to a plea bargain. Later that summer, the US Figure Skating Association stripped Tonya of her 1994 national title and banned her for life for failing to comply with "the concept of sportsmanship and fair play."

⬜⬜ What's the Score?

Regardless of how involved she was in the attack, Tonya failed to conform to certain laws—both moral and civil. Sadly, this is a problem for all humans. Each of us has failed to conform to God's laws. This problem is called sin. A true understanding of sin is extremely important for all Christians. If we don't understand sin and how it affects us, we won't understand how desperately we need a savior.

The Bible says sin entered the world through Adam and Eve's disobedience in the Garden of Eden (Genesis 3). Every human has inherited a sin nature from Adam (Romans 5:12). We all fall short of God's perfect standard (Romans 3:23). Sin affects us completely. We sin in actions, words, thoughts, and desires. What's worse, sin separates us from God because he is holy. But in an act of amazing grace, God sent his own Son, Jesus Christ, to pay the penalty for our sins by dying on the cross. God will declare guilty and eternally punish all those who do not put their faith in Jesus. But for all who do, God will forgive their sins forever!

⟩ On the Ball

Some sins are obvious—like hitting an opponent with a baton. Other times our mistakes are harder to see or understand. Ask God to help you be aware of even your little sins. Pray for him to forgive all the bad things you do.

⟩ COACH'S COMMENT

When Adam sinned, sin entered the world. Adam's sin brought death, so death spread to everyone, for everyone sinned. ROMANS 5:12

It seemed like a good idea at the time. In 2001, World Wrestling Federation chairman Vince McMahon teamed up with television network NBC to create the XFL, a professional football league that promoted itself as a mixture of football and pro wrestling. Its goal was to rival the ultrapopular NFL. The XFL consisted of eight teams and ran from February to April, including play-offs and a championship called the "Million Dollar Game."

While much of the action on the field looked familiar, the XFL did include some quirky rules to speed up play and promote exciting—and sometimes painful—physical play. Initial interest in the league was strong, but it quickly faded. Less than three weeks after the first Million Dollar Game, the XFL folded. The XFL wasn't the first pro football league that failed to match the NFL's success. In 1985, the United States Football League folded after three seasons. It seems like nothing can compete with the real NFL.

⬚⬚ What's the Score?

Like professional sports, there are plenty of knockoff religions, too. For thousands of years, there have been countless counterfeits to Christianity—belief systems that seem so close, yet are very far from the truth of the gospel. Many different groups talk about Jesus Christ, but they preach a false salvation of works or add to God's Word. In Matthew 7:15, Jesus described these as "false prophets who come disguised as harmless sheep but are really vicious wolves."

Then there are religions that are blatantly false. Some say inner peace is the chief goal in life. Some teach that Jesus is only one of many roads to heaven or that he was nothing more than a good teacher. Some say the keys to heaven are within you. Still others teach reincarnation and all sorts of nonbiblical myths. As the apostle Paul instructed in 1 Timothy 4:16, we must watch our doctrine closely. We must be on guard against false religions and misguided beliefs. We must cling to the true gospel of Jesus Christ—that salvation comes only by faith in him. To know the difference between truth and error, we must faithfully read God's Word. When it comes to Christianity, our motto should be "No knockoffs allowed!"

⟩ On the Ball

With a parent, read about several false religions online. Know what members of these false religions believe, so you can watch out for it, and be confident in your faith in Christ.

⟩ COACH'S COMMENT

Watch your life and doctrine closely. 1 TIMOTHY 4:16 (NIV)

Ahoy, matey! Batten down the hatches, and shiver me timbers. It's time to sail the high seas! Every three years at this time, dozens of professional sailors are smack-dab in the middle of the world's most famous around-the-world sailing challenge—the Volvo Ocean Race. The 2008–2009 race, which started from Alicante, Spain, covered nearly 39,000 nautical miles. With 11 crew members, each boat sailed for up to three weeks at a time between various ports in Africa, Asia, the Middle East, North America, and more before reaching St. Petersburg, Russia. Although the Netherlands has won this race more than any other country, Sweden's Ericsson 4 took top honors in the 2008–2009 race.

With the wind and waves often against them, how do the ships reach all these locations safely? The competence of the crews is vitally important. So are the sails and other important riggings. But most importantly, the rudder steers the ship. The rudder may be a small piece of equipment, but without it, crews can't properly navigate a ship.

⬜ What's the Score?

Interestingly, in his self-named New Testament book, the apostle James compared our tongues to a large ship's rudder. That comparison might sound funny at first, but it is an appropriate metaphor. Our speech can have a huge effect on the direction of our life. James doesn't stop with the rudder analogy, though. In James 3, he compares the tongue to a spark that can ignite a forest fire. He also calls it "evil," "full of deadly poison," and "a whole world of wickedness." Make no mistake: our speech can be terribly dangerous.

We must watch our words very closely, always making sure that they are filled with kindness and love. Our words have the power to build up or to tear down others. They can bring us good or get us into serious trouble. The greatest model of loving speech is Jesus, who spoke kind, gracious words even as he was being crucified for our sins. If anyone had a reason to speak harsh, unkind words, it was Jesus. Yet he chose to point his mouth's rudder in the right direction. We should do the same!

⟩ On the Ball

Try to say one encouraging thing to a sibling, a friend, or a classmate today. Tomorrow, keep your mouth on course to say two nice things.

⟩ COACH'S COMMENT

A small rudder makes a huge ship turn wherever the pilot chooses to go, even though the winds are strong. In the same way, the tongue is a small thing that makes grand speeches. JAMES 3:4-5

One of the greatest NBA players of all time is a guy you've probably never heard of. Having played in the era of Wilt Chamberlain, Kareem Abdul-Jabbar, and Bill Walton, Wes Unseld often gets lost in the conversation of the greatest centers of all time. But his statistics and accomplishments certainly prove he was one. Wes was a six-foot-seven-inch, 245-pound roadblock who lifted the Baltimore and Washington Bullets franchise to heights it never achieved before or since. In his illustrious 13-year career, Wes guided the Bullets (now called the Wizards) to the play-offs for 12 straight years, including four NBA Finals appearances in the 1970s, and to the franchise's only championship in 1978.

Wes was a five-time all-star who also won the league's Most Valuable Player and Rookie of the Year honors. He was inducted into the Basketball Hall of Fame in 1988 and named to the NBA's 50th Anniversary All-Time Team in 1996. Just as impressive, he spent his whole career with one team. After retiring as a player in 1981, he immediately took an executive position with the Bullets before serving as the team's head coach from 1987 to 1994. As he once told *Sports Illustrated*, "I've always been a Bullet, and I always will be."

What's the Score?

Wes made a lifetime commitment to the Washington, DC, basketball team. Athletes like Wes, who play for only one team and then continue with that team in a leadership role, are extremely rare. Similarly, Christians are called to an exclusive, lifetime commitment to Christ. Sadly, many people treat Christianity like a new shirt at the department store. They try it on, and if they don't like it, they try something else.

But Christianity isn't something to be returned. Following Jesus Christ is a lifetime commitment, not a random decision. In fact, the word *Christian* means "Christ follower." A true follower of something follows for life, not just for a short time. Jesus himself said in John 15:5 that true believers must "remain in me." Becoming a Christian isn't simply a matter of praying a quick prayer or having a mysterious spiritual experience. It's not about knowing the Bible or going to church regularly. Becoming a Christian means repenting of your sins, trusting in Jesus as your Savior, and committing your entire life to him. True Christians will still sin, yes, but their commitment to Christ will be for a lifetime.

On the Ball

Read John 15 to understand more about making a lifetime commitment to Jesus.

COACH'S COMMENT

I am the vine; you are the branches. Those who remain in me, and I in them, will produce much fruit. For apart from me you can do nothing. JOHN 15:5

The stench of raw sewage in the streets was almost unbearable, and the depths of poverty were shocking—like adult men bending over to brush their teeth using sand, street water, and their own fingers.

Kyle Korver's trip to India was indeed a life-changing event. Kyle, a longtime NBA veteran, flew to India in 2008 as part of the league's Basketball without Borders program. While there, he fed and bathed dying medical patients, brought hundreds of pairs of shoes to poor children, and performed other acts of kindness. Previously, Kyle had taken similar trips to South Africa, China, Brazil, and parts of the United States.

Despite his NBA riches and fame, Kyle has a true heart for others, especially the needy. He learned that trait from his family, which includes many pastors (his father, grandfather, and two uncles). Growing up in the 1980s, Kyle spent many Saturdays helping his dad, Kevin, clean up their hometown of Paramount, California. By the time Kevin's "Lookin' Good" project was finished, it had won a national award from President George H. W. Bush for transforming a dangerous, run-down city into a nice place to live. Kyle has carried that others-first attitude into his professional career. Besides his international humanitarian trips, he also started the Kyle Korver Foundation, which reaches out to needy people in several US cities.

What's the Score?

Many professional sports stars treat charity work as only an obligation. But Kyle showed he was different. For him, helping the needy around the world was one of his passions. He wanted to live out his faith and to show others the love of Christ.

This should be our attitude too. God calls his children to unselfishly help others in need. James 1:27 describes true worship of God as "caring for orphans and widows in their distress"—in other words, helping the poor and needy. Jesus Christ, God's own Son, did this when he was on earth, giving us a wonderful example to follow. He often sacrificed his personal comfort to help others. Good works don't save us (only trusting in Jesus can do that), but they are a vivid display of genuine faith.

⟩ On the Ball

Find a way to help the needy in your community. Volunteer to do yard work for the elderly or injured. Serve meals at a soup kitchen. Visit a nursing home. Come up with your own idea: _____

⟩ COACH'S COMMENT

Pure and genuine religion in the sight of God the Father means caring for orphans and widows in their distress and refusing to let the world corrupt you. JAMES 1:27

One is a game with knights, bishops, and queens, and it utilizes the brain for strategy. The other is a brutal sport with hooks, uppercuts, and jabs, and it uses the brain as a punching bag. Welcome to the wacky world of chess boxing. Just when you thought you had heard about every weird sport out there, one more pops up. Chess boxing combines—you guessed it—the thinking game of chess and the fighting sport of boxing.

This isn't just some silly weekend invention by two guys with nothing better to do. The sport, which held its first match in the Netherlands in 2003, has an official governing body, the World Chess Boxing Organization (WCBO), and is popular in Europe. In February 2010, the first North American chess-boxing club started in Los Angeles. Chess boxers alternate four-minute rounds of chess with three-minute boxing rounds, including a one-minute break in between. A fight can last up to 11 rounds. Chess boxers can win by knockout or by checkmate. The competition also concludes if a player exceeds the chess time limit or if the referee decides the fight has to be stopped. If the chess portion ends in a tie, boxing points determine the winner. If the boxing portion ends in a draw, the player who had black on the chessboard wins.

What's the Score?

Somehow, the founders of the WCBO managed to successfully combine two totally different activities into one sport. But there are certain things that don't mix well. Take, for instance, Christians and unbelievers. In 2 Corinthians 6, the apostle Paul warns Christians to avoid teaming up with unbelievers. Now, let's be clear: This doesn't mean you're never allowed to talk with non-Christians or be friends with them. And it certainly doesn't give you the right to be mean or arrogant, as if you are better than somebody else.

But as Christians, we are called to be different from those around us. God wants us to act, speak, and think differently than those who don't trust in him. Non-Christians aren't concerned about becoming more like Jesus. If you hang out too much with unbelievers, they will eventually influence you in ungodly ways. By all means, pray for unbelievers and share the Good News of Jesus Christ with them. Influence them for good, but don't allow them to influence you for bad.

) On the Ball

Non-Christians aren't concerned about becoming more like Jesus. As a Christian, you should make it your main goal to grow more and more like Jesus. Jesus helped, ate with, prayed for, and shared the truth of God with people who didn't know him. We should follow that example. Think of ways you can influence those around you for good, but be careful not to let yourself be influenced for the bad.

) COACH'S COMMENT

Don't team up with those who are unbelievers. How can righteousness be a partner with wickedness? How can light live with darkness? **2 CORINTHIANS 6:14**

Carlos Peña's career appeared to be finished in 2006. Carlos, a major-league first baseman, had suffered his worst season since having become a full-time starter in 2002. After clobbering 27 home runs and driving in 82 runs for Detroit in 2004, he was released by the Tigers during the 2006 spring training and then let go by the New York Yankees' Triple-A team that August. He signed with Boston shortly afterward but struggled in 18 games to end the year.

In 2007, Carlos was invited to spring training by the Tampa Bay Rays, but he didn't survive the final cut. However, when Greg Norton, Tampa Bay's first baseman, got injured, Carlos was placed on the Rays' roster right before opening day. Then the improbable happened. Carlos exploded with 46 home runs, 121 RBIs, and 103 walks—all club records. He won the 2007 American League Comeback Player of the Year Award. Over the next three seasons, he averaged 33 home runs and 95 RBIs to become one of baseball's premier sluggers.

What's the Score?

Ironically, Carlos's remarkable career turnaround was nothing that he initially earned himself. His big opportunity with Tampa Bay came only when someone else got injured. Similarly, our greatest spiritual opportunity (the forgiveness of our sins) came only by someone else's suffering—that of Jesus Christ. We can't earn God's favor, either before or after we become Christians. God isn't impressed with the good works we do after we're saved. As Galatians 2:16 says, "No one will ever be made right with God by obeying the law."

This is important, because a Christian's obedience to God should never be to "earn brownie points" or to get on God's good side. God doesn't work like that. His love for us doesn't fluctuate, and he is not some sort of divine teacher who nitpicks and grades everything we do. Rather, he is a loving heavenly Father who wants his children to serve him out of grateful hearts of worship. As Christians, our standing before God is not based on what we've earned. It's based on what Christ has earned for us. Praise God for that!

) On the Ball

Read a book or biographical article on Martin Luther, the great preacher from a few hundred years ago who passionately preached verses like Galatians 2:16 and taught people that salvation is by faith, not by works.

) COACH'S COMMENT

No one will ever be made right with God by obeying the law. GALATIANS 2:16

Was it a basketball game or a hockey fight? Fans at the March 23, 1993, contest between the New York Knicks and the Phoenix Suns couldn't decide. But they did witness one of the worst brawls in NBA history. It started with an offensive foul called on Knicks guard Doc Rivers, who had bumped Suns guard Kevin Johnson. Kevin trash-talked Doc a little, and they got into a shoving match. Both teams' benches had emptied onto the court by the time officials restored order. Moments later, Kevin drove to the basket against Doc and was whistled for an offensive foul. On the next play, as Doc raced down the court for a last-second shot, Kevin decked him with a flagrant forearm. Doc chased down Kevin and punched him, prompting both teams to flood the court again in a wild free-for-all.

As things were settling down, Knicks guard Greg Anthony sprinted onto the court and punched Kevin, restarting the chaos. When the fight finally ended, officials ejected six players, including Greg, Kevin, and Doc. The NBA suspended the three players and levied a total of $160,500 in fines against both teams. Oh, by the way, Phoenix won the game easily, 121–92, in case anyone cared.

What's the Score?

As Kevin and Doc learned, it can be extremely difficult to avoid retaliating when someone wrongs us. But Romans 12:17-21 clearly teaches that we should "never pay back evil with more evil" (verse 17), but instead we should leave revenge "to the righteous anger of God" (verse 19). God's anger is always without sin, but ours rarely is. When we get angry because someone has wronged us, it's easy to want revenge. But God is the ultimate judge of the universe, not us.

God wants us to repay evil with good. If someone wrongs you, try to answer back with kindness in speech and action. It's certainly not easy, but it's what we are called to do. Our perfect example of this is Jesus, who didn't retaliate even when he was unjustly mocked, beaten, and crucified. First Peter 2:23 describes Jesus this way: "He did not retaliate when he was insulted, nor threaten revenge when he suffered. He left his case in the hands of God, who always judges fairly." That's an example we should all strive to follow.

) On the Ball

Read Romans 12:17-21, and pray for God to give you a heart that wants to repay evil with good.

) COACH'S COMMENT

Never pay back evil with more evil. ROMANS 12:17

Raccoons, beware! Each year these bandit-masked furry animals are the target of excited dogs and hunters in coon-hunting events. One of the biggest in the country is the American Coon Hunters Association (ACHA) World Hunt, which started in the mid-1940s. But there are plenty of other coon-hunting organizations too. The American Kennel Club, Professional Kennel Club, and United Kennel Club, among others, all host their annual championships.

Coon hunting, which is most popular in the South and Midwest, is big business. Many national competitions feature hundreds of coonhounds, attract thousands of spectators, and bring millions of dollars into the local economy. In events like the ACHA World Hunt, raccoons aren't actually harmed. The man-dog hunting teams score points for "treeing" a coon—in other words, chasing a frightened raccoon up a tree. Dogs also compete for the best in show by breed. The winner of the 2010 ACHA World Hunt, which was held March 24-27 in Glasgow, Kentucky, was a young hound of the Treeing Walker breed named Gainesville Creek Tank. Way to go, Tank!

What's the Score?

Aren't you glad you're not a raccoon? It's nice to be at the top of the food chain. But seriously, think about the exclusive blessings God has given to humans over all other creatures. We possess a complex intellect and emotions. We have eternal souls. And we were made in God's own image. No other beings in God's creation can claim these traits. In Genesis 1, God commanded humans, "Fill the earth and govern it. Reign over the fish in the sea, the birds in the sky, and all the animals that scurry along the ground" (verse 28).

While pondering these things, David wrote in Psalm 8:4-5, "What is mankind that you are mindful of them, human beings that you care for them? You have made them a little lower than the angels and crowned them with glory and honor" (NIV). In all his creation, God poured the most detail, affection, and responsibility into humans. His love for us is beyond comprehension. He has showered us with grace and allowed us to take care of his world. The Lord God Almighty wants us to rule his world and enjoy fellowship with him through Christ. Chew on that for a while!

) On the Ball

Go enjoy an outdoor activity (hiking, fishing, bike riding) to marvel at God's creation. Thank him for his special attention in creating you.

) COACH'S COMMENT

What is mankind that you are mindful of them, human beings that you care for them?
PSALM 8:4 (NIV)

Hope. The Pittsburgh Pirates haven't enjoyed too much of that recently. But it's something they cling to desperately each year in spring training. The Pirates entered 2011 coming off their 18th consecutive losing season. No other team in North America's four major professional sports—Major League Baseball, the NFL, NBA, and NHL—has gone that many years without a winning record. The Philadelphia Phillies held the previous record of 16 losing seasons from 1933 to 1948.

Some seasons have been worse than others for Pittsburgh. Take 2010, for instance. The Pirates went a miserable 57–105 to finish a whopping 34 games out of first place. It was the longtime franchise's fourth-worst record since 1890 and its most losses since a 42–112 mark in 1952. Still, every year the Pirates travel to their spring training site in Bradenton, Florida, with renewed hope that, amid their great trials, this will be the year that they enjoy their first winning season since 1992.

🏐 What's the Score?

In the book of Lamentations, God's people were desperate for a glimmer of hope. The word *lament* means "to mourn out loud." The Bible's book of Lamentations was a cry of sorrow and repentance to God.

In the sixth century BC, when Lamentations was probably written, things looked bleak for the Israelites. The Babylonian army had destroyed Jerusalem, the nation of Judah's capital city, and God's holy temple. King Nebuchadnezzar had deported thousands of Jews to Babylon. The rest were left in poverty in a war-scarred land. The people's trials were great, and hope seemed to be in short supply.

Yet in the midst of this terrible suffering, the author of Lamentations says there was hope. How could he say such a thing? Because "the faithful love of the LORD never ends" (Lamentations 3:22). God is the author of hope. Whenever life seems out of control or things seem like they can't get any worse, remember God's great love for his children. After their 70 years of captivity, God restored his people. And he wants to restore us, too.

⟩ On the Ball

Draw a picture of a baseball diamond. Add a spot for each of the nine player positions. Next to each position, write down a reason we can hope in the Lord.

⟩ COACH'S COMMENT

I still dare to hope when I remember this: The faithful love of the LORD never ends! His mercies never cease. **LAMENTATIONS 3:21-22**

Trivia time: What do Usain Bolt, Mia Hamm, Dwight Howard, Derek Jeter, Jimmie Johnson, Peyton Manning, Candace Parker, and Serena Williams all have in common? Answer: These famous athletes have all promoted Gatorade. Gatorade is probably the most well-known sports drink in America, if not the world. Gatorade pays the world's top athletes millions of dollars each year to promote its products. If you watch enough sports on TV, you're bound to see a Gatorade commercial touting the drink's abilities to quench thirst and refresh weary athletes with important nutrients. But do you know how Gatorade got its unique name?

In 1965, a University of Florida assistant football coach asked a group of university physicians why many of his players were struggling to perform in the heat. The doctors did some research and found that the human body needs to replenish certain minerals and nutrients that are lost during exercise. Based on their findings, they created a new beverage to aid the Gators. Hence the name "Gatorade." Drinking Gatorade that football season, Florida finished 7–4. The following year, the Gators went 9–2 and won the Orange Bowl for the first time in school history. Soon other teams were ordering Gatorade by the truckload. By 2010, Gatorade was the official sports drink of the NFL, NBA, Major League Baseball, Major League Soccer, and many other organizations and teams.

What's the Score?

No, this isn't a commercial for Gatorade. It's just a helpful reminder that we all need to be refreshed occasionally. Life is hard sometimes. Things don't always go our way. We can stumble along the journey, and it's not always easy to get back up. What do you do when you're weary? Who do you turn to when you need to be refreshed?

Gatorade might replenish our carbohydrates and electrolytes, but only God can refresh our hearts and minds. There is no greater energizer than God's Word. The Bible can lift us up when we're feeling low and can provide hope during our greatest trials. The Bible is great at "refreshing the soul," as Psalm 19:7 (NIV) says. When life leaves you thirsting for refreshment, drink in Scripture deeply. Take it in big gulps, and let it nourish your soul. God's Word will always satisfy.

) On the Ball

The book of Psalms is loaded with encouraging words of refreshment. Try reading Psalms 19, 23, 27, and 34.

) COACH'S COMMENT

The law of the LORD is perfect, refreshing the soul. The statutes of the LORD are trustworthy, making wise the simple. PSALM 19:7 (NIV)

Frank Tanana's life was a mess. Athletically, Frank was on top of the world. A first-round draft pick by the California Angels in 1971, Frank quickly rocketed to stardom as a fire-balling left-handed pitcher. He led the American League in strikeouts with 269 by age 22 and was voted into three straight All-Star Games. But off the field, Frank was useless. Drinking and partying topped his postgame rituals. Despite his success in baseball, he felt terribly empty inside.

That's when God intervened. Through a series of arm injuries and the death of a teammate, Frank slowly began considering tough spiritual questions. By 1983, he had become a Christian, and his life was drastically changed. After retiring from baseball in 1993, he devoted himself to spreading the gospel. In addition to serving as an elder at his church in Michigan, he traveled nationwide to share the Good News of Jesus Christ at prisons, golf tournaments, seminars, and various church functions.

What's the Score?

Like Frank's life story, the book of Philemon is a wonderful tale of how God radically changes lives. In it, Paul pleads with Philemon to forgive a slave named Onesimus, who had apparently stolen from Philemon and run away. In the ancient world, most runaway slaves would be thrown into prison or executed. Some people would have considered Onesimus useless. But somewhere along his flight, Onesimus ran into Paul, who shared the gospel with him. In his letter, Paul encouraged Philemon to forgive Onesimus and receive him as "a brother in the Lord."

Spiritually speaking, we all start life as useless. With sin and selfishness running our lives, we are like spiritual runaways who have no hope. But God loves to change lives, just like he did with Onesimus and Frank. In his letter, Paul tells Philemon that his seemingly useless runaway slave is now "very useful to both of us." Sometimes God uses our parents, a friend, or a church to help us turn from our sins. Maybe in your life he's even using this devotional book. Regardless, God wants each of us to turn from our sins and to run to him through faith in Jesus, just like Onesimus did. Then we can go from being useless to being very useful in the Kingdom of God!

On the Ball

List three ways you can be useful to God this week, and work to accomplish each goal.

1. _____

2. _____

3. _____

COACH'S COMMENT

Onesimus hasn't been of much use to you in the past, but now he is very useful to both of us. PHILEMON 1:11

Play ball! Um, well, at least play virtual ball! At this very moment, with a new Major League Baseball season just days away, fantasy baseball leagues are taking shape all over the country. In fantasy baseball, as in other fantasy sports, you are the owner, the general manager, and the coach of a team. You "draft" players at each position and manage the team throughout the season, choosing who plays and who gets benched each day. The better that player does in real life, the more points your fantasy team scores. For instance, your fantasy team will score a lot more points with a batter who is hitting .350 with 30 home runs and 100 RBIs than one hitting .250 with 10 homers and 35 RBIs.

But fantasy sports aren't limited to baseball. Fantasy football starts in late summer as the NFL season approaches, and the fall brings new NBA and NHL fantasy seasons. There are even fantasy leagues for NASCAR! Fantasy sports are a big deal in America. In fact, a March 2010 article in *Time* magazine estimated that the fantasy sports industry is worth about $4.5 billion annually. That's right—$4.5 billion!

⬜⬜ What's the Score?

Why are fantasy sports so popular? Here's a theory: we like to be in control. Fantasy sports let the average fan make decisions like a high-rolling executive of a rich professional sports team. We like the feeling of being in charge and doing what we think is best. That might be okay in fantasy sports, but not in real life. The fact is, we are not in charge. God is.

Sure, God lets us make decisions in our lives. (After all, he didn't create us to be robots!) But that doesn't mean we can manage our lives as we see fit. As Proverbs 19:21 says, "You can make many plans, but the LORD's purpose will prevail." We must never forget that we are under the divine rule of the Lord God Almighty, the Creator of the universe. All our decisions should be made with God's will in mind. He is fully in control of our lives, whether we know it or not. To think otherwise is, well, a fantasy.

⟩ On the Ball

Create a fantasy baseball team by picking one player per position (for pitchers, choose five starters, a middle reliever, and a closer). Keep your picks until the end of the season, then check to see how well your fantasy team would've done. It's a good exercise to show how limited our knowledge and control really are.

⟩ COACH'S COMMENT

You can make many plans, but the LORD's purpose will prevail. **PROVERBS 19:21**

Moving to another state is tough. You leave behind old friends and everything you've known. But it can be even tougher when a professional sports team moves. On this day in 1984, Baltimore Colts fans awoke to some shocking news: their beloved team was gone. The night before, in the wee hours of the morning, the team had packed its belongings and left for Indianapolis in a fleet of trucks.

The Colts had been one of the NFL's greatest franchises, winning the 1958 and 1959 world championships and the 1971 Super Bowl. They were adored by Baltimoreans. But when the team struggled in the late 1970s and early 1980s, attendance dropped. To make matters worse, Colts' owner Robert Irsay couldn't convince the city to help him finance renovations to old Memorial Stadium. So when Indianapolis showed interest in becoming the Colts' new home, Robert jumped at the chance, forever breaking Baltimore's heart and outraging many fans.

What's the Score?

To this day, many fans of the old Baltimore Colts feel betrayed. Any move is hard. But Robert believed the best thing for his team was to relocate to Indiana. The Bible talks about a lot of moves. After Jesus was born, an angel appeared to Joseph in a dream and said to get out of Bethlehem and go to Egypt (Matthew 2:13). That night, Joseph got up and moved Mary and Jesus.

Jesus' move to Egypt saved his life. The Colts' move to Indianapolis may have helped save the team. They weren't getting the money they needed to be competitive in Baltimore, so they moved to a place where they could thrive. It was difficult for both cities at first. Of course, once Baltimore got the Ravens and the Colts started playing well, people felt better.

Has Jesus ever called your family to move? Maybe you moved to a new country to spread God's love. Maybe your dad got a new job that forced your family to relocate. Even when it's difficult to transition to a new place, trust God. He's with you wherever you go . . . even when you move to a new home.

) On the Ball

Think of a time of transition in your life. Maybe it was a move to a new state, a new school, or a new church. Did you fight the move or accept it? Whenever you have to make a move, remember that God is with you and knows what's best for your life.

) COACH'S COMMENT

After the wise men were gone, an angel of the Lord appeared to Joseph in a dream. "Get up! Flee to Egypt with the child and his mother," the angel said. MATTHEW 2:13

Matt Hughes proves you can't judge a book by its cover. The five-foot-nine-inch, 170-pound mixed martial arts (MMA) fighter is a nine-time world welterweight (lightweight) champion in Ultimate Fighting Championship (UFC), the most popular MMA league in the country. MMA is a timed, officiated combat sport like boxing, in which competitors fight in a ring. But unlike boxing, MMA athletes use many forms of fighting, such as jujitsu, judo, karate, boxing, kickboxing, and wrestling. It's not for the faint of heart or weak of bicep.

Fighters can win fights by decision, knockout, technical knockout, and submission. Matt has won fights in a variety of colorfully descriptive ways, including a "keylock," "armbar," "kimura," and "slam." Other victories sound a lot more ouchy for his unfortunate foes: the "side choke" and "arm triangle choke" sound like something you'd want to stay away from. Matt, who was inducted into the UFC Hall of Fame in 2010, has lost a handful of fights too. But when opponents saw Matt in the ring, they knew they'd be in for a long night.

What's the Score?

Matt's profession calls for him to attack others with fists and feet of fury. But he is quite different outside the ring. Matt, who accepted Jesus as his Savior in 2004, enjoys living peacefully and serving others. He often volunteers to help youth in his hometown of Hillsboro, Illinois, and since 2004, he has been involved with Rancho 3M, a Christian orphanage in Mexico.

We, too, are called to live peaceful lives and to love others. The Bible says we must avoid fighting and bitterness and "live at peace with everyone" (Romans 12:18, NIV). Why must Christians promote peace? Because we are representatives of Christ, who sacrificed himself on the cross so that we could achieve ultimate peace with a holy God through the forgiveness of our sins. So live peaceably with everyone . . . yes, even your brothers and sisters.

) On the Ball

Do you have any lingering anger toward a family member or a friend? Go to that person and promote peace by asking for forgiveness.

) COACH'S COMMENT

If it is possible, as far as it depends on you, live at peace with everyone.
ROMANS 12:18 (NIV)

François Bon liked to ski. But the Frenchman's version of skiing was, uh, a tad extreme. François was into speed-riding, which means he basically climbed to the top of the world's highest mountains . . . and then jumped off. Speed-riding mixes snow skiing and paragliding at ridiculously high speeds. For each run, François climbed to a mountain's peak (which often took more than a week) and then launched off with only a small, controllable paragliding sail coming out of a backpack and a pair of skis to guide him.

As François sped down sheer mountainsides at 50 to 100 miles per hour, his skis only touched down when the mountain grade leveled off a bit. When it steepened again, he went airborne. On March 31, 2008, François gained international fame by conquering Argentina's Aconcagua, the highest summit in the Western Hemisphere at 22,834 feet. By the time he stopped, he had plummeted 9,000 feet in four minutes and 50 seconds.

What's the Score?

As a speed-rider, François entrusted his life to a small nylon sail and a pair of skis. There was no guarantee he'd survive any attempt because his equipment wasn't 100 percent trustworthy. Nothing man-made in life is. If his equipment failed, he probably would have died. In the seventh century BC, the nation of Judah needed something trustworthy. The ruthless Assyrian Empire ruled the ancient world, with Egypt and Babylonia jockeying for power, too. With so much surrounding chaos, the people of Judah probably felt like they were free-falling down an icy mountain.

So God sent the prophet Nahum to comfort his people. Nahum encouraged them to trust in God, because God was strong enough to protect them in times of trouble. Nahum 1:7 says, "The LORD is good, a strong refuge when trouble comes. He is close to those who trust in him." Keeping our faith in God is an important lesson for us today, too. Things in life don't always go our way. But we should always trust God, whether circumstances are good or bad. He is always trustworthy—or dependable—because he is holy, all-knowing, and all-powerful. He will never fail.

) On the Ball

The next time something bad happens, ask God for help. Prayer is a great way to show trust in God.

) COACH'S COMMENT

The LORD is good, a strong refuge when trouble comes. He is close to those who trust in him. NAHUM 1:7

The latest Guitar Hero–*style* video game looked amazing . . . or, at least, really interesting. On April 1, 2009, Microsoft announced the release of *Alpine Legend,* an interactive yodeling-and-alphorn rhythm game for the Xbox 360. The game trailer showed two competitors dressed in German lederhosen. One was yodeling, while the other blew into a six-foot-long, curved plastic horn. *Alpine Legend* featured classic hit songs such as "Whose Spit Is in My Horn?" and "More Goat Bell." For a limited time, players could purchase a tri-horn pack and become a "tri-horn blast master."

It didn't take people long to figure out that *Alpine Legend* was an April Fool's joke from Microsoft. The silly costumes and ridiculous yodeling made people laugh when they thought about the possibility of the new game. Sure, there were rock-band games, bongo-playing games, and other rhythm titles. But the world is going to have to wait awhile longer for a yodeling-and-alphorn video game.

⬜⬜ What's the Score?

Nobody knows exactly why or when April Fool's Day started. Some historians trace it back to the 1600s in France. Others believe this wacky day sprouted up in different cultures as they celebrated the first day of spring. Even though countries celebrate differently, tricks and jokes highlight this special day around the world.

It doesn't get talked about much, but God is a big fan of joy and fun. God created everything good, and that includes laughter. The writer of Psalm 126 notes that after witnessing God's power, "We were filled with laughter, and we sang for joy." God wants us to be joyful. He loves when his children laugh. So have fun on April Fool's Day. Plan a silly stunt. Just remember to keep your pranks harmless. Laughing at somebody else's expense isn't fun; it's just mean. But when everybody is laughing together, it's way more fun than playing *Alpine Legend* or any other video game.

⟩ On the Ball

Do you like to play April Fool's jokes? If you do, make sure everybody laughs together—not at one person.

⟩ COACH'S COMMENT

We were filled with laughter, and we sang for joy. And the other nations said, "What amazing things the LORD has done for them." **PSALM 126:2**

Not many 10-year-olds can say they've played with a professional basketball team. Before Jaylin Fleming turned 11, he had played with *two*. In 2010, Jaylin practiced with the New York Knicks and worked out with Chicago Bulls guard Derrick Rose. NBA scouts and college coaches said Jaylin might be the best fifth-grade basketball player in the world.

The five-foot-one-inch point guard impressed coaches with his ballhandling skills, passing, and shooting. Although Jaylin could drive to the basket or shoot every time he had the ball, he enjoyed passing and getting his teammates involved offensively. Jaylin played on two teams in Chicago, Illinois, and went to the gym two or three times a week. But that didn't mean Jaylin's life was all about basketball. He tried hard in school to get all As and Bs. And he attended church and Bible study every week.

⬜⬜ What's the Score?

At just 10 years old, Jaylin received tons of attention for his basketball talent. While a lot of kids would get a big head, Jaylin stayed humble. Jaylin's dad wanted his son to be a better person than basketball player. Jaylin's dad played a big part in Jaylin's development as a player and a young man. He introduced his son to basketball and coached him during his younger years.

The Bible encourages children to listen to their father's instruction (Proverbs 1:8). Parents want the best for their children. So when you listen and obey what your mother and father teach, you do better in life. Jaylin followed his father's advice, and he attracted the attention of high school, college, and professional basketball coaches. Your parents can often see potential and talent in you that you might not notice. Sometimes it may seem like your parents ask a lot of you. But they do it because they want you to be your best.

⟩ On the Ball

What instruction does your father always give you?

What does your mother try to teach you?

When you pay attention to what your parents say, you'll do well in life.

⟩ COACH'S COMMENT

Listen, my son, to your father's instruction and do not forsake your mother's teaching.
PROVERBS 1:8 (NIV)

The 1983 University of Houston basketball team loved to dunk so much that it earned the nickname Phi Slama Jama. The Cougars were known for fast-breaking and slamming the ball through the basket. But in the NCAA championship game, Houston got dunked by underdog North Carolina State 54–52.

Houston entered the contest as the top-ranked team in the nation and felt they would crush the Wolfpack. NC State barely made the NCAA tournament and already had 10 losses during the season. Before the finals, Houston coach Guy Lewis said his team was so overconfident that it had its worst practice of the year. Then Houston started the game lethargically and trailed NC State 33–25 at halftime. In the second half, Houston played better and went on a 17–2 run to take the lead. However, Guy told his team to slow the pace, and the Wolfpack came back. NC State started fouling Houston, and the Cougars missed their free throws. With a minute to go, the score was tied 52–52. Four seconds were on the clock when NC State guard Dereck Whittenburg was forced to take a shot from 35 feet from the basket. The shot was obviously short, but nobody boxed out NC State forward Lorenzo Charles. Lorenzo caught the ball with two seconds left and jammed it through the hoop for the victory!

⬛⬛ What's the Score?

Little things added up to result in a huge defeat for Houston. The Cougars were overconfident and didn't practice hard before the biggest game of the year. Then they started the finals slowly and fell behind. Even when Houston started playing better, the coach decided to slow the pace instead of push ahead. Finally, the Cougars didn't make their free throws and failed to box out on the game's final shot.

Houston found out that a lot of little things make a big difference. Nearly 3,000 years ago, King Solomon warned us to guard against the little things that can mess up our lives. He said to catch the little foxes before they can ruin the vineyard (Song of Solomon 2:15). In other words, little things can have a big impact. Watch out for the little things—such as white lies, talking negatively, or having a bad attitude—that can eventually ruin your life.

⟩ On the Ball

Do you have any "little foxes" in your life? Ask God to help you identify the little things that could hurt you. Then pray to him to help you get rid of them.

- -

⟩ COACH'S COMMENT

Catch all the foxes, those little foxes, before they ruin the vineyard. SONG OF SOLOMON 2:15

- -

Before the biggest game of the National Lacrosse League (NLL) season, Washington Stealth star Lewis Ratcliff got away from everything so he could prepare himself. Lewis had scored 46 goals during the regular season, but he hadn't tallied a single goal in the play-offs. He knew his team needed a big performance from him if the Stealth hoped to defeat the five-time NLL champion Toronto Rock.

Lewis took a week off from his job in Canada to go to Everett, Washington, and focus on the game. For four days before the 2010 championship, Lewis practiced his shooting and thought about what he needed to do.

All that preparation paid off as Lewis scored 59 seconds into the game to give the Stealth a 1–0 lead. Lewis tallied again two minutes later. But the Rock didn't win five Champion's Cups by lying down. Toronto built a 10–6 lead late in the third quarter. However, Washington answered with a 9–1 flurry to win the game 15–11. Lewis ended the contest with five goals and was awarded the Most Valuable Player trophy.

What's the Score?

Lewis knew he had a big challenge ahead, so he took time to prepare himself. In the Bible, Jesus knew he faced the greatest challenge in human history. The night before he took on every human's sin and was nailed to a cross, Jesus went to the Garden of Gethsemane. He wanted to be alone to pray. Jesus knew he needed to prepare himself to do God's will. He understood that he needed the power that comes through prayer to accomplish his purpose for coming to earth.

It wasn't easy for Jesus to die for our sins. He felt pain. He cried. But he also said, "I want your will to be done, not mine" (Mark 14:36). By getting away and preparing himself in Gethsemane, Jesus achieved the greatest feat of all time—he paid the price for our sins. Whether you've already celebrated Easter or are about to, remember to praise and thank Jesus for his amazing sacrifice!

) On the Ball

Is there something coming up in your life that you need to prepare for? Maybe it's a test, tryouts for a sport, or a musical performance. Make sure to take time to get alone so you can focus and prepare yourself to do your best.

) COACH'S COMMENT

They went to the olive grove called Gethsemane, and Jesus said, "Sit here while I go and pray." MARK 14:32

Michigan's Fab Five changed the face of college basketball in the early 1990s. When Chris Webber, Jalen Rose, Juwan Howard, Jimmy King, and Ray Jackson decided to attend the University of Michigan, many considered them the best recruiting class in college basketball history. They started as freshmen and led the Wolverines to the NCAA championship game—marking the only time that five freshmen had taken a school to the finals. Michigan lost to Duke to end the season.

But the Fab Five returned with a vengeance as sophomores. With their black socks pulled high, baggy shorts riding low, and a confident attitude, Michigan cruised through the season. On this day in 1993, the Wolverines faced North Carolina in the championship game. Michigan appeared close to victory as it held a 67–63 edge with 4:32 left. But a 10–4 run by the Tar Heels gave them a 73–71 lead with 20 seconds remaining. Michigan didn't have any time-outs, but they still had plenty of time for a tying shot. However, instead of the team's point guard dribbling up the ball, Chris—a power forward—quickly dribbled past half court, picked up the ball, and called time-out. Because the Wolverines were out of time-outs, referees called a technical foul on Michigan and gave the ball to North Carolina. The Tar Heels went on to win the game 77–71.

What's the Score?
The Fab Five never won an NCAA championship. Some say they never reached their full potential. Years after they left the school, a federal investigation reported that Chris took money from a Michigan booster. All of the Fab Five's records were erased.

In sports there's a big difference between playing with confidence and being prideful. Having a little spunk on the court is a good thing. You have to believe that you can win. But when you get prideful, you might start thinking that the rules don't apply to you—that you can get away with anything. In Obadiah 1:3-4, God's prophet tells the Edomites that their pride is going to lead to a fall. That's what happened with the Fab Five. Their pride led to their falling from the heights. What started out with so much promise ended as a failure.

On the Ball
Why do you think pride is so dangerous? Write down some ideas:

Read 2 Timothy 3:1-5. Are you surprised that proud people are mentioned in this list? As you go about your life, try to stay humble.

COACH'S COMMENT
"You have been deceived by your own pride. . . . Even if you soar as high as eagles and build your nest among the stars, I will bring you crashing down," says the LORD.
OBADIAH 1:3-4

The Olympic Games can be traced back nearly 1,000 years before Jesus was born. Athletes gathered in Olympia, Greece, to run one race—a 632-foot sprint.

The modern Olympics are a fairly recent event. Baron Pierre de Coubertin organized the first modern Olympics just over 100 years ago. On this day in 1896, the modern Olympics began in Athens, Greece. Fewer than 250 athletes from 14 countries competed. James Connolly of the United States became the first Olympic champion as he won the triple jump. James received a silver medal and crown of olive branches for his achievement.

Over the years, the Olympics have grown and changed quite a bit. No women were allowed to compete in the first Olympics. And it wasn't until the third Olympics that gold, silver, and bronze medals were given to the top three finishers in each event. When the Summer Olympics returned to Athens in 2004, over 10,600 athletes from 201 nations competed in 301 events.

What's the Score?

Part of Pierre's reason for creating the modern Olympics was to foster peace. When Pierre designed the official Olympic flag in 1914, he used five connected rings to represent Africa, America, Australia, Asia, and Europe. The white background symbolized peace. The olive branches given to the winners in the first Olympics were also a symbol of peace.

According to some experts, the Bible was the first place that an olive branch was used to represent peace. When God flooded the world, Noah sent out a dove to see if the water was receding. The dove returned the first time. But the second time, the dove came back to Noah with "a fresh olive leaf in its beak" (Genesis 8:11). It was a sign that the Flood had ended and that a new life could begin on earth. God also gave Noah the sign of the rainbow, which was a covenant from God that he would never destroy all life again with a flood.

) On the Ball

Aren't you glad we can live at peace with God? Our sinful actions deserve judgment. But God gives us grace. The next time you see a rainbow or an olive tree, thank God for his covenant of peace.

) COACH'S COMMENT

This time the dove returned to him in the evening with a fresh olive leaf in its beak. Then Noah knew that the floodwaters were almost gone. GENESIS 8:11

The North Pole Marathon promoted itself as the world's coolest marathon—literally. During the 2009 race, temperatures plummeted to negative 35 degrees. That's cold. The race is run on ice—not land—floating on the Arctic Ocean. As the runners compete, the whole course moves slightly with the current. Now that *is* cool!

In 2010, it was a balmy negative four degrees. Of course, high winds and blizzard conditions didn't make the race any easier. Despite the snow, wind, and freezing temperatures, all 25 athletes finished the 26.2-mile race. Joep Rozendal, a former marine from the Netherlands, won in a time of five hours and 58 seconds. Yen-Po Chen of Taiwan was third at nearly five-and-a-half hours, which was more than double his normal marathon time.

Ireland's Emer Dooley won the women's division, finishing in just under six hours. Jamie Cuthbertson of Great Britain placed 13th, but his race might have been the most impressive. After losing his sight in an explosion in 1986, Jamie—along with his guide Alex Pavanello—showed that a disability couldn't stop somebody from completing the coolest race on earth.

What's the Score?

Jamie had to trust his guide to lead him on the rugged terrain. Much of the frozen course had little dips under the surface and mounds of snow. Plus, with whiteout conditions, Jamie had to trust Alex not to get off the path. Alex guided Jamie perfectly to an amazing accomplishment.

As Christians, we have an incredible guide who can keep us on the right path. He's called the Holy Spirit. The apostle Paul writes in Galatians 5:16 to "let the Holy Spirit guide your lives. Then you won't be doing what your sinful nature craves" (Galatians 5:16). Because we're human, we all have a sinful nature that nudges us to be jealous, hateful, angry, selfish, and engaged in other negative behaviors. But when we rely on God's Spirit to guide us, we act with goodness, love, kindness, and self-control. How would you rather live?

) On the Ball

Do you ever feel a battle inside yourself to act selfishly versus selflessly? When you act selfishly, you're not letting the Holy Spirit guide you. Pray to God to give you the strength and wisdom to follow his Spirit. The Holy Spirit is the best guide we could ever ask for!

) COACH'S COMMENT

Let the Holy Spirit guide your lives. Then you won't be doing what your sinful nature craves. GALATIANS 5:16

When Hank Aaron broke baseball's home run record, it could've cost him his life. The Atlanta Braves slugger knocked his 713th homer on September 29, 1973, which put him just one behind Babe Ruth's all-time mark. With the season over, Hank received numerous death threats and hateful letters that warned him about coming back the next season. These people didn't want an African American player to overtake Babe's record. Instead of running scared or responding in anger, Hank stayed dignified and let his bat do the talking.

On this day in 1974, Hank crushed his 715th home run in a game against the Los Angeles Dodgers. There was extra security in the stadium as Hank rounded the bases and was picked up by his teammates after crossing home plate. Hank retired two years later with 755 home runs. During Hank's 20-year career, he never hit 50 home runs in a season. Instead, he put up solid numbers year after year, until he became the greatest home-run hitter of all time. Hank hit 40 or more home runs eight times, and in 14 seasons he had a batting average above .300.

What's the Score?

Hank was a great ambassador for baseball. Shortly after retiring, he was hired by the Braves and became one of the first African American executives in Major League Baseball. In 1982 he was inducted into the Baseball Hall of Fame. Hank persevered during a long and difficult career. When he was threatened, he just kept doing what he loved to do—playing baseball.

The Bible talks about somebody who had a long career for God. The apostle Paul traveled the world telling others about Jesus Christ. When his life was threatened, he didn't back down. Paul just kept doing what he loved to do—spreading the life-changing love of Jesus Christ. Near the end of Paul's life, he wrote a letter to his friend Timothy. In it he said, "I have fought the good fight, I have finished the race, and I have remained faithful." Those same words could easily be used to describe Hank's baseball career. Wouldn't it be cool if you could say those words at the end of your life?

⟩ On the Ball

What characteristics would you have to show to live a life that could be described in such glowing terms? You'd have to be determined, consistent, faithful. . . . (Add a few ideas to the list.)

Commit yourself to living this way, and you can have a Hall of Fame faith.

⟩ COACH'S COMMENT

I have fought the good fight, I have finished the race, and I have remained faithful.
2 TIMOTHY 4:7

The Marathon des Sables (Marathon of the Sands) has been called the toughest footrace on earth. Whoever said that was right! The race lasts six days, covers 151 miles, and runs through the Sahara Desert. That's the biggest desert—not counting Antarctica—in the world. Temperatures during the race often top 120 degrees. Hot winds kick up sand and make running nearly impossible. If you want to get an idea of what it's like to compete, attach a hair dryer to a long extension cord. Then turn it on full blast, aim it at your face, and run around a school playground while a friend throws sand at you. . . . Okay, that might not be a good idea.

More than 1,000 lunatics, er, uh, racers, took part in the 25th Marathon des Sables in 2010. And when the dust had cleared—literally—on April 9, Morocco's Mohamad Ahansal had won his third straight title by completing the race in 19 hours, 55 minutes, and eight seconds. Michael Wardian of the United States crossed the finish line three hours later to claim third place—the best finish ever by an American.

⬜⬜ What's the Score?

Michael Wardian isn't a household name, like Kobe or LeBron. But he's one of the best runners to come from the United States. For two years he held the Guinness World Record for fastest marathon while pushing a baby stroller (his son, Pierce, was in the stroller).

To earn third place at the Marathon des Sables, Michael had to overcome numerous challenges. His luggage got lost. Ants infiltrated his tent one night. He suffered from heat stroke after the third stage, but he came back the next day to run an amazing 50-mile stage four.

Running a 151-mile race in the desert is amazing, but can you imagine outrunning a horse-drawn chariot for 20 miles? That's what the prophet Elijah did. Immediately after Elijah faced down 450 prophets who worshiped a false god, he tucked his cloak into his belt and beat King Ahab in a race to Jezreel. You can read the whole story in 1 Kings 18:16-46.

❯ On the Ball

Elijah must have been exhausted after hiding in the wilderness and battling against the false prophets, yet God gave him amazing strength. When you feel weak or tired, remember to pray and ask God for special power.

❯ COACH'S COMMENT

The LORD gave special strength to Elijah. He tucked his cloak into his belt and ran ahead of Ahab's chariot all the way to the entrance of Jezreel. **1 KINGS 18:46**

Why did the golfer wear two socks? In case he got a hole in one. Ha! Seriously, golf is a huge sport. You can watch golf on its own cable channel or see it on network television nearly every weekend. But golf had very humble beginnings in the United States. On this day in 1916, the Professional Golfers' Association (PGA) of America was founded in New York City with 35 members. These men wanted to see the sport of golf grow. And it has grown. Fewer than 100 years later in 2010, the PGA had 28,000 members—making it the largest sports organization in the world.

Not only does the PGA govern professional golf tournaments, but it also encourages children to get involved with the sport. It provides free lessons and equipment to underprivileged families. Plus, the PGA gives millions of dollars every year to charities.

What's the Score?

Without the PGA, golf wouldn't be the sport that it is today. This organization worked hard to bring up the next generation of young players. The PGA helped create the First Tee program, which takes golf to less-fortunate neighborhoods and supports golf education. Because of the PGA, golf has grown into one of the most popular sports in the world.

In the Bible, David's army saw massive growth. God commanded the prophet Samuel to appoint David as king because Saul was no longer following God's plan. The people had to choose sides, and many went with David.

God knows that there's strength in numbers. That's why he brought so many warriors to join David's army. David couldn't have become king without the help of his large army—just like without all of its members, the PGA couldn't do so much for so many people. When you surround yourself with people who have your same goals, you can accomplish amazing things.

) On the Ball

Can you accomplish more by yourself or with a group of people working with you? Silly question, right? Think about something you want to accomplish or somebody you might want to help. Now get together with friends who feel the same as you and make it happen!

) COACH'S COMMENT

Day after day more men joined David until he had a great army, like the army of God.
1 CHRONICLES 12:22

For years sports announcers called Phil Mickelson "the best player never to win a major." The talented left-handed golfer had won 22 PGA titles and had been on the hunt for numerous major championships. Phil finished second in the US Open in 1999 and 2002. He notched four third-place finishes at the Masters from 1996 to 2003. He was even second at the PGA Championships in 2001. But for some reason Phil never could win the big one.

That all changed on this day in the 2004 Masters. Phil entered the final round in a tie for the lead. But two eagles by Ernie Els put the South African ahead midway through the round. Phil answered Ernie's charge with birdies of his own on holes 12, 13, and 14. When Phil knocked home another birdie putt on hole 16, he was tied with Ernie with two holes to go. Instead of thinking about past failures, Phil focused on winning.

On the 18th hole, Phil's ball rested 18 feet from the cup. Another player, Chris DiMarco, blasted his ball out of the sand, and it landed right behind Phil's. Phil watched closely as Chris putted and missed. When Phil's turn came, he used what he had learned to focus on sinking the final shot. He confidently rolled in a birdie . . . and won the Masters!

☐☐ What's the Score?

Phil had recorded 17 top-10 finishes in major golf competitions. But he didn't break through for a victory until he followed his playing partner's ball. By using Chris's shot as an example, Phil earned his first green jacket for winning the Masters.

As Christians, we need to follow the example of people who have gone before us. In 1 Corinthians 11:1 the apostle Paul says, "Follow my example, as I follow the example of Christ" (NIV). If we call ourselves followers of Christ, we should do just that—follow. We don't need to blaze our own trail or try something different. God often calls us to see how other believers have lived successfully and to follow their examples. We can also learn from other people's actions and make minor adjustments to be more successful. That's what Phil did, and it gave him the victory.

) On the Ball

Think of a person in your life you want to follow. Maybe it's a parent, a youth pastor, a relative, or a coach. And, of course, remember to follow the perfect example of Jesus Christ.

) COACH'S COMMENT

Follow my example, as I follow the example of Christ. 1 CORINTHIANS 11:1 (NIV)

The sport of kabaddi looks sort of like a combination of red rover and wrestling. But instead of linking arms and calling, "Red rover, red rover, let Johnny come over," teams in kabaddi send a "raider" to the opposition's side of the field. The raider must hold his breath as he faces four opponents with linked hands, hoping to break the chain and return to his side of the field unscathed. A raider must not take a breath on the opponent's side of the field as he pulls and wrestles his foe. The sport originated in South Asia years before Jesus was born as a form of recreational combat training.

The first Kabaddi World Cup was held in 2010 in the Punjab state of northwest India. Although cricket is the most popular sport in India, kabaddi is the official sport in this area. The local fans rarely sat down as they cheered their team to the championship. India, Pakistan, Great Britain, the United States, Iran, Italy, Canada, and Australia began the tournament. But in the end, India defeated Pakistan 58–24 in the final match. Following the victory, the Punjab government awarded government jobs to each player on the winning team.

⬜⬜ What's the Score?

If you're not familiar with the sport, kabaddi looks a little strange. It's obvious there are rules, which six officials help enforce, but as an outsider it's hard to understand. For the people in Punjab, other parts of India, and Bangladesh, however, kabaddi is part of their sports tradition. When traditions pull people together and create unity, they can be good things.

During Jesus' time on earth, he ran into some bad traditions. The Pharisees created traditions and rules that went against God's laws. They acted holy, but their hearts weren't dedicated to God. When Jesus saw what they were doing, he said, "You ignore God's law and substitute your own tradition" (Mark 7:8).

As you live for God, think about the traditions you have. Maybe your family has the tradition of serving at a homeless shelter every Easter. Or perhaps you always do a family Bible study on Wednesday nights. Those are good traditions that line up perfectly with God's laws. But also be on the lookout for traditions that might not be what God wants.

〉 On the Ball

Write down one of your family's traditions: _____.
Do you think it lines up with God's teachings? Jesus wants us to inspect every area of our lives to make sure we're fully living for him.

〉 COACH'S COMMENT

You ignore God's law and substitute your own tradition. MARK 7:8

Tiger Woods may be the greatest golfer to ever pick up a club. He certainly looked that way on this day in 1997. At the age of 21, Tiger became the youngest player to win the Masters Golf Tournament. Not only that, but he earned the victory in dominating fashion. He beat Tom Kite, the next closest competitor, by 12 strokes. And Tiger's four-round score of 270 set a PGA record for lowest score ever shot at a major championship.

Surprisingly, the 1997 Masters didn't start out that well for Tiger. He shot a four-over-par 40 on his first nine holes. But then he corrected his swing and went six-under on the back nine. From there he cruised to a history-making victory. As Tiger walked up the 18th fairway during his final round, he high-fived fans. Then he spotted his parents at the back of the green. He walked toward them with tears in his eyes and hugged his father, Earl, for nearly 30 seconds. Winning the Masters and becoming the world's greatest golfer wasn't just Tiger's dream; it was Earl's dream for his son.

What's the Score?

Tiger's father pushed him to be the best. At six months old, Tiger saw his father playing golf and mimicked his swing. Less than three years later, Tiger was appearing on national television and shooting under 50 for nine holes of golf. At nine, Tiger won his first of six Optimist International Junior Golf Championships. Earl was Tiger's coach growing up. He wanted his son to be physically strong and mentally tough. Sometimes when Tiger would putt or swing, Earl would jingle his keys or rip open the Velcro on his gold glove, trying to distract his son. Instead of getting frustrated at his dad, Tiger learned to stay focused.

The Bible commands fathers not to make their children angry (Ephesians 6:4). Tiger could've easily gotten mad at his father, but he understood that Earl's actions were training him for greatness. You need to have that same attitude with your parents. Parents aren't perfect, but they do want the best for their children. When your father takes you to church or gathers the family for Bible study, join him without complaining. Parents are supposed to discipline their children and teach them about God.

) On the Ball

The next time your parents discipline you or tell you about God's Word, surprise them by saying, "Thank you for doing a good job raising me." Then see what happens.

) COACH'S COMMENT

Fathers, do not provoke your children to anger by the way you treat them. Rather, bring them up with the discipline and instruction that comes from the Lord. **EPHESIANS 6:4**

Close your eyes and imagine what it would be like to ski 100 miles per hour. The cold biting your face. Wind rushing past your ears. Shaking skis ready to skid out from under you at any moment. Adrenaline rushing through your veins as you fly down the mountain. Now keep your eyes closed and imagine doing it blind. That's right—no safety ropes, no vision, and 100 mph.

In 2006, former British soldier Kevin Alderton set a downhill-speed record for blind skiers by reaching a speed of 100.94 mph at Les Arcs in France. The back of Kevin's jacket said it all: "nosightnofear." As he stood at the top of the run known as the Flying Kilometre, Kevin was focused on showing the world that his lack of sight wasn't a barrier for his achieving an amazing record. He quickly got into a tuck and started flying down the mountain. Kevin broke 100 mph before falling and sliding 200 yards down the mountain unharmed.

What's the Score?
Kevin grew up enjoying skiing. After he was blinded by a gang of people while he protected a woman, Kevin showed a lot of courage by continuing in the sport. On that mountain in France, it took a lot of faith for Kevin to go that fast. The only guidance he received was through radio speakers in his helmet from his coach, Norman Clarke. Kevin said the sensation of skiing that fast without being able to see was "amazing."

Sometimes in our lives we can feel "blind." There are situations when we're not sure what decision to make, or we feel like it would be great to see into the future. At those points, we need to show the same faith that Kevin had. God doesn't tell us that our lives will be easy and we'll always know exactly what to do. But God is always there to guide us. In fact, the Bible says God's Word is a lamp to our feet (Psalm 119:105). A lamp won't light up a path for hundreds of yards, but it will show us the next step to take. Take that step, and then trust God to show you where to take the next.

) On the Ball
Whenever you're not sure which choice is right or what to do, turn to God's Word. The wisdom in the Bible can show you the way. Trust God and have faith in him as you zoom through this journey called life.

) COACH'S COMMENT
Your word is a lamp to guide my feet and a light for my path. PSALM 119:105

Have you ever had a major brain freeze? Maybe you've eaten ice cream too quickly or slurped a Slurpee really fast. But you know the feeling. The massive pain behind the eye. The throbbing brain. The only good part is knowing that the headache will last only about 30 seconds. Brain freeze is caused when something cold comes into contact with the roof of your mouth and triggers nerves connected to your brain. As bad a brain freeze as you've had, you've probably never experienced a brain freeze like Pat Bertoletti's.

In 2009, Sports Slurping became an official, recognized sport by Major League Eating and the International Federation of Competitive Eating. On this day in 2010, Pat traveled to Australia to take part in the world's first Sports Slurping Championships. Pat won the competition and set a world record by drinking a 22-ounce Slurpee in just nine seconds. According to the rules, the first half of the Slurpee must be consumed through a standard straw. Then the final half can be drunk straight from the cup. Pat downed his sports-flavored Slurpee in record time and then had to deal with the brain freeze.

What's the Score?

Eating doesn't seem like much of a sport. After all, people do it every day, and it doesn't take any particular skill. But recently, competitive eating has grown in popularity around the world. Pat is one of the rising stars. He's been known to eat 47 glazed, cream-filled doughnuts in five minutes or nine pounds of blueberry pie in eight minutes without using his hands. That's some impressive eating, but definitely not as painful as guzzling a Slurpee.

Brain freeze hurts, but it doesn't cause any permanent damage or hurt you in the future. It's a good idea to protect your brain. That includes what you feed your brain by watching TV or movies. In Jeremiah 17:10, God says that he examines your mind and rewards you according to your actions. When you guard your mind and fill it with good things, those good choices will be reflected in your actions. Allowing inappropriate images or dangerous ideas into your brain can negatively affect your future.

) On the Ball

Don't freeze bad images or thoughts in your brain. Fill your mind with good things. Then when God searches your heart and examines your mind, he'll be pleased with what he finds.

) COACH'S COMMENT

I the LORD search the heart and examine the mind, to reward each person according to their conduct, according to what their deeds deserve. JEREMIAH 17:10 (NIV)

For 25 years, Jack Nicklaus had been one of the biggest names in golf. Note the words "had been." Known as "The Golden Bear," Jack had won 17 major championships. But when he entered the 1986 Masters in Augusta, Georgia, many felt the legend's career was over. He was 46 years old and hadn't won a tournament in six years. But in just four days, Jack proved he wasn't a "has-been."

Heading into the final round, Jack trailed the leaders by four strokes. On the first eight holes, he missed putts of 20, 18, 5, 22, and 10 feet. Jack was frustrated and five strokes behind the leaders. Yet he knew he had to trust his putter. On the ninth hole, he sank an 11-foot birdie. He birdied the 10th and then nailed a 25-foot birdie putt on hole 11. On the 15th hole, Jack had a 12-foot putt for eagle. He had seen this exact putt in the 1975 Masters and missed it. "It's not what it looks like," Jack told his son and caddy, Jack Jr., before sinking the shot.

Just one stroke behind, Jack birdied the 16th and set himself up for an 11-foot birdie on hole 17. "This putt is impossible to read," Jack said to his son. Jack tapped the ball on the tricky downhill putt, having faith that it would go in. The ball wiggled right, shimmied left, and dropped into the hole. Jack was in the lead. His score of 65 on the last day made him the oldest Masters champion of all time!

⬜⬜ What's the Score?

For 25 years, Jack amazed fans with his golfing abilities. But at the 1986 Masters, it was his faith that pulled him through. He knew he couldn't count on his eyes to read the greens and make putts. Jack had played at Augusta National so many times that he relied on faith to sink seemingly impossible putts at incredibly stressful times.

During your life, you'll find yourself in stressful situations. Sometimes you won't be able to see a solution to your problems. At those times, you need to live by faith, not by sight. Have faith that God can help you. Trust in things you cannot see. The Bible says there's a spiritual, unseen world that's so much more important than the world we live in. Keep an eternal perspective, and pray for godly wisdom as you try to read the difficult putts in life.

〉 On the Ball

Have faith in what you cannot see. God is always with you to help you navigate tricky situations.

〉 COACH'S COMMENT

We live by faith, not by sight. 2 CORINTHIANS 5:7 (NIV)

For almost two years Gregg Treinish and Deia Schlosberg blazed their own trail and hiked 7,800 miles! On this day in 2008, they finished hiking the entire length of the Andes Mountains—the longest mountain range in the world. The couple's journey began on June 30, 2006, when they flew from Leadville, Colorado, to Ecuador. Using black-and-white photocopies of maps from the 1920s, Gregg and Deia stayed near the mountain ridges as they made their way south.

For more than a year, they didn't see another hiker. They battled bouts of intestinal problems, typhoid, and worms. Heading into their journey, they hoped to complete the hike in a year. But Gregg and Deia soon realized it would take much longer. They started focusing on smaller goals, such as making it to the next big city so they could retrieve supplies they'd shipped ahead. At times the pair thought they might die. Other times they tried to convince each other that things would get better. . . . They never did. When the couple arrived at the southernmost tip of Tierra del Fuego, Gregg dropped to a knee and asked Deia to marry him.

What's the Score?

Gregg and Deia completed an amazing journey. The couple became the first people to navigate the length of the Andes at or near its spine without the use of roads. People around the world followed their progress and celebrated when they finished.

Jesus' brother James wrote that we should honor Christians who suffer for their faith in Christ. Job was a perfect example of this. He endured the loss of his children, his house, his livestock, and his money—yet he continued to trust and praise God. A day might come during your journey as a Christ-follower when you'll suffer for your faith. When that time comes, remember that James wrote this about Job: "The Lord was kind to him at the end, for the Lord is full of tenderness and mercy" (James 5:11).

) On the Ball

Don't give up on God when you suffer. Read the first two chapters in the book of Job. Do you think you'll ever suffer like he did? Probably not. Ask God to give you the endurance to make it through any suffering you might experience with your faith firm in Jesus Christ.

) COACH'S COMMENT

We give great honor to those who endure under suffering. For instance, you know about Job, a man of great endurance. You can see how the Lord was kind to him at the end, for the Lord is full of tenderness and mercy. JAMES 5:11

In a battle between a 1,200-pound beast and a 150-pound man, who do you think would win? At the 2010 Professional Bull Riders (PBR) World Cup in Las Vegas, the man came out on top most of the time. But winning meant the bull riders only had to stay on the bucking bulls for eight seconds. Of course, when there's a massive beast thrashing around, staying on it for eight seconds can seem like an eternity. At the end of the competition, Brazil proved it had the best bull riders in the world by defeating teams from the United States, Mexico, Australia, and Canada.

Brazil scored an impressive 1,330.25 points at the PBR World Cup to easily outdistance the second-place US team (972 points). Brazil was led by Guilherme Marchi, who rode five of his six bulls and scored 432.5 points. Renato Nunes and Robson Palermo rode four of their six bulls, and each scored more than 350 points for his team. Brazilian captain Adriano Moraes said his squad "was more of a team this year." US captain J. W. Hart also felt his team had a great competition, as he told reporters, "I know that Adriano is proud of his riders, but not as proud as I am of my guys. Our guys didn't lay down and fought hard."

⬜⬜ What's the Score?

Bull riding is one of the most difficult and dangerous sports in the world. The bulls are huge and angry. All of the PBR competitors showed great strength and courage at the competition in Las Vegas, but the Brazilian team displayed the most consistency. Adriano credited the win to solid team spirit. He said the Brazilian riders showed a lot of maturity and accepted each other. J.W. had equally great things to say about his team.

The Bible says to love each other with brotherly affection and "outdo one another in showing honor" (Romans 12:10, ESV). When players work together for the success of the group instead of for individual accolades, the team does better in the end. More than wins or losses, God cares about whether you treat your teammates and opponents with respect.

⟩ On the Ball

If you play on a sports team, what do you say about your teammates? Do you show them honor? Lifting up your teammates can help you have more success.

⟩ COACH'S COMMENT

Love one another with brotherly affection. Outdo one another in showing honor.
ROMANS 12:10 (ESV)

Mallory Holtman graduated as the greatest softball player in Central Washington University history. She finished as the best home-run hitter in Great Northwest Athletic Conference history. But Mallory will be remembered for something she did in the field more than for what she accomplished with her bat. During a 2008 game that would decide a play-off spot, Mallory displayed an act of sportsmanship that grabbed national headlines.

In the second inning of a contest between Central Washington and Western Oregon, Western right fielder Sara Tucholsky belted a three-run home run over the center-field fence. Sara had never hit a home run during her four-year college career. She was so excited watching the ball that she missed first base and then twisted awkwardly when she turned to go back, which tore the ligaments in her knee. She crumpled to the ground and started to crawl back to the base. According to NCAA rules, teammates and coaches couldn't help Sara around the bases.

That's when Mallory stepped in. She called over Central Washington shortstop Liz Wallace, and the pair picked up Sara. They carried her to second base and let her touch the bag with her good leg. Then they walked to third. By the time the trio reached home plate, the entire Western Oregon bench was in tears at Mallory's act of service. Even the fans and the Central Washington coach were crying.

☐☐ What's the Score?

Western Oregon ended up winning the game 4–2, which eliminated Central Washington from play-off contention. But nobody really cared. They knew they had witnessed one of the greatest acts of sportsmanship.

The book of Titus tells us to "learn to do good by meeting the urgent needs of others." Mallory did that when she carried her opponent around the bases. Mallory said sports had taught her to be a better person. As Christians, we need to be aware of the needs of people around us. Do you have an elderly neighbor who needs help with yard work? Maybe you have a teacher who would appreciate help cleaning up the room after class. Perhaps you could share your lunch with a kid at school who can't afford to bring one. God brings people into our lives for a reason, so look for ways to serve them.

⟩ On the Ball

Can you think of somebody in your life who has urgent needs? When you help people, you're living a productive life for God.

⟩ COACH'S COMMENT

Our people must learn to do good by meeting the urgent needs of others; then they will not be unproductive. TITUS 3:14

Would you ever want to ride over Niagara Falls in a barrel? Probably not. But in 2009, Tyler Bradt plunged off an even higher waterfall without the protection of a barrel. The 22-year-old kayaker paddled over 186-foot Palouse Falls in Washington state to set a world record for highest waterfall plunge. (Note: Niagara Falls is about 170 feet tall and so powerful that riding a kayak over it would *not* be a good idea.)

Tyler took his plunge after careful planning. In 2007, he had set a world record by kayaking over Alexandra Falls in Canada, which is 107 feet high. But Brazilian Pedro Oliveira rode over a 127-foot waterfall in Brazil to break Tyler's record. Tyler had looked at Palouse Falls before and knew it was runnable.

On the day of his record-breaking plunge, Tyler got in his little red kayak and positioned himself perfectly on the right side of the falls. As Tyler went over the edge, he disappeared in white, foamy water. He fell nearly four seconds and reached speeds of more than 100 mph. After entering the water below, Tyler emerged holding half a paddle (it had broken on the way down). His only injury was a sprained wrist.

What's the Score?

Tyler didn't just wake up one day and decide to risk his life in a record-breaking stunt. He was an experienced kayaker who knew the risks and put together a great team. He had people in boats at the bottom of the falls, a friend at the top ready to rappel down for a rescue, several cameramen, and plenty of medical equipment. Tyler received a ton of media attention for his feat. His name was splashed all over the Internet and in magazines. Instead of taking all the credit, Tyler acknowledged his team.

The Bible says organizing a good team is important. In 1 Corinthians 12:18, Paul writes that the body has a lot of parts and God puts each part where he wants it. Every part of the body has a purpose, just like every member of Tyler's team did. Some members of the body get noticed more, like the hand or the eye. But for the body to be successful, each member must do its job.

On the Ball

If you're on a team and don't get a lot of attention, don't complain or quit. Remember that without your best efforts, your team could fail. And if you're a hand or an eye, remember to give your teammates credit for helping you look good.

COACH'S COMMENT

Our bodies have many parts, and God has put each part just where he wants it.
1 CORINTHIANS 12:18

Jeff Gordon's auto-racing career began when he was five. By the time he was eight, he had won his first quarter-midget championship. But Jeff would have to wait until he was 35 before he earned his 76th NASCAR victory that tied him with Dale Earnhardt as the sixth-winningest driver.

On this day in 2007, Jeff started from the pole position in the Subway Fresh Fit 500 at the Phoenix International Raceway. Known as "Wonder Boy," Jeff had claimed his 75th NASCAR victory in July 2006, but he couldn't seem to win the race he needed to tie Dale. To honor Dale, Jeff's Hendrick Motorsports team had prepared a flag with No. 4 on it, which they had planned to unveil once Jeff tied the legendary driver.

In Phoenix, Jeff led the 312-lap race early. However, Tony Stewart soon worked his way to the front. Jeff regained the lead on lap 294, but Tony made a pass to reclaim the top spot on lap 299. Jeff knew he didn't have much time. He boldly moved to the bottom of the track and passed Tony during lap 300. From there he pulled away to win the race by six car lengths.

What's the Score?

Following the victory, Jeff's crew handed him the No. 4 flag, and Jeff slowly drove around the track honoring Dale. Fans cheered on Jeff and paid their respects to Dale, who had died in a crash in 2001. It was a memorable moment for Jeff—one worth waiting for.

Have you ever heard the saying "Good things come to those who wait"? That's what Jeff experienced. He had to wait nearly nine months for his record-tying victory, but the moment was amazing. The Bible puts it this way: "Patient endurance is what you need. . . . Then you will receive all that he has promised" (Hebrews 10:36).

Have you noticed that you don't always get everything you want when you want it? That's okay. In fact, it's good to show patience. God rewards patience. Doing his will without being rewarded right away makes the payoff even sweeter in the end.

) On the Ball

Would you describe yourself as a patient person? It's not easy to wait. The next time you want something badly, purposefully wait to get it. Maybe you can wait a whole month. While you're waiting, pray to God to give you endurance and help you be more patient in life.

) COACH'S COMMENT

Patient endurance is what you need now, so that you will continue to do God's will. Then you will receive all that he has promised. HEBREWS 10:36

Nobody said Mike Bordick's job would be easy. In December 1996, the Baltimore Orioles signed Mike, a free agent from the Oakland Athletics, to be their shortstop the following season. This was huge news in Baltimore because it effectively ended superstar Cal Ripken's 14-year run as the team's shortstop. In 1997, Cal, who had redefined the shortstop position in the 1980s, shifted to third base, and Mike took over at shortstop. No pressure, right?

Actually, Mike thrived. Some of the best seasons of his 14-year career came in Baltimore. His defensive wizardry helped Orioles fans move past Cal's era at shortstop. During Mike's five-plus seasons with the Orioles, he posted a better career fielding percentage (.982) than Hall of Famers such as Cal and Ozzie Smith, who were considered two of the greatest shortstops of all time. Still, no one expected what happened in 2002. That's when Mike set major-league records for consecutive errorless games at 110. In fact, in 117 games and with 570 chances, Mike only made one error!

⬜⬜ **What's the Score?**

Defensively, Mike's 2002 season stands out as one of the best. But if you want to be nit-picky, it wasn't perfect. He still made an error. It's pretty tough to be error free, whether in baseball, on a test, or in anything really. That's what makes the Bible so amazing. The Bible has—drumroll, please—*no* errors! If the Bible had any errors, it would cease to be Holy Scripture. We couldn't rely on it. One error would turn the Bible into a book of lies because it claims to be the inspired, error-free Word of God. And who wants to live his or her life based on a mistake-filled book?

But God's Word *doesn't* contain any errors. Not a single one. Since it is "inspired by God" (2 Timothy 3:16), it is perfect in every way because God himself is perfect. When we read the Scriptures—from Genesis to Revelation—we can be fully assured that they are completely trustworthy and error free. As Psalm 33:4 says, "The word of the LORD holds true." That's a book worth reading!

⟩ **On the Ball**

Try to play your favorite video game or sport perfectly. You'll quickly realize it's not possible. Each time you make an error, consider how amazing it is that God's Word is error free.

⟩ **COACH'S COMMENT**

The word of the LORD holds true, and we can trust everything he does. **PSALM 33:4**

Imagine if your last name were fruity. Natalie Nectarine. Walter Watermelon. Janna Banana. Harry Blueberry. Life wouldn't be easy. You'd be on the wrong end of plenty of jokes. But no one was laughing at Darryl Strawberry in the 1980s.

Darryl, the New York Mets' No. 1 overall draft pick in 1980, rocketed to stardom thanks to a beautiful left-handed swing that sent baseballs soaring. With the 1983 National League Rookie of the Year Award, a World Series title, eight All-Star appearances, and 280 home runs in his first nine seasons, Strawberry appeared destined for the Hall of Fame. But injuries, a bout with colon cancer, and terrible personal choices derailed his career. Darryl was arrested for drug possession. He also abused alcohol and pled guilty to tax evasion. He spent time in baseball suspension, rehab centers, and prison. During his final eight seasons, he bounced between the Dodgers, the Giants, and the Yankees and rarely displayed the mesmerizing power and abilities he had shown in the 1980s. In 1999, his final season, he had only three home runs and six RBIs in 24 games with the Yankees.

⬚⬚ What's the Score?

Sadly, Darryl Strawberry's life was characterized by bad choices and sinful behavior. What should a Christian's life be characterized by? Well, fruit actually. But not a juicy selection from the grocery produce aisle or a delicious-sounding last name. No, look for the fruit found in Galatians 5:22-23: "Love, joy, peace, patience, kindness, goodness, faithfulness, gentleness, and self-control."

If you've ever wondered how a Christian is supposed to act—there it is! This "fruit" is the mark of true believers in Jesus Christ. When we put our faith in Christ, God's Holy Spirit enters our hearts and starts making us more like him. He starts replacing hate with love, sorrow with joy, cruelty with kindness. This transformation doesn't happen all at once. Even as Christians, we still struggle with sin. But the fruit of the Spirit should continually become more evident in our lives as time goes on. And that's just peachy!

⟩ On the Ball

Using a scale of one to nine (one being the best), rank the fruit of the Spirit in your life, from what you're best at (by God's grace) to what you need the most help with. Ask your parents to do the same for you, and compare rankings. Thank God for your strengths, and ask him for help in your weaknesses.

⟩ COACH'S COMMENT

The Holy Spirit produces this kind of fruit in our lives: love, joy, peace, patience, kindness, goodness, faithfulness, gentleness, and self-control. There is no law against these things! GALATIANS 5:22-23

Entering the 2010–2011 NBA basketball season, only five players had scored more than 70 points in a single game. How many of them can you name? If you said Kobe Bryant, that's correct. Wilt Chamberlain is another. NBA greats Elgin Baylor and David Thompson also posted 70 in a game. And on this day in 1994, San Antonio Spurs center David Robinson dropped 71 points on the Los Angeles Clippers to help him win the season-long scoring crown.

Heading into the game, David needed to score at least 33 points to pass Shaquille O'Neal for the NBA scoring lead. He did more than twice that! David made 26 of 41 shots, including a three-pointer, and sank 18 free throws. He ended the season averaging 29.8 points per game. Shaq's average was 29.3.

What's the Score?

The seven-foot-one-inch center will be remembered as one of the best players in NBA history. But David didn't always dominate on the court. He played only one year of high school basketball before attending the Naval Academy as a six-foot-four-inch forward. David grew seven inches in college and became a powerful center. He won two world championships with the Spurs, an MVP award, and countless other honors. But if you asked David about the greatest honor in his life, he would say it is serving Jesus Christ. Of course, that came with some challenges. He was often criticized for his faith, especially when his team was losing.

David never backed down, and he'd encourage you to do the same. "Don't get discouraged, because God has a wonderful work waiting for you in a challenge and it may not be what you think," David said. "Stand up and face your challenges whatever they are." God has called each of us to a special work. The apostle Paul said in Acts 20:24, "I consider my life worth nothing to me; my only aim is to finish the race and complete the task the Lord Jesus has given me" (NIV). God wants all of us to tell people about the powerful difference he's made in our lives. And he has other great plans for us as well . . . even if we never score 70 points in a game.

) On the Ball

Think about the things you've accomplished in life or want to accomplish. All of those things are meaningless unless you're living for Christ and finishing the race he has planned for you. Serving God is more important than any earthly honor.

) COACH'S COMMENT

I consider my life worth nothing to me; my only aim is to finish the race and complete the task the Lord Jesus has given me—the task of testifying to the good news of God's grace. ACTS 20:24 (NIV)

For decades, boxing has been known as "the sweet science"—a unique combination of elegant athleticism and brutal violence. Perhaps more than any other sport, it also seems to be a breeding ground for boasting. When two powerful boxers prepare for a big fight, boasting (or bragging about oneself) never seems to be far behind.

Take Floyd Mayweather Jr., for instance. During his brilliant career, Floyd was an unabashed self-promoter. As the boxing world excitedly anticipated a possible showdown between Floyd and Filipino champion Manny Pacquiao in 2009, Floyd stoked the fire with prideful comments. Here are a few samples:

+ "Can Manny Pacquiao beat me? Absolutely not. Easy work, easy fight."
+ "Floyd Mayweather is the face of boxing. All roads lead to Floyd Mayweather."
+ "There's no fighter that can beat me. The world's going to go 'wow' if Floyd Mayweather gets beat. That's what everyone's looking to see."

But Mayweather's outsized claims were nothing new to boxing. In the 1960s and 1970s, Muhammad Ali, the great heavyweight champion, made boasting an art form. Before fights, he would often taunt opponents and praise himself with rhyming poems. He once said to a foe, "I'm going to float like a butterfly and sting like a bee. George can't hit what his hands can't see."

What's the Score?

Boasting is commonplace in all sports, not just boxing. But that doesn't mean it's okay. In fact, the Bible says boasting is a sin.

We all struggle with boasting, even if we're not athletic. It's part of our nature that we must fight to control. We like bringing attention to ourselves and telling others what we can do.

Actually, when you think about it, boasting is quite silly. Any skill or ability we have comes from God, not us. We can't even breathe or make our heart beat without God's help! Therefore, as 2 Corinthians 10:17 tells us, the only place for boasting is boasting in the Lord. In other words, instead of talking about what we can do, we should talk about what *God* can do. He created us and sustains our lives. He provides for all our needs and gives us unique abilities. And he provided a Savior for our sins in his Son, Jesus Christ.

Let's boast in the Lord!

) On the Ball

Make a list of all the things you're good at. Then one by one, thank God for giving you each talent.

) COACH'S COMMENT

As the Scriptures say, "If you want to boast, boast only about the LORD."

2 CORINTHIANS 10:17

It should have been a season of enjoyment and elation. Instead, it was one of exhaustion and anxiety. Today in 1961, New York Yankees outfielder Roger Maris hit the first of 61 home runs, which broke the single-season record of beloved Yankees icon Babe Ruth. For 34 years, Babe's 60 home runs in 1927 were the most hallowed record in Major League Baseball. As the 1961 season continued, it became clear that many New York fans and sportswriters did not want to see Roger break the record. He was a New York outsider—a quiet Midwesterner who had come to the noisy Big Apple from the Kansas City Athletics. The public wanted to see the record broken by superstar Mickey Mantle, who spent his whole 18-year Hall of Fame career in New York.

Mickey's and Roger's race for the record took a severe toll on Roger. Reporters hounded him, and fans booed him while cheering for Mickey. Roger even received letters that threatened him and his family. The pressure became so great that Roger lost some of his hair and didn't eat much. In the last two weeks of the season, he twice asked Yankees manager Ralph Houk for a day off. In the end, though, Roger did it. While Mickey suffered a hip injury in September and finished with 54 homers, Roger hit number 61 in the final game of the season.

What's the Score?

In his greatest season, Roger dealt with crippling anxiety. After retiring, he once said of his New York celebrity, "All it brought me was headaches." Have you ever felt anxious or worried about something? Of course you have. It's a natural human response to problems. But the Bible tells us not to be anxious.

First Peter 5:7 says to cast *all* our anxiety on God. That leaves no room for us to hold on to any—not even a smidgen. If we do, it's basically telling God that he's not good, wise, or strong enough to help us, or that we think we can solve our problems better than he can. And both of those assumptions are untrue. No matter what you are facing, cast all your cares on God through prayer and trust. He loves you and wants to help!

On the Ball

A great way to cast anxiety on God is to pray something like this: "God, I'm concerned about (*insert problem here*). But I know you care about me. Please help me trust in you and make it through this difficult situation."

COACH'S COMMENT

Cast all your anxiety on him because he cares for you. 1 PETER 5:7 (NIV)

Chugga-chugga, chugga-chugga, choo-choo! Batters beware—here comes the Ryan Express! On this day in 1983, Houston Astros right-hander Nolan Ryan, nicknamed the Ryan Express for his blazing fastballs, became Major League Baseball's all-time strikeout king with 3,509. A five-strikeout performance against the Montreal Expos was all Nolan needed to surpass Washington Senators great Walter Johnson.

After the historic pitch, Nolan's teammates rushed to the mound to celebrate with him. The baseball that Nolan used for the record-breaking whiff was sent to the Hall of Fame. But Ryan wasn't done. Not by a long shot. The Ryan Express kept chugging along for 10 more seasons and 2,205 strikeouts. The eight-time All-Star finished his Hall of Fame career in 1993 with 324 wins, a record 5,714 strikeouts, and seven no-hitters. Even at an age when most pitchers break down, Nolan was marvelous. He led the league in strikeouts four times while in his 40s, fanned 203 batters when he was 44, and finally retired at age 46, after a record-tying 27 major-league seasons. *Wow!*

🏏 What's the Score?

Plenty of good pitchers entered the major leagues in the early 1990s as Nolan's career was winding down. But even in his 40s, he was still as powerful as any of them. As opposing hitters found out, newer is not always better. That is certainly true with Christianity. For 2,000 years people have looked for ways to improve the gospel message. But that's impossible. You don't need a new model when there's nothing wrong with the original.

The gospel—that is, the Good News of salvation from our sins through faith in Jesus—is a simple yet powerful message. It cannot be improved upon. The writers of the New Testament knew this and defended the gospel against all sorts of false doctrines in the first century AD. In fact, the apostle Paul said anyone who supports an untrue gospel will be "under God's curse" (Galatians 1:8, NIV). Avoid anything, or anyone, who seems to be promoting a better or more current version of Christianity. There's nothing wrong with God's original plan of salvation. The amazing gospel of Jesus is just as relevant and true today as it was 2,000 years ago.

How do we know? Because God's Word says so.

⟩ On the Ball

Pray to God for wisdom and discernment to follow the one true gospel of the Bible.

⟩ COACH'S COMMENT

Evidently some people are throwing you into confusion and are trying to pervert the gospel of Christ. But even if we or an angel from heaven should preach a gospel other than the one we preached to you, let them be under God's curse! **GALATIANS 1:7-8 (NIV)**

Brooks Laich was stunned. The Washington Capitals' veteran center couldn't believe the season was over—not this quickly. With a 54-15-13 record, the Capitals had entered the 2010 play-offs as a favorite to win the franchise's first Stanley Cup. In the first round of the play-offs, they took a commanding three-games-to-one lead against the Montreal Canadiens. Then everything fell apart. Washington dropped three straight games, including a 2–1 heartbreaker at home in game seven. The season was done.

Brooks could have retreated into a self-absorbed cocoon of sadness and self-pity. Instead, in a heartwarming display of kindness, he reached out to others. While driving home after the season-ending loss, he noticed a mother and her teenage daughter stranded with a flat tire. Many cars drove past. Brooks pulled over. Still in his postgame dress clothes, Brooks changed the greasy tire. The women, who had attended the Capitals' game that night, were thrilled that a millionaire NHL star would perform such a kind act. When he was done, Brooks hugged the ladies and drove off, leaving a lasting memory.

⬜⬜ What's the Score?

Like Brooks, we should watch for ways to show kindness to others, even if it means going out of our way or doing it when we don't want to. There's never a bad time to be kind. Colossians 3:12 says we are to wear kindness like clothing. That doesn't mean being kind is always easy. We might have to inconvenience ourselves to help someone. But kindness isn't worth much if it doesn't cost us something.

Other times we may think certain people don't deserve our kindness. Maybe someone said or did something nasty to you. It's tough to be kind to those people. But the Bible commands us to love everyone, not just those who treat us well.

The ultimate expert on kindness was Jesus. He showed love and compassion to everyone—children, adults, rich, poor, sick, and healthy. He even showed kindness to his enemies, asking his heavenly Father to forgive those who mocked him while he hung on the cross for their sins. To be like Jesus, we must show kindness to others.

⟩ On the Ball

Surprise someone with one of the following acts of kindness this week:

1. Offer to do yard work for a neighbor.
2. Bake cookies for a friend.
3. Give some of your old toys to a kid less fortunate than you.
4. Write a note of appreciation to someone.
5. Tell your family how much you love them.

⟩ COACH'S COMMENT

Since God chose you to be the holy people he loves, you must clothe yourselves with tenderhearted mercy, kindness, humility, gentleness, and patience. **COLOSSIANS 3:12**

Team spirit can get kind of silly, can't it? Cheering on their favorite team makes normal people do some pretty wacky stuff. It makes girls do dangerous flips in the air and adults wear body paint to display their team's colors. It causes muscular, grown men to start wildly hopping and chanting in a circle before kickoff and 300-pound linemen to sing something called an "alma mater" at the end of games. It makes tens of thousands of people line city streets and others drop confetti from skyscrapers as championship players slowly drive by in a parade.

In baseball, team spirit produced the Rally Monkey, Thunderstix, and Sausage Race. In the NFL, it produced the Lambeau Leap, the Black Hole, and the Hogettes. In case you were wondering, the Hogettes are a group of male Washington Redskins fans who have worn hats, dresses, and pig snouts to Redskins games since the 1980s, when a group of beefy offensive linemen nicknamed "the Hogs" led Washington to several Super Bowl titles. Team spirit never looked so, uh, unique.

⬜⬜ What's the Score?

The Bible talks a lot about spirit, but in a completely different context than face paint and team cheers. Scripture often uses "spirit" to describe angelic beings, a person's soul, or the Holy Spirit. But did you know it also describes God the Father? It's true. In John 4:24, Jesus himself says, "God is Spirit."

God is not like us. He is not human and doesn't possess a physical body. He doesn't have size or dimension. His being is not like anything else in creation. That's why he forbids us in Exodus 20:4 to worship him with any man-made images. Sometimes the Bible talks about God's hands, arms, eyes, and mouth. But this is always because the biblical authors were trying to describe God in ways that humans could understand.

It's not possible for us to fully comprehend God. He's too large, and our brains are too small. But believing everything about God mentioned in the Bible is extremely important because we must worship God as he truly exists, not as we *think* he exists. That said, the Bible promises that Christians will see God's face in heaven (Revelation 22:4). What that truly means is a mystery, but it is certainly something to get excited about!

⟩ On the Ball

Occasionally, God took visible form in the Old Testament. Check out these amazing Scripture passages to learn more:

1. Genesis 18:1-33
2. Genesis 32:24-30
3. Exodus 13:21-22
4. Exodus 24:9-11
5. Exodus 33:18-23
6. Judges 13:21-22
7. Isaiah 6:1

⟩ COACH'S COMMENT

God is Spirit, so those who worship him must worship in spirit and in truth. JOHN 4:24

A zero on the scoreboard had never looked so imposing. Less than nine minutes into the 2010 NCAA women's lacrosse championship game, the University of Maryland trailed Northwestern 6–0. This was uncharted territory for the Terrapins, who had dominated their competition virtually all season and lost only once in the previous 22 games. But Northwestern was not like any other team Maryland had faced. The Wildcats entered the championship game as the sport's reigning dynasty with an eight-game winning streak and five straight NCAA titles to their credit.

So when the mighty Wildcats took a six-goal lead, the game appeared over. Except to Maryland. The Terrapins never gave up and eventually took a 10–8 lead that they would never relinquish in a shocking 13–11 victory. It was the Terrapins' 11th national title but their first since 2001. Later that year, ESPN ranked Maryland's comeback as the ninth-best women's sports story of 2010. "After the 6–0 run, we never gave up," Maryland's Caitlyn McFadden, the game's Most Outstanding Player, told reporters. "[After] each [Northwestern] goal, we came together and said [to] keep fighting and stay in it."

What's the Score?
Maryland enjoyed a lot of blowout wins in 2010, but it learned a vital lesson in the NCAA final against Northwestern: trouble is bound to come. The question is, what will you do when it happens? It's a question everyone must answer in life, not just in sports. Ever since Adam and Eve sinned in the Garden of Eden, trouble has been part of the daily human experience.

Sometimes trouble is as small as a stubbed toe or a lost toy. Other times, it's as big as the death of a loved one. Trouble comes in all shapes and sizes. But it certainly will come. Fortunately, there is a God who wants to help. When trouble pelts us like an angry hailstorm, we can call out to him. Scripture says, "The LORD is a shelter for the oppressed, a refuge in times of trouble" (Psalm 9:9). He might not always bring relief right away or answer your prayer exactly the way you want. But he knows what's best for you and will help. Trouble is inevitable. But like the Terrapins, don't give up when it knocks you down. Trust in God.

On the Ball
Keep a prayer journal, and write down every time you cry out to God for help. When he answers your prayer, record it as a testimony of his help in times of trouble.

COACH'S COMMENT
The LORD is a shelter for the oppressed, a refuge in times of trouble. PSALM 9:9

Pro athletes make millions of dollars. When you play professional sports, you're loaded with cash, right? Not Troy Ready. He played professional soccer for free. Troy had wanted to be a soccer pro since he was five. He even had green carpet in his bedroom to look like grass. Troy was a soccer star at the University of Washington, and he played semipro for the Portland Timbers. His desire to play soccer was matched only by his desire to spread God's love. So he and his young family moved to Tajikistan in 2009 to help people in one of the poorest nations in the world.

Troy went to one of Tajikistan's top pro teams, FC Vakhsh, and volunteered to play. He didn't mind that his permit to be in the country didn't allow him to be paid. Troy just wanted to be part of the team and to connect with the people. Soccer was the perfect bridge. Troy couldn't speak the language well, but he could play the game they all loved. He organized local soccer events for kids and got involved with some coaching, too. Bringing hope to people in Tajikistan was much more valuable to Troy than making lots of money.

What's the Score?

Troy's choices may seem crazy to some. They might say he gave up so much. But his life is what Jesus was talking about when he said, "If you try to hang on to your life, you will lose it. But if you give up your life for my sake, you will save it" (Matthew 16:25). It might sound confusing, but it's pretty simple. Jesus said we gain true life and real joy when we give everything to him.

Jesus wants nothing to be more important than him. That can be hard sometimes. We get hung up on our stuff. It's okay to have an iPod or a Wii, but it's not okay to love them more than we love God or other people. When we're willing to give up everything for God, he fills us with a peace that's much better than any possession. Ask him for help to have an attitude like Troy's.

) On the Ball

Bounce a soccer ball on your knee. Notice that it's only when you bounce the ball away from yourself that it can come back. Our lives are kind of like that. When we give freely to others, God's true plan for our lives can come back and fill us up. What can you use to give to others?

) COACH'S COMMENT

If you try to hang on to your life, you will lose it. But if you give up your life for my sake, you will save it. MATTHEW 16:25

Fifteen-year-old Rick Hoyt came home from school and asked his dad if they could run a five-mile race together to benefit a local college student who had been paralyzed in a car accident. There's nothing odd about that—until you discover that Rick was a quadriplegic with cerebral palsy. He couldn't control most of the muscles in his body and was confined to a wheelchair. Rick had to type out his question to his dad on a special computer that allowed him to select letters by the slightest motion of his head.

Rick's father, Dick, agreed. He had never run a race before, but he ran that race pushing Rick's wheelchair. It changed their lives forever. Rick loved the race. He told his dad that when they ran, he didn't feel disabled. That was in 1977. Since then Team Hoyt has completed more than 1,000 endurance events around the world, including marathons and Ironman triathlons. What kept them going? The delight of a son and the love of a father. Many people thought Dick should have started a solo career in endurance sports. If he could go so fast pushing and pulling his middle-aged son, think how fast he could go alone! Not a chance. Dick said he only did it because of Rick. His only motivation was a father's incredible love for his son.

What's the Score?

Team Hoyt is an inspiring example of a father's love and dedication. But even more amazing is that it doesn't even come close to the love God has for us. God loves us so much that he sent his own Son to die on the cross for us (John 3:16). There's no reason God had to call us his children—except his love caused him to do just that. We can't imagine how much God loves us. He could have chosen to be an almighty ruler who controlled us like a bunch of robots. Instead, "see how very much our Father loves us, for he calls us his children, and that is what we are!" (1 John 3:1). Isn't it awesome to be one of God's children?

On the Ball

Your earthly father isn't perfect, but he probably loves you more than you understand. Connect with him today. Ask him to do something fun together. Call or Skype him if he's far away, and set up a long-distance project you can do together: maybe reading the same book or creating a video together.

COACH'S COMMENT

See how very much our Father loves us, for he calls us his children, and that is what we are! 1 JOHN 3:1

Ever try bowling with your eyes closed? Dale Davis didn't have to imagine what it would be like. He was blind, but he loved to bowl. On this day in 2008, the 78-year-old achieved bowling perfection by throwing 12 strikes in a row. Even though he couldn't see the pins fall, he heard and enjoyed every crash and tumble.

Dale lost his eyesight to the eye disorder macular degeneration. He had been a good bowler before but understandably gave up the sport when he couldn't see anymore. His sister convinced him to try again, and he fell in love with the game once more. Dale had a small sliver of peripheral vision in the corner of his right eye. To bowl, he turned his head to find the big dot on the floor. He lined up, took four steps, released the ball, and listened. By his 10th frame on May 3, everyone in the bowling alley was gathered around to watch and cheer for Dale. Everybody went crazy when his ball hit the pins. They celebrated not only a perfect game, but the courage, commitment, and blind faith of the man who had achieved it. Even with all the celebrating, Dale had no trouble hearing that he'd hit the last strike.

What's the Score?
Sometimes we can have trouble trusting in things we can't see. But that's what we have to do with Jesus. First Peter 1:8 says, "You love him even though you have never seen him. Though you do not see him now, you trust him; and you rejoice with a glorious, inexpressible joy." We may not be able to see God, but we know that he's there.

For now, we catch glimpses of God at work out of the corner of our eye, kind of like Dale. We have to rely on our other senses and faith to see and hear God. Of course, we can hear God in his Word and feel his Spirit move in us. But we can also know that our faith won't always be blind. Someday we'll see God with perfect vision, and everything will be clear.

) On the Ball
Do something blindfolded, maybe something you're already good at. Concentrate on using your other senses. And remind yourself how clear God will make everything someday.

) COACH'S COMMENT
You love him even though you have never seen him. Though you do not see him now, you trust him; and you rejoice with a glorious, inexpressible joy. 1 PETER 1:8

Think of great athletes. Who comes to mind? Maybe LeBron James, Michael Phelps, Peyton Manning, or Lance Armstrong? Probably not Calvin Borel. What? You've never heard of Calvin Borel?

Calvin was as dominant in horse racing as the Los Angeles Lakers were in basketball. He was the jockey who rode three of the four Kentucky Derby winners between 2006 and 2010. The horses he rode—Street Sense, Mine That Bird, and Super Saver—might be better known than Calvin. Weighing in at 110 pounds, Calvin was tougher pound for pound than any other athlete out there. A jockey's job requires mental skill, physical strength, and a willingness to take great risks. Jockeys plunge their horses into the pack of 1,000-pound beasts stampeding at 35 miles per hour. Talk about toughness.

Calvin's skills and accomplishments should be enough to put him into discussions of the greatest athletes of all time. But most people have never heard of him. Whether he gets all the glory or none, we can learn a lot from an athlete like Calvin. His lack of fame doesn't erase his greatness.

What's the Score?

Now think about heroes of the Christian faith. Who comes to mind? Abraham, David, Peter, and Paul? Probably not Jephthah. Who? Jephthah is the great warrior and leader who ruled as a judge.

You can find Jephthah's story in Judges 11–12. And even though others may have forgotten his greatness, God did not. Jephthah is recognized alongside Gideon and Samuel (1 Samuel 12:11) as well as Samson, David, and all the prophets (Hebrews 11:32). God counted Jephthah as one of the greats of faith. He ruled with justice and trusted God. "By faith these people overthrew kingdoms, ruled with justice, and received what God had promised them" (Hebrews 11:33). Those heroes of faith included Jephthah.

On the Ball

List the people who have had the biggest impact on your life. Then think again about whom you might have forgotten—someone who has made a huge contribution to your life but has done it more quietly. E-mail or text that person to say thank you.

COACH'S COMMENT

By faith these people overthrew kingdoms, ruled with justice, and received what God had promised them. HEBREWS 11:33

The first seat on the plane was empty. It belonged to Los Angeles Lakers captain and team leader Kareem Abdul-Jabbar. But Kareem had injured his ankle so badly in game five of the 1980 NBA finals that he couldn't make the trip for game six to play the 76ers in Philadelphia. The Lakers' mood was glum. Without Kareem, they didn't have a good chance of winning.

That's when a rookie stepped up. Twenty-year-old Earvin "Magic" Johnson sat in his seat with his big trademark grin and told his team, "No fear. E.J. is here." In Philly, he backed up his words. Magic was normally the point guard, but he played all over the court that night, including center where Kareem usually dominated. He made moves like Kareem, including the Big Man's signature "skyhook." That night Magic did it all, including pouring in nine points in the final 2:22. The Lakers won the game and claimed the NBA title. Magic's performance was the best ever by an NBA rookie: 42 points, including 14 of 14 free throws, 15 rebounds, seven assists, and three steals. Back home in California, Kareem danced around on his one good leg.

⬜ What's the Score?

Magic Johnson was ready to lead, and he knew it. He didn't hesitate; he stepped up and performed. We need to be ready like Magic in the game of life. Our time will come, even if it seems like it's nowhere near. And now is the time to get ready.

The apostle Peter tells us, "Always be prepared to give an answer to everyone who asks you to give the reason for the hope that you have" (1 Peter 3:15, NIV). We do that by staying close with God, reading his Word, talking with him, and getting to know him better. We also need to remember the big story of how he saved the world and how he's writing that story in our lives. As we live out our faith, people will notice. And when they wonder what makes us different, we can explain God's love and hope inside us. We don't do that by arguing with people. We "do this with gentleness and respect" (1 Peter 3:15, NIV) by explaining what God means to us.

⟩ On the Ball

Get a piece of paper, and write the story of God's work in your life. Write how you fit in his big story of the world. It will help you be prepared to tell others.

⟩ COACH'S COMMENT

Always be prepared to give an answer to everyone who asks you to give the reason for the hope that you have. But do this with gentleness and respect. 1 PETER 3:15 (NIV)

Blink and you'd miss him. Well, almost. On this day in 1954, a British medical student named Roger Bannister became the first person to run a mile in under four minutes. His new world record was 3:59.4, to be exact. Roger will always be remembered as the first person to break the four-minute barrier, but he didn't do it alone. Two other racers ran with him to help him keep up the fast pace.

Some runners might have called off the record attempt that day. The wind was blowing, and it could have slowed down the runners. But with 3,000 spectators watching, Roger went for it and became the fastest man in the world in the mile. His record didn't last long, though. His rival, Australian John Landy, set a new record a month later by running the mile in 3:57.9. Since then the record has been broken a number of times. In 1999, Moroccan Hicham El Guerrouj ran the mile in 3:43.13. That's fast!

⬜⬜ What's the Score?

The Bible talks a lot about running. It usually encourages us to run toward something, to keep running, or not to give up. But Amos 5:14 has a different message: "Do what is good and run from evil so that you may live!" That's smart advice.

Too often, we try to get as close to sin as we can without actually sinning. It's in our nature to get close to the line, but it's also something we should fight against. Temptation is like a poisonous snake. If you poke it with a stick, you will get bitten. The best way to deal with a viper? Run away. Fast. That's what Amos is telling us to do with evil. Get as far away from temptation as possible, as quickly as possible—like Roger Bannister sprinting for the four-minute mile. Think of him the next time you're staring at temptation. Then get up and run away—fast—for your life.

⟩ On the Ball

Run a mile and write down your time. The next time you're facing a big temptation, get up, and go run another mile. The bigger the temptation, the faster you should go. See if you can beat your personal record.

⟩ COACH'S COMMENT

Do what is good and run from evil so that you may live! Then the LORD God of Heaven's Armies will be your helper, just as you have claimed. AMOS 5:14

The United States has developed some of the world's best athletes in basketball, baseball, football, track, swimming, hockey, and a multitude of other sports. But in 2009, the United States officially became a world power of . . . facial hair. It was during this month that the United States dominated the World Beard and Moustache Championship in Anchorage, Alaska, winning championships in 12 of the 18 categories. Go, team USA!

So what does it take to be a facial hair champ? A beard styled to look like an Alaskan snowshoe took the top freestyle spot. An elaborate boat-shaped moustache stretched wider than its owner's shoulders, but it was only good enough for second place. And a long (to the belly button), red (all-natural color) beard took third.

Believe it or not, there are more than 30 international beard and moustache clubs that compete around the world. The United States has more than 50 local chapters. If you're a boy, you'd better start working on your beard now—or at least start planning crazy shapes for when you get some peach fuzz growing on your upper lip.

What's the Score?

When it comes to facial hair, judging by appearance is the way to go. (Really, is there any other way?) But when it comes to faith and character, we have to dive below the surface. Things aren't always as they seem.

When religious leaders criticized Jesus for healing a man on the Sabbath, Jesus responded, "Stop judging by mere appearances, but instead judge correctly" (John 7:24, NIV). So what is the correct way to judge? By looking at the heart of the matter instead of seeing only the outward appearance.

Jesus was telling the religious leaders that they were sticking to the rules so tightly that they couldn't see the true meaning. The point of God's laws and commands is to draw us closer to God. Jesus healed a man to help connect him with God. That should be our goal with other people, too. God wants us to see and love others for what's inside their hearts, not for what they look like or what they wear on the outside.

⟩ On the Ball

Turn your mirrors around. Try going for a week, or even a day, without looking in the mirror. Use it as a reminder to stop judging yourself, others, and situations by mere appearances. Try using your energy instead to get to the heart of the matter.

⟩ COACH'S COMMENT

Stop judging by mere appearances, but instead judge correctly. JOHN 7:24 (NIV)

Does being lost in the Amazon jungle sound like fun? Ed Stafford wasn't exactly lost, but the former British army captain spent a couple of years sleeping in mosquito-covered hammocks and eating piranhas and smoked turtle. If anything had gone wrong, he would have died without any hope of rescue. And Ed loved it!

Ed did some searching on the Internet and found that no one had ever walked the length of the Amazon River from source to sea. People told him it was impossible, but that just made Ed want to do it more. He started in 2008 with a friend, but his friend quit after three months. A Peruvian man named Gadiel "Cho" Sanchez Rivera agreed to walk Ed through the Red Zone, a dangerous area notorious for drug trafficking and terrorism. The pair ran into some scary situations, but Cho enjoyed his time with Ed. Cho agreed to walk a few more days, and he kept walking the rest of the Amazon with Ed.

The trust between the two transformed the trek. Without Cho's knowledge of the jungle and surrounding cultures, Ed probably wouldn't have made it. Almost two and a half years and 4,000 miles later, the two men reached the end of the Amazon River.

⬜ What's the Score?

A challenge that feels like a jungle can arise in our lives. When we feel unsure of what to do next, we can take a lesson from Ed. The best way to survive is to surround ourselves with people who have the experience, knowledge, and wisdom to help.

Moses learned that strategy. In a battle between the Israelites and the Amalekites, Moses went to a hillside overlooking the battle. When he held up his arms, the Israelites dominated. When he let his arms down, they began losing ground. Moses knew he couldn't do it alone. When Moses got so tired he could no longer hold up his arms, Aaron and Hur helped. "They stood on each side of Moses, holding up his hands. So his hands held steady until sunset" (Exodus 17:12). Moses found strength in his friends, and you can do the same.

⟩ On the Ball

Who holds up your arms when you are tired or lost in life's jungles? Write those people a note or a message today to say thanks. Then hold up someone else's arms when he or she needs support or encouragement.

⟩ COACH'S COMMENT

Moses' arms soon became so tired he could no longer hold them up. So Aaron and Hur found a stone for him to sit on. Then they stood on each side of Moses, holding up his hands. So his hands held steady until sunset. EXODUS 17:12

Juan Uribe never met a pitch he didn't like to swing at. The San Francisco Giants short-stop swung at the second highest percentage of pitches in the National League during the 2010 season. His batting average of .248 wasn't horrible, but he struck out about once for every five times he batted.

On May 9, 2010, Juan recorded a first in his 10-year career. The New York Mets threw him 21 pitches, and Juan swung at . . . zero. Juan walked four times in one game for the first time in his 1,136 Major League contests. His patience at the plate helped the Giants win 6–5.

What's the Score?

Juan normally didn't show a lot of self-control at the plate. He loved to swing away, even at pitches that were out of the strike zone. Often his lack of discipline made him look silly and resulted in his getting out. But by earning four walks in one game, Juan displayed discernment and self-control. Proverbs 25:28 says, "A person without self-control is like a city with broken-down walls." In other words, he or she is going to get beat.

In Bible days, a city's walls were its main protection from enemies. The people lived inside the walls where it was safe and guarded. Remember Jericho? The people there were confident because their city had big, strong walls—they just couldn't stand up to God's power.

How's your self-control? There are many areas in our lives where we need it: control-ling our mouths from hurtful words, keeping ourselves from eating too much junk food, not losing our tempers, and more. When we lose control, we often do things we regret later. It takes practice to learn discipline and to avoid making mistakes where we're weak. But like Juan, we can master self-control even in our weakest areas—with God's help.

) On the Ball

What's your weakness? Make today the day you beat it all day. Ask for God's help. Plan now for how you'll respond when you're tempted to lose control.

) COACH'S COMMENT

A person without self-control is like a city with broken-down walls. PROVERBS 25:28

You've heard the story of five loaves, two fish, and 5,000 people who were fed. But have you heard the one about the nine-year-old, 2,057 free throws, and $2 million raised? It's the story of Austin Gutwein and Hoops of Hope.

When Austin was nine, he heard about the millions of kids in Africa orphaned by AIDS. Austin decided to use his favorite sport, basketball, to help. On World AIDS Day 2004, Austin shot 2,057 free throws—one for each child whose parents would die that day. He raised $3,000 through sponsorships. It was a huge success, so Austin kept the idea going. Since then thousands of kids and adults have joined Hoops of Hope in shoot-a-thons all over the country. Altogether they raised almost $2 million by 2010 to benefit children in Africa. The money has helped build schools and medical clinics, and it has provided food, water, and shelter.

What's the Score?

When you think about showing love, basketball isn't usually the first thing that comes to mind. It's a competitive sport where athletes play to win. But for Austin, shooting hoops was his way of living out 1 John 3:18: "Dear children, let's not merely say that we love each other; let us show the truth by our actions." Basketball was Austin's love in action.

What does your love in action look like? You don't have to shoot hoops or raise millions of dollars, but God wants each of us to do something. The Bible says, "If someone has enough money to live well and sees a brother or sister in need but shows no compassion—how can God's love be in that person?" (1 John 3:17). Most of our families have enough money to live well. How can we use our resources and skills to help those who don't? Put your love into action.

) On the Ball

Live out love today.

1. I will live out love for my parents by _____ .
2. I will live out love for my friends by _____ .
3. I will live out love for kids around the world by _____ .

) COACH'S COMMENT

Dear children, let's not merely say that we love each other; let us show the truth by our actions. 1 JOHN 3:18

One of the greatest thrills in baseball is clobbering a grand slam. The crack of the bat. Watching the ball go over the fence. Starting the home-run trot. Being greeted at home plate by teammates as four runs get posted on the scoreboard. Pittsburgh Pirates outfielder Lastings Milledge felt the thrill of hitting his first career grand slam in May 2010, but his ecstasy quickly turned to agony.

Lastings had just blasted a 1-2 pitch deep into left field. Chicago Cubs outfielder Alfonso Soriano just turned around and watched the line drive fly over his head. "The ball is back," shouted the TV announcer. "It is gone!" Lastings rounded first base in a home-run trot as fireworks went off in PNC Park. Pirate fans cheered like crazy.

"Not so fast," said the Cubs. Alfonso picked up the ball after it hit high off the wall and threw it back to the infield. As Lastings rounded second base, the Cubs tagged him out. What happened? Even though the stadium started celebrating a homer, the umpires never signaled a home run. The ball had bounced high off the wall but apparently not on top of it, so it wasn't a home run. Lastings was totally confused, but he hadn't paid attention. He was out.

☐☐ What's the Score?

It's easy to get caught unexpectedly by temptation or evil. Lots of times it can feel like everybody is cheering for us to do what's wrong. Hebrews 2:1 says, "We must pay the most careful attention, therefore, to what we have heard, so that we do not drift away" (NIV).

Lastings got caught up hearing the fans cheer and watching fireworks explode in the sky. But his attention should've been on the umpires, because it's their opinion that matters. In our own lives, we have to listen to the right voices to make sure we follow the truth. We have to look to God and seek him with all our strength, because it's only his opinion that matters. If we don't pay attention, we'll drift away with the misguided crowd and be tagged out without even realizing what's happening. Don't get taken by surprise. Pay attention to God and his commands.

⟩ On the Ball

Pay attention, and listen to the right voices. Spend some time listening and singing along with your favorite praise songs. Focus on God by worshiping him with all your heart.

⟩ COACH'S COMMENT

We must pay the most careful attention, therefore, to what we have heard, so that we do not drift away. HEBREWS 2:1 (NIV)

It was the mountaintops that Ed Viesturs didn't reach that made the biggest difference. Those were the ones that kept him alive to climb all the rest. On this day in 2005, Ed stood on top of Annapurna, a Himalayan mountain that is 26,545 feet high. It was the last of the world's 14 tallest mountains—those over 26,000 feet—that Ed had left to climb. Ed was the first American to accomplish this feat without using extra oxygen and only the fifth person in the whole world to complete this challenge.

It took Ed 16 years to climb the 14 tallest peaks. *Why didn't he rush to finish sooner?* Because Ed likes to live. He had attempted Annapurna three years earlier but had turned around because of dangerous conditions. He also once turned around only 300 feet below the summit of Mount Everest. That would have been a hard decision for most people to make. But Ed knew it was the best call.

Mountain climbing is a dangerous sport. Ed knew that reaching the top is only half the accomplishment—the other half is making it back down alive. That's especially true above 26,000 feet, where it's called the "death zone" because there's so little oxygen in the air that the human body starts to slowly shut down. Most climbers use extra oxygen bottles that high. Ed didn't. He believed if he couldn't make it totally on his own physical strength, then he couldn't make it. Other climbers greatly respected Ed for his patience, experience, and wisdom—especially in the highest, most dangerous places.

☐☐ What's the Score?

Ed showed wisdom as a mountain climber. He not only had knowledge and strength, but he had the wisdom to make good decisions while he was climbing. The Bible says a lot about wisdom. Proverbs 4:6 says, "Don't turn your back on wisdom, for she will protect you. Love her, and she will guard you."

Wisdom definitely protected Ed. And wisdom will protect us in life. A lot of wisdom is learned through patience and experience. But you can also gain wisdom by following good advice from the Bible, your parents, and other older Christians. Your good decisions will lead to good results. The more you learn, the wiser you'll become.

) On the Ball

Learn from your mistakes, too. What was the last thing you got in trouble for? How could you have avoided it? How will you avoid it next time by showing wisdom?

) COACH'S COMMENT

Don't turn your back on wisdom, for she will protect you. Love her, and she will guard you. PROVERBS 4:6

Morgan Pressel was 12 when she first qualified for the US Women's Open. She was the youngest golfer ever to play in the tournament, even though she was a ripe old 13 when she actually stepped onto the first tee at Pine Needles Lodge and Golf Club in North Carolina in 2001. Morgan's mom was there to watch—even though she had breast cancer. No one outside the family knew it then. But everyone knew by 2003 that Kathy Pressel was very sick because her cancer had returned. Still, that wasn't enough to stop Morgan's mom from bundling up with blankets in chilly 30-degree temps to watch her daughter play the Doherty Championship. Nothing was going to keep her from being there to support her daughter and cheer her toward her dream of being a professional golfer.

Kathy died in 2003 when Morgan was 15. It was a heartbreaking loss. But Kathy's love and support had given Morgan the strength to pursue and achieve her dream. As soon as Morgan was 18, the LPGA welcomed her to the pro tour. In 2007, Morgan became the youngest professional golfer to win a major women's championship. Morgan's mother was always close to her heart, and Morgan stayed passionate about fighting breast cancer. Using golf as a platform, she raised millions of dollars toward finding a cure for the disease that took her mom's life. She dreamed of a day when no one would lose her mother to breast cancer.

☐☐ What's the Score?

When a kid falls down, who does he run to? When a teenager experiences heartbreak, whose shoulder does she cry on? There's a special relationship between mothers and children. No one can comfort us like our moms.

God is our heavenly Father, but he loves us like a mother, too. "I will comfort you there in Jerusalem as a mother comforts her child," he says in Isaiah 66:13. He can hold us, understand us, and wipe away our tears even better than our moms can. God uses mothers in our lives in many, many ways, but we can turn to God and trust him even when our mothers let us down or can't be around.

⟩ On the Ball

Show your mom today how much you love her. Give her a hug, and tell her you love her. If she is far away, call or write. If your mom is no longer a part of your life, write a letter to her or to someone who has filled that role. Thank God for his perfect love too.

⟩ COACH'S COMMENT

I will comfort you there in Jerusalem as a mother comforts her child. ISAIAH 66:13

The waves at the Coronado Bay Resort in Imperial Beach, California, had the competitors barking with excitement. The stormy conditions at the 2010 Surf Dog Competition didn't stop the furry competitors from itching with anticipation . . . and maybe even chasing their tails a bit. That's right—all the surfers had four legs and a whole lot of fur.

These salty dogs really were dogs. More than 60 pooches showed up to catch some waves. The dogs wore flotation vests and stood on their surfboards while their owners pushed them into the breaking waves. Fans cheered from the shore as these canines "hung 20." The dogs ranged in size from a five-pound Pomeranian to an 85-pound Bernese mountain dog. An Australian kelpie named Abbie Girl won the under-40-pound division. And all the surfers seemed to have fun as they raised money for the San Diego Police Department's canine unit.

☐☐ What's the Score?

Dogs are just plain cool. (Sorry, cat lovers!) They can do so much: catch Frisbees and balls, track things with their sense of smell, rescue people or chase down criminals, and surf. Plus, they're man's best friend. They'll love you no matter what. If you have a dog, you know.

But dogs are still dogs. And dogs have some pretty gross habits, too. Proverbs 26:11 reminds us of one of those: "As a dog returns to its vomit, so a fool repeats his foolish-ness." *Eeeewwww!* That gross mental image gives us a good lesson: things can get ugly (and a little disgusting) when we return over and over to our foolish ways without learning from our mistakes. Don't be like a dog. Stop making the same mistake over and over.

) On the Ball

Can you imagine eating dog food until you throw up . . . and then eating that? That would be a horrible idea. But it's also horrible to keep repeating the same mistake. Remember the image of dog vomit the next time you're toying around with doing something foolish—and make a wiser decision.

) COACH'S COMMENT

As a dog returns to its vomit, so a fool repeats his foolishness. PROVERBS 26:11

Sydney Harbor looked like it was ready to celebrate one of Australia's biggest holidays. Boats packed the waters, and tens of thousands of people lined the shores. But this wasn't New Year's Eve or Australia Day. These crowds were gathered on this day in 2010 to cheer the arrival of 16-year-old Jessica Watson. Why? Because she was the youngest person ever to sail all the way around the world without assistance.

Jessica's journey aboard her sailboat, *Ella's Pink Lady*, lasted seven months and carried her 24,000 nautical miles. During that time, she had to deal with not sleeping very much and being completely alone. Even worse, she had to overcome mountainous waves and fierce storms. Jessica's boat was knocked over six times, and its mast was dunked underwater once. One particularly bad storm near the southern tip of South America brought 30-foot waves and 80-mile-per-hour winds.

But no matter how scary the situation, Jessica sailed on. When she made it safely back to Australia, she was praised for her courage. "When I was young, I was pretty much afraid of everything," Jessica wrote in *True Spirit*, her book about the adventure. Clearly, she had come a long way—even farther than around the world.

⬜⬜ What's the Score?

We often call people heroes when they demonstrate courage, especially in the face of danger. People called Jessica Watson a hero, but she disagreed, saying she was "just an ordinary girl who had a dream, worked hard at it, and proved that anything is possible."

Most "ordinary heroes" tell us they get scared but simply do the right thing anyway. God knows that it's normal for us to be afraid, but he has promised to always be with us. His Spirit helps us, gives us the peace to remain calm, and strengthens us to act bravely and obediently even when the storms of life are raging.

⟩ On the Ball

What is your biggest fear? No matter what it is, always remember: God is even bigger!

⟩ COACH'S COMMENT

I am leaving you with a gift—peace of mind and heart. And the peace I give is a gift the world cannot give. So don't be troubled or afraid. JOHN 14:27

Elena Myers had a need for speed. In May 2010, she became the first female to win a race in the 76 years of American Motorcyclist Association (AMA) Pro Racing. She was also only 17.

The AMA Supersport Race One at Infineon Raceway was called short due to a crash, so Elena won because she was leading at that point. But she had battled her way to the front of the pack from her start in the seventh position. Many people doubted the five-foot-three-inch, 116-pound girl could compete with the bigger and stronger men. Some felt she didn't have the strength to be racing motorcycles. But Elena had been riding for Kawasaki three years before she could even get a driver's license. What did the guys she raced against think? They respected her and wanted to beat her just like anybody else.

⬜⬜ What's the Score?

Elena broke through stereotypes and earned some respect in the process. Our world is full of stereotypes. Those are usually unfair ways we judge other people. For example, a stereotype is that girls are weaker and no good at motorcycle racing. That's true of some girls—and some boys—but not of Elena.

God calls us to respect people even before their performance demands it. In 1 Timothy 5:1-2, we're told to respect all kinds of people regardless of age or gender. The verses include guidance about how to treat both boys and girls: "Talk to younger men as you would to your own brothers. . . . Treat younger women with all purity as you would your own sisters."

We should respect and honor people as if they were our family members. The more we show respect like that to others, the more others will respect us.

⟩ On the Ball

Show respect for another boy or girl today by saying something nice about him or her in front of other people.

⟩ COACH'S COMMENT

Never speak harshly to an older man, but appeal to him respectfully as you would to your own father. Talk to younger men as you would to your own brothers. Treat older women as you would your mother, and treat younger women with all purity as you would your own sisters. 1 TIMOTHY 5:1-2

Edurne Pasabán didn't care much about the record. It wasn't why she climbed mountains. Maybe earlier on it had been part of her motivation, but not anymore. When the Spanish mountaineer summited Annapurna (26,545 feet) and Shishapangma (26,289 feet) in the spring of 2010, she became the first woman to officially climb all 14 of the world's 8,000-meter mountains. Those are the ones taller than 26,247 feet. Only 21 men and women had ever accomplished this feat of endurance. (There was some debate and a little controversy about whether or not Edurne was indeed the first woman.)

Edurne didn't worry about the controversy or the recognition. She was just happy to have fulfilled her dream. Six years earlier, frostbite had taken part of her toes after she had climbed K2. She grew depressed and almost quit climbing. But she realized that going back to the mountains brought her peace and gave her a clearer perspective about life.

What's the Score?

Where do you go to clear your head? What helps you regain focus? Getting into the mountains or other beautiful places God has created can be a great way to gain a fresh perspective. The writer of Psalm 121 knew that. He said, "I look up to the mountains—does my help come from there? My help comes from the LORD, who made heaven and earth!" (Psalm 121:1-2).

Mountains are majestic and powerful. They can't help us, but they remind us of God's incredible power. He made mountains. He made our earth and the entire universe. And he helps us with the same strength! Let the wonders of mountains, oceans, forests, rivers, swamps, prairies—the creation—remind you of the power of the Creator.

) On the Ball

Go for a hike or a walk outside. Listen to the wind, and watch stars. Sing out praise songs to God. Take a picture to remind you of the beauty and strength of God all around you.

) COACH'S COMMENT

I look up to the mountains—does my help come from there? My help comes from the LORD, who made heaven and earth! PSALM 121:1-2

John Smoltz didn't want to become a relief pitcher for the Atlanta Braves in 2002. The best major-league pitchers are starters, and John was one of the best. He won the 1996 Cy Young Award, was a six-time All-Star, and had the winningest postseason pitching record in baseball history. Yes, John had missed the entire 2000 season and part of 2001 due to shoulder surgery. But he felt great in 2002. The New York Yankees and Arizona Diamondbacks both offered him fat contracts as a starter. But the Braves wanted him to be their closer and to come in at the end of a game to protect a lead and get the final few outs.

So why did John agree to go to the Braves' bull pen? Because he prayed and asked God to show him what was best—even if he didn't like it. John submitted to God's authority and his coaches' authority and put the good of the team ahead of his desires. God blessed his decision. John dominated as a closer. From May 2002 to May 2003, the Braves didn't lose a single game that John pitched in. And he broke the National League record for most saves in a season with 55.

▢▢ What's the Score?

John moved back to the starting lineup in 2005 and proved he was one of the best in baseball no matter when he pitched. Some pitchers would have been too proud to move to the bull pen. But John showed he was humble enough to obey the Bible's command to "submit yourselves for the Lord's sake to every human authority" (1 Peter 2:13, NIV).

Sometimes we may think we know better than our parents, teachers, and coaches. But God wants us to respect and follow the leaders who have been put in our lives—unless they tell us to do something that clearly goes against God's Word. We don't have to like all rules, but we have to listen respectfully and obey. Sometimes our leaders will make mistakes, but they usually have a bigger picture in their minds that will help us in the end. If one of the big league's best can submit to authority, you can too.

) On the Ball

What's your least favorite rule or authority figure? Obey without complaining. Change your attitude, and you might be surprised that your teacher or parent will too.

) COACH'S COMMENT

Submit yourselves for the Lord's sake to every human authority: whether to the emperor, as the supreme authority, or to governors, who are sent by him to punish those who do wrong and to commend those who do right. 1 PETER 2:13-14 (NIV)

"Happy Mother's Day, Mom. I'm going to ride my kayak over an 82-foot waterfall." Can you imagine telling your mom something like that? Christie Glissmeyer's mom might have seen it coming. Her daughter was a professional white-water kayaker. Christie's mom probably still wasn't thrilled by the idea, but on Mother's Day in 2009, Christie paddled right over the edge of Metlako Falls on Oregon's Eagle Creek. The 82-foot plummet set a new record for the highest kayak drop by a woman.

It was definitely a "don't try this at home" kind of event. Christie had carefully planned and studied the best route over the falls. And she went with experienced professional friends. Christie's biggest challenge was not freaking out at the top. She paddled hard with the "green tongue," the flow of the main current, and let the water launch her over the edge. Christie threw her paddle away, tucked forward, and closed her eyes. Then she let gravity and the water do the work. She splashed into the pool below and was surprised at how soft the landing felt.

☐☐ What's the Score?

Have you ever been to a big waterfall? You can feel and hear it before you see it. There's an amazing amount of energy in flowing water. If you've ever been white-water rafting, you know the feeling.

Jesus described the life he offers as "rivers of living water" flowing from our hearts (John 7:38). God's Spirit is like a thundering waterfall pouring out of us, full of power, strength, and refreshment. Don't let fear or embarrassment dam up the power inside you. Let God's love and life pour out of you like an 80-foot waterfall. Other people will feel it and hear it before they even see you, and they'll want to dive in!

⟩ On the Ball

Ask God to give you a chance to share his love with someone today. Dive in. Get in God's powerful current. And watch for the opportunity he brings to share about him.

⟩ COACH'S COMMENT

Anyone who believes in me may come and drink! For the Scriptures declare, "Rivers of living water will flow from his heart." JOHN 7:38

How would you travel around the world—jet, cruise ship, helicopter, submarine? Colin Angus biked, hiked, skied, canoed, and rowed during a totally self-powered circumnavigation of the globe. The Canadian adventurer trekked through 17 countries. He and his fiancée, Julie Wafaei, rowed unsupported across two oceans. The route went from Canada to Alaska, across the Bering Sea and Siberia (in the winter), from Moscow to Portugal, across the Atlantic Ocean to Costa Rica, and then back up to Canada. Makes you tired just reading about it, doesn't it?

So, you may be wondering, *why'd he do it?* Besides the obvious love of adventure and exploration, Colin wanted to raise awareness for our amazing world. His message was that if he could spend nearly two years and travel 26,000 miles without polluting the earth, the rest of us should be able to try to reduce pollution in our everyday travels.

⬚⬚ What's the Score?

For followers of Jesus, the earth is more than a good cause or a challenging adventure. It's God's handiwork that he put in our care since the creation of the world. And it's one of the ways God is revealed to us.

Romans 1:20 says that nobody has an excuse for not believing in God because "ever since the world was created, people have seen the earth and sky. Through everything God made, they can clearly see his invisible qualities—his eternal power and divine nature." That's good reason for us to live in ways that protect creation and keep it reflecting the pure, majestic, and unspoiled nature of its creator.

⟩ On the Ball

Do everything you can today to travel everywhere by your own power. Walk, bike, skateboard, or ski. Then consider walking or biking to school more often.

⟩ COACH'S COMMENT

Ever since the world was created, people have seen the earth and sky. Through everything God made, they can clearly see his invisible qualities—his eternal power and divine nature. So they have no excuse for not knowing God. ROMANS 1:20

Josiah Viera loved baseball. The six-year-old's one dream was to play the sport. The problem was Josiah's disease, progeria. This rare condition caused Josiah's body to function more like a 60- or 70-year-old's. It was why the six-year-old boy was bald, only a little taller than two feet, and weighed 15 pounds. His body was wearing out about 10 times faster than normal. Only about 50 kids in the whole world have the disease, and most only live until they're eight to 13 years old.

The disease had almost killed Josiah before he was two. He had lots of surgeries. Somehow he had miraculously survived. And the older he got, the more he wanted to play baseball. A local T-ball team heard about Josiah and let him come play a game with them. Josiah told the coach to pitch him the ball—he didn't need the tee—and he hit it every time. Josiah was in heaven. He just didn't want it to end.

On May 21, 2010, the Tri-Valley White Sox threw Josiah a surprise birthday party and invited him to be on their team for the rest of the season. The little slugger's story spread, and 1,000 people showed up for Josiah's last game. Afterward, they all lined up around the diamond, and Josiah high-fived every one of them. His mom said he was put here to touch people's lives.

What's the Score?

Josiah knew he wouldn't live as long as most people. His greatest hope on earth was to play baseball. He also hoped for more when his life did end. When ESPN asked him what heaven looked like, Josiah answered, "Jesus."

That's the same hope we have—to one day see Jesus and know that the salvation he promised us comes true. The Bible says, "If we already have something, we don't need to hope for it. But if we look forward to something we don't yet have, we must wait patiently and confidently" (Romans 8:24-25). Someday we'll see God's work in us completed. In the meantime, we give our faith and our life and our dreams—everything we have—to Jesus . . . just like Josiah did.

) On the Ball

What do you hope for most? Give it to God. Ask him and trust him for it.

) COACH'S COMMENT

We were given this hope when we were saved. (If we already have something, we don't need to hope for it. But if we look forward to something we don't yet have, we must wait patiently and confidently.) ROMANS 8:24-25

Jordan Romero was on top of the world—literally—on this day in 2010. And the 13-year-old became the youngest climber to scale Mount Everest, the world's highest mountain at 29,035 feet above sea level. At the top, he hugged his dad and stepmom, cried, and said, "I love you." Then he called his mom on a satellite phone.

The Everest expedition was another step toward Jordan's ultimate goal to climb the Seven Summits, the highest peaks on all seven continents. But many people criticized his Everest climb. They said he was too young. They said Everest was too dangerous for a 13-year-old. They blamed his father. But Jordan's parents insisted that the inspiration and motivation were all Jordan's. They were simply helping him fulfill his dreams. Other people defended Jordan's actions. They praised his vision and dedication. Everyone was glad Jordan stayed safe on Everest. His accomplishment was inspiring. It was hard for anyone to argue against that.

⬜ What's the Score?

Jordan wasn't the first young person to be looked down on because of his youth. In the Bible, Paul encouraged Timothy to be an example to all believers in his life, love, faith, and purity (1 Timothy 4:12). Even though Timothy was young, he could still be a leader.

It's not an easy challenge to lead at a young age. But the good news is that God doesn't consider youth to be a limitation. His promises of protection and guidance don't have any minimum age requirement. When you're feeling too young or inexperienced on life's mountains, be encouraged by the words of 2 Samuel 22:34: "He makes me as surefooted as a deer, enabling me to stand on mountain heights." Trust that God is always walking next to you, and keep climbing.

⟩ On the Ball

What's your dream? What do you feel God is calling you to do? Take one step today toward fulfilling that dream. Write it on a rock, and put it in a visible place. Mark and add a new rock for each step you take. Watch your mountain take shape as you pursue your dream.

⟩ COACH'S COMMENT

He makes me as surefooted as a deer, enabling me to stand on mountain heights.

2 SAMUEL 22:34

Imagine if the NBA champions played the best basketball teams from different leagues around the world until the best of the best was the final winner. That's the idea of the UEFA Champions League. The top soccer teams from each European nation play until there's one champion.

On this day in 2007, the Italian club A.C. Milan battled England's Liverpool in the UEFA final. At the center of Milan's offense was its Brazilian striker, Kaká. Liverpool covered him well. But with less than 10 minutes left, Kaká made a perfect pass to assist a goal that put Milan up 2–0. Liverpool scored in the final minute, but Milan held on for the victory. Confetti showered the field. As Milan celebrated, Kaká pulled off his jersey to show his undershirt. It read in big, black letters, "I belong to Jesus." He ran a lap around the field waving to fans and celebrating. There was no mistaking his message of thanks to God.

The victory was part of an amazing year for Kaká. He received several prestigious awards, including soccer's highest honor, the World Player of the Year. As usual, the humble star was gracious and quickly gave thanks and praise to God.

☐☐ What's the Score?

Kaká made a name for himself off the soccer field for his devotion and obedience to God. His example was way different from the examples of many other soccer pros who made headlines for their bad behavior. Kaká's actions backed up his words, and his words were bold.

The Bible tells us, "Never be ashamed to tell others about our Lord" (2 Timothy 1:8). As you can tell by his T-shirt, Kaká did whatever he could to use his fame to tell people about Jesus. In what creative ways can you bring attention to Jesus? Words are good. Actions are good. And sometimes there are other unique ways: art, songs, fiction, and poetry. The options are endless. What's important is to be willing and prepared to tell others about your faith in Jesus.

⟩ On the Ball

Choose a creative way to let others know about God's love. Choose one of the ideas mentioned above, or create your own.

⟩ COACH'S COMMENT

Never be ashamed to tell others about our Lord. And don't be ashamed of me, either, even though I'm in prison for him. With the strength God gives you, be ready to suffer with me for the sake of the Good News. 2 TIMOTHY 1:8

In surfing there are waves and there are BIG waves. Big waves are taller than your house. They can be taller than five-story buildings, reaching 50 or 60 feet or more! But that doesn't stop big-wave riders from surfing them. For them, the bigger the wave, the bigger the adrenaline rush.

Most big-wave riders are men. But Maya Gabeira is a Brazilian woman who lives for supersized surf. In 2009, she caught the biggest ride of her life when she rode a 45-foot wave off the coast of South Africa. It proved to be the largest wave ever surfed by a woman. Later that year, Maya earned her third straight women's Billabong XXL award, which is given for the biggest ride of the year.

Maya's surfing performance was even more impressive when you realize that she had been surfing only five years. She tried riding the waves when she was 14, but she couldn't learn even after a month of lessons. At 17, she finally picked up the sport and has been breaking records ever since.

What's the Score?

Maya's courage in the face of giant waves was amazing. The Bible tells us to be courageous too: "Be strong and courageous, all you who put your hope in the LORD!" (Psalm 31:24). When we put our hope in the Lord, we tap into a power source that's way stronger than the ocean.

You may never surf 40-foot waves, but you will face plenty of intimidating situations in life. No matter what gets your knees knocking, you have the greatest source of courage possible: God. He is far stronger than your toughest challenges, and he can do more than all your ability, determination, or bravery—combined! Turn to him when you're nervous about a school test, an important competition, or standing up to pressure from your friends. When your hope is in God, you have nothing to fear.

) On the Ball

Write down the things you're afraid of. Stick the list inside your Bible by Psalm 31. Notice how small your list is compared to God and his Word.

) COACH'S COMMENT

Be strong and courageous, all you who put your hope in the LORD! PSALM 31:24

Any athlete who wants to play goalie in lacrosse may need to get his or her head examined. Wearing little padding and facing shots exceeding 100 miles per hour, lacrosse goalies have a difficult chore. Still, a good goalie makes the difference between winning and losing. That fact was proven during the 2003 NCAA Division I men's lacrosse championships. Virginia Cavaliers goalie Tillman Johnson got on a roll and led his team to the title.

The Cavaliers entered the postseason ranked No. 2 in the nation. After battling through the early rounds, Virginia met top-ranked Johns Hopkins in the finals at M&T Bank Stadium in Baltimore. The Blue Jays had beaten Virginia 8–7 during the regular season, but Tillman made sure the outcome was different this time.

The Cavs got on the board early as their first two shots found the back of the net. They built a 5–0 edge in the second quarter thanks to three goals by A. J. Shannon, but Johns Hopkins narrowed things to 5–3. Virginia still held a 6–4 margin at halftime. Tillman stepped up in the second half. With his team ahead 8–5, he made three monster saves early in the fourth. His 13 saves in the game helped the Cavaliers earn a 9–7 victory.

▢▢ What's the Score?

Many people think lacrosse goalies don't have a prayer trying to stop bouncing, speedy, well-placed shots. But Tillman Johnson showed it's possible. With a career-high 18 stops in the semifinals and 13 saves in the finals, Tillman helped Virginia win the national title and earned himself first-team All-American status.

Many of us wouldn't have a prayer trying to guard a lacrosse goal, but we can all pray to God. We can share our problems with him, ask for his comfort, or just tell him about our day. God cares about all our needs. The Bible tells us to pray all the time about all kinds of things (Ephesians 6:18). Because the Holy Spirit is in our lives, our prayers have power. But God doesn't want us to pray only for ourselves. He wants us to pray for other people, too.

⟩ On the Ball

How often do you pray? What do you pray about? Remember to constantly communicate with God.

⟩ COACH'S COMMENT

At all times, pray by the power of the Spirit. Pray all kinds of prayers. Be watchful, so that you can pray. Always keep on praying for all of God's people. **EPHESIANS 6:18 (NIrV)**

Dan Mazur was a Mount Everest veteran, but he didn't expect *this* on his climb to the top. About two hours from the highest summit in the world, Dan found a man sitting on the trail. The climber's jacket was around his waist. He wasn't wearing a hat or gloves. A lack of oxygen had him a little confused, but that wasn't the strangest part. This climber, named Lincoln Hall, had collapsed the day before after reaching the summit and had been left for dead.

Somehow Lincoln survived the night without freezing or falling over the steep drop-offs on either side of the ridge. At about 28,500 feet high, the Australian was in the death zone, where lack of oxygen slowly shuts down a person's body. He was suffering from cerebral edema, which is swelling of the brain, along with frostbite and dehydration. But he was miraculously alive. Dan's team quickly gave up their lifetime dreams of reaching the summit to save Lincoln's life. They sacrificed their own oxygen, gear, and food and coordinated a rescue of the man who had already been declared dead on Everest. Dan and his climbing partners were real-life Good Samaritans.

☐☐ What's the Score?

You probably know the story Jesus told about the Good Samaritan. It begins with a man who was beaten by robbers and left for dead by the side of a road. People you would expect to help him, a priest and a Temple worker, walked right by. Then a Samaritan came by. The Jewish people and Samaritans despised each other, yet this man stopped and saved the victim's life.

Jesus used this story to teach us to love our neighbor and to show us that our neighbors aren't just the people like us—they're everybody, even the people we dislike. Jesus finished his story by asking who had acted as the neighbor to the man in need. His listener answered, "'The one who showed him mercy.' Then Jesus said, 'Yes, now go and do the same'" (Luke 10:37). That's the same thing we're supposed to do when we find someone in need . . . even when that person is 28,500 feet up on a mountain.

❭ On the Ball

Keep your eyes open at school this week for someone who is rejected or struggling. Go beyond your normal group of friends to reach out to someone who needs a hand or a friend.

❭ COACH'S COMMENT

The man replied, "The one who showed him mercy." Then Jesus said, "Yes, now go and do the same." LUKE 10:37

How badly would you want to beat your brother or sister in the finals of a major tournament with the whole world watching? Would you want to humiliate him? Or would you go easy on her? That was a real question for Venus and Serena Williams.

Venus and Serena faced off in the 2002 French Open finals. They were two of the best tennis players in the world. Venus held the top woman's ranking, while Serena was ranked second in the world. They had faced each other before, but this was the first time either of them had reached the French Open finals. Both sisters normally were merciless against opponents. But they didn't seem to have the same edge against each other. The match was actually on the sloppy side. Both players made numerous unforced errors. The momentum swung back and forth. In the end Serena beat her older sister 7–5, 6–3. She celebrated, but not as much as normal.

The sisters hugged at center court and said, "I love you." On the winner's podium, Venus took pictures of Serena with their mom's camera. Then they went back to traveling the tour together—and stealing toothpaste from the other's hotel room. After all, they were still sisters.

What's the Score?

It's an amazing achievement to reach No. 1 in any pro sport. Having two members of one family reach that level is almost unheard of. Venus and Serena showed the strength of their relationship by staying close even as they battled for the world's top spot.

How well do you get along with your siblings? Psalms says, "How wonderful and pleasant it is when brothers live together in harmony!" (Psalm 133:1). That includes sisters, too. Your parents would agree with that verse. You have the ability to bring peace—or war—to your whole house. All brothers and sisters will fight sometimes, but finding the power to forgive each other can open the door to finding a best friend who lives in the same house. Take the first step to bring peace and to show appreciation for your brother or sister. Talk to your parents for some ideas if you need help.

) On the Ball

Surprise your brother or sister today by going out of your way to do something nice or helpful for him or her.

) COACH'S COMMENT
How wonderful and pleasant it is when brothers live together in harmony! PSALM 133:1

Victory celebrations in sports can look a little funny. A coach gets drenched with a bucket of Gatorade. Players spray each other with champagne. Soccer players rip off their jerseys and run around the field. Someone grabs a bottle of milk and drinks it. Yeah, you read correctly; drinking milk is a long-standing victory celebration at the Indianapolis 500. Every year the winner of the Indy 500 drinks milk in Victory Lane.

Milk has nothing specific to do with open-wheel racing—or any racing for that matter. But it has everything to do with tradition. It goes back to 1936. That's when three-time Indy 500 winner, Louis Meyer, drank buttermilk in Victory Lane after his second win. Why? Because the weather was hot and he was thirsty. An executive of the Milk Foundation saw it and jumped at the chance to promote milk to racing fans. And like a good milk mustache, drinking milk stuck. Although in 1993, Emerson Fittipaldi bucked tradition by drinking orange juice at the finish. He owned some orange groves and wanted to promote the citrus industry. Fans booed. Newspapers criticized him. They didn't have anything against orange juice, but Emerson's act went against the tradition that bound Indy drivers and fans together through the years.

⛶ What's the Score?

Your family probably has traditions, ways you do and celebrate things like Christmas, vacations, birthdays, or ways to worship God. Traditions help us remember and connect with our ancestors and with other Christians who have gone before us. They are good for us because they give us a better perspective about our lives and where we fit in God's big picture.

The Israelites were reminded all through the Old Testament to follow their traditions and remember how God had worked in the past. Those memories encouraged and challenged them. Hebrews 13:7 tells us, "Remember your leaders who taught you the word of God. Think of all the good that has come from their lives, and follow the example of their faith." We should do the same as the Israelites, using our traditions to remind us of God's goodness.

⟩ On the Ball

Drink a glass of milk and answer these questions:

My favorite family traditions are _____ .

They remind me_____ .

My favorite worship traditions are _____ .

They remind me_____ .

⟩ COACH'S COMMENT

Remember your leaders who taught you the word of God. Think of all the good that has come from their lives, and follow the example of their faith. HEBREWS 13:7

Perfect games don't come often in baseball—probably because they're, well, so perfect. Not one little thing can go wrong. A perfect game is when a pitcher gets every batter out. No hits. No walks. No batters struck by wild pitches. It's 27 up and 27 down. As of Mother's Day 2010, there had been only 19 perfect games pitched in Major League Baseball's modern era (that's since 1900 when the rules were made consistent). But on that day, Oakland A's pitcher Dallas Braden threw a perfect game against the Tampa Bay Rays. It was a rare and special moment in baseball.

Then only 20 days later on May 29, Roy Halladay of the Philadelphia Phillies threw a perfect game against the Florida Marlins. It was the first season in the modern era that included two perfect games—and they happened in the same month! As if that wasn't enough, Roy took it another step. During the first game of the National League Division Series on October 6, he pitched another perfect game against the Cincinnati Reds. That marked only the second postseason perfect game in baseball history. Talk about a career high.

☐☐ What's the Score?

Having three perfect games in a single season is extremely rare. Psalm 119:96 says, "To all perfection I see a limit, but your commands are boundless" (NIV). It tells us that all perfection comes to an end eventually. We can tell that by how rare perfect games are, even though pitchers practice every single day to try to reach that goal every time they step on the mound.

Only God is perfect. He calls us into his perfection, but we won't be fully perfect until we're with him in heaven someday. Sometimes we get frustrated with ourselves because we fall short or make mistakes. As long as we're still on earth, that's going to happen—both in our sports games and in our spiritual lives. We should always try our best, but we should also remember that God understands our human weaknesses. When we come up short, we can confess our sins to God and enjoy his perfect forgiveness. Then we need to forgive ourselves, too.

⟩ On the Ball

Are you having trouble forgiving yourself for something? Write down what it was. Then run the paper through a paper shredder. Your failure is gone. Let go of it like God has.

⟩ COACH'S COMMENT

To all perfection I see a limit, but your commands are boundless. PSALM 119:96 (NIV)

Do you like to ride your bike? What's the farthest you've ever ridden? How does riding 125 miles sound? Not too bad. Now do it every day for three weeks straight with many of the rides going over super-steep mountain passes. Pretty intense, huh? Welcome to the Giro d'Italia, Italy's version of the Tour de France.

Ivan Basso was sure glad to be back at the 2010 Giro. Ivan had been banned from cycling for two years as part of a blood-doping scandal. (Blood doping is an illegal way to enhance the body's performance by giving it extra oxygen.) Ivan had been a top rider before the scandal. He wanted to come back and prove to people that he was riding clean: no cheating, no doping. He expected that fans wouldn't trust him, so he knew his only chance was complete honesty and transparency. He underwent regular blood tests like all cyclists, but Ivan posted all of his results online for everyone to see.

The Giro came down to the final few mountain stages. They were difficult climbs up steep mountains. That was where Ivan made his move to claim the lead. Two days later he won the race . . . this time with his integrity intact.

⬜ What's the Score?

The world knew about Ivan's failures. He knew it would take a long time for people to trust him again. But he was willing to take extra steps to help rebuild his reputation. If only he had kept his integrity true in the first place, he wouldn't have had to prove anything.

Psalm 25:21 says, "May integrity and honesty protect me, for I put my hope in you." We usually try to keep our sin a secret. We try to cover it up dishonestly. But honesty keeps our actions out in the open. Don't cut corners even if doing so looks like a shortcut to success. Your truthful, consistent actions help give you a good reputation. Any dishonesty or cheating only leads to trouble.

⟩ On the Ball

What secrets are you hiding? How are you tempted to cut corners? Write down where you're tempted. Seal the paper in an envelope. Then tear open the envelope as a symbol that you're letting it out. Confess to a good friend or parent, and live your life in the open.

⟩ COACH'S COMMENT

May integrity and honesty protect me, for I put my hope in you. PSALM 25:21

The mayor of Clarkston, Georgia, said no more soccer playing was allowed in the park. That was a problem for the Fugees Family soccer club, who had no other place to practice in 2006. The club is made up of refugees, and the team name is a short form of the word *refugees.* The boys' families had been relocated to the small Atlanta suburb from 24 troubled countries all over the world, mostly Africa. But the residents of Clarkston didn't exactly want them there.

Soccer was all the Fugees had. Their coach made them follow strict rules to stay on the team. Soccer kept many of the boys out of gangs or off drugs. Many of them struggled in school because they didn't know any English, but they had to make good grades to be a Fugee. Some of the players' fathers were still political prisoners in their home countries. Some had seen parents executed or had been forced themselves to fight in wars before they came to the United States. They were safer in their new home, but they were poor. Coach Luma Mufleh, a Jordanian-American woman who started the club, appealed to the city council to allow the Fugees to play in the park grass. The mayor agreed to let the Fugees play there for six months, but two months later the mayor said they couldn't. When Coach Luma questioned him, he said they could use the field for another three months. Coach Luma was forced to find the Fugees a new, permanent practice field. Nothing came easily for the Fugees.

What's the Score?

God cares a lot about refugees and immigrants. He told his people, "You must not oppress foreigners. You know what it's like to be a foreigner, for you yourselves were once foreigners in the land of Egypt" (Exodus 23:9). The same still applies to us.

Did you do anything to be born in America? No, it's only by God's grace that we were born in a peaceful, free nation with lots of material blessings. On the flip side, poor immigrants had no say about their home countries. They were simply born in a part of the world filled with war and poverty. Many who arrived in the United States and Canada came with little except their clothes, and they face an uphill battle to earn a living. We are called to help.

) On the Ball

Look around your community for refugees in need. You can start a campaign at school or at church to help meet their needs. Even soccer gear can make a big difference.

) COACH'S COMMENT

You must not oppress foreigners. You know what it's like to be a foreigner, for you yourselves were once foreigners in the land of Egypt. EXODUS 23:9

Talk about seeing double! Since winning the French Open in 2003, Bob and Mike Bryan have established themselves as possibly the greatest doubles team in ATP World Tour history. Through the 2010 season, the identical twins, who were born three minutes apart in 1978, had won more doubles-tournament titles than any other pair—ever. More often than not, they were ranked the tour's No. 1 duo between 2003 and 2010. They even broke double digits in Grand Slam victories when they won their third straight Australian Open doubles championship in 2011.

Besides their similar physical appearances and tennis skills, Bob and Mike are quite similar off the court, too. They both play guitar, like Mexican food, and cheer for the Los Angeles Lakers.

What's the Score?

Unlike the Bryan brothers, the Bible's most famous twins—Jacob and Esau—had virtually nothing in common, all the way down to their physical traits. Esau was brash and hairy, and he liked to hunt. Jacob was quieter and smooth skinned, and he preferred to hang out in the family tent. Theirs was a sobering tale of two vastly different paths in life.

While Jacob was far from perfect (he was a pretty good liar), he had 12 sons whose descendants became the 12 tribes of Israel. Jacob had a strong faith and chose to worship God. Esau, meanwhile, chose a bad path. He carelessly sold his birthright to Jacob for a bowl of stew and married many pagan wives who worshiped false gods. His descendants—like the Edomites and the Amalekites—became bitter enemies of the Israelites. Thousands of years later, the writer of Hebrews summarized Esau's unfortunate life by calling him "godless" (Hebrews 12:16).

We all have similar choices in life. Like Esau, we can ignore God's call of salvation and choose a path of selfish pleasure that leads to ruin. Or we can follow Jacob's example and worship the one true God and live for him. Joshua 24:15 says, "Choose for yourselves this day whom you will serve. . . . But as for me and my household, we will serve the LORD" (NIV). Now that's a good decision!

) On the Ball

List three good choices you can make today, such as "speak kindly to others," "obey Mom and Dad," etc. Pray that God will help you do them.

1. _____

2. _____

3. _____

) COACH'S COMMENT

Choose for yourselves this day whom you will serve. . . . But as for me and my household, we will serve the LORD. JOSHUA 24:15 (NIV)

To say the 1925 baseball season was a tough one for Wally Pipp would be a severe under-statement. For 11 previous seasons, Wally had been a very good first baseman, mostly for the New York Yankees. In 1924, he hit .295 with 114 RBIs and led the American League with 19 triples. But on June 2, 1925, with Wally and the Yankees struggling, Lou Gehrig replaced him at first base. One story says that Wally asked to sit out the game because of a bad headache. Another says Yankees manager Miller Huggins benched Wally to shake up his slumping team.

Either way, it was the most famous substitution in American sports history. Wally never regained his starting job because Lou went on to play 2,130 consecutive games. Nicknamed "The Iron Horse," Lou entered the Hall of Fame as one of the greatest first basemen of all time. Wally, meanwhile, only played three more unexceptional years and is largely remembered for that fateful day when he sat out. His name, in fact, has become a sort of saying. In baseball jargon, to be "Wally Pipped" means to get replaced by a better substitute.

What's the Score?

The Bible features a remarkable tale of substitution too. Only this substitute is far greater than a Hall of Fame baseball player. He is Jesus Christ, God's own Son.

The Bible says we all deserve death and eternal separation from God because of our sins. But Jesus died in our place—as a substitute—to pay the penalty for our sins. His death on the cross paid for the death we deserve, appeased God's holy wrath, and made it possible for us to spend eternity in heaven through faith in him. As a wonderful passage in Isaiah says, "He was pierced for *our* transgressions" and "crushed for *our* iniquities" (53:5, NIV, emphasis added). Jesus' coming to earth to die for us is a substitution worth cheering for!

On the Ball

Every time you have a substitute teacher at school or experience a substitution on your sports team, thank Jesus for dying on the cross as the substitute for your sins.

COACH'S COMMENT

He was pierced for our transgressions, he was crushed for our iniquities; the punishment that brought us peace was on him, and by his wounds we are healed. ISAIAH 53:5 (NIV)

Call him "Mr. Versatility." Ashrita Furman, a resident of Queens, New York, has jumped on a pogo stick underwater in the Amazon River for three hours and 40 minutes, balanced a pool cue on his index finger for seven miles in Egypt, and bounced on a kangaroo ball for a mile on the Great Wall of China. You might call him eccentric, goofy, or even crazy. But Guinness World Records calls him its greatest record holder.

Ashrita, who was born in 1954, has set more than 300 official Guinness records since 1979. During the fall of 2010, he held 123 world records at the same time—which was another record! Obviously Ashrita's achievements weren't normal athletic feats like the fastest 100-meter dash, most touchdowns in a season, or highest career batting average. His records were a bit more, uh, unique, like most Jell-O eaten with chopsticks in a minute (16.04 ounces), the fastest mile traveled while balancing a milk bottle on your head (13 minutes, 51 seconds), and most apples sliced in midair with a samurai sword in one minute (27).

Hey, everybody needs a hobby, right? Ashrita's off-the-wall endeavors have been featured by *Sports Illustrated*, the *New York Times,* and HBO's *Real Sports with Bryant Gumbel.*

"You get to a point where you're doing stuff you never dreamed you could do," Ashrita told Bryant in October 2009.

What's the Score?

While you probably have never set world records like Ashrita has for racing a yak while hopping in a sack or duct-taping yourself to a wall faster than any other human being, you certainly enjoy various activities. Maybe you love playing sports or listening to music or reading. Maybe you love to draw, play video games, or collect things.

In creating the world, God filled it with countless things for us to enjoy. We all have different interests, hobbies, and skills. But whatever we do—no matter how normal or bizarre—we should do it for God's glory. The apostle Paul says in 1 Corinthians 10:31 that we should glorify God even when we eat. God created us to bring praise and glory to his name. So no matter where you are or what you're doing, remember to glorify him . . . even if you love seeing how many grapes you can catch in your mouth in a minute (Ashrita caught 80).

) On the Ball

Make two columns on a sheet of paper. On the left, list your favorite things to do. On the right, list how you can glorify God when doing them.

) COACH'S COMMENT

Whether you eat or drink, or whatever you do, do it all for the glory of God.
1 CORINTHIANS 10:31

There's no denying maple bars are delicious. But are they really *this* good? On June 4, 2010, Seattle Seahawks wide receiver Golden Tate and a friend made headlines for entering the Top Pot gourmet doughnut café in Bellevue, Washington, and eating some maple bars. No big deal, right?

Well, it *is* a big deal when it's three in the morning and the shop is closed.

Top Pot was on the bottom floor of a residential building where Golden lived. Apparently, Golden and his buddy entered the bakery through a door that was left open and accessible to building residents. They saw some freshly baked maple bars and couldn't resist a late-night sugar fix. A Top Pot baker working the night shift saw the two men and called Bellevue police, who only issued a warning for trespassing to Golden and his friend.

"A buddy made the mistake going in and grabbing a couple," Golden later told reporters. "We ate them." Golden admitted it was "a foolish mistake that won't happen again.

"But," he added, "If you ever want maple bars, that's the place to go."

⬜⬜ What's the Score?

Those must have been some *really* tasty maple bars. Why else would an NFL star with a contract worth $3.26 million steal doughnuts in the middle of the night? The incident was so ridiculous it was almost laughable. But this is no laughing matter: we must choose our friends carefully. To hear Golden tell it, he followed his friend's lead, and it got him in trouble. Why did Golden follow his friend into the café? Maybe Golden shouldn't hang out with guys who have no problem breaking the law. He should've known better.

We should know better too. The Bible, especially the book of Proverbs, is filled with warnings about associating with fools. In fact, Proverbs 13:20 warns us: "Associate with fools and get in trouble." God knows how easily others can influence us, and he wants us to make wise decisions in life. Choose your friends carefully. Don't assume you can hang out with troublemakers and be unaffected by them. You might think you can change them for the better, but most likely they will change you for the worse. Avoid fools, and befriend people who will help you grow in godliness. It's not always easy, but it pleases your heavenly Father and helps you avoid trouble in life.

⟩ On the Ball

Think about your friends. Are you mixed up with any troublemakers? If so, talk to your parents or a trusted adult about how to honor God with your friendships.

⟩ COACH'S COMMENT

Walk with the wise and become wise; associate with fools and get in trouble.
PROVERBS 13:20

More than any other sport, baseball is a game of numbers. Statistics and records help define players, teams, and entire eras of the game.

Hitters are judged by statistics like batting average, slugging percentage, and RBIs (runs batted in). Pitchers are measured by win-loss records, strikeouts, and ERA (earned runs allowed). Records help provide perspective and history for the game. For years, numbers like 714 and 2,130 were considered untouchable baseball benchmarks.

The number 714 was the great Babe Ruth's career home run total, a record that stood for 39 years until Hank Aaron broke it in 1974. And 2,130 represented the number of consecutive games played by another New York Yankees Hall of Famer, Lou Gehrig, until Cal Ripken Jr. broke his mark in 1995. Today, records like .406, 56, 4,256, and 5,714 define baseball. In 1941, Ted Williams set the modern-day record for batting average by hitting .406, and Joe DiMaggio set the record for consecutive games with a hit at 56. Pete Rose became baseball's all-time hit king with 4,256, and Nolan Ryan notched the career strikeout record with 5,714.

⬜⬜ What's the Score?

Yes, baseball loves its record keeping. Aren't you glad that God doesn't keep a record of all our performances? If God kept track of all our sins, we'd be in serious trouble. The book of Romans says we have all fallen far short of God's holy standard and deserve death. Based on our sinful records, we are all headed for the Hall of Shame. But God doesn't want to hold our sins against us. He wants to erase our record book of disobedience (Psalm 103:12).

So where does God put all our sins? On his Son, Jesus Christ! When we place our faith in Jesus, God wipes away all the old records of sin and gives us a fresh start. Now that's an achievement worth remembering!

⟩ On the Ball

Chances are, you've committed a number of sins today even before reading this devotional. List all the wrong things you've done today on a piece of paper. Then crumple it up and throw it in the trash, signifying what God does with our sins when we put our faith in Jesus. Finally, thank God for this amazing truth!

⟩ COACH'S COMMENT

As far as the east is from the west, so far has he removed our transgressions from us.
PSALM 103:12 (NIV)

Yesterday you learned how serious Major League Baseball is about its record keeping. But baseball isn't the only sport with records and statistics. All sports keep them, and they are an important part of each sport's history.

See if you can answer some of these trivia questions (answers are below, but don't peek!):

1. Who is the NFL's all-time rushing leader?
2. Who is the NBA's all-time scoring leader?
3. Who is the WNBA's all-time leader in rebounds?
4. Who has won the most major titles in PGA Tour history?
5. Who was the youngest girl to play for the US national women's soccer team?

☐☐ What's the Score?

Baseball and other sports may keep records, but God doesn't keep a record of wrongs for any true follower of Christ. Because of Jesus' sacrificial death on the cross, God doesn't hold the sins of his children against them anymore. What an amazing promise! But as important as this truth is, the Bible has much more to say about the subject of records. When it comes to record keeping, we are very good at remembering other people's sins against us. If people wrong us, it's easy for us to hold on to anger toward them. Maybe we speak unkindly to him or ignore her. Or maybe we just silently seethe with bitterness.

But if God doesn't hold our sins against us, we shouldn't hold other people's sins against them. That would be hypocritical. In Matthew 18, Jesus told a story about a servant who was forgiven a great debt by the king. But that servant went out and treated one of his fellow servants unkindly because of a much smaller debt. When the king found out, he punished the wicked servant severely. The moral of the story is clear: we must forgive others since we have been forgiven of much more than anything anyone could do to us. Record keeping might be fun in sports, but don't hold records of wrong-doing against others!

) On the Ball

Read Jesus' parable of the unforgiving debtor in Matthew 18:21-35.

) COACH'S COMMENT

The master called the servant in. "You wicked servant," he said, "I canceled all that debt of yours because you begged me to. Shouldn't you have had mercy on your fellow servant just as I had on you?" MATTHEW 18:32-33 (NIV)

Trivia Answers:
1. Emmitt Smith (1990–2004), 18,355 yards; 2. Kareem Abdul-Jabbar (1969–89), 38,387 points; 3. Lisa Leslie (1997–2009), 3,307 rebounds; 4. Jack Nicklaus, 18 major PGA titles; 5. Mia Hamm, age 15 in 1987

The smeared eye black down both cheeks made Bryce Harper look like a fearsome tribal warrior. The home runs he launched into the sky were like towering rockets. Grown men's mouths dropped when they witnessed his amazing talents firsthand. Bryce certainly didn't look like a teenager at the College of Southern Nevada. On June 7, 2010, after Bryce's remarkable freshman season, the Washington Nationals selected him as the first overall pick in Major League Baseball's draft. At the time, Bryce was only 17 years old. He would have barely qualified for a Washington, DC, driver's license, and he wasn't old enough to vote.

But age and normal expectations never meant much to Bryce. After leaving high school early, he hit .443 with a school-record 31 home runs and 98 RBIs to lead Southern Nevada to the National Junior College Athletic Association World Series. In August 2010, Bryce signed a record five-year, $9.9 million deal with the Nationals.

⬜ What's the Score?

Time will tell if Bryce was worth the top pick. But he certainly accomplished everything possible in his short, amateur career. From a young age, Bryce proved he had major-league talent, so the Nationals took a chance on the teenager. As Christians, age shouldn't matter to us, either. Look at all the youngsters in the Bible who did great things for God.

Samuel was just a boy when God called him into ministry (1 Samuel 3). David was probably a teen when he killed Goliath (1 Samuel 17:41-42). Daniel was one of the "young men" (Daniel 1:4) who stood for righteousness as exiles in Babylon. And because of the kindness of a "young girl from Israel" (2 Kings 5:2, NIV), Naaman, the commander of Aram's army, was healed of leprosy.

The lesson? When God searches for willing servants, he doesn't look at your birth certificate. He looks at your heart. As 1 Timothy 4:12 says, you should "set an example for the believers in speech, in conduct, in love, in faith and in purity" (NIV) no matter how old you are.

⟩ On the Ball

What's one area where you can be an example to your family? Write it down here: _____. Maybe you can try hard to serve others, take care of the pets, dish out compliments, or pray for your family. If you can't think of an idea, ask your parents for help.

- -

⟩ COACH'S COMMENT

Don't let anyone look down on you because you are young, but set an example for the believers in speech, in conduct, in love, in faith and in purity. 1 TIMOTHY 4:12 (NIV)

- -

Fans love to honor their favorite athletes. Regardless of the sport, we honor—or show respect to—the best performers in countless ways. We cheer wildly for them when they make a game-changing play. We hang their posters on our walls or buy the same kind of shoes that they wear. We thank them for their efforts with standing ovations and curtain calls.

Media professionals do the same thing. They bestow honors like "Player of the Game," "Player of the Week," "Player of the Month," and "Player of the Year." Athletes get voted into all-star games. Books and magazine articles are written about them. We collect their jerseys, trading cards, and bobblehead dolls.

For certain achievements, some athletes receive luxury cars or large bonus checks. League champions are often met at the airport by crowds of screaming fans and given ticker-tape parades through downtown city streets. Of course, the greatest athletes of all time are honored by being inducted into their sports' Hall of Fame.

⬜⬜ What's the Score?

It's natural to honor our favorite athletes. But according to the Bible, the greatest honor should be given to one set of people: your parents. Scripture is filled with commands to honor, love, and obey your parents. God places such a priority on children honoring their parents that he made it one of the Ten Commandments. In Deuteronomy 5, he promised a long life to Israelite children who honored their parents.

The author of Proverbs reminded his son many times to "pay attention to what I say." Jesus mentioned the fifth commandment numerous times, and the apostle Paul commanded children to "always obey your parents, for this pleases the Lord" (Colossians 3:20). Is honoring your parents always easy? No, of course not. But it's not optional. It's a command of the Lord God Almighty. Other than God himself, there is no one you should honor, love, and obey more than your parents.

⟩ On the Ball

Memorize Colossians 3:20, recite it to your parents, and ask them how you can best fulfill this biblical command. Watch their jaws drop as you do it!

⟩ COACH'S COMMENT

Children, always obey your parents, for this pleases the Lord. **COLOSSIANS 3:20**

Not many horses get a movie made about their lives. Because of the way Secretariat ran, he deserved to have one made about his life. On this day in 1973, Secretariat, a large, three-year-old chestnut colt, set a world record with a history-making victory at the Belmont Stakes. With his first-place finish, he became the first horse in 25 years to win the Triple Crown. That's the title given to a horse that wins the Kentucky Derby, the Preakness Stakes, and the Belmont in the same year.

Before entering the Belmont, Secretariat had already enjoyed a fantastic season, with wins in the first two Triple Crown races. But his performance at Belmont Park in New York made him a legend. With Ron Turcotte, the 1972 Belmont-winning jockey aboard him, Secretariat set the world record for a mile-and-a-half race on dirt in two minutes, 24 seconds and finished a whopping 31 lengths ahead of his nearest challenger. Many experts consider Secretariat to be the greatest racehorse of all time.

What's the Score?

Humans have always been fascinated with horses because of their speed, power, and majesty. In ancient times, horses also served many practical purposes. Any country whose army lacked horses was in danger of being attacked. Before the invention of tanks, fighter planes, and other modern vehicles of warfare, horses were vital for national defense. A horse-drawn chariot, for instance, was one of the most feared weapons in ancient times.

Despite this, we read something very interesting in Deuteronomy 17:16, where God commanded that "the king must not build up a large stable of horses for himself or send his people to Egypt to buy horses." Why would God command this when horses were crucial for a nation's survival? The answer is simple: He wanted his people to entrust their lives to him, not to military might. He would fight their battles if they trusted him. He wanted Israel to "boast in the name of the LORD," as Psalm 20:7 says.

The same is true today. God wants his children to trust him above all else. Nothing can protect and save us besides God. He is stronger than the most powerful king or the mightiest army. Are you trusting something for your safety other than God? Maybe your parents or your country's military? Neither of these things are bad, but they also can't ultimately protect you. Only God can. And that's no horsing around.

) On the Ball

Ask God to help you trust in him alone.

) COACH'S COMMENT

Some nations boast of their chariots and horses, but we boast in the name of the LORD our God. PSALM 20:7

When the sun rose on June 10, 2010, life was quite different for fans of the Chicago Blackhawks. Suddenly, all the years of frustration had vanished. The Blackhawks were Stanley Cup champions again! One night earlier, right-winger Patrick Kane's sneaky goal 4:06 into overtime propelled Chicago to a 4–3 victory over the Philadelphia Flyers in game six of the Stanley Cup Finals. The win gave Chicago its first NHL championship since 1961.

The Blackhawks are one of the league's oldest and proudest franchises. They won the Stanley Cup in 1934 and 1938. Then future–Hall of Famer Bobby Hull led the Blackhawks to a championship in 1961. But after the 1961 season, the Chicago team endured an agonizingly long stretch of 35 straight play-off appearances without a Stanley Cup. For Chicago fans, it was like listening to a broken record . . . for three-and-a-half decades. Then, starting in 1998, things got worse. For the next 10 years, Chicagoans watched as their beloved Blackhawks missed the play-offs every year but one. For fans used to their team making the play-offs each year, it was torment. At last, thanks to Patrick's goal and the 2009–2010 team, the wait for another Stanley Cup was over.

⬜⬜ What's the Score?

All the near misses of not winning a championship for 49 years took a toll on Chicago fans. But they remained faithful to their team. Even in tough years, the Blackhawks had a crowd of rowdy and excited fans packing the stands. They knew things would eventually get better.

When Jesus came to earth, he knew things would get better too. His purpose for humbling himself, living a sinless life, and enduring rejection was to win victory over death. At the end of Jesus' ministry, he suffered shameful ridicule and unspeakable torture. He willingly died a horrific, undeserved death on the cross because of "the joy awaiting him" (Hebrews 12:2). In other words, the hardship was worth the reward. This wonderful truth should encourage us to trust in Jesus and follow him, even when it feels like we can never win. Our worst defeats in life don't compare to what Jesus endured to save us from our sins!

⟩ On the Ball

The next time you feel the sting of defeat personally or mourn a tough loss by your favorite team, thank Jesus for enduring the shame of the cross on your behalf.

⟩ COACH'S COMMENT

Because of the joy awaiting him, he endured the cross, disregarding its shame. Now he is seated in the place of honor beside God's throne. Think of all the hostility he endured from sinful people; then you won't become weary and give up. **HEBREWS 12:2-3**

Who's hungry for a Strasburger? Washington Nationals fans, that's who. On June 11, 2009, the buzz around Stephen Strasburg made him one of the biggest pitching prospects in Major League Baseball history. The Nationals drafted him first overall and awarded him a record $15.1 million contract. In his major league debut a year later, he struck out a whopping 14 batters—a team record for a rookie. His 100-mph fastball easily earned him a 5–2 win over Pittsburgh.

Washington fans dubbed the evening "Strasmas." Newspaper and magazine headlines read, "Dazzling debut," "Amazing arm," and "National treasure." DC-area restaurants sold "Strasburgers." Even the National Baseball Hall of Fame requested items from the historic evening. The good times kept rolling. In his first 11 games, Stephen went 5–3 with a 2.97 ERA and 86 strikeouts in just over 63 innings. He seemed to be well on his way to the National League Rookie of the Year Award and a fabulous career. Then disaster struck. On August 21, 2010, Stephen threw a pitch and felt pain in his arm. He left the game and found out a week later that he needed season-ending elbow ligament replacement surgery. Just like that, his season was over, and question marks surrounded his future.

What's the Score?

Stephen's injury was a sobering reminder that many things in life are out of our control. No matter how much we want things to be a certain way, life often takes us in a different direction. Sometimes bad things happen just because we live in a broken world. But God can use even those situations to humble us and remind us that he is in charge. As the Bible says, "In their hearts humans plan their course, but the LORD establishes their steps" (Proverbs 16:9, NIV).

The fact that we are not the boss can be tough to swallow. Most people like to feel they are in control. But the more quickly we learn this important lesson, the better off we'll be. The Lord wants us to remember that he is God, not us.

) On the Ball

List three things you want really badly in life.

1. _____

2. _____

3. _____

Now pray that God would help you loosen your grip on them and understand that he is in control.

) COACH'S COMMENT

In their hearts humans plan their course, but the LORD establishes their steps.
PROVERBS 16:9 (NIV)

When traveling coast-to-coast, most people decide to fly. But every June a group of sturdy (crazy, perhaps?) athletes opt to make the trip on bikes. And they do it as fast as humanly possible. Say hello to the Race Across America (RAAM), the most famous transcontinental cycling race in the United States. Starting in 1982, cyclists covered approximately 3,000 miles from Oceanside, California, to Annapolis, Maryland. They battled each other, but the bigger competition may have come from the wind, rain, heat, and extreme fatigue.

There are various race categories, but the solo class is the most demanding. Unlike team racing, in which teammates take turns riding and sleeping, a solo racer must complete the grueling journey alone within 12 days to qualify as an official RAAM finisher. Because the clock doesn't stop, elite solo racers often sleep as little as 90 minutes a day. Typically, racers can't sleep more than about four hours a day in order to finish within the 12-day limit.

While sleep is an afterthought for the better part of two weeks, nutrition and fluid intake are crucial. To replenish the energy they're burning, riders usually consume about three gallons of fluids and 8,000 calories a day. Clearly, RAAM isn't for the lazy, weak, or faint of heart. Austria's Wolfgang Fasching, who won RAAM's solo competition three times and who also climbed Mount Everest, said RAAM was the harder of the two endeavors.

☐☐ What's the Score?

For RAAM racers, rest is a luxury they can't afford. Fatigue is not an option. Idleness won't get them anywhere. The same thing is true in our Christian life. God's people are called to be movers, not sitters. We are to be people of action, not inactivity.

Does that mean God wants us to never plop down on the couch? Does that mean we should sleep only 90 minutes a night, like some RAAM riders? No, of course not. The point is, we are always to be on the lookout for opportunities to show kindness and love to others. The Bible exhorts us to "never get tired of doing good" (2 Thessalonians 3:13). That's what Jesus did. During his three-year ministry on earth, Jesus was constantly on the move, teaching his disciples, performing miracles, and proclaiming the Good News of God's Kingdom. He was never too busy to help someone, and he was always searching for ways to show God's love.

） On the Ball

Do you have a normal time each week for relaxation? This week, use that time to do something nice for someone.

） COACH'S COMMENT

As for the rest of you, dear brothers and sisters, never get tired of doing good.
2 THESSALONIANS 3:13

Muscle-bound jocks often ask each other, "How much can you bench press?" Nobody asked Bill Gillespie that, because his answer would have just made anyone else feel like a weakling. Bill worked as the head strength and conditioning coordinator at Liberty University in Lynchburg, Virginia. As of 2010, he was a 40-time world-record holder and a 17-time world champion in the bench press. The bench press is a weight-lifting competition where competitors lie on a flat bench and push a bar of weights up from their chest.

For a little perspective on Bill's power, the average teenage boy would do well to bench-press his own body weight. The 200-pound plateau is a highly coveted mark among many high school athletes. With that in mind, consider this: in 2009, at the World Cup Bench Press and Deadlift Championships, Bill set an age-group world record by bench pressing 804.5 pounds. That's the equivalent of lifting four full-grown men stacked on top of each other. Even more amazing, he did it at age 49!

Ever since his childhood, Bill had wanted to become the strongest man in the world. He started weight lifting at age 14 and devoted much of his life to building physical strength in himself and others, including football players for Liberty, the University of Washington, and the NFL's Seattle Seahawks.

⬜⬜ What's the Score?

Bill was a muscle-bound marvel of power and strength. But even he had his limits. He never bench-pressed a car or a grown elephant. Even the strongest man in the world can't do everything he wants.

God's power, though, has no limits. He is omnipotent, which means all-powerful. "Nothing is too hard for you!" Jeremiah 32:17 says. Think about that for a moment. That knowledge can change your life. There is no living being or force of nature that is outside of God's control. By his limitless power, God created and sustains the universe, rules over all living beings (including angels, demons, and Satan), and raised Jesus from the dead. Most gloriously, this same infinite, incomprehensible power can change us from sinful rebels to sanctified children of God, bound for heaven. What should our response be to this? To worship the all-powerful Lord God Almighty! He alone is worthy of our praise.

) On the Ball

Think about the many ways that God's power is evident in your life: he keeps your heart beating, provides daily food for you, and gives you the ability to play sports and learn in school. Now do as many push-ups as you can, praising God for a different part of his power during each push-up.

) COACH'S COMMENT

O Sovereign LORD! You made the heavens and earth by your strong hand and powerful arm. Nothing is too hard for you! JEREMIAH 32:17

In 490 BC, a Greek man named Pheidippides ran 40 kilometers (about 25 miles) from the Battle of Marathon to Athens, the capital of Greece. The reason? To announce a remarkable victory for the fledgling Greek city-states over a vastly superior Persian army. After giving his report, Pheidippides immediately fell over dead. Or that's how the story goes. Although historians for centuries have debated the authenticity of this account, it has inspired one of the most enduring athletic competitions in the world—the marathon. In 1896, the organizers of the first modern Olympics, which were held in Athens, staged a 25-mile race over what they believed was the route that Pheidippides had run nearly 2,400 years earlier.

At the 1908 London Olympics, British officials lengthened the race to its current length of 26.2 miles. The marathon is now a world-famous event. Hundreds of marathons are held annually in the United States alone. In fact, the world's largest, the New York City Marathon, typically draws more than 100,000 runners each year. In 2008, Ethiopia's Haile Gebrselassie set the men's marathon world record in a lightning-quick time of 2:03.59. Great Britain's Paula Radcliffe set the women's record in 2:15.25 at the 2003 London Marathon. Pheidippides would be proud!

⬜ What's the Score?

The marathon is a difficult race that tests the limits of human endurance. It takes months, if not years, for competitors to train their bodies to withstand the grueling physical toll it takes to race more than 26 miles. In 1 Corinthians 9, the apostle Paul describes Christianity as a long race. Like a marathon, the Christian life requires lots of training, discipline, and hard work. Just as a marathoner can't reach elite status without thousands of miles of training runs, a Christian can't be truly effective without consistently reading the Bible, praying to God, and going to church.

All of this training isn't just for the short term. Marathoners often complain of "hitting the wall"—a phrase used to describe the point when their body feels like it's shutting down. The best runners push through the pain and keep going. Christians must do the same. Even when things aren't going well, we must stay obedient to God and persevere in our faith. Remember, there's a wonderful prize waiting for all believers at the end—eternal life and blessings in heaven!

⟩ On the Ball

Take a run at your school or local park. While you're running, ask God to help you race to win the prize!

⟩ COACH'S COMMENT

Don't you realize that in a race everyone runs, but only one person gets the prize? So run to win! 1 CORINTHIANS 9:24

Michael Chang never possessed the fastest serve, the greatest backhand, or the nastiest topspin. But he sure seemed to be everywhere on a tennis court at once. Michael, a former professional tennis player, played on the ATP World Tour from 1988 to 2003, a period that is often referred to as "The Greatest Generation" of American players, thanks to superstars such as Andre Agassi, Pete Sampras, and Jim Courier.

But the smallish Michael (he stood five feet nine inches and weighed 160 pounds) held his own, thanks to a strong all-around game and lightning-quick speed. At age 17 he became the youngest Grand Slam winner ever when he won the 1989 French Open. Over his illustrious career, he won 33 more tournaments and reached the No. 2 ranking in the world. In 2008, Michael was inducted into the International Tennis Hall of Fame.

What's the Score?

Michael, of course, couldn't be everywhere at once. He was human. But there is Someone—and *only* one person—who can be everywhere at once: God. God is not confined by time or space. He is omnipresent, which means he exists everywhere in the universe all at once. We see this when God asked the prophet Jeremiah, "Am I not everywhere in all the heavens and earth?" (Jeremiah 23:24).

Think about any place on earth, and God is there. Think about any planet or star in the universe. God is there, too. (Is this hard to understand? It's okay. This is a deep theological concept.) How is God omnipresent? Well, as the creator of time and space, he also rules over time and space. By understanding this important concept, it helps us worship God for how awesome he really is. It helps us understand his creation better. It gives us comfort knowing that God is always near. It lets us know there is nowhere we can flee from God (just ask Jonah). And it provides a needed perspective on how small we are and how big God is. God truly exists everywhere, and that's great news!

) On the Ball

Besides today's passage from Jeremiah, Psalm 139 also speaks of God's omnipresence. Memorize verses 7-10 in Psalm 139.

) COACH'S COMMENT

"Am I a God who is only close at hand?" says the LORD. "No, I am far away at the same time. Can anyone hide from me in a secret place? Am I not everywhere in all the heavens and earth?" says the LORD. JEREMIAH 23:23-24

If you thought cardboard was worthless, think again. In 2007, a California man paid a record $2.35 million for the world's most famous piece of cardboard—a 1909 baseball card of Honus Wagner, the Pittsburgh Pirates' Hall of Fame second baseman.

Whoa. That's a lot of money for something that could fit in your back pocket. Imagine if that collector had gone home and realized he had bought a fake. He probably would have been a bit upset. In the popular world of sports memorabilia, originals are important. Whether it's trading cards, player autographs, game-worn jerseys, or actual equipment used in a contest, no collector wants to buy a knockoff. Fakes aren't worth anything. All collectors strive for the original because originals hold their value.

What's the Score?

Did you know you can own the world's greatest original collectible—a priceless object worth far more than a 100-year-old baseball card? It's true. In fact, you might even have it already. It's the Bible! The Bible is the most valuable object on earth because it is the original, inspired Word of God. Over the centuries, there have been many people who falsely claimed to speak for God. But the Bible is the authentic message from God to us.

In Exodus 31:18, God presents the Ten Commandments to Moses. The two stone tablets were actually "inscribed by the finger of God" (NIV). In 2 Timothy 3:15-16, the apostle Paul calls the Bible "holy Scriptures" and affirms that "all Scripture is God-breathed" (NIV). The Bible is made up of 66 books—from Genesis to Revelation—and was written over a couple thousand years by about 40 men, who were all inspired by the Holy Spirit. As the apostle Peter says in 2 Peter 1:20-21: "Above all, you must realize that no prophecy in Scripture ever came from the prophet's own understanding, or from human initiative. No, those prophets were moved by the Holy Spirit, and they spoke from God." When it comes to your faith, avoid all counterfeits and go to the original Word of God, the Bible!

) On the Ball

Since the Bible is the world's most precious original, commit to reading it every day!

) COACH'S COMMENT

All Scripture is God-breathed and is useful for teaching, rebuking, correcting and training in righteousness. 2 TIMOTHY 3:16 (NIV)

Talk about having a cool dad. Brian Bannister's dad, Floyd, was a Major League Baseball pitcher. But he wasn't just any pitcher. Floyd was the No. 1 overall pick in the 1976 draft, pitched for 15 seasons, and finished with a 134–143 career record. He also appeared in the 1982 All-Star Game and the 1983 American League Championship Series. Some of Brian's earliest memories were hanging out with Hall of Famer George Brett, slugger Bo Jackson, and pitcher Bret Saberhagen when Floyd played for the Kansas City Royals in the late 1980s.

Brian followed in his dad's footsteps, making his major league debut in 2006 with the New York Mets. He then spent the next four seasons, coincidentally, in Kansas City. Floyd was a loving father who taught his three sons about the Bible and baseball. Floyd never pushed baseball on his sons, but they all excelled in the sport. Brian enjoyed the most success, having finished third in the 2007 American League Rookie of the Year Award voting. In 2004, Floyd even helped Brian, who studied art and design in college, start a photo studio called Loft 19 in Phoenix, Arizona.

What's the Score?

Because of his demanding baseball schedule, Brian doesn't get to see much of Floyd on Father's Day, which is celebrated on the third Sunday of June. But Brian and Floyd remain close and share a deep love for each other.

The greatest love in the universe between father and son is seen in the Bible between God the Father and Jesus Christ. God expresses his love for his Son in passages like Matthew 3:17 (Jesus' baptism) and Matthew 17:5 (Jesus' Transfiguration). But despite God's perfect love for his Son, he was still willing to sacrifice him for our sins. This amazing love for us is seen in John 3:16, "God loved the world so much that he gave his one and only Son, so that everyone who believes in him will not perish but have eternal life."

Maybe as you read about Floyd and Brian, you have a loving, supportive father. Sadly, some of you do not. But regardless of your family situation, you have a loving heavenly Father who spared nothing, not even his own sinless Son, to bring you near to him. This is reason for praise to God—not only on Father's Day, but every day!

) On the Ball

Write a Father's Day card to God, thanking him for being an indescribably loving heavenly Father.

) COACH'S COMMENT

God loved the world so much that he gave his one and only Son, so that everyone who believes in him will not perish but have eternal life. JOHN 3:16

The 2010 NBA Finals renewed professional basketball's greatest rivalry. Led by Kobe Bryant, the Los Angeles Lakers won an epic seven-game series against the Boston Celtics. Entering the 2010–2011 season, Boston and Los Angeles had a combined 33 championships (the Celtics held a slight edge with 17). The 2010 NBA Finals marked the 12th time the Celtics and Lakers faced off in the championship—a rivalry that started in 1959 when the Celtics swept the Lakers (then located in Minneapolis) in four games.

The two famous franchises tussled in the finals six times in the 1960s (with the Celtics winning them all) and three more times in the 1980s (with the Lakers taking two). In 2008, the teams renewed the rivalry as Boston's Big Three of Ray Allen, Kevin Garnett, and Paul Pierce led the Celtics to another championship. But the Lakers got revenge in 2010. The rivalry has also featured great Hall of Famers like the Celtics' John Havlicek, Bill Russell, and Larry Bird, and the Lakers' Jerry West, Magic Johnson, and Kareem Abdul-Jabbar. As basketball rivalries go, it doesn't get any better than Celtics and Lakers.

☐☐ What's the Score?

Did you know the Bible features an epic rivalry? It's the showdown between God and Satan. But this rivalry is completely one sided. In fact, its outcome was determined ages ago. We read of Satan's initial challenge to God in Isaiah 14:12-15, which describes Satan (also known as "the devil") falling from his heavenly position because of rebellious pride. In Genesis 3, Satan helped introduce sin into the world by getting Adam and Eve to eat the Garden of Eden's forbidden fruit. Satan is the "father of lies" (John 8:44) who attempts to deceive (2 Corinthians 11:3), attack (Ephesians 6:16), and accuse (Revelation 12:10) Christians.

With so many bad things happening in the world, it might seem as if Satan has won the battle. But that's not true! Satan is a defeated enemy. Immediately after the Fall, God foretold Jesus' defeat of Satan through the Cross (Genesis 3:15), and Revelation 20:10 clearly details Satan's future doom. When it comes to God versus Satan, there is no rivalry. God is already victorious, which means Christians are on the winning team!

) On the Ball

To learn more about God's ultimate victory and Satan's final defeat, read Revelation 19:11–20:15.

) COACH'S COMMENT

The devil, who had deceived them, was thrown into the fiery lake of burning sulfur, joining the beast and the false prophet. There they will be tormented day and night forever and ever. REVELATION 20:10

In the NBA, "big men" is an expression used to describe the tallest players who typically stay close to the basket. But that term doesn't do justice to Manute Bol. Manute, who played in the pros for 11 years, is considered one of the two tallest players in NBA history. He and former Washington Bullets teammate Gheorghe Muresan were both listed at seven feet seven inches tall during their playing days. Talk about your "big men"—that's more like a human skyscraper!

Thanks to Manute's tremendous height and long arms, he became the only NBA player in history to tally more blocked shots (2,086) than points (1,599). His arm span measured a whopping eight feet six inches from the tip of his left finger to the tip of his right. He could even put his hands above the rim without jumping! Manute, who died on June 19, 2010, at age 47, was not only an amazing basketball player, but he also lived an amazing life. He claimed to descend from tribal chieftains in his native Sudan, where he once killed a lion with a spear while herding cattle as a youth.

☐☐ What's the Score?

Manute earned lots of money and basketball fame because of his impressive physical traits. But when it comes to being a follower of Jesus Christ, appearance doesn't matter. You don't have to be tall, strong, fast, or good looking to serve God. In fact, the Bible includes many examples of weak, unimpressive men and women who did great things for God.

Take Moses, for instance. He didn't speak well. When God called him to lead Israel out of Egypt, Moses replied, "I am slow of speech and tongue" (Exodus 4:10, NIV). But he eventually helped save Israel and became a great leader. David was "only a boy" when he defeated the Philistine giant, Goliath (1 Samuel 17:33). Elisha, a great miracle-working prophet, was made fun of for his baldness (2 Kings 2:23).

God can use ordinary people to do extraordinary things! He doesn't care what we look like. What he wants most are people with willing hearts who want to obey him.

) On the Ball

Do you have any impressive physical characteristics? Even if you think you're just average, you can accomplish super things for God. Pray that God would use you for his glory, no matter what you look like!

) COACH'S COMMENT

The LORD said to Samuel, "Don't judge by his appearance or height, for I have rejected him. The LORD doesn't see things the way you see them. People judge by outward appearance, but the LORD looks at the heart." 1 SAMUEL 16:7

Graeme McDowell didn't wow PGA crowds with massive blasts from his driver or seemingly impossible saves from the woods. But his steady play and gritty attitude helped him win the 2010 US Open. Graeme, a native of Portrush, Northern Ireland, barely qualified for the Open and came to coastal California's famed Pebble Beach Golf Links as the 37th-ranked player in the world. He had done well in Europe but had never won on the PGA Tour. That was about to change.

As the tournament progressed, Graeme faced several challenges. The leaderboard included some of the biggest names in golf, like former major winners Tiger Woods, Phil Mickelson, Ernie Els, and Davis Love III. What's more, no European had won America's golf championship since 1970. Yet, one by one, all of Graeme's challengers dropped off in the final round. Despite shooting a three-over-par 74, Graeme won by a stroke over Grégory Havret. It was the biggest victory of his career.

What's the Score?

Graeme was a relative no-name who overcame great odds to score a huge victory. That's kind of like Gideon in Judges 6. Gideon was an Israelite judge during one of the low points in the nation's history. The people consistently turned to idol worship, so God disciplined them by allowing Canaanite armies to invade the land. The enemy during Gideon's lifetime was Midian, a powerful eastern nation that was so oppressive, they forced many Israelites to hide in caves. To save his people, God didn't select a mighty warrior. He chose Gideon, an unimportant man from a weak clan who was hiding from the Midianites when God called him.

But God did mighty things through Gideon. Before Gideon attacked Midian, God downsized his army from 32,000 men to 300 and commanded the tiny group to use only trumpets, empty jars, and torches as weapons. One by one, God removed all the challenges in front of Gideon. He gave Gideon a miraculous victory by routing the Midianites and bringing peace to Israel. God didn't need Gideon to be powerful or have amazing skill; he just wanted somebody to faithfully follow him. Our responsibility is to "be strong and courageous," as 1 Chronicles 22:13 implores us, and to trust God. He can use us in mighty ways if we have faith and don't give up.

On the Ball

Looking for more stories about how godly men and women accomplished seemingly impossible things through faith in God? Read the stories of Joshua, Nehemiah, and Esther.

COACH'S COMMENT

Be strong and courageous; do not be afraid or lose heart! 1 CHRONICLES 22:13

In 1943, baseball went pink. As World War II pressed many major leaguers into military duty and forced certain minor league teams to shut down, Chicago Cubs owner Philip K. Wrigley worried that the war would cripple his franchise, and maybe all of Major League Baseball. So Philip and other businessmen started the All-American Girls Professional Baseball League. The league ran from 1943 to 1954 and featured a 108-game regular-season schedule from mid-May to September 1, followed by the play-offs. At the height of its popularity in 1948, it boasted 10 teams playing at minor league ballparks throughout the Midwest and averaging several thousand fans a game.

League officials wanted players to retain their femininity and "all-American girl next door" image. So each player received a beauty kit and attended a mandatory charm school. Uniforms were one-piece short-skirted tunics. After 12 seasons, because of various social and economic factors, the league folded in 1954. But it remains a unique part of America's baseball history.

☐☐ What's the Score?

Like the All-American Girls Professional Baseball League, the Bible features many tales of women doing extraordinary things in difficult times. Ruth is one of those women. The book of Ruth tells an amazing account of human kindness and God's sovereignty. When the husband and two sons of Ruth's mother-in-law, Naomi, died (including Ruth's husband), Ruth could have returned to her home country of Moab. But fearing for Naomi's welfare as a widow, Ruth traveled with Naomi to her hometown in Judea.

Soon Ruth met Boaz, a distant relative of Naomi, who showed great kindness to the women and who eventually married Ruth. Boaz fulfilled the ancient kinsman-redeemer laws of Israel, where a man would marry a female relative in order to preserve the family line and land. Like Ruth, Boaz didn't have to show kindness, but he did so abundantly. This caused great celebration in Naomi's town (Ruth 4:14). Ultimately, because of Ruth's and Boaz's exceeding kindness toward others, Jesus' ancestral family line remained intact. Boaz and Ruth had a son named Obed, the grandfather of King David, whose royal earthly line would one day include Jesus. In his wisdom, God used Ruth's and Boaz's compassion to ensure that his plan of salvation would eventually be fulfilled in the ultimate Redeemer, Jesus Christ!

❭ On the Ball

Read the entire book of Ruth. Then surprise someone with an act of exceeding kindness.

❭ COACH'S COMMENT

The women of the town said to Naomi, "Praise the LORD, who has now provided a redeemer for your family! May this child be famous in Israel." RUTH 4:14

When his final backhand mercifully landed in bounds, John Isner tumbled to the All England Club's famed grass and lifted his weary arms in triumph. He had just won the longest tennis match in history. For 11 hours and five minutes, John, an American, battled Frenchman Nicolas Mahut in a first-round match during the 2010 Wimbledon tournament. It was an exhausting marathon that spanned three days thanks to two suspensions for darkness. Finally, on day three, John prevailed by the craziest tennis score ever seen: 6–4, 3–6, 6–7 (9–7), 7–6 (7–3), 70–68. Yes, that's 70–68, because rules at Wimbledon state the final set can't go to a tiebreaker and must be won by two games.

It sure took a lot of waiting and stamina to decide the winner. Consider these absurd statistics: A total of 980 points were scored in the match. The final fifth set alone took eight hours and 11 minutes, crushing the previous single-set time record of six hours and 33 minutes at the 2004 French Open. One sports physiologist estimated that John and Nicolas each ran the equivalent of 15½ miles and expended about 8,500 calories of energy—more than what it takes to run two full marathons.

What's the Score?

Life often requires lots of spiritual stamina, or the ability to wait and endure hardship. By nature, we want things right away. We don't like our dreams to be delayed. And we certainly don't enjoy having to wait through difficult trials. But God often calls us to wait for his goodness. There are plenty of examples in the Bible: The Israelites waited through 400 years of Egyptian slavery and 40 years of wilderness wandering to reach the Promised Land. Abraham waited until he turned 100 before God gave him his promised son, Isaac.

Believe it or not, waiting is a good thing. As Micah 7:7 says, "I wait confidently for God to save me." Waiting is God's way of teaching us to trust in him. He knows if we receive everything we want immediately, we will quickly forget about him. So in his infinite wisdom, he often makes us wait for his goodness. Like John found out, waiting can be a very good thing!

) On the Ball

Make a list of important prayer requests (not just toys or video games!), and ask God to fulfill those desires—if it's his will—while helping you to wait for his answer. Keep the list and mark it down when God answers the prayer.

) COACH'S COMMENT

As for me, I look to the LORD for help. I wait confidently for God to save me, and my God will certainly hear me. MICAH 7:7

The goal didn't count! In a heartbeat, the US Men's National Soccer Team went from joy-fully celebrating a 1–0 lead against Algeria to frustrated disbelief. Millions of fans around the world howled as replays clearly showed that the referee's offside call was wrong. On the world's biggest stage—the World Cup—the American team had suffered from a ref-ereeing mistake . . . again. Five days earlier, a different referee called a "mystery" foul against the Americans that disallowed a winning goal. Now with this bad call, it appeared as if the US team would be going home. The United States needed to beat Algeria to advance to the next round of the 2010 World Cup. A loss or a tie would send the Americans out of the tournament. It seemed that everything was going against them.

Instead of giving up, the Americans attacked the Algerian goal. They fired shot after shot—but each one missed, bounced off the goalpost, or was saved by the Desert Foxes' goalkeeper. Time was running out. Fans were desperate. Failure was looming. The clock ticked past the 90-minute mark and into four minutes of extra time allowed because of earlier injuries. The Algerians created a good scoring chance, but US goalkeeper Tim Howard made the save and quickly threw the ball to Landon Donovan. Landon dribbled down the right side of the field. He passed to Jozy Altidore, who crossed it to Clint Dempsey in the center. Clint fired, but the Algerian keeper blocked the shot. The ball rebounded to the center of the box, where Landon sprinted in and shot. *Goooooal!*

⬜⬜ What's the Score?
The Americans did it! They refused to give up even when things weren't going their way. The players had devoted the past four years toward achieving their dreams, and their per-severance paid off.

It's easy to get discouraged when circumstances aren't going our way in a game, at school, in friendships, or with life in general. Even when we're trying our hardest, we sometimes face struggles that we can't control. The Bible tells us that's the time to thank God and keep going (Romans 5:3). To persevere means to keep trying to reach our goal no matter what obstacles we face. The good news is that God has promised to help us. And the more we keep going, the stronger we get.

⟩ On the Ball
What challenge are you facing? Do you feel like you've been treated unfairly? Ask God for the strength to keep going.

⟩ COACH'S COMMENT
We also glory in our sufferings, because we know that suffering produces perseverance; perseverance, character; and character, hope. ROMANS 5:3-4 (NIV)

On this day, the Washington Wizards selected University of Kentucky freshman John Wall as the first overall pick in the 2010 NBA draft. Immediately, John was heralded as the Wizards' franchise savior. This team certainly needed some help. Earlier in the 2009–2010 season, star guard Gilbert Arenas was suspended for the final 50 games after bringing guns into the locker room. The Wizards finished with a miserable 26–56 record, which wasn't unusual. The team had only won one play-off series (2005) in the previous 27 years.

So when the 19-year-old arrived in Washington, DC, a day after the draft, the Wizards gave John a red-carpet welcome—literally. A police-escorted limousine chauffeured him from the airport to the team's home arena, Verizon Center, where hundreds of fans awaited him under hanging banners that read, "Wall: Game Changer." He walked into his new home court on a red carpet. DC Mayor Adrian M. Fenty proclaimed June 25 "John Wall Day," and the Wizards showed a "Welcome to DC" video that featured some of the city's top professional athletes, including Redskins quarterback Donovan McNabb.

⬚⬚ What's the Score?

On average, most No. 1 draft picks who are dubbed franchise saviors never live up to expectations. For every top selection who turns into a superstar, such as Dwight Howard (2004) or Tim Duncan (1997), there's a Kwame Brown (2001) or Pervis Ellison (1989). (If you're wondering who those last two players are, that's the point.) And that's just in the NBA. The NFL, the NHL, Major League Baseball, and other professional sports leagues all have similar stories. Doling out "franchise savior" labels in sports is always risky business.

Thankfully, when it comes to our eternal salvation, there is one true, unquestioned Savior—Jesus Christ. He alone can save us because he is the only person who lived a sinless life, died, and rose again from the grave. Jesus, who was both fully God and fully man, is our Savior because he provided forgiveness of sins when no one else could.

⟩ On the Ball

Get a piece of paper and ask your parents to help you list 10 reasons why Jesus Christ is an awesome Savior.

- -

⟩ COACH'S COMMENT

They said to the woman, "Now we believe, not just because of what you told us, but because we have heard him ourselves. Now we know that he is indeed the Savior of the world." JOHN 4:42

- -

When Arizona Diamondbacks right-hander Edwin Jackson threw his final pitch on June 25, 2010, he joined an elite fraternity: he became the 267th pitcher in Major League Baseball history to throw a no-hitter. After Jackson hit a game-ending groundout for a 1–0 victory over the Tampa Bay Rays, his teammates mobbed him in celebration. Then, during a postgame TV interview, a teammate playfully threw a pie in his face.

But as joyous as the occasion was for Edwin, his performance was one of the ugliest no-hitters ever. He threw an astounding 149 pitches—the most of any major-league pitcher since 2005—and gave up eight walks, including seven in the first three innings. Edwin suffered with so many control problems that the Diamondbacks had relievers warming up in the bull pen from the sixth inning until the end of the game.

What's the Score?

Like Edwin's no-hitter, when it comes to our righteousness before God, even our best performance has major flaws. Many people think that if they do enough good deeds and don't commit any "major" sins like murder or stealing, they'll get to heaven. But the Bible clearly teaches that our best isn't good enough to earn God's favor. In fact, Isaiah 64:6 says our righteousness is "nothing but filthy rags" before God.

That's because God is holy—meaning he is perfect, sinless, and set apart from us in every way. We, on the other hand, are utterly sinful. We can't earn a relationship with a holy God by what we do. Our righteousness before God has to come from someone else. That someone is Jesus! God's own Son, Jesus Christ, died to take away our sins and clothe us in his righteousness. If we put our faith in Jesus, God forgives our sins, looks past our flaws, and credits Jesus' righteousness to us. So don't try to earn your salvation from God. Trust in Jesus—the only person who can turn filthy rags into spotlessly clean clothes!

) On the Ball

Put a fancy, clean shirt over what you're wearing and look in the mirror. What do you see? Just the clean shirt, right? If you've accepted Jesus as your Savior, that's what God sees—Jesus' righteousness—when he looks at you.

) COACH'S COMMENT

We are all infected and impure with sin. When we display our righteous deeds, they are nothing but filthy rags. Like autumn leaves, we wither and fall, and our sins sweep us away like the wind. ISAIAH 64:6

Many athletes talk about how the game "slows down" when they're on a hot streak. For PGA Tour veteran Ben Crane, though, a slow game resulted in one of the biggest controversies of his professional career. PGA Tour golfers usually play in pairs or trios. When one player prepares to swing or putt, the others must wait silently. The problem was, Ben was one of the slowest players on the tour.

At the 2005 Booz Allen Classic in Bethesda, Maryland, Ben was paired in the final round with South African Rory Sabbatini, a notoriously fast player. When tournament officials gave the duo a warning because of Ben's lethargic pace, Rory fumed and walked ahead to the 18th tee even though Ben was still on the 17th fairway. By golf's gentlemanly code of conduct, Rory's act was rude. After their round, Rory had heated words for his playing partner. To play with Ben, patience was required, and Rory struggled to have it that day.

⬜ What's the Score?

Just like in golf, patience is needed in everyday life. That doesn't mean it's easy. People can be tough to love. On any given day, they can be annoying, cranky, or downright mean. (Does that sound familiar?) But guess what? It's hypocritical for us to be impatient with others because we have plenty of flaws ourselves. Just because someone is obnoxious or unkind or clumsy doesn't mean you have a right to treat that person rudely.

God commands us to be patient with others in Ephesians 4:2. Patience is the mark of a true follower of Jesus Christ. It is one of the descriptions of true, godly love in 1 Corinthians 13, and it is listed as a fruit of the Spirit in Galatians 5. Most importantly, we must remember that God has been exceedingly patient with us. Our sins deserve punishment and death, but instead, he has shown great patience by offering us the free gift of salvation through Jesus Christ. With that as our example, let's be patient with others!

〉 On the Ball

On a sheet of paper, list the things that annoy you the most. Then make another column and list ways you can be patient with people whenever they do things that bother you.

〉 COACH'S COMMENT

Always be humble and gentle. Be patient with each other, making allowance for each other's faults because of your love. EPHESIANS 4:2

Brian Roberts screamed in fear. As a five-year-old, he didn't know all the details of his upcoming surgery. It was better that way. Doctors were about to cut a Y-shaped incision in his chest and briefly stop his heartbeat to patch a hole in his heart. Brian didn't understand all this, but he knew enough to be scared. So as the doctors wheeled him into the operating room, he reached out and cried for his parents.

Nearly 30 years later, things turned out quite well for Brian. After the successful surgery, he eventually became one of the best leadoff hitters and second basemen in Major League Baseball. In his first 10 seasons, he made two all-star teams, and in 2009, he became only the fourth player in major league history to hit 50 doubles in at least three seasons. Not bad for a guy who had a bad ticker as a kid.

What's the Score?

The truth is that, like Brian, we were all born with a heart problem. But our problem is not a medical condition. It's far worse. It's a spiritual crisis that threatens our eternal standing before God. We were born with sinful hearts. King David understood this well. In Psalm 51:5, he wrote, "Surely I was sinful at birth, sinful from the time my mother conceived me" (NIV). And the writer of Proverbs 20:9 said, "Who can say, 'I have kept my heart pure; I am clean and without sin'?" (NIV). The obvious answer is no one. This is a major problem, because the Bible also says that only the pure in heart will see God in heaven (Matthew 5:8).

Without help, our wicked hearts separate us from God forever. That's why later in Psalm 51, David pleads with God to "create in me a pure heart." Thankfully for us, God mercifully answers this prayer. *How?* you ask. By providing the perfect heart-cleaning remedy in his Son, Jesus Christ. Jesus died on the cross for our sins, and when we put our faith in him, he cleans our hearts and makes them acceptable to God. And you can take this wonderful truth to heart!

) On the Ball

Read Psalm 51 as a prayer to God. Ask your parents for help with any words or phrases you don't understand.

) COACH'S COMMENT

Create in me a pure heart, O God, and renew a steadfast spirit within me.
PSALM 51:10 (NIV)

Look out for giant, killer mosquitoes! That's probably what players at the 2010 FIFA World Cup in South Africa were thinking. In the summer of 2010, a simple musical instrument made international headlines as big as the soccer being played. A small plastic horn called the *vuvuzela* created quite a controversy during the biggest sporting event in the world. Blown by itself, a vuvuzela sounds innocent enough. But when excited soccer fans blow thousands of vuvuzelas at once, they sound like a deafening swarm of insects.

Many South Africans felt the vuvuzela was a vital part of the first World Cup hosted on African soil, saying it represented the freedom and racial equality that South Africa had struggled for decades earlier. Others complained that the vuvuzela sounded like a dying goat. Many coaches and players called for vuvuzelas to be banned, and TV executives worried that people wouldn't be able to hear the announcer's voice because of the instruments. In the end, tournament officials allowed fans to blow vuvuzelas during games. Although their loud drone could distinctively be heard on TV, they weren't loud enough to drown out the exciting action.

What's the Score?

Thousands of years ago, horns and trumpets played an important part of life in ancient Israel. Various trumpet sounds were signals for the Israelites to gather at the tabernacle, to pack up their belongings for relocation, or to prepare for battle. The Israelites heard a piercing trumpet sound after receiving the Ten Commandments. Rams' horns were used as priestly trumpets when the walls of Jericho fell. They were also blown to commemorate festivals and to hold the oil that anointed the head of a new king.

Even today, Christians wait in great anticipation for a special trumpet sound. In 1 Thessalonians 4, the Bible promises a future day when a great trumpet will blast to signal Christ's return to earth. He will come in incredible majesty and power to gather all Christians and take them back to heaven to live with him forever. That's a sound worth listening for!

) On the Ball

The next time you hear a trumpet being played, remember the wonderful promise of Jesus' future return.

) COACH'S COMMENT

The Lord himself will come down from heaven with a commanding shout, with the voice of the archangel, and with the trumpet call of God. First, the Christians who have died will rise from their graves. Then, together with them, we who are still alive and remain on the earth will be caught up in the clouds to meet the Lord in the air. Then we will be with the Lord forever. 1 THESSALONIANS 4:16-17

En garde! For you non–French speakers, that means "On guard!" It's a phrase that has become closely associated with swordplay over the years. You might have heard someone use those words while you were watching a TV show or movie. Swords were the weapon of choice for thousands of years. But these days, swordplay is mainly an athletic endeavor.

The art of fencing, a combat sport using swords, has been around for hundreds of years. Some historians believe fencing was one of the sports in the original Olympic Games in ancient Greece. It is also one of only four sports that have been included in every modern Olympics, which started in 1896. The sport of fencing has been called "physical chess" for its strategic emphasis and importance of quick moves and counter-attacks. Fencers use one of three types of swords—the foil, épée, or saber—to score points by touching an opponent with their weapon. But fear not, future fencers—fencing is not a fight to the death. Competitors wear protective clothing and masks to avoid injury.

What's the Score?

Did you know that the Bible teaches Christians to be *en garde* against sin by using a sword? It's true! In Ephesians 6, the apostle Paul describes the armor of God that all Christians should put on daily to protect themselves against the devil's attacks. Almost all the armor is defensive in nature (helmet, breastplate, and shield), except for one important offensive weapon—the "sword of the Spirit," the Bible!

God's Word is a very powerful weapon we are to use to fight sin. Reading the Bible helps us know right and wrong. Memorizing Scripture verses gives us important reminders when we are tempted to disobey. Hebrews 4:12 goes into even greater detail about the sword of God's Word, saying it "is alive and powerful" and that "it is sharper than the sharpest two-edged sword, cutting between soul and spirit." If you want to be victorious in the fight against sin, you must use the sword of the Spirit well!

) On the Ball

Ask your parents to help you start a good Bible memory program. This will help sharpen your spiritual swordplay!

) COACH'S COMMENT

The word of God is alive and powerful. It is sharper than the sharpest two-edged sword, cutting between soul and spirit, between joint and marrow. It exposes our innermost thoughts and desires. HEBREWS 4:12

They call him Mr. Irrelevant. Not a very flattering title, is it? *Irrelevant* means "immaterial" or "it doesn't matter." When applied to an NFL player, it basically means "that guy isn't going to amount to anything in the league." Each June, a California organization throws a four-day party called "Irrelevant Week" for the last player picked in that year's NFL Draft. Historically, that player has been known as Mr. Irrelevant. The player—often an athlete from a little-known college—enjoys a party in his honor and takes part in other activities like a boat trip and a trip to Disneyland.

Irrelevant Week was the brainchild of Paul Salata, a bench-warming NFL wide receiver in 1949–1950 who wanted to provide a little recognition to the underdog. Since he first started Irrelevant Week in 1976, Paul has raised more than $1 million for local charities. A few Mr. Irrelevants have found success in the NFL. Kansas City Chiefs kicker Ryan Succop, the 2009 Mr. Irrelevant, set a franchise rookie record with 25 field goals that year after being picked 256th in the draft. But most players who earn this dubious title never make an NFL roster and have to find another career. But at least for one week in Southern California, they are treated like kings.

☐☐ What's the Score?

Have you ever felt alone, unloved, or unwanted? To put it another way, have you ever felt irrelevant? It's a feeling many of us struggle with at some point in life. We wonder if God is there and if he really cares. Take heart! There are no Mr. (or Miss) Irrelevants to God. He considers every single person on earth important, including you. We see evidence of this throughout Scripture. He formed you in your mother's womb (Psalm 139:13-15) and directs your life (Proverbs 16:9). In fact, in Luke 12, Jesus himself testifies to God's love and personal care for all people, telling us that he has numbered the very hairs of our heads.

If the all-powerful, all-knowing God knows the smallest of details about us, clearly we are very relevant to him . . . even if we're the last pick in the NFL Draft!

⟩ On the Ball

Try counting the number of hairs on your head. (Hint: it's impossible.) Once you realize God knows the number, thank him for loving you so personally and considering you very relevant to him!

- -

⟩ COACH'S COMMENT

What is the price of five sparrows—two copper coins? Yet God does not forget a single one of them. And the very hairs on your head are all numbered. So don't be afraid; you are more valuable to God than a whole flock of sparrows. **LUKE 12:6-7**

- -

Alex Honnold and Sean Leary had been rock climbing for 24 hours straight in Yosemite National Park. By the time they finally decided to stop, the pair had broken the speed record for consecutive ascents. That sounds impressive, doesn't it? It was downright mindblowing to the climbing world because the guys had been climbing El Capitan, which rises 3,000 feet almost straight up. Most climbers take three to five *days* to climb the iconic mountain, setting up platforms to sleep in at night. Alex and Sean climbed it three times in just one day!

Alex and Sean followed three major routes called The Nose, Salathe Wall, and Lurking Fear. By the time they were done, they had covered 85 pitches, or big sections, and 8,200 vertical feet. Alex normally did a lot of free-climbing without using ropes. (If he had fallen, he would have died—so he tried hard not to fall.) But he and Sean used ropes on El Cap. They may be insane but they weren't stupid. Would you want to fall 3,000 feet? They were understandably tired when they finished on July 1, 2010—and ready to eat some pizza.

What's the Score?

Have you ever rock climbed? It can be scary, and it's hard. But it's an awesome feeling when you reach the top! A big part of climbing is mental. As long as you're connected to a safety rope, you can't fall. Sure, you can slip off the rock, but the rope is there to catch you and keep you safe. Convincing your brain of that fact when you're way off the ground can be tricky. You have to put your trust in your rope and keep moving.

In a similar way, we have to step out and trust that God is with us. Peter gave us a good example in the Bible when he walked on water in Matthew 14:22-32. Sure, he sank when he stopped looking at Jesus and got scared. But Peter put his faith into real action by getting out of the boat. None of the other disciples even tried.

Don't be content to stay in the boat or on the ground. Put your faith into action, and trust Jesus to hold up your climbing rope. You'll be amazed by the view at the top.

) On the Ball

Go rock climbing if you can, and think about how the experience is like trusting God. If you can't go climbing, take a step of faith and do something that you've been hesitant about.

) COACH'S COMMENT

"Yes, come," Jesus said. So Peter went over the side of the boat and walked on the water toward Jesus. MATTHEW 14:29

Once you experience the freedom and power of surfing, it becomes something you long to do again and again. At the Hurley US Open of Surfing in 2009, some pro surfers helped a few friends to enjoy a ride on the waves. There was nothing unusual about that. But what was unusual was that the people they helped were paralyzed. Some couldn't move their legs. Some couldn't move their arms or legs. But with the help of special equipment and knowledgeable friends pushing their surfboards, these disabled people were able to surf the ocean waves.

A surfer named Jesse Billauer knew just how they felt. He was the quadriplegic who started this "They Will Surf Again" event through his Life Rolls On Foundation (LRO). Jesse was a promising surfer with his sights set on the pros. But when he was 17, a wipeout snapped his spinal cord and left him paralyzed. He didn't let that keep him out of the waves. With the help of some friends and professional surfers, Jesse relearned to surf by lying on his board and being pushed into the breaking waves. He started LRO to inspire and help other disabled people follow their passions. He loves helping them learn to surf, too.

⬜⬜ What's the Score?

Jesse's story is similar to a Bible story in Mark 2: "Four men arrived carrying a paralyzed man on a mat. They couldn't bring him to Jesus because of the crowd, so they dug a hole through the roof above his head. Then they lowered the man on his mat, right down in front of Jesus." Jesus was impressed by their faith and probably by their commitment to help their friend. He healed the paralyzed man and forgave his sins.

Those four guys were good friends, like the surfers who carried the disabled people into the water. They knew Jesus was the only hope for their paralyzed buddy, and they didn't let anything stop them from making sure he got help. We all need friends like that. And we each need to be a friend like that. Friends like that turn the waves of life from intimidating to enjoyable.

⟩ On the Ball

Spend your energy today helping a friend in need. You may not be able to totally solve the problem, but don't give up until your friend knows he or she is not alone.

⟩ COACH'S COMMENT

Four men arrived carrying a paralyzed man on a mat. They couldn't bring him to Jesus because of the crowd, so they dug a hole through the roof above his head. Then they lowered the man on his mat, right down in front of Jesus. MARK 2:3-4

The Henley Royal Regatta is rowing royalty. The history, setting, and traditions all point to a romantic image of royal tea parties, elegant fishing lodges, and fancy rowing races. The regatta started in 1839 as a one-day event just in the town of Henley, England, on the Thames River. But it grew into a premiere, five-day international amateur rowing tournament.

The regatta is still unlike any other rowing event in the world. Because it's so old, the tournament uses its own rules instead of national or international rowing federation guidelines. One difference is Henley's one-on-one racing instead of multi-lane competitions. The "royal" part of the name came about because the king or queen of England is an official sponsor of the event.

The race starts at beautiful Temple Island, named for the restored temple that was turned into a fancy fishing lodge. Its rolling meadows and wooded hills are just part of the river's natural beauty that the regatta has committed to preserve. Regatta organizers maintain a sanctuary for plants and animals, and they plant trees along the river. They also build and remove all the race structures each year. In July the area is packed with people for the festivities. But from September through March, all you can see is the river's natural habitat.

⬛ What's the Score?

When Adam and Eve were placed in the Garden of Eden, God instructed them to care for his creation. Genesis 2:15 tells us, "The LORD God placed the man in the Garden of Eden to tend and watch over it." Too bad we don't still live in Eden. But we do still have the job of taking care of God's creation. We are free to enjoy and use the resources of the world, but we have to remember we are only stewards of what belongs to God. "He holds in his hands the depths of the earth and the mightiest mountains. The sea belongs to him, for he made it. His hands formed the dry land, too" (Psalm 95:4-5).

The Henley Royal Regatta uses the river for fun, but its organizers also are careful to take care of the natural environment. We should do our best to avoid wasting energy and natural resources and to protect areas and animals that are in danger of being destroyed. After all, they are part of God's amazing creation.

) On the Ball

Get a group of friends and family and buy a tree together. Choose a place in your yard or in a public place approved by your local government and plant the tree.

) COACH'S COMMENT

The LORD God placed the man in the Garden of Eden to tend and watch over it.
GENESIS 2:15

One of the most touching moments in sports history took place on July 4, 1939, when Lou Gehrig retired. The New York Yankees first baseman was one of the best players in the game. It wasn't that he wanted to retire. He had to. Lou had been diagnosed with amyotrophic lateral sclerosis (ALS). It's a disease of the brain and spine that causes the muscles to slowly quit working. There's no cure, and Lou knew it would painfully break down his body and kill him.

But Lou wasn't bitter. He was thankful. He spoke to the full stadium and said, "Fans, for the past two weeks you have been reading about the bad break I got. Yet today I consider myself the luckiest man on the face of this earth." He thanked everyone for his opportunities in baseball and for the blessings in his life. Everyone cried. Babe Ruth walked over, put his arm around Lou, and spoke to his former teammate for the first time in five years. Lou died only two years later. He is still remembered as one of the greatest players of all time—and for his kindness and gracious attitude.

What's the Score?

Lou epitomized 1 Thessalonians 5:18: "Be thankful in all circumstances, for this is God's will for you who belong to Christ Jesus." He could have been bitter and angry. He could have focused on all he was losing. No one would have blamed him. Instead he kept his attention on all the goodness he had experienced.

That's the kind of attitude God calls us to have. We will all face bad times, and they can sometimes feel overwhelming. But with God's help, we can find good to focus on. If nothing else, we can be thankful because God will always be there for us. And that makes us some of the most blessed people on earth.

) On the Ball

Start thanking God no matter what is going on in your life. Focus on his goodness, and let him fill your heart with thankfulness.

) COACH'S COMMENT

Be thankful in all circumstances, for this is God's will for you who belong to Christ Jesus. 1 THESSALONIANS 5:18

Joey Chestnut knew how to pig out! In July of 2009, Joey set a world record by eating 68 hot dogs in 10 minutes. Nicknamed "Jaws," he took home $20,000 by eating all those hot dogs in Coney Island, New York. Eating competitions have come a long way since the first hot-dog-eating contest was held in 1916. The winner of that one only had to put away 13 frankfurters to claim first place. Joey's modern accomplishments are enough to make your stomach hurt!

And if it doesn't hurt now, just think about eating eight pounds of pork ribs in 12 minutes. That's what Joey did to win the Best in the West Nugget Rib Cook-Off's eating competition in 2010. It was the skinny 26-year-old's fourth win in five years at the event. And this victory was all about technique. Joey slid the meat off each bone with his hands and ate it in a ball instead of taking individual bites off the bone.

🏈 What's the Score?

Joey was America's top professional eater, holding world eating records for hot dogs, hamburgers, ribs, steak, asparagus, macaroni and cheese, and jalapeño peppers. You might think Joey's accomplishments are disgusting, amazing, entertaining, or all of the above. But millions of people around the world would give anything for just a small portion of what he ate in one contest.

Joey ate a whopping amount of food for the sake of competition, but for some people, gluttony (greedy or excessive overeating) is a real physical and spiritual problem. The city of Sodom in the Bible is famous for its evil ways, and the Bible tells us gluttony was one of its big sins. Ezekiel makes it clear that it isn't just overeating that is sinful, but overindulging at the expense of those in need: "Sodom's sins were pride, gluttony, and laziness, while the poor and needy suffered outside her door" (Ezekiel 16:49).

It's easy for us to take our plenty, including food, for granted. God cares about our attitudes in all things, even eating. Instead of pigging out as much as you can, watch for ways to share food with others around you . . . and around the world.

) On the Ball

Instead of counting how many hot dogs you can eat, count how many you can give away. Volunteer at a local food pantry. Or organize a cookout at your church or a local shelter for people in need of a meal.

) COACH'S COMMENT

Sodom's sins were pride, gluttony, and laziness, while the poor and needy suffered outside her door. EZEKIEL 16:49

The tennis match was like two gladiators battling back and forth. Roger Federer and Rafael Nadal, the two top players in the world and arguably two of the best of all time, waged an epic battle on the grass court of the 2008 Wimbledon final. It just kept going. The rivalry between Roger and Rafael was already strong. Roger had won the last five Wimbledons. Rafael had won the previous four French Opens, beating Roger every time. In this match, they battled fiercely for every point. Rain delayed the match twice and probably helped each player get some rest and regain momentum.

Rafael won the first two sets 6–4, 6–4. Then Roger narrowly took the next two sets in tiebreakers 7–6, 7–6. The match went on and on, and the fifth set went to extra games. Finally, Rafael prevailed 9–7. At nearly five hours, it was the longest Wimbledon final in history. Rafael won this classic battle of endurance. You can read about an even longer first-round match in the June 22 devo.

What's the Score?
Staying strong to the end was worth the cost. Both Rafael's and Roger's talent, dedication, and love of the game kept them going, even in one of the longest, toughest competitions of their lives. What in your life is worth enduring to the end for?

Jesus talked about endurance when he said, "The one who endures to the end will be saved" (Matthew 24:13). He was talking about enduring persecution and hardship. But staying strong in our faith also applies to any situation when we're tempted to quit. Giving up often looks like the easiest way out. But when you quit, you might be missing out on God's blessing or something he wants to teach you. Be encouraged by Jesus' words, and stay strong.

On the Ball
Write some of your current challenges on a tennis ball. Then bounce the ball on a racket as many times as you can without letting it drop. Try to get to 100. Keep trying even if it's tough. As you bounce, think about how you can apply endurance to your life situations.

COACH'S COMMENT
The one who endures to the end will be saved. MATTHEW 24:13

Have you ever counted how many times you can make a stone skip across the water? When you find the right lake or river with the right rocks, you can spend hours skipping stones. Flat stones are best. They can skim and zoom across the waves. If you're really serious about your stone skipping, you should head to the Mackinac Island Stone Skipping and Gerplunking contest every July. It's one of the biggest contests in the nation. (Gerplunking is the kids' version of the contest.)

Russell "Rock Bottom" Byars has won the Mackinac and other contests multiple times. But his most rockin' accomplishment came closer to home on the Allegheny River north of Pittsburgh, Pennsylvania. In July 2007, Russell set the stone-skipping world record with 51 skips. He estimated that the stone traveled 250 feet. The stone-skipping master threw 40 times that day, but he never bettered his first throw. He didn't have to.

⬚⬚ What's the Score?

Guinness World Records used video to verify Russell's record by counting the rings on the water from each skip. You know how the ripples spread out in circles across water. Something similar happens in our lives. It's called the ripple effect.

The Bible tells us that "the love of the LORD remains forever with those who fear him. His salvation extends to the children's children" (Psalm 103:17). God's love and faithfulness are basically ripple effects that spread through people, especially families. And our actions have a ripple effect too. Think of our actions as the stones we throw that send out ripples to other people. We can spread God's love and goodness if that's what we "throw." Or we can spread hurt and pain if we're tossing out negative rocks. Choose your stones wisely, and make sure they keep spreading godly ripples.

⟩ On the Ball

Go skip some stones and watch the ripples spread. Come home and do something unexpected and kind for each of your family members. See how your kindness ripples through your family.

⟩ COACH'S COMMENT

The love of the LORD remains forever with those who fear him. His salvation extends to the children's children. PSALM 103:17

The summer of 2010 brought World Cup fever to all corners of the world. But on the Caribbean island of Barbados, a different world championship was firing up a lot of excitement. The Woz Challenge Cup rolled onto the field to the delight of millions, er, actually, hundreds of fans. The Woz Cup is the World Cup of Segway polo. That's right—those two-wheeled, electric-powered, gyroscopically steered, stand-up vehicles.

At first glance the competition seemed to be between old dudes with enough money to spend on high-tech toys. But take a closer look before you write off these guys. One of the competitors was Steve Wozniak, cofounder of Apple Computers. He's the Woz in Woz Cup. Many of his teammates and opponents worked for Apple. Others were engineers, Segway shop owners, or retirees.

The Segway polo players all shared a self-proclaimed geekiness that made them want to ride a Segway and swing a mallet at the same time. They didn't care if people thought it was cool or not. Maybe it was that attitude that helped them follow their own paths in life. And maybe that attitude led them to achieve enough success that they could spend time cruising around on two wheels and relaxing in the tropical island breezes.

⬜⬜ What's the Score?

Many of the most inventive, influential people in history never measured up to the cool kids' checklist. Instead, they redefined cool by being exactly who they were made to be.

Ephesians 2:10 says, "We are God's handiwork, created in Christ Jesus to do good works, which God prepared in advance for us to do" (NIV). God made you just the way he wants so you can do the special things he has prepared for you. That's truly cool! But sometimes we have to walk away from the pressures of our world to discover the identity God has given us. When we follow God's design for us instead of what the world calls cool, we might even find some amazing friends who have done the same thing.

⟩ On the Ball

What are you doing just because it's the cool thing? Talking or dressing a certain way? Ask God for the courage to stop. I'm going to stop _____ and start _____ instead.

- -

⟩ COACH'S COMMENT

We are God's handiwork, created in Christ Jesus to do good works, which God prepared in advance for us to do. EPHESIANS 2:10 (NIV)

- -

It all started with the jokes around the 1996 Atlanta Olympics, wisecracks about a bunch of rednecks hosting the world's biggest sporting event. So some self-described rednecks from East Dublin, Georgia, decided to host some real redneck games. They thought it would be a funny way to raise some money for charity and to celebrate their Southern heritage. They expected 500 people, but 5,000 showed up. The legendary Redneck Games were born.

The games have been held every July since then. They're a lot like the Olympics, with feats of strength and competitions of, um . . . well, at least they're funny. The usual events include the Hubcap Hurl (okay, that's like the discus), Bobbin' for Pigs' Feet (yes, real pigs' feet), Redneck Horseshoes (played with toilet seats), Mud Pit Belly Flop (like diving except it's all about a big splash), and Watermelon Seed Spitting (lots of baseball players spit too).

And no epic competition is complete without its traditions. These games are started with the ceremonial lighting of a barbecue grill. Of course, there's also an Olympic-inspired torch, but this one is made out of empty cans. Fans have even been known to get all nostalgic about a boy who serenaded the crowd by playing "Dixie" with his armpit. As they say in East Dublin, "Let the games begin, y'all!"

What's the Score?

Do the Redneck Games sound fun or repulsive to you? Either way, it's definitely a group of people playing up the stereotypes about their culture.

As humans, we are notorious for forming cliques and groups. There's nothing wrong with hanging with people whom you like and who share the same interests. But it is wrong to exclude others and to put down people based on how they look, how much money they have, or what games they like to play. Jesus taught his followers, "I am giving you a new commandment: Love each other. Just as I have loved you, you should love each other" (John 13:34). God's love isn't based on our shallow human judgments. Look past your preconceived ideas and focus on people's hearts. See others as individuals God made. Treat them like you'd want to be treated—no matter the color of their neck.

) On the Ball

Who have you judged unfairly? Talk to him or her today. Ask questions to find out what you have in common.

) COACH'S COMMENT

I am giving you a new commandment: Love each other. Just as I have loved you, you should love each other. JOHN 13:34

The sun proved to be the winner through 120 minutes of soccer in the 1999 Women's World Cup finals. The United States and China couldn't manage a goal, but the sun managed to push temperatures to nearly 100 degrees at the Rose Bowl in Pasadena, California. The players were exhausted. The 90,185 fans were about to collapse as well. As the teams prepared to take turns shooting penalty kicks, the players sat on the grass, guzzling water.

When the best players in the world shoot at the goal from just 12 yards away, the goalie doesn't have much of a chance to block the ball. China went first and scored against US goalie Briana Scurry. US captain Carla Overbeck answered with a goal. The teams traded goals again. Then Brianna made a diving save, punching away China's third attempt. The next four shooters all scored, which made it 4–4 with just Brandi Chastain left to shoot. The US defender approached the ball and pounded it with her left foot into the lower-right corner on the net. The United States had won their second World Cup championship!

What's the Score?

Brandi's goal clinched the championship. But without her teammates, she wouldn't have had the opportunity to win at all. Carla Overbeck, Joy Fawcett, Kristine Lilly, and Mia Hamm also scored. Plus, Brianna made a brilliant save. All these players were extremely tired after playing 120 minutes of soccer in very hot temperatures. But they all reached deep and found the extra strength to pull out the victory.

In the Bible, David needed an extra dose of strength from time to time, such as when he killed a lion, defeated Goliath, and hid from King Saul. In Psalm 18:32 he writes, "God arms me with strength." David knew his strength came from God. God designed our bodies with an amazing capacity for strength and endurance. Sometimes when we think we can't go on anymore, if we bear down and trust God, we discover the ability to keep going. That's what happened for the US women's soccer team, and it can happen for you, too.

) On the Ball

Think of a time when you were really tired. Maybe it was on a family hike or bike ride. Perhaps it was during gym class or during a sports game. Were you able to find extra energy that you didn't know you had? Thank God for giving you strength.

) COACH'S COMMENT

God arms me with strength, and he makes my way perfect. He makes me as surefooted as a deer, enabling me to stand on mountain heights. PSALM 18:32-33

God made Eric Liddell fast. The Scottish sprinter won a gold medal in the 1924 Summer Olympics. But Eric will always be remembered for his faith in Jesus Christ more than for his speed. In 1924, Eric was one of the best 100-meter sprinters in the world. He qualified for the Summer Games and was a favorite to win gold. There was just one problem: the 100-meter schedule called for the final heats to be run on Sunday—and Eric said he wouldn't run on the Sabbath, which God commanded to be a day of rest.

At first Eric was criticized for his decision. People begged him to reconsider for the good of his country. Eric stood firm. He trained and qualified for the 200 and 400 meters instead, but no one gave him much chance in those events. Yet Eric had faith that God would honor his decision. On this day in 1924, when the gun sounded for the 400 finals, Eric bolted from the blocks. He never trailed as he flew around the track and finished with a time of 47.6 seconds—a new world record!

☐☐ What's the Score?
Just before the start of the 400 finals, a British trainer handed a piece of paper to Eric. On it was written, "It says in the Old Book, 'Him that honours me, I will honour.' Wishing you the best of success always." Eric ran with that message in his mind as he captured the gold. That moment was highlighted in the Academy Award–winning movie *Chariots of Fire*, which was about Eric's life. In the movie, Eric's character says he could feel God's pleasure when he ran.

It does feel good to follow God. Making decisions that honor God gives us a good feeling inside. Eric's life proved that God honors those who honor him (1 Samuel 2:30). He stood up for his beliefs and didn't run on Sunday. And then Eric pulled off one of the best races in Olympic history.

) On the Ball
Have you ever been tempted to go against one of God's commands? It would've been easy for Eric to agree to run on Sunday and take part in his best event. Instead he risked not winning a gold medal and suffered the ridicule of other athletes and people in the media. When you're in a situation in which you are tempted to compromise your faith, remember what Eric did. And remember that God honors those who honor him.

) COACH'S COMMENT
The LORD, the God of Israel, says: . . . I will honor those who honor me, and I will despise those who think lightly of me. 1 SAMUEL 2:30

How long can you hold your breath? Get a watch and time yourself. What did you get? Thirty seconds? Forty-five? A minute? Studies show the average person can hold his or her breath for about 45 seconds. So can you imagine what it would be like to hold your breath for nearly 20 minutes? In July 2009, Karol Meyer held her breath for 18 minutes and 32 seconds while being submerged under 300 feet of water.

Karol has had the nickname "Fish" since she was a young girl. She started diving when she was little and began competing in free diving (in which an athlete holds his or her breath and dives as far as possible underwater) in 1996. By 2009, Karol held five world records, including longest time holding breath underwater. Before Karol went under the water, she inhaled pure oxygen to help her body get ready for the feat.

⬜⬜ What's the Score?

Karol trained her body to go without oxygen for a long time . . . a really, really long time. (And she used special techniques to allow her body to go deep underwater, so don't try this at home.) The human body needs oxygen to live. That's the way God created us. We naturally breathe in and out to sustain our lives. By breathing in pure oxygen before heading underwater, Karol was able to set a world record. She also holds the world record for holding her breath without first breathing in pure oxygen at seven minutes and 18 seconds.

The Bible says that God is ultimately in control of our lives. You've probably sung the song "He's Got the Whole World in His Hands." Well, in the book of Job it says, "The life of every living thing is in his hand, and the breath of every human being" (Job 12:10). Other verses in the Bible say that God knows how many days we will live. God is in control of everything. His power is limitless. God has big plans for your life. Who knows? Maybe someday you'll set your own world record.

⟩ On the Ball

Breathing comes naturally. For the next minute, every time you breathe in and out thank God for your life. Breath is a gift from God, and he deserves our praise.

⟩ COACH'S COMMENT

The life of every living thing is in his hand, and the breath of every human being.
JOB 12:10

Chelsey Kipping was head-over-heels excited about breaking a world record in July 2010. That's because she hoped to make a new mark for consecutive back handsprings. Chelsey had enjoyed gymnastics since she was four years old. She practiced more than nine hours a week at Barron Gymnastics in St. Louis, Missouri. So when the 13-year-old showed up to the Mon-Clair League's Valmeyer Mid-Summer Classic baseball tournament, where organizers had arranged for her to perform before the game, she was confident that she could beat the old record of 26 and raise some money for the league.

Chelsey started near third base and flipped toward right field. The baseball announcer and fans started counting as she began her first back handspring. "One, two, three . . ." The crowd kept counting until she hit 32! Chelsey had set a world record.

⬜ What's the Score?

Chelsey's main reason for back handspringing across a baseball field wasn't to set a record. Her motivation was to honor former Mon-Clair League president Mel Patton. Mel had been killed the previous year by a drunk driver. Chelsey, her family, and her friends showed up at the field wearing shirts that said, "This one's for you, Mel!" At the end of her record-breaking performance, Chelsey had raised more than $700 for Valmeyer's Mon-Clair baseball team and her gymnastics club.

In the Bible, God's people often did things to honor him. In the beginning of the book of Joshua, the Israelites crossed into the Promised Land as God held back the Jordan River. God commanded Joshua to choose one man from each of Israel's 12 tribes to pick up a stone from the middle of the river. The men carried these stones to the Israelite camp. Joshua set up these stones as a reminder of God's power and of the fact that God always keeps his promise.

⟩ On the Ball

Read Joshua 3:7–4:18. Sometimes it's important to create "standing stones" in your life so you can remember what God has done for you. Is there a time in your life when you really saw God's power at work? Maybe he didn't stop a river, but perhaps God kept you safe in an accident or healed somebody you love. Never forget that God is alive and active in your life. You may want to go outside and set up some stones in your yard so that every time you look at them, you'll be reminded of God's power.

⟩ COACH'S COMMENT

In the future your children will ask you, "What do these stones mean?" Then you can tell them, "They remind us that the Jordan River stopped flowing when the Ark of the LORD's Covenant went across." These stones will stand as a memorial among the people of Israel forever. JOSHUA 4:6-7

What do you get when you combine 150 school-aged children and thousands of LEGOs? Well, if you add a pastor and an architect, you might get the world's largest LEGO model of Noah's Ark. At least that's what happened when all these ingredients combined during a 2009 summer camp at Harvest Bible Chapel in Elgin, Illinois.

More than 150 kids helped build a replica of Noah's Ark that was a 1:37 scale of the original. That means for every foot of the LEGO ark, Noah's boat was 37 times bigger! In the end, the kids built a LEGO model that was 12 feet long, two feet high, and three feet wide. Based on computerized architectural plans, LEGO shipped the blocks to Harvest Bible Chapel from its headquarters in Denmark. The record-breaking boat was the biggest LEGO Noah's Ark ever created based on its size and the number of bricks used.

⬜⬜ What's the Score?

Everybody seems to know the story of Noah. Even kids who have never set foot in a church know that Noah built a huge boat to save the world's animals during a great flood. You might even think the story is a little childish. But we can learn a lot from Noah—and not just about boat building or how to care for thousands of animals in a confined space.

Noah stood up for his beliefs. People mocked him for building a gigantic boat in the middle of nowhere. But Noah didn't listen to them; he listened to God. God told him to build the ark, so that's what he did. The Bible notes that Noah was a righteous man who "walked in close fellowship with God" (Genesis 6:9). Wouldn't you want to be described as "righteous" and "in close fellowship with God"? By listening to God and following his commands, you can be.

⟩ On the Ball

Read about Noah's life in Genesis 6–8. What are the highlights for you? Write down some ways that you can follow Noah's example:

- -

⟩ COACH'S COMMENT

This is the account of Noah and his family. Noah was a righteous man, the only blameless person living on earth at the time, and he walked in close fellowship with God. GENESIS 6:9

- -

Surprisingly, the World Toe-Wrestling Championships were not held in Tokyo. Get it? Toe-kyo. Ha! At the 2010 competition in Ashbourne, England, two of the sport's best competitors successfully defended their titles by showing a lot of toe-nacity. In the men's division, Alan Nash claimed another world championship. For more than a decade, he had been one of the best at the sport. On the ladies' side, it was Lisa Shenton who earned her second title in as many years.

The sport of toe wrestling began in 1976 when a group of walkers in northern England took off their socks and put up their feet. The rules are very similar to arm wrestling. Opponents lock big toes and try to push the outside edge of their foe's foot to the side of the table. The winner of two-out-of-three rounds advances. Rules state that the foot not being used must be held in the air and the heel of the foot locked in battle must stay on the table. Although the sport may look a little silly, Alan said it requires strategy and strength. "You really feel it the next day," Alan added, "when your feet ache and start to swell."

What's the Score?

Feet are funny looking. They can even look a little gross. Before someone can compete in the World Toe-Wrestling Championships, his or her feet must be inspected. Athletes have been turned away due to corns, calluses, bunions, and athlete's foot fungus. *Yuck.*

The book of Isaiah says it's possible to have beautiful feet: "How beautiful on the mountains are the feet of the messenger who brings good news, the good news of peace and salvation" (Isaiah 52:7). God sees our feet as beautiful when we tell others about him. It doesn't take nail polish and a pedicure to create terrific looking tootsies. Just living for Jesus can give you fantastic feet—and lead you to fantastic feats.

) On the Ball

Think of some ways you can use your feet for Jesus. Tonight ask your parents to walk with you around your neighborhood and pray for your neighbors. Or use your feet to walk cookies over to some neighbors you don't know very well.

) COACH'S COMMENT

How beautiful on the mountains are the feet of the messenger who brings good news, the good news of peace and salvation, the news that the God of Israel reigns! ISAIAH 52:7

Matt Moniz was awestruck as he stood on top of Mauna Kea in Hawaii. The view from 13,796 feet on the Big Island would inspire anybody. But what made this moment extra special to Matt was the fact that he'd just climbed, walked, or biked to the highest point in all fifty states in a record 43 days, three hours, 51 minutes, and nine seconds! Oh yeah—it probably should be mentioned that Matt was just 12 years old.

Matt began his historic journey with his dad by climbing Mount McKinley in Alaska. At 20,320 feet, it's the highest point in North America. But he ran into a lot of trouble on Mount Rainier in Washington. Near the 14,410-foot summit, a storm blew in and stopped his progress. Matt said Guadalupe Peak (8,749 feet) in Texas was one of the prettiest. And when he summited Mauna Kea on this day in 2010, his journey was complete.

⬜⬜ What's the Score?

Matt proved that his age couldn't stop him from completing an amazing challenge. He made it even more fun by trying to discover the best root beer and hot chocolate on his trip. He decided the best root beer was found at the base of Mount Rainier, while the best hot chocolate was in Salt Lake City, Utah. During his adventure, Matt also made a stop in New York City's Central Park, where he spoke to a crowd of 25,000 people about the importance of getting outside and enjoying nature. Sure, Matt wanted to break a record and reach the highest point in every state, but his biggest goal was to get kids excited about being outside.

The Bible tells us that inspiring and caring for people is one of the most important things we can do with our lives. The apostle Paul wrote, "If I had such faith that I could move mountains, but didn't love others, I would be nothing" (1 Corinthians 13:2). It took a lot of faith for Matt to climb the highest mountains (of course, 345-foot Britton Hill in Florida wasn't too tough). But Matt's goal wasn't personal glory. He wanted to help other kids live healthier lives by getting outside. We need to be as committed to helping others and showing them Jesus' love.

⟩ On the Ball

How often do you exercise? Make sure you're keeping your body healthy. Get outside today to ride your bike, throw a Frisbee, or go swimming. Bring some friends along to show that you care about their health too.

⟩ COACH'S COMMENT

If I had such faith that I could move mountains, but didn't love others, I would be nothing.
1 CORINTHIANS 13:2

In the entire history of Major League Baseball, just over 50 players have strung together hitting streaks of 30 games or more. But in the summer of 1941, New York Yankees slugger Joe DiMaggio put on a hitting clinic. He hit safely in 56 straight games—an MLB record!

Joe started the streak against the Chicago White Sox on May 15. Over the next two months, Joe hit a blistering .408. He had 22 multihit games, 15 home runs, five three-hit games, and four four-hit games. But on this day in 1941, Joe's streak came to an end. In a game against Cleveland, Joltin' Joe went 0-for-3 at the plate. He even hit into a double play with the bases loaded. "I can't say I'm glad it's over," Joe told reporters after the game. "Of course, I wanted it to go on as long as I could."

What's the Score?

Joe didn't let that one bad game ruin the rest of his season. He hit safely in the next 16 games. At the end of the season, Joe won the American League Most Valuable Player award. When sports fans look back at Joe's record, they think one thing: consistency. Joe brought a consistent intensity every time he stepped into the batter's box. His 56 straight games with a hit totally eclipsed the old record of 45, which had been set by Willie Keeler from 1896 to 1897.

Consistency is also important in our relationship with Jesus. He wants us to consistently follow his commands. Of course we'll make mistakes. But we shouldn't let one bad day or bad decision mess up our walk with Christ. We need to ask forgiveness, put our mistake behind us, and push ahead. The longest chapter of the Bible, Psalm 119, encourages us to act consistently to reflect God's laws. When our actions line up with God's commands, we can be confident that we're living the way he wants us to.

) On the Ball

Doing anything 56 times in a row is difficult. Try batting a balloon in the air 56 times or throwing a ball in the air and catching it 56 times. Ask yourself if there's anything you can do to help your actions consistently line up with God's commands.

) COACH'S COMMENT

Oh, that my actions would consistently reflect your decrees! Then I will not be ashamed when I compare my life with your commands. PSALM 119:5-6

Think of a sport that takes a lot of strength. Football? That's a good answer. Weight lifting? Of course. But there may not be any greater display of strength than ripping a tree out of the ground and seeing how far you can throw it. Okay, the caber toss isn't exactly tree throwing. For starters, most cabers look more like telephone poles than trees, but they are wooden. They come in different weights, and each competitor is judged for how straight he can throw his caber. First, he balances the caber and then tosses it into the air, where it rotates, hits its opposite end on the ground, and continues falling over. If the end of the caber that starts in the thrower's hands ends up pointing directly away from him at the end, that's a great toss!

The caber toss is actually just one of the events that takes a lot of strength in the Highland games, which date back to 11th-century Scotland. The competitions, dances, and other festivities tie heavily into Scottish culture. At the 2009 Lochcarron Highland Games in Scotland, Sinclair Patience displayed an immense amount of strength. He won the shot put and the heavy shot. He also placed first in the hammer throw and the heavy hammer throw. And his caber toss tied him for second. Overall, Sinclair was named the Champion of the Day.

☐☐ What's the Score?

Highland games competitions take place all over the world. But at the Lochcarron games, spectators get a true feeling of history. They can almost close their eyes and imagine being at a festival 500 years ago.

The caber toss is the signature event of the games. But you couldn't have cabers without trees. Trees play a huge role in the Bible, too. Sin entered the world when Adam and Eve disobeyed God and ate from the tree of the knowledge of good and evil. Jesus died for our sins by being nailed to a tree. And when Jesus walked the earth, he talked a lot about trees. In Matthew 7:16-20, Jesus says you can recognize people by their fruit. Good people, just like good trees, produce good fruit. Evil people create nasty fruit and are eventually cut down and thrown into the fire.

) On the Ball

What kind of fruit do you produce? Do people find it sweet and appealing to hang around with you? Plant yourself in good soil with other good people so you will always produce good fruit. Make a list of the fruit your life is producing now. Ask yourself, "Am I a good tree?"

) COACH'S COMMENT

A good tree produces good fruit, and a bad tree produces bad fruit. MATTHEW 7:17

Jake Drummond turned a school project into a world record. Jake was just 14 when he had to look through the *Guinness Book of World Records* to do a report in school. He noticed that a man in Barbados had recorded a 100-meter time of 16.68 seconds while riding a wheelie on a bicycle. *I think I could beat that,* Jake thought. Jake had always loved bike riding. He had jumps, ramps, and berms built up in his backyard in Oshkosh, Wisconsin.

About a year later, Jake had taken all the steps to attempt to break the 100-meter wheelie world record. Electronic timing was set up on Oshkosh West High School's outdoor track. The proper video equipment was ready. Guinness officials had been informed. Riding his beloved mountain bike, Jake took off on his first attempt, but he couldn't hold his wheelie the entire 100 meters. On his second try, he posted a time of 16.01—a new world record. But Jake wasn't done. He pedaled out a time of 15.21 to break the old record by more than one second!

What's the Score?

Jake had always shown a natural ability on a bicycle. When he told his mother that he wanted to go for a world record, she thought it was a great idea. "He has loved bicycles his whole life," Jake's mom told reporters. "It just made sense. When we happened to come across the fact he could ride this fast, it was easy."

When things come easily for you, it's natural to think they're simple for everybody else. But that's not the case. God gives everybody different abilities and talents. Even if math is easy for you, your friend might struggle in it. From a young age, Jesus understood God's Word. When he was 12, Jesus' parents took him to Jerusalem. He ended up at the Temple, listening to and asking questions of the religious leaders. The Bible says, "All who heard him were amazed at his understanding and his answers" (Luke 2:47). Jesus didn't look down on people who didn't understand the Scriptures. He spent much of his ministry teaching people about God's Word and helping them understand it. God wants us all to use the abilities he gives us to help the people around us too.

) On the Ball

God wants you to develop your talents—whether those include math, bike riding, or playing a musical instrument. And we can all follow Jesus' example of digging into God's Word and gaining a better understanding of his commands. Practice your skill today, and thank God for the unique abilities he has given you.

) COACH'S COMMENT

All who heard him were amazed at his understanding and his answers. LUKE 2:47

Wilma Rudolph was the 20th of 22 children. Born prematurely, she weighed just four-and-a-half pounds. Before she turned five, she had battled through measles, mumps, chicken pox, scarlet fever, polio, and double pneumonia. Most of her childhood was spent in bed. Doctors told her she'd never walk normally. At age six, Wilma was fitted with a leg brace so she could get around a little better.

But less than 14 years later, Wilma would do more than "get around." At the 1960 Summer Olympics in Rome, Italy, Wilma won three gold medals and became the "fastest woman in the world." She won the 100-meter and 200-meter sprints, and she anchored the 400-meter-relay team to a first-place finish. In every event, Wilma set a world record with her time!

What's the Score?

Wilma had a difficult time growing up. She just wanted to play and run with the other kids, but all her illnesses kept her stuck inside. When she was diagnosed with polio, doctors put her left leg in a brace. But Wilma didn't give up on her dream. She rubbed her withered leg as she watched kids play outside. Her brothers and sisters took turns massaging her leg too. Every week, Wilma's mom took her to the hospital for treatments. By the time Wilma turned 11, her leg was strong enough to walk without the brace. And once the brace was off, she couldn't be stopped. She became an all-state basketball and track athlete in high school. Then she went on to Olympic glory.

Wilma had a lot of faith that she'd get better, but she also got a lot of help from her family. The Bible says, "A brother is born to help in time of need" (Proverbs 17:17). Wilma had plenty of brothers . . . and plenty of needs! Her brothers and sisters helped her heal, and they were there to play with her and to encourage her. Later in life Wilma said, "When you're from a large, wonderful family, there's always a way to achieve your goals."

On the Ball

Can you think of a time when a brother or a sister has helped you? What could you do to help him or her? This week do something special for your family so they will know that you'll always be there to help.

COACH'S COMMENT

A friend is always loyal, and a brother is born to help in time of need. PROVERBS 17:17

If you thought riding your bike with no hands down the street was hard, just imagine the difficulty of zooming off a nearly vertical ramp and spinning around two full times. That was just one of the tricks Jamie Bestwick threw down at X Games 16. By winning his fourth-straight gold in BMX Vert, the British-born rider made X Games history. Although some of the riders matched the height that Jamie soared above the ramp, none could compete with his array of technical stunts. He nailed an alley-oop 540, tossed in a few other 540 variations, and completed tailwhip flairs with ease. The smoothness and the complexity of his ride earned him 90 points—10 more than his closest competitor.

His victory at the 2010 X Games gave him seven gold medals in BMX Vert. In a radio interview before the X Games, Jamie had said, "I respect all the guys that I ride against, and I have a great time regardless of what the outcome is. But I put a lot of work into my riding. . . . I want Vert to look as good as it can be so that it will inspire a new generation of Vert riders."

☐☐ What's the Score?

Jamie wanted to be a role model with his BMX Vert ramp riding. Soaring nearly 20 feet above the edge of the ramp made his hard work obvious. He respected the sport and the other riders enough to put in the effort to be the best. By being a leader, working hard, and showing respect, Jamie made X Games history.

In the Old Testament, the prophet Micah tells God's people three things they need to do. He says that you're required "to do what is right, to love mercy, and to walk humbly with your God" (Micah 6:8). By showing these three characteristics, you can live power-fully for God. You don't have to do a lot of stunts and draw attention to yourself. You must simply do what is right, love mercy, and humbly follow God. Keep those three things in mind as you go about your daily life, and people will take notice.

) On the Ball

Memorize Micah 6:8. Whenever you're not sure how to act, keep that verse in mind. It'll go a long way in helping you live the way God wants you to.

) COACH'S COMMENT

O people, the LORD has told you what is good, and this is what he requires of you: to do what is right, to love mercy, and to walk humbly with your God. MICAH 6:8

Lance Armstrong only had a 50 percent chance of living. In 1996, doctors discovered Lance had cancer that had traveled to his lungs, abdomen, and brain. He had 12 tumors, some golf-ball sized, in his abdomen and two lesions on his brain. It appeared as if the career—and possibly the life—of one of the most promising American cyclists was over. Lance went through two surgeries, four rounds of chemotherapy, and numerous radiation treatments. Amazingly, by the summer of 1997, he was cancer free!

Lance started training with renewed dedication. In July 1999, he accomplished something that nobody thought was possible. He won the Tour de France, the biggest bike race in the world. The Tour de France takes 22 days, twists through super-steep mountain ranges, and covers more than 2,000 miles. Lance took the lead for good on July 13 as he pounded his way up the Alps. He continued to win stage after stage in the mountains, proving he was one of the best hill climbers in the world. When Lance rode into Paris near the end of the month, nobody could catch him. More than 500,000 people watched Lance win his first Tour de France.

☐☐ What's the Score?

After winning the Tour de France, Lance told reporters that his determination to do well was fueled by a desire to show cancer patients that anything is possible.

As Christians we know that all things are possible through Christ. There are count-less stories in the Bible of Jesus healing somebody. But God is more concerned about our eternal souls than our physical bodies. In the book of Jeremiah, the prophet says, "O LORD, if you heal me, I will be truly healed; if you save me, I will be truly saved" (17:14). God wants to heal our bodies and save our souls. If you think about it, our time on earth is pretty short. Even if we live 90 years, that's nothing compared to an eternity in heaven. So when you're sick or when somebody you love is fighting a disease, pray to God for his miraculous healing. At the same time, pray to be closer to Jesus and more dedicated to following him.

⟩ On the Ball

No matter what happens, trust God. We can't always explain why things happen, such as illnesses or other difficulties. But God has a plan. And like Jeremiah says . . . our praises should be for God alone!

⟩ COACH'S COMMENT

O LORD, if you heal me, I will be truly healed; if you save me, I will be truly saved.
My praises are for you alone! JEREMIAH 17:14

Before the Summer Olympics in Atlanta, Georgia, the US women's gymnastics team had never won a gold medal. But that changed on this day in 1996, thanks to a courageous performance by Kerri Strug. The four-foot-eleven-inch gymnast stood in the shadow of her more famous teammates Dominique Moceanu, Shannon Miller, and Dominique Dawes for most of the Games. But in the vault, her efforts—and her heart—shone like gold.

The United States entered its final event, the vault, with a .897 lead over Russia, a country that had won the team gold at every Olympics since 1948. Early in the vault, the US team struggled. One girl fell twice and posted a 9.2. Meanwhile, the Russian gymnasts churned out high scores on the floor exercise. Kerri needed a good score. But on her first vault, she landed awkwardly, slipped, fell, and heard a snap in her left ankle. Kerri could barely walk, but when she saw her score of 9.162, she knew she had to go again. Kerri quickly iced her ankle, said a prayer to God, and prepared for her next vault. As best she could, Kerri sprinted down the 75-foot runway, hit the vault, spun, flipped, and landed on two feet! Her ankle cracked with pain. But she managed to smile at the judges before collapsing in agony. Kerri's coach rushed to the mat and carried her away. Her score flashed on the scoreboard: 9.712. The United States had won the gold!

⬜ What's the Score?

Everybody in the Georgia Dome and watching on TV could feel Kerri's pain. It was one of the gutsiest performances in Olympic history.

The Bible encourages Christians to feel each other's pain. Hebrews 13:3 says, "Remember also those being mistreated, as if you felt their pain in your own bodies." There may be times in your life when you're treated badly because you believe in Jesus. In some countries, Christians are thrown in jail and beat up. God wants us to remember and pray for other believers who are mistreated. Feeling another person's pain is called empathy. Try to show empathy to people who are hurting, and then figure out something to make them feel better.

⟩ On the Ball

Can you think of somebody who's hurting now? Maybe it's a friend, a family member, or a teacher. Make a card, bake some cookies, or do something nice for that person to show you care.

⟩ COACH'S COMMENT

Remember those in prison, as if you were there yourself. Remember also those being mistreated, as if you felt their pain in your own bodies. HEBREWS 13:3

Tractors are designed for plowing, pulling, and performing other farm work. But Mike Hagan from Whitehall, Montana, used his tractor to set a world record. On July 24, 2008, Mike popped a wheelie on his tractor and drove for 5.3 miles with the front wheels off the ground! The truck driver didn't accomplish this by accident. He knew the world record for longest tractor wheelie had been set in 1995 at a distance of three miles. For four years, Mike worked and planned to accomplish this feat.

First, he knew he had to find the perfect tractor. It took him two years until he found a 1994 Ford 4630, 55-horsepower farm tractor. Then he worked for two years on the tractor, figuring out the safest and best way to drive it with two wheels off the ground. When the day came to attempt the record, Mike had his nine-year-old son, Layne, work as his crew chief. With family and friends watching, Mike popped the front wheels off the ground and drove that way for 30 minutes to set the world record.

What's the Score?

Mike knew the key to breaking the world record for tractor wheelie was to find the right equipment. He searched for two years. When he found the 1994 Ford tractor, it was like striking gold! He knew he had to have it. Mike bought it and put a lot of time into understanding how it worked, and it helped him reach his goal.

Jesus compared the Kingdom of Heaven to finding a treasure. In the book of Matthew, Jesus told the story of a man who discovered treasure in a field. The man went home, sold everything he had, and bought the field. Just like Mike's excitement at finding the perfect tractor, we need to be willing to sell everything and to buy in when we discover the truth of God's Kingdom. Discovering the depth of Jesus' love and forgiveness is like finding treasure. And the cool part is, once we find this treasure, nobody can steal it away.

) On the Ball

Do you treat your relationship with Jesus like a treasure? It's easy to take God's love for granted and to forget to treat him specially. Think of a way you can show God that you treasure your relationship with him. Then do it!

) COACH'S COMMENT

The Kingdom of Heaven is like a treasure that a man discovered hidden in a field. In his excitement, he hid it again and sold everything he owned to get enough money to buy the field. MATTHEW 13:44

Hawaii's Molokai Channel is considered one of the most challenging and treacherous stretches of water in the world. It's filled with big ocean swells and unpredictable waves and wind. These 32 miles of water between Molokai and Oahu consistently test the best paddleboarders in the world. At the 2010 paddleboarding championship, Australia's Jamie Mitchell proved he was still the "King of Paddleboard." Jamie won his ninth consecutive Molokai-2-Oahu World Paddleboard title on this day. Despite extremely challenging conditions, Jamie finished the race in four hours, 52 minutes, and 45 seconds—just four minutes slower than the record time he had set in 2007.

In the women's race, Kanesa Duncan-Seraphin proved she was equally dominant. The Hawaiian paddleboarder won her eighth title, with a time just over six hours.

⬜⬜ What's the Score?

Jamie earned his title of "King of Paddleboard." From 2002 through 2010, he rarely lost a race. And he was a perfect nine-for-nine at the world championships.

The apostle Paul encouraged the Christians in Corinth to "try to be perfect" (2 Corinthians 13:11, NIrV). Perfection doesn't come naturally. Just ask Jamie. It takes hard work. Even though the Molokai-2-Oahu race took place in July, he started seriously training in March. Waking up at 5 a.m., Jamie swam every day and then went on a long paddle (often more than 30 miles) each week. It takes similar effort to strive for perfection in our faith. We'll never be completely perfect until we reach heaven with Jesus, but until then we can work to become more like him. We need to build our spiritual muscle by reading the Bible and praying—even if that might mean waking up early every morning. We need to train ourselves to do the right thing by always telling the truth and by trying to follow God's laws. By putting in hours of effort and making good choices, we can see ourselves moving closer to perfection.

⟩ On the Ball

Even though no human can achieve perfection, you should strive to grow more like Jesus by knowing and following God's commands. Is there an area of your life that you need to work on? Maybe you struggle with anger, lack of patience, or pride. Through God's love and peace, you can conquer this area and live more like Jesus—which is perfect.

⟩ COACH'S COMMENT

Try to be perfect. Pay attention to what I'm saying. Agree with one another. Live in peace. And the God who gives love and peace will be with you. 2 CORINTHIANS 13:11 (NIrV)

David de Rothschild dreamed of crossing the Pacific Ocean in a boat made entirely out of plastic bottles. No kidding. Although most people thought it was a joke, especially after early versions of the ship kept breaking, David kept his dream alive. And on this day in 2010, David and his crew sailed into Sydney Harbor—completing their amazing 9,500-mile journey onboard a 60-foot ship named *Plastiki*.

It took four years to perfect the technique of holding the plastic bottles together to form the ship's hull. In the *Plastiki,* a boat made from 12,500 plastic bottles, David set sail from San Francisco in April. For four months he and his crew battled tough seas and uncomfortable conditions. David said the plastic bottles made a ton of noise as they sailed over ocean waves. "It was 100 degrees in [the cabin]—a plastic sweat lodge," David told reporters. "The creaking and slamming and banging was like trying to fall asleep on the side of a highway." All the sound did have a benefit, however. It attracted a lot of dolphins and whales that swam up to see what all the noise was about.

What's the Score?

David had a greater purpose behind his ocean journey than just achieving something amazing . . . and a little strange. He wanted to encourage people to stop polluting the world's oceans.

The Bible tells us that God gave life to everything (Nehemiah 9:6). He made the earth, every animal that walks on it, and every creature that swims in its seas. And when God created humans, he put us in charge (Genesis 1:26). He expects us to take care of his creation. That means we shouldn't abuse the planet. To be good stewards of God's creation, we can conserve its resources by taking shorter showers and make it more beautiful by not littering. By treating God's planet with care, we show him our appreciation for making such a wonderful world.

) On the Ball

What can you do in your area to be a good steward of God's creation? Maybe you could get a group of friends to pick up trash or start a recycling program at your school. Write down an idea or two:

1.
2.

) COACH'S COMMENT

You alone are the LORD. You made the heavens, even the highest heavens, and all their starry host, the earth and all that is on it, the seas and all that is in them. You give life to everything. NEHEMIAH 9:6 (NIV)

Pedro Barros entered X Games 16 as a virtual unknown. He left Los Angeles as an X Games gold medalist. The 15-year-old from Brazil showed a dizzying array of tricks and endless energy to win Skateboard Park. With the victory, Pedro became the first athlete who hadn't been born when the X Games first began to win gold.

Heading into the finals, Pedro knew he'd have to beat X Games veteran Andy Macdonald. Andy, who was 37, had won 20 X Games medals over the years. In the finals, Pedro pulled ahead by landing several 540s, flying over small and large gaps, and executing a low-to-high frontside smith grind on the biggest wall of the course. Pedro varied his runs and looked for different ways to showcase his talents on the curvy gray-and-red course in downtown LA. Andy didn't show as much creativity and fell on his fifth run. Pedro's final score of 86 proved to be five points better than Andy's 81.

What's the Score?

Pedro brought a lot of energy to the 2010 X Games. He had qualified for the finals of Skateboard Big Air but failed to medal. However, Pedro made the most of his opportunity in Skateboard Park. The excitement he showed made him an immediate crowd favorite as he walked away with the gold.

The Bible says everybody is judged by his or her actions. If you want to have a good reputation, be honorable in the way you act and treat others. King Solomon wrote, "Even children are known by the way they act, whether their conduct is pure, and whether it is right" (Proverbs 20:11). Your parents, teachers, and other adults will notice when you do the right thing. Try your best to represent Jesus in everything you say and do. As you consistently live out your Christian beliefs, people will become fans of yours, too.

) On the Ball

What kind of reputation do you have? When your conduct is pure and you do the right thing, people will know you as a good person. And as one of God's children, that's exactly the reputation you want to have. Write down three words you want people to use when they describe you.

) COACH'S COMMENT

Even children are known by the way they act, whether their conduct is pure, and whether it is right. PROVERBS 20:11

At the 2004 Summer Olympics, US super heavyweight weight lifter Shane Hamman stood five-feet-nine-inches tall and measured five-feet-two-inches around. Shane's barrel-sized chest had been built through years of farm work in Mustang, Oklahoma, and years of weight lifting in the gym. Heading into the Olympics, the 350-pound athlete had won seven straight US championships and had set numerous American weight lifting records.

In Athens, Greece, Shane broke two of his own records. He lifted 524 pounds in the clean and jerk, and he ended with a total weight of 948 pounds. However, Iran's Hossein Rezazadeh proved he was the world's strongest man as he lifted a combined 1,041.7 pounds to win the gold medal. Shane had to settle for seventh.

What's the Score?

Shane had dreamed of being an Olympian from the time he was eight years old. He played football and wrestled in high school and then fell in love with weight lifting. Pretty soon he was breaking world records in power lifting—even bench pressing 551 pounds and squatting more than 1,000 pounds! In 1996, Shane watched the Summer Games and decided to switch to Olympic weight lifting. Shane quickly mastered the new techniques and broke more than 30 American records. Shane knew God had blessed him athletically. Even at 350 pounds, Shane could do a standing backflip and dunk a basketball. Often during competitions, Shane would write "Jesus" on one of his shoes and "Can" on the other.

Shane always credited God with his success. "I feel really blessed that I was raised in a Christian home," Shane said. "I was able to keep my eyes straight on God my whole life, which was really cool." Shane saw God answer prayers and give him strength that he didn't know he had. At the 1999 National Weightlifting Championships, he took first place even though he had two dislocated wrists! The Bible says in Lamentations that "the LORD is good to those who depend on him. . . . It is good for people to submit at an early age to the yoke of his discipline" (3:25-27). Shane followed God from a young age. By putting God first, he experienced a multitude of blessings.

On the Ball

Do you put God first in your life? Make a commitment to be disciplined and to always follow him. Depending on God from a young age will make your life better.

COACH'S COMMENT

The LORD is good to those who depend on him, to those who search for him. . . .
And it is good for people to submit at an early age to the yoke of his discipline.
LAMENTATIONS 3:25-27

Carl Lewis may have grown up as a scrawny kid, but he turned into one of the best track athletes in US history. At the 1996 Summer Olympics in Atlanta, Georgia, Carl won his fourth consecutive gold medal in the long jump—proving his dominance in the sport for more than a decade!

As a child in New Jersey, Carl was small for his age and not as good in sports as his brothers and sisters. His parents coached track but encouraged Carl to take music lessons instead of playing sports. When Carl grew to six-feet two-inches in high school, he quickly became one of the best track athletes in the nation. At the age of 23, Carl won four gold medals at the 1984 Olympics (long jump, 100-meter run, 200-meter run, and 400-meter relay). But he was an underdog at the 1996 Games. Heading into his final jump, Carl was two inches behind the long jump leader. He sprinted down the runway, took off, and landed cleanly. Then he quickly sprang to his feet and put his arms in the air. The jump measured nearly 27 feet and 11 inches! That put him a foot ahead of the competition and earned him his ninth overall gold medal.

What's the Score?

Carl couldn't hold back his joy after winning his fourth straight gold medal in long jump. The Bible says God's followers won't be able to contain their joy when he returns. The prophet Malachi wrote, "For you who fear my name, the Sun of Righteousness will rise with healing in his wings. And you will go free, leaping with joy like calves let out to pasture" (Malachi 4:2).

Fearing God's name doesn't mean being afraid of him; it means being in awe of his power and giving him the respect he deserves. The Bible is clear that Jesus is coming back. When that happens, those who believe in him will be rewarded for their faith. We will leap for joy. Maybe we'll even jump farther than Carl Lewis.

) On the Ball

It's not always easy to be a Christian. Sometimes daily problems can get you down. At those times, look to the future. Have hope, and trust God that one day you will leap for joy. What's one problem you can give to God? Write it down: _____.

Now jump in the air, because God is bigger!

) COACH'S COMMENT

For you who fear my name, the Sun of Righteousness will rise with healing in his wings. And you will go free, leaping with joy like calves let out to pasture. MALACHI 4:2

When the pressure was on, Pierre-Luc Gagnon raised his game. On July 30, 2010, the crowd at Nokia Theater in Los Angeles was buzzing in the Skate Vert finals at X Games 16. Shaun White had pulled a frontside heelflip 540 varial (among other high-flying tricks) to score a 44 in his fourth run and take the lead. But Pierre-Luc stayed focused. He answered with back-to-back scores of 47 and 46 on his fourth and fifth attempts, for a total of 93 points—eight more than Shaun. The victory marked Pierre-Luc's third straight in Skate Vert.

Going into X Games 16, Pierre-Luc was the heavy favorite. He'd been putting together entire runs of tricks that none of the other competitors could perform. But when Shaun decided to compete after a long layoff from skateboarding, fans knew the competition could be close. Pierre-Luc pulled out the win with a 720 kickflip body varial and a massive body varial McTwist.

What's the Score?

Pierre-Luc's technical abilities and complexity of tricks were unmatched on the half-pipe. Later in the day, he added another X Games gold for Best Trick. The Canadian-born skater developed his skills through years of practice. While Pierre-Luc was growing up in Quebec, his father was a driving force in getting an indoor skate park built in his hometown of Boucherville. Pierre-Luc's father wanted his son concentrating on skateboarding and school, instead of getting caught up in negative behaviors. In fact, Pierre-Luc wasn't allowed to go to the skate park unless he got good grades and stayed out of trouble.

The Bible tells us what we should concentrate on if we want to avoid negative influences. Philippians 4:8 says to think about whatever is true, honorable, just, pure, lovely, commendable, excellent, and praiseworthy. What we put in our minds makes a big difference in our actions. When we focus our mind on good things, we're more able to stay out of trouble, make positive choices, and accomplish great things.

❯ On the Ball

What things are you focused on? Popularity? Being the best at a sport? The Bible says your thoughts should focus on truth, purity, and excellence. Write down a few good things you want to focus on more.

❯ COACH'S COMMENT

Whatever is true, whatever is honorable, whatever is just, whatever is pure, whatever is lovely, whatever is commendable, if there is any excellence, if there is anything worthy of praise, think about these things. PHILIPPIANS 4:8 (ESV)

What happens when 40-foot waves hit a 23-foot boat? You get a dangerous situation. Just ask Leven Brown, who led a group of four men in rowing a boat across the north Atlantic Ocean. The men took turns rowing for nearly 44 days to break a 114-year-old world record. Two Norwegian fishermen had set the old record of 55 days in 1896.

Leven and his crew left New York and soon encountered 40-foot waves and gale force winds. At times the boat would zoom down a wave going 17 miles per hour. It capsized twice! If the crew hadn't had safety lines connected to the boat, some of the men could've been killed. But Leven, Don Lennox, Ray Carroll, and Livar Nysted were all experienced rowers and knew what they were getting into. On this day in 2010, they reached the safety of St. Mary's Harbor in Great Britain's Isles of Scilly to complete their 3,500-mile journey.

What's the Score?

Leven already had earned three world records in ocean rowing before starting this trip. But even with all of his experience, he admitted the rough seas had him a bit scared.

The book of Mark tells the story of Jesus and his disciples getting caught in a storm. Jesus had finished a long day of teaching and wanted to go to the other side of the Sea of Galilee. As Jesus slept in the back of the boat, a storm came up that threatened to sink it. The disciples woke up Jesus, who promptly told the storm, "Silence! Be still!" The wind immediately stopped, and the waters calmed (Mark 4:39). The disciples were terrified by Jesus' power and asked each other, "Who is this man? . . . Even the wind and waves obey him!" (Mark 4:41). Of course, we know the answer to their question. Jesus was God's Son who has power over all creation. Don't you think Leven would've loved to have Jesus as a member of his crew?

) On the Ball

Read this story for yourself in Mark 4:35-41. Do any parts of the story surprise you? Why were the disciples scared with Jesus so close by? Why did Jesus ask the disciples, "Why are you afraid?" Take a minute or two to think about God's power. Then thank God that you can be a member of his crew!

) COACH'S COMMENT

When Jesus woke up, he rebuked the wind and said to the waves, "Silence! Be still!" Suddenly the wind stopped, and there was a great calm. MARK 4:39

Derek Redmond thought he'd been shot. That's what it felt like. One second he had been ahead of the pack in a 400-meter semifinal at the 1992 Barcelona Olympics. The next second he felt a snap in the back of his leg, and he fell. Derek was hurt—badly. Derek had torn his hamstring muscle. A previous injury had forced him out of the 1988 Seoul Olympics 10 minutes before his race. After surgeries and countless hours of rehabilitation, he had returned to training and qualified for the 1992 Games to finally achieve his dream of Olympic gold. Heading into the 400, he was the favorite to win.

The other runners blew by. Derek struggled back to his feet and began hopping. He knew he wasn't going to win, but he was going to finish. The crowd of 65,000 began to roar, urging Derek on. Suddenly he felt a familiar arm and heard a familiar voice. Derek's dad, Jim, had bolted from the stands, past security guards, to reach his son on the track. Derek leaned on his dad and sobbed bitterly. Together, father and son headed for the finish line.

"I'm the proudest father alive," Jim told the media. "I'm prouder of him than I would have been if he had won the gold medal. It took a lot of guts for him to do what he did."

☐☐ What's the Score?

Jim Redmond wasn't going to let anything or anyone stop him from reaching his son. He wanted to help his son any way he could. He gave Derek comfort and strength. That's the kind of father God is. The Bible calls him "our merciful Father and the source of all comfort" (2 Corinthians 1:3). He's there for us no matter what. He comforts us when our dreams shatter. He holds us and carries us on. And the Bible tells us he even uses our troubles to comfort and help others later.

Derek went on to become a motivational speaker who encouraged others to pursue and achieve their dreams. What did he show when he spoke? The video of his—and his father's—Olympic moment.

) On the Ball

If your dad is around, read today's story with him, and thank him for being there. And if you notice friends struggling with a problem you've been through, put an arm around them and help them out.

) COACH'S COMMENT

God is our merciful Father and the source of all comfort. He comforts us in all our troubles so that we can comfort others. When they are troubled, we will be able to give them the same comfort God has given us. 2 CORINTHIANS 1:3-4

Have you learned about the famous explorer Marco Polo and the great warlord Genghis Khan in school? If not, you probably will. Tim Cope had studied the historic pair, but he wasn't satisfied to just read about them in history books. In 2004, Tim set out to travel from Mongolia to Hungary on horseback—all 6,214 miles! For a year and a half the explorer followed the route Genghis Khan had used more than 700 years ago to build the largest empire in the world.

Tim quickly found himself alone in a ginormous wilderness scattered with nomads and herdsmen. When a local man returned Tim's lost horses early in the trip, he realized he would have to rely on others to survive. He stayed with more than 160 families during his journey. By the end of his trip, people started showing up to ride their horses along with him. Even though he was crossing a vast, lonely land, Tim succeeded on his journey by relying on the gracious hospitality of the local people.

⏸ What's the Score?

Do you ever feel alone? Do you ever feel like no one else cares about living for God? The famous Old Testament prophet Elijah did. After God's great victory on Mount Carmel (1 Kings 18), Elijah ran and hid in the wilderness. He complained to God, "I am the only one left, and now they are trying to kill me, too." But God reminded Elijah that there were still many more faithful people despite the persecution they all faced. And God brought Elijah another prophet, a man named Elisha, to help him (1 Kings 19:15-18).

We all need other people, especially on our loneliest quests. God encouraged Elijah and used other people to support him. We all have someone who cares about us and wants to help. Sometimes we just need to look up and reach out to realize it.

⟩ On the Ball

List the family members, friends, and others who love and care about you. When you're tempted to feel sorry for yourself, ask one of them for help.

⟩ COACH'S COMMENT

He replied again, "I have zealously served the LORD God Almighty. But the people of Israel have broken their covenant with you, torn down your altars, and killed every one of your prophets. I am the only one left, and now they are trying to kill me, too." 1 KINGS 19:14

No American gymnast had ever won an Olympic all-around gold medal. Not a single man or woman. But Mary Lou Retton had a chance at the 1984 Games in Los Angeles, California. The 16-year-old was in the lead on August 3, 1984. Ecaterina Szabo of Romania trailed by only .15 of a point. The two traded the lead as they moved through the four rotations. It all came down to Mary Lou on the vault. Ecaterina led by .05 of a point. Mary Lou could win gold, but only if she scored a perfect 10. "I'm going to stick it," she told her coach, Béla Karolyi.

The four-foot-eight-inch gymnast sprinted toward the vault as fast as she could. She leaped and sprang into an airborne, laid-out backflip with a twist. Both feet landed—and didn't budge. She stuck it. A perfect 10! The crowd erupted in cheers and applause. Mary Lou was a national hero. She brought home a gold that no other American had ever been able to claim.

☐☐ What's the Score?
There's nothing like gold. In sports, it's first place—the best. For treasure seekers, it's the ultimate prize. Throughout history, it's been used for money. It's what other valuables are compared to. If something's worth a lot, we say it's "as good as gold."

But there's something even better: God's Word. God's laws are "more desirable than gold, even the finest gold" (Psalm 19:10). Why? Because they satisfy much more deeply. Gold can be spent, and it's gone. Gold can be stolen or lost. But God's Word is good forever. God's ways are never used up. They keep bringing life, peace, satisfaction, meaning, and blessing. When the richest billionaires and winningest athletes die, their gold is worthless to them. It's done and gone. But after death is when God's Word begins to pay off treasures we can only imagine. Go for more than gold. Stick with God's Word, and you'll be truly blessed.

❭ On the Ball
Track your time this week. How much do you spend trying to be a better athlete, musician, artist, or student? How much do you spend trying to learn and follow God's Word?

❭ COACH'S COMMENT
The laws of the LORD are true; each one is fair. They are more desirable than gold, even the finest gold. They are sweeter than honey, even honey dripping from the comb.
PSALM 19:9-10

Samantha Larson thought it would be fun to go on a mountain climbing adventure with her dad—and not just because it meant she would get to miss a week of school. The 12-year-old and her dad climbed Mount Kilimanjaro, the highest peak in Africa at 19,340 feet. Samantha was no mountaineer. She was a good student who also played the oboe and danced. But she loved her African experience. She kept climbing with her dad. Then she set a goal: to climb the Seven Summits. Those are the collection of the highest peaks on each of the world's continents.

For the next eight years, Samantha and her dad tackled the rooftops of the world. She worked toward her goal literally one step at a time. She walked up and down mountains, including Russia's Mount Elbrus (18,510 feet), Alaska's Mount McKinley (20,320 feet), and the 16,864-foot Vinson Massif in Antarctica. Samantha was so committed to her goal that she put off going to college for a year after graduating from high school to train for her final mountain: Mount Everest. She saved the highest for last, and when Samantha and her dad reached the top in 2007, she was the youngest person to have climbed all the Seven Summits. Her goal was achieved!

What's the Score?

A goal is a target. It's something you decide to accomplish or work toward. Goals are good for us in all areas of life because they help us set our priorities and choose what's important to us.

There was nothing more important to the apostle Paul than knowing Jesus better and helping other people know Jesus too. He said, "I press on toward the goal to win the prize for which God has called me heavenward in Christ Jesus" (Philippians 3:14, NIV). It was his No. 1 goal. He was committed to it 100 percent. So he made sure that everything he did pointed him in that direction. We should make different kinds of goals in our lives. Goals can help us achieve greatness. But our No. 1 goal should always be living for God.

) On the Ball

Set three goals. Make one of them something about serving God.

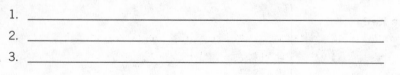

1. _____

2. _____

3. _____

) COACH'S COMMENT

I press on toward the goal to win the prize for which God has called me heavenward in Christ Jesus. **PHILIPPIANS 3:14 (NIV)**

It's the ultimate rags-to-riches story. One year Bébé was living in a homeless youth shelter. A few years later he had signed a contract to play for one of the most powerful soccer teams in the world, Manchester United. Oh, and they paid him $11.4 million!

How did that happen? Bébé was noticed by scouts while playing for Portugal in the Homeless World Cup. The Homeless World Cup happens every year in August. It's the brainchild of a South African man named Mel Young. He wanted to do something to fight homelessness, so he got creative. Homeless soccer organizations in more than 70 countries play year-round. So Mel planned a yearly tournament for them. Homeless World Cup games take place in the street or on the beach, not in fancy stadiums. Crowds often gather to cheer on the action. The experience is enough to change players' lives. Organizers say many of the homeless players break their drug and alcohol addictions, get educations, jobs, and homes. The story of Bébé going from homeless to millionaire is straight out of his—and Mel's—wildest dreams.

⬜ What's the Score?

What a creative way to help the homeless! The Bible commands us to help the poor. Psalm 82:4 says, "Rescue the poor and helpless." There are people in our towns with no place to live or eat. Most of them aren't poor by choice. They may have made some bad choices in life, but they've also probably endured hard times or sicknesses beyond their control. It can be difficult sometimes to know how to help. Talk to your parents, and try some of these ideas:

1. Pack snack bags to carry in the car. Share them with people asking for help on street corners. You might even include information about a local church or shelter that can help more.

2. Do an underwear or toiletries drive. Those aren't easy items for the homeless to get. And no one wants them secondhand.

3. Do a laundry-a-thon at a church or a coin-operated laundromat. Clean clothes are also hard for the homeless to come by. Think up your own ideas. There wasn't a Homeless World Cup either, until Mel started one to change lives.

⟩ On the Ball

Talk with your parents about how your family can help poor or less fortunate families around you. Try one of the above ideas, or come up with your own.

⟩ COACH'S COMMENT

Rescue the poor and helpless; deliver them from the grasp of evil people. PSALM 82:4

Richard Rodriguez was scared of roller coasters when he was a kid. He got over his fear. In August 2007, Richard rode a roller coaster for 401 hours straight to set a new world record for the longest roller-coaster marathon! Richard set the mark riding the Pepsi Max Big One at Blackpool Pleasure Beach in England. He rode the Big One almost 8,000 times and covered a distance equal to 6,300 miles! At 235 feet, the Big One is one of Europe's tallest roller coasters, and it reaches speeds of 75 miles per hour. It plunges 205 feet down its first drop, and riders experience a g-force 3½ times stronger than normal gravity.

Richard's mark of almost 17 days blew away the old record of nine and a half days. The new king of coasters could only get off the Big One for five minutes every hour. That meant he had to sleep, eat, and drink on the coaster. As far as it's known, he never threw up. That's a bonus accomplishment!

What's the Score?

Roller coasters are a blast. But it's also a good feeling to step off a roller coaster onto solid ground. Sometimes in life things can get so crazy and turbulent that we might say it feels like we're on "a roller-coaster ride" or "an emotional roller coaster." Most of us try to avoid those situations. But you may experience times when life jerks you around or throws you for an unexpected loop. One minute you're zooming along just fine. The next minute you're slammed into a free-falling corkscrew.

Those are the times we need to remember that "Jesus Christ is the same yesterday, today, and forever" (Hebrews 13:8). No matter what surprises or changes come our way, God stays the same. He is faithful and solid. We can hold on to him when our world feels like it's spinning. He will always hold us tightly and straighten out our track.

) On the Ball

On a separate piece of paper, draw a picture of a time your life felt like an out-of-control roller coaster. Then change the picture to show God keeping you safe and protected.

> COACH'S COMMENT

Jesus Christ is the same yesterday, today, and forever. HEBREWS 13:8

Have you heard people say they would die trying? Unfortunately, that's what happened at the World Sauna Championships. Russian Vladimir Ladyzhenskiy died August 7, 2010, in the finals. Saunas are popular around the world and especially in Finland. Steam is a good way to stay warm in the country's cold climate. But the sauna competition has always been too extreme. The idea is to see who can last the longest sitting in a steam-filled room where the temperatures can reach 230 degrees or more. It's basically a stubborn fest. Remember, water boils at 212 degrees. During past competitions, contestants had suffered medical problems, including burns and blisters. That kind of heat can essentially boil the skin.

Vladimir and five-time champion Timo Kaukonen were the last two competitors remaining in the 2010 finals. Sadly, Vladimir didn't make it out alive. Even Timo had to be put in the hospital for serious burns. Organizers said they would never hold the event again after Vladimir's death. It's sad that the stubbornness cost a life first.

⬜⬜ What's the Score?

There's a difference between persistence and stubbornness. Persistence can be a good thing as you keep trying to accomplish a goal. Stubbornness is persistence mixed with stupidity. Stubbornness refuses to listen to wisdom or common sense even when the results could be dangerous.

The ancient Israelites were stubborn as they kept disobeying God. The Bible also uses the phrase *stiff-necked* (Deuteronomy 9:13, NIV) to describe them. It's like the people gritted their teeth, clenched all their muscles, and shouted "I won't!" to God. Not smart. Their disobedience caused them pain, problems, and suffering. We often act the same way. We might know the right thing to do but refuse to do it. Don't be stupid—"Do not be stubborn, as they were, but submit yourselves to the LORD" (2 Chronicles 30:8). Choose obedience and God's peace, strength, and blessing. Choose to harvest good results from good decisions.

) On the Ball

Can you remember a specific situation where you were stubborn? Is there a certain area of your life where you show a lot of stubbornness? Obey God by obeying your parents in an area that you've been fighting them about.

) COACH'S COMMENT

Do not be stubborn, as they were, but submit yourselves to the LORD. Come to his Temple, which he has set apart as holy forever. Worship the LORD your God so that his fierce anger will turn away from you. **2 CHRONICLES 30:8**

Pork and beans are delicious. Pork and car is a little weird. But that's the idea behind the annual Pig N Ford Race at the Tillamook County Fair in Tillamook, Oregon. The winner of this yearly race is the person who can make it three laps around a track while driving a Model T Ford with a pig on his or her lap. Yep, a live animal. As in, "This little piggy went to the races."

The county has been holding this ridiculous event since 1925 when a couple of farmers had to chase down some pigs and thought, *Hey, good idea for a race.* Some of the same cars and families have been competing since the beginning. Competitors start by running across the track, grabbing a 20-pound porker and hand cranking their engines. Pause for a moment and remember that the Model T was the first affordable car built back in 1908—way before auto ignition. Okay, back to the race: next the drivers jump into their cars, drive a lap, turn off their engines, put the pig back in the pen, grab another pig, and do it all again, three times. *Phew!* There's a lot that can go wrong in this race, and it usually does. No word on what the pigs think, but they do seem to squeal with delight.

What's the Score?

You've probably grown up eating bacon, pork chops, or *carnitas* burritos. But the early Christians didn't. Pigs were declared unclean in God's law, so the Jews wouldn't touch them. That was a smart move, because it meant they were obeying God. That all changed when God sent Peter a vision and told him that Christians could eat anything: "The voice spoke again: 'Do not call something unclean if God has made it clean'" (Acts 10:15).

That doesn't sound like a big deal in our world of pizza and microwave meals, but it was huge for Peter and the early Jewish Christians. Why? Well, it showed that Jesus had brought freedom from the old law. He fulfilled and completed the old law so people like us can connect with God without having to follow tons of rules and regulations. Jesus gave us the chance to know God personally. The next time you bite into a bacon, lettuce, and tomato sandwich, remember you have extra reason to thank God.

) On the Ball

Can you imagine trying to follow all of the Old Testament laws? Thank Jesus for coming and setting you free from so many rules. Celebrate your freedom by cooking bacon and eggs (or another favorite meal) for your family.

) COACH'S COMMENT

The voice spoke again: "Do not call something unclean if God has made it clean."
ACTS 10:15

Jesse Owens was a soft-spoken man, but his performance at the 1936 Olympics made a statement loud enough for the whole world to hear. The Olympics that year were in Germany—Adolf Hitler's Germany, not long before World War II. Hitler proclaimed that the German race was superior to all others. He was especially prejudiced toward black and Jewish people. The Nazis and their swastika symbols were everywhere. They wanted to use the Olympics to prove that Germans were the best.

Talk about a hostile crowd! But Jesse, an African American sprinter, demolished Hitler's racist lies. He did it by winning not just one gold medal, but four! Between August 3 and 9, Jesse won the 100 meters, long jump, 200 meters, and 400-meter relay. No athlete had ever won four Olympic gold medals before. It took until 1984 for American Carl Lewis to repeat the feat in track and field. Jesse's medals were a great sports accomplishment, but an even greater victory for humanity. He showed the world that the color of a person's skin doesn't matter.

What's the Score?

Jesse received a ticker-tape parade in New York City after the Olympics, but he still couldn't ride the elevator with white people. Unfortunately, even the United States didn't treat all people equally in those days.

God designed all colors and races of people. The variety is part of the beauty of his creation. Jesus made it clear that he brought God's salvation and Kingdom to all people and cultures. Paul said it doesn't matter what our race, heritage, or social status is. He said, "There is no longer Jew or Gentile, slave or free, male and female. For you are all one in Christ Jesus" (Galatians 3:28). It's our job as his followers to treat all people equally with God's love. We might not win a medal, but our actions of reaching out to people of different colors can speak loudly.

On the Ball

Make friends with someone from another race, culture, or country. If everyone around looks the same as you, talk to your parents about finding a way to connect with other kids from different races.

COACH'S COMMENT

There is no longer Jew or Gentile, slave or free, male and female. For you are all one in Christ Jesus. GALATIANS 3:28

Oh, those silly Brits! They're head over heels for cheese. For hundreds of years people in the English countryside have been celebrating cheese by running down steep hills to chase after it. It's a traditional cheese roll. The cheese-loving race starts on top of an extremely steep hill. Someone rolls a wheel of cheese, and everybody runs after it. Bodies tumble. Cheese rolls. Injuries occur. Everyone laughs; well maybe not *everyone*. But the person who reaches the bottom first is certainly all smiles, because he or she wins . . . cheese, of course.

Sadly, the famous cheese-rolling event on Cooper's Hill in Gloucester was shut down in 2010 because no insurance company would cover the event. Organizers were worried about injuries during this extreme sport. But devoted cheese rollers wouldn't be stopped. Competitors came from around the world anyway and staged their own unofficial event.

What's the Score?

God calls us to live for him with the same reckless abandon shown by the cheese rollers—no holding back. On the hill of life, we should be willing to make sacrifices and take risks in order to follow God, no matter what. We must run after God with the same abandon as the cheese rollers who sprinted after the cheese.

And the cool part is that we receive something far greater than cheddar at the end of our race. First Kings 8:23 reminds us that God will "keep [his] covenant and show unfailing love to all who walk before [him] in wholehearted devotion." God shows us his faithfulness and love, and one day we'll receive his ultimate reward of eternal life. And there won't be any moldy cheese in heaven!

) On the Ball

What have you been holding back from God because of fear, selfishness, or embarrassment? Let go of it and go for what God is calling you to. "Lord, I give up _____ for you." Now remember your commitment to God every time you eat a piece of cheese.

) COACH'S COMMENT

O LORD, God of Israel, there is no God like you in all of heaven above or on the earth below. You keep your covenant and show unfailing love to all who walk before you in wholehearted devotion. 1 KINGS 8:23

Zach Nash was on top of the world. The 14-year-old had won a junior Wisconsin PGA tournament. He was proud. Later that day, as he talked with one of his golf mentors, they discovered 15 clubs in Zach's bag. Golf rules allow a golfer to carry only 14 clubs in a tournament. The penalty strokes Zach should have been charged would have kept him from winning.

What should I do? Zach thought. He could keep quiet and keep his medal. After all, Zach hadn't used the extra club. It belonged to a friend who had stuck it in Zach's bag the day before. But he knew golf prides itself on honesty and fair play. Zach was so upset he couldn't help but cry. That night Zach called PGA officials, told them what had happened, and surrendered his medal. It wasn't an easy decision, but it was the right decision. In the next tournament he played in, Zach counted his clubs three times.

⬜⬜ What's the Score?

What would you do? Keep quiet and keep your trophy or do the right thing and follow the rules? When no one is looking, it's tempting to make a bad decision. Satan often tempts us with the lie "No one will know." But lies and dishonesty have a way of always getting discovered sooner or later.

God calls us to live truthfully all the time. Jesus taught us, "If you are faithful in little things, you will be faithful in large ones" (Luke 16:10). In other words, when we handle little situations honestly, we show that we're ready for bigger responsibilities. You might have heard something like that from your parents. That's good advice. Follow through on the little things in your life, such as finishing homework or cleaning your room. By being faithful in these little actions, you develop good habits. And remember to tell the truth always, especially when no one is looking.

⟩ On the Ball

Are you hiding any lies or dishonesty? Come clean by confessing them today.

⟩ COACH'S COMMENT

If you are faithful in little things, you will be faithful in large ones. But if you are dishonest in little things, you won't be honest with greater responsibilities. LUKE 16:10

Dave Wiens had won Colorado's Leadville 100 mountain-bike race five times. That was before Lance Armstrong came to ride in 2008. Yes, that Lance Armstrong . . . the guy who won seven straight Tour de France races. Dave was a retired pro mountain biker, but it looked like his Leadville reign was over.

The Leadville 100 is intense. It's 100 miles on rugged mountain trails. Known as the "Race Across the Sky," it starts at 10,200 feet above sea level and rises to 12,600 feet—the highest elevation race in the United States. Air that high has less oxygen. If you lived in Florida and tried to run a 100-yard sprint at that elevation, you would be sucking wind like an industrial vacuum cleaner. Dave and Lance led the race together for about 90 miles. Finally, Dave pushed ahead and crossed the finish line first with a new record: a little under seven hours. Lance came in second almost two minutes later. So did Dave spike his bike and taunt the legendary pro? Not a chance. He credited Lance for a great race and acknowledged that he never could have set a new record without Lance's pushing him.

⬜ What's the Score?

Dave was obviously an incredible biker. Winning the Leadville 100 six times shows dominance. But Dave didn't have a big head, even when he beat the world's greatest cyclist. He respected Lance, and Dave knew that if Lance had been in peak condition he couldn't have defeated him. Dave's humility and honesty only made the win more satisfying.

The Bible tells us to have a similar attitude. Romans 12:3 says, "Don't think you are better than you really are. Be honest in your evaluation of yourselves." That kind of attitude starts with realizing that everything we have comes from God and with being thankful for all the help he gives us. A thankful, humble attitude also reminds us that God loves us no matter what—when we succeed fantastically or fail miserably. Be honest about your strengths and weaknesses. Be thankful for what you're good at and hopeful about what you're not.

⟩ On the Ball

Grab a piece of paper and make a list with two columns: 1. Things I'm Good At; and 2. Things I'm Not So Good At. Thank God for each strength, and ask him for help with each weakness.

⟩ COACH'S COMMENT

Because of the privilege and authority God has given me, I give each of you this warning: Don't think you are better than you really are. Be honest in your evaluation of yourselves, measuring yourselves by the faith God has given us. ROMANS 12:3

Pro snowboarder Andy Finch was on vacation with his wife in Europe when he received the kind of text you never want to get: "Emergency! Call now!" Andy's dad, Cliff, had led police on a high-speed chase. Shots were fired. Seven bullets hit Cliff, three in the head. Doctors didn't expect him to make it. Andy wasn't afraid of launching big air above the half-pipe, but this rocked his world. It was hard to figure out what happened. Cliff was a great dad who loved God, but depression and mental illness took over.

Praying was the only—and best—thing Andy could do. He immediately turned to God. His father's recovery and legal process was a long ordeal, but it was miraculous. Cliff ended up partially paralyzed, but his mental illness was controllable with medication. Andy and his family prayed for justice. They were thankful that Cliff's court sentence was probation, community service, and fines. About a year and a half later, Andy took his dad snowboarding using a special harness to support him. The Finch family's ordeal was terrible, but God stayed faithful through their darkest days.

⬜⬜ What's the Score?

There's no pain or tragedy that's too deep for God. He feels our pain and has compassion. Psalm 34:18 says, "The LORD is close to the brokenhearted; he rescues those whose spirits are crushed." In our worst moments, he's able to give us comfort and peace that are unexplainable. Remember when you were little and all you wanted to do was climb on your mom's lap when you got hurt? That made everything better. It's kind of like that with God.

What is breaking your heart? A friend who's ignoring you? A divorce or death in your family? Take it to God. Climb onto his lap. Cry and tell him how you feel. Let him wipe away your tears and give you comfort. He's the God who can work miracles in our most terrible times.

⟩ On the Ball

Write a psalm or poem to God. Be totally honest and tell him exactly how you feel. But thank him and praise him too. Let him help you like no one else can.

⟩ COACH'S COMMENT

The LORD is close to the brokenhearted; he rescues those whose spirits are crushed.

PSALM 34:18

At the 2010 World Yo-Yo Contest, Jensen Kimmitt turned the yo-yo into an art form. Jensen made that little circle dance. Actually, it was like he was dancing along with it. While music played, Jensen choreographed about three minutes of phenomenal moves that had his yo-yo zigging and zagging in unimaginable ways. He slung his yo-yo and slid it, tied and untied it. He yo-yoed behind his back and yo-yoed around his neck. He twisted and looped the string into boxes and triangles while the yo-yo spun at the end. Jensen threw his yo-yo around like a rodeo cowboy's lariat and even jump roped it without missing a beat. His performance brought the house to its feet and earned Jensen the world championship.

The tall, lanky Canadian looked like he was made to yo-yo. He became interested in yo-yo tricks when he was 10 and got hooked when his grandfather took him to see a master perform. He won contests and did street performances. During high school, he quit performing. But Jensen couldn't stay away long. He picked the yo-yo back up and quickly worked his way into the world ranks. The best part of Jensen's 2010 routine was how much fun it looked like he was having.

What's the Score?

What crazy, offbeat thing do you like to do? What's your quirky skill? Many athletes say they feel like they're worshiping God when they use the athletic skills he gave them. The truth is . . . they are.

You can worship God by making good use of what he's given you. There's a great image in 2 Samuel 6:5 of David and the Israelites dancing, singing, and playing music to God. They played "all kinds of musical instruments," probably whatever they could get their hands on. They were singing and banging with all their might. God must have loved it because they used what they had. Use whatever gifts you have—even the odd ones— to praise and worship God.

) On the Ball

Commit your talents to God, no matter how strange or unusual they are. Thank God for all of your abilities, and tell him you want to use them for his glory.

) COACH'S COMMENT

David and all the people of Israel were celebrating before the LORD, singing songs and playing all kinds of musical instruments—lyres, harps, tambourines, castanets, and cymbals. 2 SAMUEL 6:5

Michael Phelps became the greatest Olympic athlete of all time at the 2008 Beijing Games. In eight races, he won eight gold medals and set seven world records. It was an unbelievable accomplishment. Michael found all sorts of ways to win, including blowouts and relays when his teammates had to come from behind. He won the 200-meter butterfly without being able to see when his goggles leaked. But his closest and most famous victory was in the 100-meter butterfly.

Michael was losing on the last lap. He slowly closed the gap, but it looked like Milorad Čavić of Serbia would win the race. From an underwater view, it appeared as if Milorad touched the wall first. But the scoreboard showed a victory for Michael. Michael screamed and slapped the water in excitement. What happened? Michael chopped his normal last stroke short and flapped his long arms an extra time. It was enough to throw him forward to touch the wall before Milorad by 0.01 second—that's one one-hundredth of a second! Whatever it took, Michael found a way to win.

⬜⬜ What's the Score?

Paul is one of the most famous apostles. You could say he was the champion of the early church. Maybe that's because he was willing to do whatever it took to spread the good news about Jesus and to help the early Christians grow in their faith. In 1 Corinthians 9:19-23, Paul wrote about how he tried to make connections with all types of people. "I try to find common ground with everyone, doing everything I can to save some," he said in verse 22.

Paul wasn't two faced. He was true to Jesus and communicated in ways people could understand. What about you? Are you willing to do whatever it takes to show and tell others that you know Jesus? Are you willing to listen to others so you can best understand how to communicate God's love to them? Do you spend time doing activities they like? Do you try to understand their cultures? Do whatever it takes to love others like God does.

⟩ On the Ball

Think of a group of people you don't know that well. How can you get to know them better? How can you show them God's love? Put those ideas in practice.

⟩ COACH'S COMMENT

When I am with those who are weak, I share their weakness, for I want to bring the weak to Christ. Yes, I try to find common ground with everyone, doing everything I can to save some. 1 CORINTHIANS 9:22

Usain Bolt blew out of the starting blocks in the 100-meter finals at the 2008 Beijing Olympics. The long strides of the six-foot-five-inch Jamaican gobbled up track like a high-speed train. Midway through the race he had pulled ahead of his competitors. By 60 meters nobody could catch him. By 85 meters he knew it. Usain eased up and spread his arms, even before he crossed the finish line. His time was 9.69 seconds, a new world record!

Many people criticized Usain. They said he showboated and could have gotten a faster time if he'd run hard the whole way. Usain denied he was bragging. He said he was just so happy that he started celebrating early. A few days later, Usain tore through the 200 meters in the same way. But this time he pushed to the finish, stretching for every millisecond. It was another world record. Usain checked the clock, then took an exuberant victory lap. He leaped, danced, posed, and pointed like a man who, well, had just won one of the greatest sporting events in the world.

⬚⬚ What's the Score?

In the Bible book of Nehemiah, the nation of Israel had just returned home to Jerusalem after 50 years of captivity in Babylon—that's good. But their country was trashed—that's bad. They weren't jumping and leaping about. They had tons of work to do to rebuild their city, its wall, and the Temple. They all got together to read God's Law. Many of them cried, but Nehemiah reminded them that it was a time to celebrate.

Nehemiah pointed to the true source of strength. He told the people, "The joy of the LORD is your strength" (Nehemiah 8:10). Israel had started the race strong by making it back to Jerusalem, but they still had to keep their heads down to reach the finish line. God's people weren't running for a medal or a world record; they were working to stay safe and to build for the future. No matter what you're working on, remember to finish strong. You may run into difficulties and sadness, but in the end let the joy of the Lord bubble out in celebration.

⟩ On the Ball

Celebrate the good God has done for you. Sing songs to him even if you're feeling sad. Sing songs that thank him if you're feeling happy.

⟩ COACH'S COMMENT

Nehemiah continued, "Go and celebrate with a feast of rich foods and sweet drinks, and share gifts of food with people who have nothing prepared. This is a sacred day before our Lord. Don't be dejected and sad, for the joy of the LORD is your strength!" NEHEMIAH 8:10

Chelsea Baker prefers baseball to softball. That's bad news for the boys. In August 2010, the National Baseball Hall of Fame and Museum honored her as one of the best Little League players in the country. The right-handed pitcher had recorded two perfect games and posted a 12–0 record. It was her fourth-straight undefeated season for her team in Plant City, Florida. The seventh-grader could have played with a girls' softball team, but a baseball is much better for throwing her signature knuckleball. She learned the pitch from the former major-leaguer Joe Niekro.

Not everyone likes a girl playing against boys. Chelsea got used to lots of unkind comments from opponents. Many told her to go play softball. Chelsea learned to ignore them and let her game do the talking. Instead of getting mad or shouting back, she calmly and quietly kept striking out the boys. She struck out 127 batters in 60 innings in 2010. No matter what people said, Chelsea kept working to be the best at the game she loves.

⬜ What's the Score?

It's hard to face criticism and insults. They make us mad, and we want to scream or shove back. But reacting emotionally throws us off our game, both in sports and in life.

God told his people, "Only in returning to me and resting in me will you be saved. In quietness and confidence is your strength" (Isaiah 30:15). It's a great reminder of where our source of power is: God. No matter what's going on around us, we can turn to him. We don't have to fight back or defend ourselves against mean words or taunts. We can be confident that God will help us. We can trust him and use the talents he's given us— and keep getting the job done, just like Chelsea did.

⟩ On the Ball

Memorize Isaiah 30:15. Say it to yourself when someone makes fun of you or when you're nervous about something.

⟩ COACH'S COMMENT

This is what the Sovereign LORD, the Holy One of Israel, says: "Only in returning to me and resting in me will you be saved. In quietness and confidence is your strength."
ISAIAH 30:15

Big-league baseball players are the best in the sport, right? Sure, but even the best players have slumps. During the summer of 2010, Jayson Werth found himself in a big slump. The outfielder went three months without getting a hit with runners in scoring position and two outs. Every time he came to bat from May 19 to August 18 with a chance to knock in some runs, he made the third out. It was an 0-for-35 run. The Philadelphia Phillies even kept him out of games because of his struggling offense.

Slumps are a dreaded part of baseball. Players try all sorts of funny things to break them. Tim Naehring trimmed the word *hit* into his scalp in 1991. Ozzie Guillén dripped eye drops on bats to help them "see" the ball. Babe Ruth thought eating scallions would help. Don Baylor shaved his mustache in 1972. None of those tricks helped. *Hmmmm.* How did things work out for Jayson? He broke his slump and led the league in doubles for the year. And he ended up signing a new contract with the Washington Nationals for $126 million.

☐☐ What's the Score?

Slumps happen in baseball and in life, too. Some people call it bad luck. Others say things just aren't going their way. It can feel like God is a long way off. It's almost like your prayers bounce off the ceiling right back at you. Some of the Bible's greatest heroes went through spiritual slumps. David even asked God, "Why have you forsaken me?" (Psalm 22:1, NIV).

At times when you feel like you're in a horrible slump, remember that God never leaves you. He never changes even when our feelings do. He's always faithful. And he uses those times when we feel like we're alone in the wilderness to teach us new things. Hold on to God. Cling to his promises like they're your oasis in the desert. God is able to help us feel better even in our worst times—it's like he can pour a new, refreshing river through the driest desert. That's exactly what he told his people in Isaiah 43.

⟩ On the Ball

Search an online Bible for verses about hope and comfort. Choose one to memorize— or start with Isaiah 43:19. Don't get discouraged when you're slumping. God will always provide a way out. ·

⟩ COACH'S COMMENT

I am about to do something new. See, I have already begun! Do you not see it? I will make a pathway through the wilderness. I will create rivers in the dry wasteland. ISAIAH 43:19

Some teams are so good that they're simply unbeatable. In 1992 the United States assembled a basketball team that was unparalleled in its skill, talent, size, strength, and depth. It was simply called the Dream Team. But playing against it was a nightmare for the rest of the world.

Until 1989, NBA players weren't allowed to play in the Olympics. After a rule change, USA Basketball assembled its top all-stars, including Michael Jordan, Magic Johnson, David Robinson, Larry Bird, Charles Barkley, Karl Malone, and more. At the Olympics in Barcelona, even the other teams were in awe. It's not that they didn't want to beat the Dream Team; they just couldn't even come close. The Dream Team won every game by an average of 44 points! Croatia came closest to the Americans in the gold-medal game. They only lost by 32. NBA players still play in the Olympics, but no team has dominated like the 1992 Dream Team.

What's the Score?

The Dream Team was impressive, but it couldn't come close to God's dominance. The Bible tells us, "If God is for us, who can ever be against us?" (Romans 8:31). No one stands a chance against his plans—because Jesus won the biggest, world-changing victory in the universe. Jesus defeated death (how's that for a tough opponent?) when he rose from the dead after hanging on a cross.

Remembering that truth can give us confidence, hope, and strength when we feel like we're facing an overpowering opponent or problem. Try it. Who or what is making you feel like a loser? What problem is dragging you down? What are you worried about? God is bigger and more powerful than them all. Romans 8:37 goes on to say that even in the problems we face now, "overwhelming victory is ours through Christ, who loved us." If you're a Christian, you're a member of his dream team, and one day you'll celebrate the ultimate victory with him.

) On the Ball

Write a cheer or a song about God's ultimate celebration. Perform your cheer for your family after dinner. Maybe you can even get your other family members involved.

) COACH'S COMMENT

What shall we say about such wonderful things as these? If God is for us, who can ever be against us? ROMANS 8:31

Have you ever tried sailing without the water? It doesn't sound fun . . . or even possible. But at the annual Henley-On-Todd Regatta in Alice Springs, Australia, they have a blast! The whole series of boat races takes place in a sandy bed of the dried-up Todd River. When the bring-your-own-boat competition runs, it really runs. Racers run on foot and carry their homemade watercraft. Of course, there are also rowboats on train tracks, boogie-board towing, and sand skis that four people try to walk on at once. And the Battle Boat Spectacular is always a crowd favorite. It's a massive water fight between Pirates, Vikings, and the Navy.

As you can probably tell, no part of the Henley-On-Todd takes itself too seriously. The whole event is about having fun and raising money for charity. The local Rotary Club sponsors the regatta to raise money for local, national, and international charity projects. Since 1962, the regatta has raised more than $1 million!

🏈 What's the Score?

If the Henley-On-Todd Regatta teaches us anything, it's that earning money to give to others can be fun. That's something that God agrees with. The Bible tells us that "God loves a person who gives cheerfully" (2 Corinthians 9:7). Have you ever gotten a birthday gift from someone who really didn't want to give it to you? Maybe he threw it at you and snarled, "Take it!" Or maybe you had to pry the gift-wrapped box out of her hands. Greedy attitudes like that make you not even want the gift.

How's your attitude when you give to God? He doesn't need our money. Giving to his work is for our own good, not God's. It helps us remember who really owns all our stuff. And it helps us to be thankful to God and generous toward others. Check your attitude the next time the offering plate passes at church. Plan ahead how much of your allowance you will give. Picture all the good your money can help a church or ministry do. Picture the kids or families it can help. Worship God in your heart as you hand over your cash . . . and get excited about giving.

⟩ On the Ball

List three ways you'd like to see the money you give help people. Then give it.

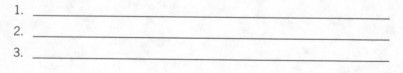

1. _____

2. _____

3. _____

⟩ COACH'S COMMENT

You must each decide in your heart how much to give. And don't give reluctantly or in response to pressure. "For God loves a person who gives cheerfully." **2 CORINTHIANS 9:7**

Surfing can be peaceful, but it can also create peace. Just look at Dorian "Doc" Paskowitz. This 80-something-year-old founded Surfing for Peace to unite surfers in the Middle East. Doc loves the sport of surfing. Although he lived in the United States, he has been credited with introducing surfing to Israel. The retired doctor first visited the Holy Land in the 1950s and has taken trips and surfed there ever since.

On this day in 2007, Doc went on a surf mission trip to the Middle East. He and world-champion surfer Kelly Slater brought 14 surfboards to a fortresslike border crossing between Israel and the Palestinian city of Gaza. Gaza was a place where Israelis and Palestinians constantly fought. The Israeli guards didn't want to open the gates and barriers for Doc and his friends. It took five hours of persuading before the surfers were allowed through. Finally, Doc walked through the barricades and he and his friends handed the boards and the shirts off their backs to a group of grateful Palestinian surfers on the other side. It was one small gesture with big significance. Doc hoped the boards would create more surfers who could unite with their enemies over their love for waves.

What's the Score?

There are plenty of conflicts in the world. They happen between nations, tribes, families, and schools. They probably even happen in your class. The Bible records a lot of fighting in the Old Testament. But Jesus brought a different approach in the New Testament. He taught us to live in peace. He said that people who work for peace will be called God's children (Matthew 5:9). And James said, "Those who are peacemakers will plant seeds of peace and reap a harvest of righteousness" (James 3:18).

Sometimes we think of peace as being wimpy. Wrong. Creating peace takes hard work. It's hard to forgive when we get mad and want revenge. It takes courage to get in the middle and keep others from fighting—or to stand up for someone against a bully. It shows wisdom to not pick a fight with your sister, even if she has wronged you. Making peace is often braver than making war. And it's following Jesus' way.

) On the Ball

Choose to take a peacemaking action toward the person you fight with most. I'm going to _____ for _____.

) COACH'S COMMENT

Those who are peacemakers will plant seeds of peace and reap a harvest of righteousness. JAMES 3:18

Bryan Clay was exhausted, and rightfully so. He had just won the Olympic gold in the decathlon—one of the Olympics' most demanding sports. On August 22, 2008, in Beijing, China, Bryan became the 12th American to win decathlon gold. His score of 8,791 points beat Belarus's Andrei Krauchanka by 240 points, the biggest winning margin in the Olympics since 1972.

Simply competing in an Olympic decathlon, let alone winning it, is no easy feat. Decathletes must master not one . . . not two . . . but 10 different track-and-field events! To win, athletes like Bryan must excel in the 100-meter dash, long jump, shot put, high jump, 400-meter dash, 110-meter hurdles, discus, pole vault, javelin, and the 1,500-meter run.

Phew! Makes you tired just reading the list of all those events!

⬜⬜ **What's the Score?**

As a decathlete, Bryan showcased quite a few special abilities that God had given him. Instead of being prideful, Bryan was thankful to God for all of his gifts. Bryan is a strong Christian who gave glory to God for his skills. As fellow believers, we should do the same. You might not be able to run as fast or jump as high or throw as far as Bryan can, but God has given you unique gifts to use for his glory.

How? Great question! First, identify your gifts. It's not a matter of *if* you have gifts, but *which* ones you have. First Corinthians 12:7 says, "A spiritual gift is given to each of us so we can help each other." Maybe your gifts are athletic or musical. Maybe you're good with your hands or you excel in math, science, or art. Maybe you just like helping others. Maybe you like to write. Pray for God to reveal to you what gifts he has given you.

Then use them for God's glory, not yours. You can follow Bryan's example. He often spoke to others about how God gave him skills as a decathlete. He also used his fame and money to create the Bryan Clay Foundation that helps kids in need. He used his gifts to show other people the love of Christ. You can too!

⟩ **On the Ball**

Make a list of your interests and the things you are good at. Then read 1 Corinthians 12 and Romans 12:6-8 to identify if any of your interests and abilities are actually spiritual gifts.

⟩ **COACH'S COMMENT**

A spiritual gift is given to each of us so we can help each other. 1 CORINTHIANS 12:7

Brazilians have a reputation for being the best soccer players in the world. Even blind Brazilian players have mastered the "beautiful game." Yes, you read that correctly. Brazil won the World Blind Football Championship on this day in 2010. They held a tough squad from Spain scoreless to win 2–0.

Having a hard time believing there's such a thing as blind soccer? It's pretty amazing. Five players from each team play at a time. They all wear blindfolds to make sure everyone's vision is completely blocked. (Some of the legally blind players have a little bit of vision.) Only goalkeepers are allowed to have sight, but they still get scored on. That's because these players are good! These blind athletes show fantastic footwork as they dribble down the field.

But how do they know where the ball is? Crowds have to stay silent except after goals. Players listen for ball bearings rattling inside the soccer ball to know where to run. Each team also has a coach who stands behind the goal to shout instructions to the players. You could say these amazing players keep their "ears" on the ball, not their eyes.

What's the Score?

Do you think about what you want to do when you grow up? There are a lot of options. Even deciding which sport to play or if you want to try out for the school play can be hard. Do you get confused about what's right or wrong? In Isaiah 30, God promised his people, "Right behind you a voice will say, 'This is the way you should go,' whether to the right or to the left." He was promising to help and guide his people. In a lot of ways, God's Spirit is just like the coach of the blind soccer team who can see the whole field and tell his players which way to go.

Our job, just like the soccer players' job, is to listen for that voice. God usually won't speak to us out loud, but his Spirit guides our conscience. He also uses the Bible and wise people like our parents to direct us with trustworthy advice. Turn to those sources for help when you're confused or questioning, and sharpen your spiritual ears to hear your heavenly Coach.

⟩ On the Ball

Ask your parents or church leaders about a time when God helped them make an important decision.

⟩ COACH'S COMMENT

Your own ears will hear him. Right behind you a voice will say, "This is the way you should go," whether to the right or to the left. ISAIAH 30:21

Allyson Felix had big dreams heading toward the Beijing Olympics in 2008. She wanted to win gold medals running in the 100 meters, 200 meters, 400-meter relay, and the 1,600-meter relay. But things didn't go as she planned. First, Allyson narrowly missed qualifying for the 100 meters at the US Olympic Trials, so that race was out and so was the 400-meter relay. At least she still had her specialty, the 200 meters. Allyson had won silver in that race at the 2004 Olympics in Greece. She was the reigning world champion and the clear favorite at the distance. But on race day, Jamaica's Veronica Campbell Brown finished first. Allyson was second. The 22-year-old American went home with one gold from her only other race, the 1,600-meter relay. But losing the 200 stung.

Allyson was disappointed, but she stayed gracious. One reason that made it easier for her to stay positive was Allyson had made it clear she was running for God's glory—whether she won or lost. She saw her speed as a gift from God. She welcomed her attention as a world-class runner so she could point others to her Savior. "Whatever I can do to bring someone to him, whether it's through my actions or if I'm able to say something to affect someone, I realize that's what he's given me this gift for," she said.

What's the Score?

The eyes of the world were on Allyson. She knew about "a huge crowd of witnesses to the life of faith," both on the track and in everyday life. And she was determined to "run with endurance the race God has set before [her]" (Hebrews 12:1).

God wants us to do the same. We won't win every race, but we can still keep trying and giving it our best. We should train our spirits to follow Christ, just like Allyson trains her body on the track. Don't let anything slow you down. Get rid of sin or bad influences that hold you back. Let the support and cheers of Christians around you give you a boost, and keep going for God!

) On the Ball

Is there anything holding you back in God's race? Doubt? Fear? Laziness? Write it down. Then determine to overcome it and run with endurance.

) COACH'S COMMENT

Since we are surrounded by such a huge crowd of witnesses to the life of faith, let us strip off every weight that slows us down, especially the sin that so easily trips us up. And let us run with endurance the race God has set before us. HEBREWS 12:1

For years, Mary Decker was the queen of American distance running. She was considered the best in the world, but she had never won an Olympic medal. An injury kept Mary out of the 1976 Games. An American boycott kept her from competing in the 1980 Olympics. But in 1984, she was favored to win the 3,000 meters when the Olympics came to Los Angeles.

Mary and two other runners jumped to an early lead. About halfway through the race, the barefoot 18-year-old Zola Budd from South Africa moved slightly ahead of Mary. Zola cut over sharply. Mary's toe hit Zola's foot, and she fell—tearing a hip muscle in the crash. Mary's hopes for an Olympic medal shattered. The crowd booed. Zola felt awful and gave up the race. After the race, Zola attempted to make an apology, but the heartbroken Mary told her not to bother. Much later, both runners apologized and admitted they should have handled the whole event differently.

What's the Score?

Life can get heated, just like a close race. We have to stay alert and keep our guard up. There are many obstacles that can trip us and keep us from obeying God. Sometimes temptations snag us. Sometimes we believe lies that contradict God's Word. Sometimes other people cause us to stumble, either on accident or on purpose. That's what happened to Mary and to the Christians in the city of Galatia. Paul wrote to them, "You were running a good race. Who cut in on you to keep you from obeying the truth?" (Galatians 5:7, NIV).

We need to choose friends who will run beside us, not cut us off. Think of them as your teammates. They can help you run your fastest and avoid obstacles. And remember, when you do hit an obstacle, to keep obeying the truth. That's the best way to run a good race.

) On the Ball

Do you have a friend who cuts you off and keeps you from obeying God's truth? You might need to stop hanging out with that person.

) COACH'S COMMENT

You were running a good race. Who cut in on you to keep you from obeying the truth?
GALATIANS 5:7 (NIV)

It's the way you dream of winning a game. Georgia's Dalton Carriker stepped to the plate in extra innings of the 2007 Little League World Series and belted a walk-off home run. The final score was Southeast 3, Japan 2. Dalton's teammates from Warner Robins, Georgia, mobbed him as he crossed home plate. They hugged and jumped and shouted and celebrated.

But the Japanese players were crushed. On the field, some of them fell to their knees, crying. The Georgia players noticed how distraught the Japanese were and cut their celebration short. They walked over and began hugging their Japanese opponents. It was a classy display of true sportsmanship.

▢▢ **What's the Score?**

The Warner Robins Little League team showed a lot of sportsmanship by consoling the Japanese team. Not only did a lot of players on the team want to show they were good sports, but they also wanted to show how they lived out their faith in God. "I'm a very religious person," Dalton said. "I go to church and just got to thank the Lord for all he's given us."

It's easy to get caught up in sports rivalries and not live out our faith on the playing field. Sometimes you may even think of the other team as enemies, but they're not. They're actually a lot like you. If you were on the same team, you might even be friends. But even if they were enemies, Jesus told us to love them. He said, "Love your enemies! Do good to them" (Luke 6:35). He told us to bless those who hurt us, give more to people who demand from us, and do good to those who hate us. That goes against our human nature. We want to hate our enemies and pay them back. Loving them takes God's help and strength, but he always gives it to us. Start living out your faith by reaching out with kindness to your opponents.

⟩ **On the Ball**

Make a point of congratulating the other team and players whether you win or lose.

⟩ **COACH'S COMMENT**

Love your enemies! Do good to them. Lend to them without expecting to be repaid. Then your reward from heaven will be very great, and you will truly be acting as children of the Most High, for he is kind to those who are unthankful and wicked. LUKE 6:35

Do you ever have dreams in which you can fly? A lot of kids do. Many people have wished they could fly like the birds. Way back in the 1480s, Leonardo da Vinci studied flight and sketched flying machines. Centuries before that, the ancient Greeks made up the story of Icarus, who got airborne but flew too close to the sun. The dream of human-powered flight lives on, even with all our modern aircraft.

At the Red Bull Flugtag in August 2010, 34 teams of wannabe pilots came to California to launch their homemade flyers off the Long Beach Pier. *Flugtag* means "flying day" in German. Good description. The goal of Flugtag was to see who could fly the farthest off the 30-foot-high pier. Everyone eventually crashed into the ocean, but Team Peepin' It Real claimed victory by soaring 98 feet. You know those sugary marshmallow birds called Peeps that are famous at Easter? The winning aircraft was a giant yellow Peep with a cockpit and propeller. The all-female team was a group of mechanical and aerospace engineering students. Seems like their education is paying off.

⬚⬚ What's the Score?

When Jesus looked at the birds, he probably didn't wish he could fly. Instead he taught his disciples—and us—an important lesson. "Look at the birds," he said in Matthew 6:26. "They don't plant or harvest or store food in barns, for your heavenly Father feeds them. And aren't you far more valuable to him than they are?" In other words, don't worry. Even though you can't fly, you are much more important to God than the birds. He will take care of you and give you what you need.

What do you get worried about? Grades? Friends? Popularity? Your family? God cares about all the details of your life. He wants to work them out for your best. He also sees the big picture and knows what's the best overall. Not everything will work out exactly like you would want it, but God promises to take care of you no matter what. Keeping that truth in mind can help keep you soaring.

⟩ On the Ball

Every time you see a bird today, thank God for how much he values you.

⟩ COACH'S COMMENT

Look at the birds. They don't plant or harvest or store food in barns, for your heavenly Father feeds them. And aren't you far more valuable to him than they are? MATTHEW 6:26

The Olympic racer had only learned to swim nine months earlier. But Eric Moussambani had been invited to the 2000 Olympics in Sydney, Australia, through a special program to spread sports around the world. He had never even swum in an Olympic-sized pool, which is 164 feet long. His small country in Africa—Equatorial Guinea—only had two swimming pools. He trained at a hotel pool that was 65 feet across.

In Sydney, the other two swimmers in Eric's 100-meter freestyle heat both false-started and were disqualified. So when the gun sounded, Eric dove in to swim alone. His stroke looked more average Joe than Olympian. Spectators began to notice Eric's struggle after his awkward turn. As Eric flailed along, the crowd began to roar, urging him toward the finish. They weren't sure if he'd make it or drown. Eric the Eel, as he was later nick-named by reporters, splashed to the finish. His time was more than a minute slower than other racers, but he became a hero. After the race he thanked the crowd, saying it was their cheering that had kept him going.

What's the Score?

Eric the Eel gave his best, but he needed more. He needed the crowd. Their cheers gave him new strength, and he was able to race farther than he ever had before.

We need other people in our spiritual lives, too. That's why church is so important. The Bible tells us, "Let us not neglect our meeting together, as some people do, but encourage one another" (Hebrews 10:25). Worshiping together helps build our spiritual muscles and pumps us up for the rest of our week. Our family and Christian friends cheer us on. They help us stay on course in life's race for God. When we get tired or feel like giving up, we can hear their support and keep going. We can give the same kind of encouragement to others, too. Together we can reach the finish like a whole pack of "eels."

) On the Ball

Look around church this week at the people who cheer for you. How can you pass the same kind of encouragement to others?

) COACH'S COMMENT

Let us think of ways to motivate one another to acts of love and good works. And let us not neglect our meeting together, as some people do, but encourage one another, especially now that the day of his return is drawing near. HEBREWS 10:24-25

Have you ever been snorkeling? If so, you probably did it in warm, tropical waters filled with brilliantly colored reefs. You might have seen swarming schools of exotic fish or even sea turtles, sharks, eels, or rays. Bog snorkeling is nothing like that.

The World Bog Snorkeling Championships take place each August in the smallest town in Great Britain: Llanwrtyd Wells, in Wales. What's a bog? Think of a peat bog as a type of spongy, grassy swamp. There's a canal cut through it for the competition, and the water is like a bug-infested soup. Swimmers have zero visibility in the murky, brown liquid. Wet suits are highly recommended. Competitors swim two lengths in the 60-foot canal but can't use traditional swimming strokes. It's no aquatic paradise, but at least the money raised goes to charity.

⬜⬜ What's the Score?

You could say bog snorkeling is a cheap imposter of ocean snorkeling. If all you ever knew was splashing around blindly in muddy, slimy bog waters, you would miss out on the wonderful sights found in the ocean. Being able to tell the difference between the real thing and an imposter takes discernment, which means being able to see and tell the difference; it's a skill God wants us to have.

We need discernment every day to tell the difference between God's truth and and others' lies. We're bombarded by all sorts of messages. Movies, music, TV, video games, and advertisements all look and sound cool, but many of the messages are directly opposite of the Bible. It's like they're telling us that bog water is the best around. If we believe it, we'll miss out on God's see-through-blue tropical pools. As Paul wrote, we need "to understand what really matters" (Philippians 1:10). When we do, we can choose messages that pull us closer to God and help us obey and reflect him. Otherwise we're just swimming in a stinking swamp.

⟩ On the Ball

Practice discernment. List a few of your favorite songs, movies, games, or shows. Think carefully. What are they really about? Do they push you closer to God or pull you away from him?

1. _____
2. _____
3. _____

⟩ COACH'S COMMENT

I want you to understand what really matters, so that you may live pure and blameless lives until the day of Christ's return. PHILIPPIANS 1:10

Some people work and sweat and practice for years to reach the Olympics. Once they're in, they get one chance to give it all and win a medal. Lawrence Lemieux had his chance in the 1988 Seoul Games. Things were going well for the Canadian sailor even though 40-mile-per-hour winds whipped up choppy waves. Lawrence was in second place. That's when he saw two other sailors from a different race who were in the water. Their boat was upside down. Lawrence knew they needed help. He veered off course and abandoned his race to rescue them. Once Olympic officials took the two sailors from Singapore ashore, Lawrence finished his race. He finished last.

Lawrence was disappointed but knew he had done what he had to do. The International Olympic Committee (IOC) gave Lawrence an honorary silver medal. It was one of only nine that had ever been handed out. The IOC said Lawrence's rescue represented the true spirit of the Olympics. Twenty years after his Olympics, Lawrence said he would still do the same thing and make the rescue.

⬜⬜ **What's the Score?**

Lawrence is a perfect example of what the apostle Paul meant when he told us, "Don't look out only for your own interests, but take an interest in others, too" (Philippians 2:4). What would you have done if you had trained for years to reach your Olympic dream? It's easy for us to go after what we want, but how often do we look around? Who's having a bad day? Who is hurting? Who needs a hug or a high five? Who needs some help with homework or extra practice on the court?

There are many easy ways to help people around us. But sometimes helping another person means we have to sacrifice. Are you willing to give up something that means a lot to you in order to help someone else? Start by looking around to see who is in need. Then ask God to give you his strength—and offer to help.

⟩ **On the Ball**

The people I know who need help are

    1. _____

    2. _____

    3. _____

I can _____ to help them.

- -

⟩ COACH'S COMMENT

Don't look out only for your own interests, but take an interest in others, too.
PHILIPPIANS 2:4

- -

If Bob Burnquist was going to do a 900, he was going to do it differently. Four other people in the world—all friends of his—had already perfected a trick that required the skateboarder to spin two and a half times on a skateboard. But different has always been Bob's style. So at the end of the summer in 2010, the Brazilian-American pro skateboarder did the world's first 900 on a MegaRamp, fakie to fakie. (Translation: Bob rode down the 180-foot-long supersized ramp and flew over a 70-foot gap of open space with a giant trapeze net below. Then he landed on and slid down a curved rail and shot onto a lower ramp. He landed backward, rolled up, and flew straight up a 25-foot quarterpipe wall. As he launched above its edge, Bob spun the 900, reaching about 40 feet above the ground, and landed backwards.) Impressive.

Oh, and Bob did this in his backyard. He owns the world's only permanent Mega Ramp. Skaters from all over the world can try it or practice on it, if they're brave enough. Skateboarding has always respected innovation. If there was any doubt, Bob sealed his legacy as a skater willing to reach new heights by taking different paths.

☐☐ What's the Score?

It's much easier to go with the crowd and do what everyone else is doing. But Jesus calls us to live differently. The world wants us to cruise down its wide, comfortable road. It promises feel-good fun, parties, and riches—but it all ends in pain and destruction. Jesus said, "The gateway to life is very narrow and the road is difficult" (Matthew 7:14). There won't be as many people on it, so it could be lonely sometimes. But the end reward is life with God that will go beyond what you can imagine.

The next time you feel like you're the only one not going with the crowd, look past the here and now. Focus on God's future payoff, and know that Jesus is with you on the narrow road.

⟩ On the Ball

What are the people around you doing that you know is wrong in God's eyes? Draw a picture of how God sees those activities.

⟩ COACH'S COMMENT

You can enter God's Kingdom only through the narrow gate. The highway to hell is broad, and its gate is wide for the many who choose that way. But the gateway to life is very narrow and the road is difficult, and only a few ever find it. MATTHEW 7:13-14

The final score made sportswriters all across America reach for their thesauruses. It was *stunning, astonishing, unthinkable, inconceivable*, and virtually any other word you can think of to describe what was once thought impossible: Appalachian State 34, Michigan 32.

On this day in 2007, Appalachian State's football team pulled off possibly the greatest upset in the history of college football. The virtually unknown Mountaineers, a Division I-AA team from Boone, North Carolina, traveled to "The Big House"—Michigan's intimidating 110,000-seat football stadium in Ann Arbor—and beat the mighty Wolverines. Michigan, then ranked No. 5 in the country, was considered a national-championship contender with a roster loaded with future NFL players. Appalachian State was the two-time defending I-AA champ, but no one expected them to beat Michigan. The Mountaineers' victory was the first win for a Division I-AA team over a I-A team in 18 years!

⬜ What's the Score?

The Bible includes many shocking stories and miracles. But there's one that tops them all: the resurrection of Jesus Christ. Jesus' resurrection, though, isn't just a cool ending to a feel-good fairy tale. It's an actual, real-life event that concluded a difficult journey on earth for God's Son. The Bible says that after dying on the cross, Jesus rose from the dead three days later and then appeared to hundreds of eyewitnesses. On Resurrection Sunday, Jesus appeared to at least five women near his tomb (Luke 24:10), two travelers on the road to Emmaus (Luke 24:13-15), and some of his disciples (Luke 24:35-36). Over the next 40 days, Jesus appeared to his disciples at least twice more (John 21:14), to 500 other believers at once (1 Corinthians 15:6), and to his half-brother James (1 Corinthians 15:7). Years later, Jesus also appeared to the apostle Paul in a miraculous vision (Acts 9).

The truth of Jesus' resurrection is essential to the Christian faith. In fact, Paul says in 1 Corinthians 15:3 that it is "most important." If Jesus wasn't raised from the dead, the Christian faith would be "useless" (1 Corinthians 15:14). But Jesus isn't dead—he's alive! And that means Jesus really is God's Son who can take away sins. Praise God!

⟩ On the Ball

Hold an "Easter in September" party! Read the Resurrection accounts in Luke and John, and thank Jesus for dying on the cross and rising from the dead.

⟩ COACH'S COMMENT

I passed on to you what was most important and what had also been passed on to me. Christ died for our sins, just as the Scriptures said. He was buried, and he was raised from the dead on the third day, just as the Scriptures said. **1 CORINTHIANS 15:3-4**

Chicago Cubs fans know what it's like to suffer under "The Curse of the Billy Goat." Seriously. The Cubs, more than any other Major League Baseball team, know heartache. Heading into the 2011 season, their last World Series title had come in 1908, making it baseball's longest streak of futility. To give a little perspective, the Cubs' last championship came before World War I, the invention of the television, and before most Americans owned a car. We're talking ancient history!

According to legend, it's all because of a goat. During game four of the 1945 World Series between the Cubs and the Detroit Tigers, a man named Billy Sianis and his pet goat were kicked out of Wrigley Field by Cubs owner Philip Wrigley. Angry about being ejected, Billy placed a curse on the Cubs that they would never win another National League pennant. The Cubs lost that World Series and, over the next 65 years, never returned.

What's the Score?

Still, the Curse of the Billy Goat? It sure sounds ridiculous. Lots of teams fail to win championships. That doesn't mean they are all cursed. Believing in sports curses is just silly superstition. But there *is* a curse in the Bible that's true. In fact, it is one of the most profound, wonderful truths in all of Scripture. Are you ready? It might shock you. . . . Jesus was cursed by God.

You're probably shaking your head right now thinking, *No way! How could God the Father curse his own Son?* It's simple: he had to. Galatians 3 tells us that anyone who breaks God's law is cursed—or cut off from God. That's bad news for us because we have all sinned (Romans 3:23). But here's the good news. Jesus paid for our sins by becoming the curse for us. He died on the cross so we wouldn't have to be separated from God if we put our faith in Jesus. And God accepted Jesus' sacrifice. That's evident because God raised him from the dead. What amazing love Jesus showed us by taking the curse of sin upon himself!

On the Ball

Read Galatians 3 to more fully understand this incredible truth.

COACH'S COMMENT

Christ has rescued us from the curse pronounced by the law. When he was hung on the cross, he took upon himself the curse for our wrongdoing. For it is written in the Scriptures, "Cursed is everyone who is hung on a tree." GALATIANS 3:13

Whisper. Go ahead. Whatever comes to mind, just say it in a whisper. Are you done? Reed Doughty wouldn't have been able to hear you. Sometimes Reed can't hear someone speaking in a normal voice when he is standing a few feet away. You see, Reed has severe hearing loss in both ears. That alone is not unique. Lots of people have hearing problems. But Reed is a safety for the Washington Redskins.

Football, more than most major sports, is a game of communication. At any given time, there are 22 players on the field, each with a vital role. Instructions are relayed from the sideline and discussed among players before every play. Then moments before each snap, both teams shout out other information, based on how the other team lines up. All this happens while 70,000 fans are screaming at the top of their lungs. It doesn't sound like the ideal job for a person with hearing difficulties, does it? Yet Reed has played more than five NFL seasons. He overcame his challenges by memorizing hand signals, reading lips, and immersing himself in his playbook.

☐☐ What's the Score?

Reed, a Christian, trusted in God to help him through his challenges. Maybe you have some type of special need like Reed. Or maybe your difficulty is completely unrelated to physical ailments. Whatever you are facing in life, there is a God who is bigger than your problems and wants to use you for his glory.

In Exodus 3 and 4, God called Moses to lead the Israelites out of Egyptian slavery. But Moses hesitated, claiming he was slow of speech. God reminded Moses that he had made him and could put words into his mouth. Moses eventually obeyed and became one of the Bible's greatest heroes. No matter what your challenge, God can do mighty things through you if you trust in him. Just like Reed Doughty and Moses did.

⟩ On the Ball

Write down any challenges (physical or otherwise) you might have:

Now look up Bible verses to speak truth into your life and encourage you.

⟩ COACH'S COMMENT

The LORD asked Moses, "Who makes a person's mouth? Who decides whether people speak or do not speak, hear or do not hear, see or do not see? Is it not I, the LORD? Now go! I will be with you as you speak, and I will instruct you in what to say." **EXODUS 4:11-12**

Mark Herzlich was used to tough opponents. As a star linebacker at Boston College, he regularly faced some of the best football teams in the country. But in 2009, Mark encountered his greatest foe yet: cancer. Doctors discovered a large cancerous tumor in Mark's left leg. He was forced to undergo six months of chemotherapy and four weeks of radiation treatment. He also had to have a 12-inch titanium rod inserted into his leg. In October 2009, he was pronounced cancer free, but he had missed the entire season while recovering.

Finally, on September 4, 2010, Mark played in his first game in 21 months, making four tackles in Boston College's 38–20 win over Weber State. His inspirational comeback story made national headlines. "Not many of us have experienced miracles," Boston College head coach Frank Spaziani told reporters. "Mark experienced one."

☐☐ What's the Score?

Jesus was in the business of miracles. During his public ministry on earth, he healed the deaf, blind, mute, sick, leprous, paralyzed, demon possessed, and those with all other sorts of maladies. He even raised the dead. But Jesus had a greater purpose than healing sickness. His greatest concern was healing people's hearts.

As scary as cancer (or any other life-threatening disease) is, each of us faces a far more deadly foe—our sin. Disease can kill the body, but sin can destroy our souls and separate us from God forever. When Jesus healed people, he wanted to see their faith more than anything. We see one example of this in Mark 2, when Jesus heals a paralytic, who went to great lengths to see Jesus. Interestingly, Jesus didn't heal him right away, but rather told him, "My child, your sins are forgiven." Only later did Jesus heal the man physically.

Jesus knew the man's greatest need was to be reconciled to God through the forgiveness of his sins. We also must remember that our greatest need is not our physical health, but the salvation of our souls.

⟩ On the Ball

Pray for people you know who are sick. And if they aren't Christians, pray for God to save them from their sins.

⟩ COACH'S COMMENT

"I will prove to you that the Son of Man has the authority on earth to forgive sins." Then Jesus turned to the paralyzed man and said, "Stand up, pick up your mat, and go home!"

MARK 2:10-11

Bethany Hamilton never saw the shark coming. Bethany, a native of the small Hawaiian island of Kauai, was a born surfer. By age eight, she was winning surfing competitions and seemed destined for a career as a star professional surfer. But one fall day in 2003, as she was surfing with several friends off Kauai's North Shore, a 14-foot tiger shark attacked her, severing her left arm. Her friends bravely paddled her back to shore, where she passed out waiting for the ambulance after losing 60 percent of her blood.

Incredibly, after several surgeries, a one-armed Bethany was back on her surfboard within a month. She even fulfilled her lifelong dream by competing on several different professional surfing tours. She gained international fame for her incredible tale of survival and perseverance. In 2011 a feature-length movie about her life entitled *Soul Surfer* was released in theaters around the world.

Bethany tried to honor God throughout her trial. She has traveled the world to share her faith and to encourage others to overcome obstacles for God's glory.

☐☐ What's the Score?

Bethany was a great example of God using human weakness to show his power. Most people would doubt that a one-armed surfer could win in a sport that relies heavily on balance. But Bethany did just that. God has worked through her physical limitations to bring glory to his name.

He wants to do that with you, too. God often puts us in difficult situations to humble us and to show us where we truly draw our strength from. When you run into a difficult time, don't resist him. Thank him for the great things he is about to accomplish through you!

) On the Ball

Think about one area in life in which you are weak: sports? math? reading? music? Now think about how God can show his power through your weakness.

) COACH'S COMMENT

Each time he said, "My grace is all you need. My power works best in weakness." So now I am glad to boast about my weaknesses, so that the power of Christ can work through me.
2 CORINTHIANS 12:9

Imagine going to school for seven straight years without taking a sick day. Yikes! Not exactly your idea of fun, right? But that's the equivalent of what Baltimore Orioles Hall of Fame shortstop Cal Ripken Jr. did during his career. From May 1982 to September 1998, Ripken played in 2,632 consecutive games, breaking what was once considered one of Major League Baseball's untouchable records—the 2,130 consecutive games played by New York Yankees Hall of Famer Lou Gehrig, who retired in 1939. (Divide 2,632 by 365—the number of days in a year—and it equals roughly seven years!)

As surely as a baseball is round, Cal laced up his spikes and took the field every day for 16 straight seasons, often playing through nagging pain and injuries. For his toughness, faithfulness, and dependability, he earned the nickname "Iron Man." When Cal finally broke Gehrig's record on September 6, 1995, the Orioles honored him in a memorable way at Camden Yards. At the end of the fifth inning, when it became official, the game was paused for more than 20 minutes as banners reading "2,131" were unfurled on the iconic warehouse behind the outfield bleachers. Cal enjoyed the moment by taking a victory lap around the stadium, high-fiving fans along the way.

What's the Score?

No matter how he felt, Cal did his job every day in a faithful, dependable manner. His manager and teammates could always count on him. And he eventually got rewarded with an unforgettable night and a Hall of Fame statue in Cooperstown, New York.

Christians are supposed to be like that too. There are no days off in the Christian life. God calls his children to a lifetime of obedience marked by serving him and loving others, no matter how we feel. At the end of our lives, if we have been faithful to do what God has asked of us, we will receive a rich reward. He will bring us into heaven and shower us with unimaginable blessings!

⟩ On the Ball

Think of one thing you can do each day this week to faithfully serve God and others. Write down your ideas:

+ Monday: _____
+ Tuesday: _____
+ Wednesday: _____
+ Thursday: _____
+ Friday: _____
+ Saturday: _____
+ Sunday: _____

⟩ COACH'S COMMENT

The master was full of praise. "Well done, my good and faithful servant. You have been faithful in handling this small amount, so now I will give you many more responsibilities. Let's celebrate together!" MATTHEW 25:21

Angel McCoughtry was on fire. The Atlanta Dream's star forward had enjoyed a fantastic 2010 WNBA regular season, averaging 21.1 points to finish as the league's third-highest scorer. But on this night—game two of the Eastern Conference Finals on September 7, 2010—she was otherworldly, doubling her regular-season average and setting a WNBA play-off record with 42 points in a 105–93 win over the New York Liberty that sent the Dream to its first WNBA Finals.

Angel continued her superhuman pace in the finals against the Seattle Storm, averaging 25 points over three games. In fact, in game three, she poured in a WNBA Finals–record 35 points and nearly rallied Atlanta to victory with nine points in the final 2:30 of the game. But it wasn't enough. Seattle held on for an 87–84 victory to win its second league championship.

☐☐ What's the Score?

Angel's impressive performance in an overall losing effort by her team is a good reminder of an important spiritual truth. Life isn't always going to work out the way we hope, even when we give our best effort. In a fallen world, occasional failure is just a fact of life.

But that's okay. The final score is not ultimately what should inspire us. No matter what we do, our motivation should never come from a desire for personal glory, worldly success, or any other selfish reasons. Winning is not the top priority. We are called to honor God in every aspect of our lives, regardless of the outcome. Whether it's sports, school, or other activities, God wants us to give our best effort for him. We should strive for excellence in everything because God gave us our talents and it glorifies him when we use them to the fullest.

) On the Ball

Make a list of how you can glorify God in your favorite activities and hobbies. Review that list before you participate in each one.

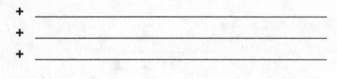

+ _____

+ _____

+ _____

) COACH'S COMMENT

Whatever you do, work at it with all your heart, as working for the Lord, not for human masters, since you know that you will receive an inheritance from the Lord as a reward. It is the Lord Christ you are serving. COLOSSIANS 3:23-24 (NIV)

You had to feel a little sorry for Donovan McNabb. Philadelphia Eagles fans didn't even give him a chance. In 1999, a group of Eagles fans traveled to New York City for the NFL Draft. Philadelphia had the second overall pick, and many of its fans—including the rowdy group in New York—were hoping the team would select Ricky Williams, the dynamic running back from the University of Texas. Instead, the Eagles chose Donovan, a quarterback from Syracuse.

As soon as the selection was announced, the Eagles fans booed. Yep, that's right. Before Donovan had a chance to prove himself, he was met with frustrated, cynical jeers. It was the start of a complicated love-hate relationship between Donovan and the team's fans.

There were plenty of good times. From 1999 through 2009, Donovan became the most successful quarterback in Eagles history by setting the team's all-time records for pass attempts, completions, yards, and touchdowns. During his 11 seasons in Philadelphia, he went to six Pro Bowls and led the Eagles to six play-off appearances and one Super Bowl. But some fans never fully embraced Donovan since he failed to win a championship. Before the 2010 season, the Eagles traded him to their NFC East rival, the Washington Redskins.

What's the Score?

Did Donovan deserve the boos and negative fan reaction over the years? Probably not, given his overall performance. Most NFL quarterbacks would love to have his career numbers and accomplishments. But nobody ever said NFL fans were fair.

It's the same for followers of Jesus. The Bible says that Christians will be teased, persecuted, and even hated—all because of their faith. If you are willing to talk about Jesus publicly, you should expect negative reactions. It might not be fair, but that's the way this sinful, messed-up world works. Jesus warned his disciples of this in John 17. As funny as it sounds, being persecuted for your faith is a good thing. When people treat you unkindly for your faith, it means you are different from the world. And that is exactly what God calls you to be (John 17:15-17). Donovan didn't let the boos stop him from doing well in the NFL. Neither should we in our Christian lives.

) On the Ball

Pray that God would give you the strength and courage to honor him when people make fun of you for your faith.

) COACH'S COMMENT

I have given them your word. And the world hates them because they do not belong to the world, just as I do not belong to the world. JOHN 17:14

Talk about girl power. The 2010 football season was a historical one for Calvin Coolidge High School in Washington, DC. The head coach wore earrings, had long, braided hair, and spoke in a high-pitched voice. That's because the head coach was a woman. When Coolidge had hired Natalie Randolph the previous March, it created a wave of headlines nationwide for her gender-busting efforts in a male-dominated sport. In 2010, she was believed to be the only female head coach of a high school football team in the country, and one of the only women *ever* to have the job.

Natalie, who had played for a semipro female football team called the DC Divas before coaching, was featured on several national TV shows and on the cover of *Parade* magazine. Coolidge received media credential requests for its 2010 season opener from all four major DC-area TV stations, as well as HBO, ESPN, the *New York Times*, the *Los Angeles Times,* and *Forbes* magazine, among others.

What's the Score?

Natalie dared to be different, despite the pressure and gender-biased comments that swirled around her and questioned her abilities. She stood up for what she believed in.

God wants his children to do the same. No matter what other people say or think of Christians, we are to obey God—not cave in to the pressure around us. That's kind of like Daniel. He was a young man among the Jewish exiles deported to Babylon after King Nebuchadnezzar's army overthrew Jerusalem in the sixth century BC. The king ordered Daniel and three friends—Shadrach, Meshach, and Abednego—to eat food that was forbidden by Old Testament law. Rather than going with the flow and avoiding harassment, Daniel and his friends obeyed God's law. In doing so, their very lives were in danger. But God protected and blessed them. Daniel and his friends pleased God by being different from the world around them.

⟩ On the Ball

Pray that God would give you courage to be different from the world.

⟩ COACH'S COMMENT

Daniel was determined not to defile himself by eating the food and wine given to them by the king. He asked the chief of staff for permission not to eat these unacceptable foods. DANIEL 1:8

Some do a silly dance. Others flex their biceps. Some let out a primal scream like the Incredible Hulk's. Once, a player took a Sharpie pen out of his sock, signed the football, and presented it to his agent behind the end zone after a touchdown. Regardless of how they do it, NFL players seem to perform a self-promoting celebration after every big play they make. It doesn't matter if it's a touchdown, a sack, or a big catch. Players have even been known to excessively celebrate after a simple first down when their team is losing by three touchdowns.

Perhaps the NFL's most well-known showman is wide receiver Terrell Owens, who performed the infamous "Sharpie Touchdown." The list of Terrell's post-touchdown antics includes mocking an opposing player's pregame entrance, dancing with a cheerleader's pom-poms, and pretending to take a nap in the end zone, using the football as a pillow. You've got to hand it to Terrell: he is nothing if not original.

What's the Score?

But there's a problem with all these look-at-me actions. Even if their antics make us laugh, this kind of behavior reveals pride (or thinking too highly of yourself). According to the Bible, pride isn't funny at all. It is a very dangerous sin.

God takes pride seriously. Because of pride, sin entered the world when Adam and Eve ate the forbidden fruit in the Garden of Eden, thinking that they knew better than God. Because of pride, the nations of Israel and Judah fell to enemy armies in the Old Testament. In fact, pride is so dangerous that, in Mark 7:20-22, Jesus equates it to other sins that can "defile you," like theft, greed, and murder. To avoid pride, we must avoid thinking too highly of ourselves, whether in sports or elsewhere in life. We must work hard not to bring attention to ourselves. Everything we have is a gracious gift from God, including our athletic talents. And we should never presume to know more than God.

⟩ On the Ball

Make it a habit to verbally give glory to God, rather than to yourself, whenever you do something well. Try to remain humble even when you do something outstanding.

⟩ COACH'S COMMENT

Pride goes before destruction, and haughtiness before a fall. PROVERBS 16:18

Warning: Trying to pronounce the names in today's devotional could be hazardous to your health. On September 11, 2010, in a matchup featuring players with tongue-twisting names, Belgium's Kim Clijsters defeated Russia's Vera Zvonareva, 6–2, 6–1, to win the 2010 US Open. Kim's two-set victory was the most lopsided US Open women's final since 1976.

Amazingly, Kim didn't play competitive tennis at all in 2008, making her achievements as hard to explain as the pronunciation of her name. It was like she had never left. In August 2003, at the young age of 20, Kim reached the world's No. 1 ranking. She won her first Grand Slam event, the US Open, two years later. In 2007, she got married and retired from tennis as she prepared for the birth of her first child in February 2008.

Many elite female athletes never reach their previous level of competitiveness—if they come back at all—after having a baby. But Kim returned to the WTA Tour in 2009 and won her second US Open that season. Two years later, Kim won the 2011 Australian Open, her fourth major championship.

What's the Score?

Do you ever feel as if God has taken a break from his job, like Kim did from hers? As if he has deserted you and can't be found? As if he's not watching over you or taking care of you anymore?

Sometimes in life we might ask, "Where's God?" We might feel all alone. But we never are. If we don't feel like God is around, we're just not looking for him. The Bible says God exists everywhere and all the time. There's nothing he can't see or doesn't know. There's nothing that escapes his notice, including you. The Bible also says God loves you more than you can understand. Christians are never alone. The all-knowing, all-present God of the universe will always be near his children. What a wonderful truth!

On the Ball

Read Psalm 139, paying careful attention to what it says about God's nearness.

COACH'S COMMENT

Do not be afraid or discouraged, for the LORD will personally go ahead of you. He will be with you; he will neither fail you nor abandon you. DEUTERONOMY 31:8

An NFL quarterback's helmet does more than protect his skull. It also provides a vital link between the player and the coach. Since 1994, a quarterback's helmet has contained a speaker that allows a coach to call the next play right into the quarterback's ear. While this allows for quicker communication than using hand signals or running in the next play from the sidelines, sometimes technical difficulties arise.

On September 12, 2010, the San Francisco 49ers suffered a demoralizing 31–6 loss in their season opener at Seattle. Part of the 49ers' offensive woes stemmed from some poor communication between offensive coordinator Jimmy Raye and quarterback Alex Smith. On several occasions, Jimmy didn't give the next play to Alex before the radio in his helmet cut off, which happened with 15 seconds left on the play clock (per NFL rules). San Francisco had to burn several time-outs, and the offense never really got going. Later in the season, the Jacksonville Jaguars lost 34–24 to the Indianapolis Colts, and a helmet radio malfunction caused Jaguars quarterback David Garrard to miss part of a play call on a fourth-and-one situation. "The headsets were going in and out and weren't working," David told reporters after the game. "I had to switch to a different helmet."

⬜⬜ What's the Score?

In the NFL, communication between coaches and the quarterback is essential for success. Communication is also key in our Christian life. The way we communicate to God is through prayer. If we are to grow in obedience and faith, we must pray often to God.

How can you get to know someone and deepen a relationship if you never talk to him? You can't. We can't know our heavenly Father on a deeper level and become more like him if we don't talk to him. Some people pray, but do it reluctantly—like it's punishment. But prayer is a great privilege. We don't deserve to talk to a holy God, but that's exactly the opportunity we have through God's grace. If we put our faith in Jesus, God's Spirit enters our hearts and allows us to speak with God himself. Jude 1:20 instructs us to "pray in the power of the Holy Spirit." Now that's some powerful communication that will always get through!

⟩ On the Ball

To grow in godliness, we must pray more. Find a time that works well, and pray at least once a day.

⟩ COACH'S COMMENT

You, dear friends, must build each other up in your most holy faith, pray in the power of the Holy Spirit, and await the mercy of our Lord Jesus Christ, who will bring you eternal life. JUDE 1:20-21

Rafael Nadal had every reason to brag. On September 13, 2010, the ultratalented Spaniard wrote his name in professional tennis's history books with a win at the US Open. His 6–4, 5–7, 6–4, 6–2 victory over Novak Djokovic gave him a career Grand Slam, which means he had won all four "major" tennis titles—the Australian Open, the French Open, Wimbledon, and the US Open. He became only the seventh man in history to accomplish this feat.

Rafael's US Open triumph also further cemented his status as the world's top tennis player and a worthy challenger to Swiss star Roger Federer's claim to being "the greatest of all time." Rafael's victory gave him nine Grand Slam titles, while Roger held the all-time record at 16. But Rafael, who is five years younger than Roger, earned the career Grand Slam three years earlier in his life than Roger did. What's more, Rafael held a 5–2 record over Roger in Grand Slam finals. Despite all this, Rafael didn't take the opportunity to boast in his achievements. He said that he "never imagined having all four grand slams." Given the chance to compare himself to Roger, Rafael said, "The titles say he's much better than me. I think that will be true all my life."

What's the Score?

Rafael's humility is impressive given his tennis greatness. There is much to be learned from a star athlete who refuses to talk big about himself despite his utter dominance.

This is the attitude God wants us to have in our lives too. The Bible often talks about how God loves humility but hates pride. We are created beings with no power of our own. Everything we can do—even the breaths we take—comes from God. There is no room for boasting, no matter how good we are at something, because it is God who gives us all our abilities. He wants us to praise him for what we can do, not talk about ourselves.

) On the Ball

Write a list of five things you are good at, and then thank God in prayer for giving you the ability to do them.

1. _____ .
2. _____
3. _____
4. _____
5. _____

) COACH'S COMMENT

You rescue the humble, but your eyes watch the proud and humiliate them.

2 SAMUEL 22:28

He was an escape artist in shoulder pads, a slippery phantom in helmet and cleats. He was there one minute and gone the next. At least, that's the way Gale Sayers seemed to would-be tacklers. Gale was one of the NFL's all-time great running backs. In 1965, he burst onto the scene with the Chicago Bears as a 22-year-old rookie, rushing for 867 yards and 14 touchdowns and catching 29 passes for an additional 509 yards and six touchdowns. The next season, he racked up 1,678 all-purpose yards and 10 touchdowns. He appeared well on his way to breaking Jim Brown's all-time rushing record of 12,312 yards.

But injuries cut short his career. He suffered torn knee ligaments in 1968. By 1972, after several other injuries, he retired at age 29. Despite only playing in 68 games over seven seasons, Gale was a Hall-of-Fame shoo-in, with 9,435 combined yards, 57 total touchdowns, and four Pro Bowl appearances. Yet football fans were left to wonder what could have been if he had remained healthy.

What's the Score?

Like Gale's amazing but brief and injury-stained football career, we are often confronted with unexplainable circumstances in our lives. Maybe a close family member has died. Or perhaps you have to endure a chronic illness. Maybe your parents got divorced. Whatever the trial, it is there for a reason—and it's for our good. However, God doesn't always explain why it's there. Consider Job. He was a rich, righteous man, yet God allowed terrible disasters to afflict his health, family, and finances. After much suffering, Job finally cried out, "Why me?"

Interestingly, when God answered Job, he never gave a reason for the calamities. God only affirmed his holiness, power, and authority over the entire universe, including Job's life. Then he showered Job with greater blessings than before. The message is clear: God doesn't have to explain why he allows us to experience hardships. But when they come, we are called to trust in the sovereign Lord, not to question his motives or goodness.

❯ On the Ball

Identify one area of difficulty in your life, and pray that God would help you trust him through it.

❯ COACH'S COMMENT

You asked, "Who is this that questions my wisdom with such ignorance?" It is I—and I was talking about things I knew nothing about, things far too wonderful for me. JOB 42:3

The Baltimore Orioles were in a world of hurt. A poor start, weak pitching, an unreliable bull pen, an utter lack of clutch hitting, and an unfortunate rash of injuries all conspired to wreck the team's promising 2010 season. From the outset, the Orioles went into a nosedive like an airplane that has lost all its engines. Eighteen games into the season, the team was 2–16 and in danger of posting the worst record in the franchise's 56-year history in Baltimore.

Then, on July 29, the Orioles hired Buck Showalter as their new manager. In his first game, he led the team to a 6–3 win over the Los Angeles Angels, which began a four-game winning streak. The Orioles ended up winning eight of their first nine games under Buck's leadership. A spark had been lit seemingly overnight. Baltimore improved in all phases of its game: hitting, pitching, and defense. Before Buck became the manager, the Orioles had gone 32–73 for a miserable .305 winning percentage. Under Buck, the team went 34–23 (.596) in the last two months—a drastic turnaround rarely seen with midseason managerial changes.

⬚⬚ What's the Score?

As Christians, we experience a similarly radical turnaround. In Ephesians 2:1, the Bible says we were once "dead in [our] transgressions and sins" (NIV). But when Christ comes into our lives through our repentance and faith, we are radically changed. God starts the turnaround process by forgiving all our sins (both past and future), changing our hearts, and giving us his Holy Spirit to guide us into righteousness.

The Bible describes this transformation with some vivid imagery. John 3:3 calls it being "born again." Ephesians 2:5 says we are made "alive with Christ" (NIV). And 2 Corinthians 5:17 describes us as a "new person." However you describe it, it's an incredible turnaround that is possible only because of the sinless Son of God's death, burial, and resurrection on our behalf. Praise God!

❭ On the Ball

Read Ephesians 2 and John 3 to gain a greater understanding of how God radically changes lives.

❭ COACH'S COMMENT

Anyone who belongs to Christ has become a new person. The old life is gone; a new life has begun! 2 CORINTHIANS 5:17

It was party time in the Emerald City. On September 16, 2010, the Seattle Storm won its second WNBA championship with an 87–84 victory over the Atlanta Dream, completing a dream season. With a 7–0 record in three play-off series, the Storm became the first WNBA champion to go undefeated in the postseason since the Los Angeles Sparks went 6–0 in 2002. The Storm's 35–6 overall mark set a WNBA record for wins.

Seattle won all 21 games it played on its home court, KeyArena, and six-foot-five-inch forward Lauren Jackson won both the season's and the finals' Most Valuable Player awards. A day after the championship, rain couldn't stop the celebration. The team reveled in its championship with a police-escorted parade from the city's famous landmark, the Space Needle, to KeyArena, where 5,000 people anxiously awaited them and danced to music. When the team arrived, people greeted them with cheers. Storm chief executive officer Karen Bryant yelled, "We did not lose a game in this building!" and fans waved brooms to commemorate the team's 21–0 record at KeyArena that season. Confetti fell as a highlight video of the title game played on the jumbo screen, and fans took pictures with the championship trophy. Head coach Brian Agler even did a dance at center court with three players.

☐☐ What's the Score?

Seattle Storm fans enjoyed a unique championship, but Christians have something far greater than a shiny trophy to celebrate. Followers of Christ can rejoice in the fact that their sins are forgiven and that they will one day spend eternity in heaven in the presence of God.

This is great news! It's why Christians are called to worship God with music and songs. And while church is a great place to do that, we can worship God anywhere. You can sing in your bedroom, in the car, or even in the shower! It's never a bad time to celebrate God's victory over sin. Sing praises to the Lord for the amazing things he has done for us—and for the amazing things he's going to do!

⟩ On the Ball

Memorize a new worship song that you can sing to yourself anytime, anywhere, to remind yourself of God's goodness.

⟩ COACH'S COMMENT

Be filled with the Holy Spirit, singing psalms and hymns and spiritual songs among yourselves, and making music to the Lord in your hearts. EPHESIANS 5:18-19

It's not that difficult to pop a wheelie on a bicycle. But imagine riding on only the back wheel of your bike for more than a third of a mile! Now picture yourself doing it down a mountain. In 2004, that's exactly what Gilles Cruchaud of Switzerland did. Gilles traveled 1,640 feet down a mountain at an average speed of 42.45 miles per hour to set the Guinness World Record for the fastest downhill bicycle wheelie ever. Hey, everybody's got to be good at something, right?

It's not every day that you run across someone who is a wheelie-popping expert. You have to wonder how many days, months, or even years of practice went into such a daring, high-speed accomplishment. After all, one wrong twitch of his muscles or gust of wind and Gilles could have suffered a gnarly face-plant.

What's the Score?

Let's examine this one-wheeled feat a little more closely. Was it interesting? Sure. Dangerous? Yes. Bizarre? Absolutely. Important? Not so much. In the grand scheme of things, Gilles's high-speed wheelie wonder ride doesn't amount to much. It's a fun novelty that has no real lasting value, other than being a little entertainment.

This is often true of our lives. We can often be guilty of spending too much time on unimportant activities. Evaluate your favorite activities for a moment. Do you spend too much time doing trivial things, or are you putting your efforts toward things of eternal significance? Let's be a little more specific: How much TV do you watch? How many video games do you play? How much time do you spend playing with toys? There is nothing immediately wrong with these activities. They can all be harmless and fun. But ultimately, they aren't very important, and they don't necessarily help us love God more or become more like Christ. They pale in comparison to helping others or studying God's Word. As Colossians 3:2 reminds us, "Set your minds on things above, not on earthly things" (NIV). It's time we reevaluate all the insignificant things in our lives and place a higher priority on growing in godliness.

) On the Ball

Identify your favorite hobby, interest, or chilling-out activity, and commit to spending more time this week reading your Bible and praying.

) COACH'S COMMENT

The world and its desires pass away, but whoever does the will of God lives forever.

1 JOHN 2:17 (NIV)

Think you've played on a bad team before? Think again. At least you didn't play baseball for the 1899 Cleveland Spiders. On this date in 1899, the Spiders registered the final win of their historically atrocious season, beating the Washington Senators 5–4 in the first game of a doubleheader. (They lost the second game 8–5.) It was a short-lived moment of joy. Overall, the Spiders finished the season at 20–134—the worst record in the history of Major League Baseball.

Among the wreckage of that season, the Spiders endured six losing streaks of at least 11 games, including a 24-game slide. And they won consecutive games only once. Their best pitcher, Jim Hughey, led the National League . . . in losses, with 30. Their best hitter, second baseman Joe Quinn, only batted .286, with no home runs. The Spiders finished dead last in the National League standings—35 games behind 11th-place Washington (54–98) and a jaw-dropping 84 games out of first. The Spiders were one of four teams to be removed from the National League at the end of the 1899 season.

☐☐ What's the Score?

Life can sometimes feel like you're on the 1899 Cleveland Spiders team—nothing goes right. Your mom forgot to pack a dessert in your lunch. Your friends made fun of your outfit. Your hamster died.

Maybe it's worse than that. Perhaps your family is struggling to pay the bills. Or your parents are fighting constantly.

We've all experienced times when our world seems to be falling apart. King David certainly did. That's why he wrote Psalm 40. It was a testament to God's protection and faithfulness in the midst of great troubles. As David found out, God is always with us, even during our darkest hour. He will never leave us. If we call on him, he will answer and give us help from above.

⟩ On the Ball

Read Psalm 40. Write down a few of your favorite passages:

- -

⟩ COACH'S COMMENT

I waited patiently for the LORD to help me, and he turned to me and heard my cry. He lifted me out of the pit of despair, out of the mud and the mire. He set my feet on solid ground and steadied me as I walked along. PSALM 40:1-2

- -

Holy cow! It's competitive cow milking! Yup, you heard that correctly. Although competitive cow milking sounds "udderly" ridiculous, to some people it is "moo-sic" to their ears. Okay, enough bad cow jokes. Did you know that companies sell cow-milking games for birthday parties? One business sells a fake, life-size cow named "Ol' Bessie," featuring a replica udder that, according to a website, "can be played by one person using a timer or two contestants in 'hand to hand' combat."

Competitive cow milking isn't just for birthday parties, though. The Charleston RiverDogs, a minor league baseball team in South Carolina, holds a cow-milking contest each year during their "Dairy Day" promotion. And the Tennessee State Fair has taken competitive cow milking to another level. The fair, which started in 1906, added its first cow-milking contest in 2010. That year, four two-person teams consisting of TV and radio personalities from stations around central Tennessee competed on four cows. Each team had four minutes (two minutes per person) to squeeze as much milk as possible into a bucket. The winning team received "The Golden Udder" trophy. If that's not a sweet prize, what is?

🎯 What's the Score?

Milk was no laughing matter to the writer of the book of Hebrews. His readers were immature, acting like spiritual infants. So he used a food-and-milk analogy to describe their juvenile faith: "You are like babies who need milk and cannot eat solid food" (Hebrews 5:12). In 1 Corinthians 3, Paul used the same word picture to describe the childish Christians in Corinth.

Like newborn children, all Christians start with baby food. We must learn the basics of the faith—like believing that God created all things, that the Bible is the true Word of God, that Jesus is the only way to heaven, etc. But like children, we should grow in our faith in God and our obedience to him. God doesn't want us to remain baby Christians. He wants mature followers who truly understand what it means to love and worship him. How do we do this? Read the Bible and pray every day. Attend a Bible-believing church each week. Make good Christian friends. Ask trusted adults your spiritual questions. Do what it takes to keep growing in godliness!

⟩ On the Ball

Challenge yourself to grow spiritually by committing to an annual Bible reading or memorization plan.

⟩ COACH'S COMMENT

Solid food is for those who are mature, who through training have the skill to recognize the difference between right and wrong. HEBREWS 5:14

"She plays like a girl." How many times have you heard that phrase? It's not very flattering to women. Well, Billie Jean King heard it one too many times. Billie Jean, a professional tennis star in the 1960s and 1970s, certainly didn't need to prove her skills. During her career, she won 12 Grand Slam singles championships and was ranked No. 1 in the world for five years. But she is best remembered for beating a man on the tennis court.

On this day in 1973 in Houston, Texas, Billie Jean played Bobby Riggs in a highly publicized exhibition match. Bobby was a good player—he had won the 1939 Wimbledon championship—but Billie Jean whooped him, 6–4, 6–3, 6–3. Billie Jean's victory was a milestone for women in sports. In 1990, *Life* magazine named her one of the "100 Most Important Americans of the 20th Century." And the International Tennis Hall of Fame, where she was inducted in 1987, called her "arguably the single most important female athlete of all time" on its website.

What's the Score?

Billie Jean's historic victory proved that even at the highest levels of tennis, skill and heart matter more than gender. In this respect, serving God is not much different from serving a tennis ball: it doesn't matter what gender you are as long as you want to obey God.

Did you know the Bible includes a story about a woman beating a man too? Judges 4 and 5 tells the story of Deborah, Jael, and Barak—two women and a man. The Israelites were being oppressed by a Canaanite king, Jabin, and his general, Sisera, whose superior army boasted 900 iron chariots—the tanks of ancient warfare. Deborah, a prophetess, asked Barak to fight Jabin's army, but Barak said he would do it only if Deborah joined him.

Barak's army eventually defeated Jabin's forces and won Israel's freedom. But because Barak showed some fear and didn't fully trust God, the glory of the victory went to two women. Deborah helped win the battle, and Jael tricked Sisera when he was tired from fighting, killing him in his sleep. The Bible is full of stories of how God uses men to accomplish great things for him. But as this story shows, God uses women, too!

) On the Ball

It doesn't matter if you're a boy or a girl; it only matters if you are willing to serve him! Pray that God would show you the best way to make a difference for him.

) COACH'S COMMENT

There were few people left in the villages of Israel—until Deborah arose as a mother for Israel. JUDGES 5:7

Have you ever tried to walk with swim flippers on your feet? It's not very easy to do. In fact, you are almost guaranteed to fall if you try it. Running in flippers is even harder. But running *and* jumping over obstacles in flippers? Well, that's just downright impossible. It would be silly to even try. But that didn't stop Maren Zonker.

In 2008, Maren, a woman from Germany, set a Guinness World Record by completing the fastest 100-meter hurdles race . . . while wearing swim fins on her feet. Her world-record time was 22.35 seconds, more than twice as slow as the world record for the normal 100-meter hurdles. Talk about flipping out.

⬜⬜ What's the Score?

Why, you might wonder, *did Maren Zonker try to tackle this unique feat with flippered feet?* Good question. The 100-meter hurdles and swim flippers don't really seem to go well together, do they? The hurdles are an Olympic race that tests speed and agility. Swim fins help scuba divers swim well underwater and make people look like ducks. And our web-footed friends weren't really meant to run the 100-meter hurdles.

There are some things that shouldn't be mixed. It's kind of like that in our spiritual lives. God calls Christians to be different from the world—meaning Christians are supposed to be easily distinguished from non-Christians by how they think, act, and speak. If we go to church, read our Bibles, and pray on Sundays, but then use bad language, disobey our parents, and get into fights the rest of the week, how are we different from people who don't know Jesus? Instead we should follow Christ's example and be different from the world. Because, after all, just like hurdles and flippers, godliness and worldliness don't mix.

❯ On the Ball

List three ways you struggle with worldliness and pray for God's help to change:

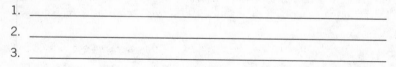

1. _____
2. _____
3. _____

❯ COACH'S COMMENT

Do not love this world nor the things it offers you, for when you love the world, you do not have the love of the Father in you. **1 JOHN 2:15**

At the time, it didn't seem like a historic baseball game. On September 22, 1911, the dreadful Boston Rustlers were concluding a three-game series in Pittsburgh. Boston was about to finish last in the National League at 44–107. The Pirates would finish in only third place. Just 1,208 fans came out to see the game at old Forbes Field. Little did the tiny crowd know what it was about to witness. Pittsburgh's twenty-nine-year-old ace, Babe Adams, threw a good game. But Babe lost a 1–0 decision to the grand old man of baseball, forty-four-year-old Cy Young. That victory ended up being the final win of Cy's incomparable career—number 511.

Cy was one of baseball's first true superstars. From 1890 to 1911, the six-foot-two-inch right-hander went 511–316, an astounding wins record that likely will never be broken. The next pitcher on the career wins list is Washington Senators great Walter Johnson with 417, but he retired after the 1927 season! No current pitcher is close to 300 career wins. Cy won 30 games in a season five times and topped 20 wins 15 times. Besides his total-victories mark, Cy's 7,356 total innings pitched and 749 complete games are also virtually unbreakable records.

What's the Score?

Cy not only recorded the most victories in baseball history, but he also gave up the most hits (7,092). His legacy of hard work, durability, and faithfulness to his craft over a long period of time paid off with the reward of elite recognition. In 1936, he was elected into Baseball Hall of Fame's first induction class. Even today, baseball's most prestigious annual pitching honor is called the Cy Young Award.

According to the Bible, Christians also will receive a great reward for a life of hard work and faithfulness to God. He has given all of us different abilities—athletic, academic, artistic, musical, etc.—and he wants us to use them for his glory. Life isn't always easy, and like Cy, we won't always win. But if we are faithful to obey him and serve him with our gifts over our lifetimes, we, too, will receive a great reward at the end—in heaven!

) On the Ball

List your strengths and abilities in one column and how you can use them for God's glory in another.

Ability	How I Can Use It for God
_____	_____
_____	_____
_____	_____
_____	_____

) COACH'S COMMENT

The LORD gives his own reward for doing good and for being loyal. **1 SAMUEL 26:23**

The hits just kept on coming. And for Ichiro Suzuki, the Seattle Mariners star outfielder, that was a good thing. Ichiro may not be as well known as a middle-of-the-order slugger or a flame-throwing strikeout pitcher, but he has been better than any other Major League Baseball player in recent history at one thing: getting base hits. On September 23, 2010, baseball's "Hit Machine" recorded his 200th hit for the 10th consecutive season to set a major league record!

Ichiro has been going about his art quietly ever since he smacked 242 hits in 2001 to win American League Rookie of the Year and Most Valuable Player honors. Most of his hits are singles, the least exciting of all hits in baseball. Through his first 10 seasons, he never totaled more than 15 home runs or 69 RBIs. He is not overly talkative with reporters and has spent his entire career with Seattle, which last made the play-offs in 2001. Yet, Ichiro will likely be a shoo-in for the Hall of Fame when he retires. All because he quietly went about his business of getting on base. Hit . . . after hit . . . after hit.

🔲 What's the Score?

Do you want to be the most popular kid at school? Do you always want to be picked first for teams or be praised by others? Receiving recognition for what we do isn't wrong, but it's not something we should crave. Like Ichiro's quiet, steady work doing something that's not overly exciting, there's great value in Christians working hard at obeying God without wanting personal glory or fame.

We can achieve great things for God by quietly serving him day by day. In doing this, we will please him and draw the attention of unbelievers who will wonder why we do what we do.

⟩ On the Ball

Find a behind-the-scenes way to serve others, like doing yard work for an elderly couple in your neighborhood, serving food at a soup kitchen, or writing letters to children in third-world countries.

⟩ COACH'S COMMENT

Make it your goal to live a quiet life, minding your own business and working with your hands, just as we instructed you before. Then people who are not Christians will respect the way you live, and you will not need to depend on others. 1 THESSALONIANS 4:11-12

Running a marathon is never easy. A marathon is a 26.2-mile road race that takes even the fastest, most skilled runners more than two hours to complete. It's a grueling test of speed, physical stamina, and mental toughness. Many people who start a marathon race never even finish. In 1999, Mike Cuzzacrea completed the Casino Niagara International Marathon at Niagara Falls in three hours, two minutes, and 27 seconds. That's an impressive time . . . especially when you consider that he ran the entire race while continuously flipping a pancake in a frying pan.

Now, you might be thinking to yourself, *Why on earth would someone do something so ridiculous?* A valid question indeed. But Mike, who is nicknamed "The Pancake Man," isn't just some flipped-out flapjack flipper. He runs for good reasons. Mike has run about 30 marathons and raised more than $55,000 for children's charities such as the March of Dimes, the Ronald McDonald House, and the United Way. He has appeared on TV and flipped pancakes with famous former-heavyweight-boxing champion Muhammad Ali. He's even carried the Olympic torch.

⬜⬜ What's the Score?

Mike took something that looked foolish to many people and did great things with it. Christians are called to do the same thing. First Corinthians 1 talks about how Christianity sounds ridiculous to the rest of the world. Not many people want to believe that their sins are putting them at risk of spending eternity apart from God when they die. They mock Christians for believing in a Savior who was crucified 2,000 years ago as a sacrifice for their sins.

Yet God, who owns all wisdom and knowledge, calls us to believe exactly that—and to share this great news with other people. God's plan of salvation might sound silly to some, but what appears to be foolish to others is actually the wisdom of almighty God.

⟩ On the Ball

Thank God for the "foolishness" of the gospel of Jesus Christ, and ask for his strength to help you share it with others.

⟩ COACH'S COMMENT

The message of the cross is foolish to those who are headed for destruction! But we who are being saved know it is the very power of God. 1 CORINTHIANS 1:18

On one of the greatest nights of his life, Josh Hamilton chose to be alone. On this date in 2010, the Texas Rangers clinched their first play-off berth in 11 years with a 4–3 win over Oakland. It was a huge night for the team. After the game, the Rangers followed an annual baseball tradition by spraying champagne all over each other in the clubhouse.

Many baseball players live for this moment—celebrating the thrill of success after a long season. But Josh chose the solitude of the team's training room. The thought of being soaked in alcohol brought back too many painful memories. In 1999, Josh had been the top prospect in baseball, having been drafted first overall by Tampa Bay. But after abusing drugs and alcohol, he was out of the game by 2003 and had nearly wrecked his marriage. God mercifully intervened and saved Josh from his deadly spiral. In 2007, Josh reached the major leagues with Cincinnati and has since become one of the best power hitters in the game.

What's the Score?

Even though Josh was a Christian, he knew his weaknesses. He understood how easy it would be to drift back into drug and alcohol abuse. So he went to great lengths to stay away from those temptations. We all have certain sins that are more difficult to overcome. The Bible calls these troublesome patterns "the old self." It refers to a Christian's former sinful lifestyle before putting his or her faith in Jesus.

Like Josh, we must be willing to go to great lengths to defeat the difficult sins in our lives. Maybe it means not watching certain TV shows, or speaking a certain way, or hanging out with certain friends. Whatever it is, we must put on "the new self" (Ephesians 4:24, NIV). In other words, we must choose to obey God and to say no to the sins of our past.

) On the Ball

List one sin that you consistently struggle with. Then write down what actions you can take to overcome this sin with God's help.

) COACH'S COMMENT

Throw off your old sinful nature and your former way of life, which is corrupted by lust and deception. Instead, let the Spirit renew your thoughts and attitudes. Put on your new nature, created to be like God—truly righteous and holy. **EPHESIANS 4:22-24**

First place is a whole lot more fun than last place. Just ask the FC Gold Pride. On September 26, 2010, the Pride, a Women's Professional Soccer (WPS) team from California's Bay Area, completed a stunning worst-to-first turnaround by winning the league championship with a 4–0 shutout of the Philadelphia Independence in Hayward, California.

Led by two star forwards, Brazil's Marta and Canada's Christine Sinclair, the Pride finished the season with a 17–3–5 overall record, including a league-record 14-game unbeaten streak. That's a far cry from their 2009 season, when they finished last in the WPS with a 4–10–6 record.

What's the Score?

When it comes to worst-to-first stories, the apostle Paul might have the greatest one in the entire Bible. We first meet Paul in Acts 7:58 as he gives approval for the brutal stoning of Stephen—the first Christian who died for his faith in Jesus. Paul (then known as Saul) was a wicked, legalistic Pharisee who thought that serving God meant following Old Testament law and imprisoning Christians.

But Jesus miraculously appeared to Paul as he was traveling one day and radically changed his life. Paul went from being a passionate Jesus-hater to a passionate Jesus-lover. He took three different missionary journeys, spreading the gospel message to most of the known world in the first century AD. He wrote 13 New Testament books. That's more than anyone else. He preached the Good News of Jesus Christ in Jewish synagogues, in Greek cities, and in Roman prisons. Even today, he is considered by many to be the greatest missionary who ever lived.

If you are a Christian, regardless of your particular background, you have a worst-to-first story too. It's true! The Bible says every believer was once far from God. But through Christ, we experienced a radical transformation. What's your worst-to-first story?

) On the Ball

Write down your worst-to-first salvation story of God coming into your life, and read it to a friend or family member.

) COACH'S COMMENT

This includes you who were once far away from God. You were his enemies, separated from him by your evil thoughts and actions. Yet now he has reconciled you to himself through the death of Christ in his physical body. As a result, he has brought you into his own presence, and you are holy and blameless as you stand before him without a single fault. COLOSSIANS 1:21-22

When Jim Furyk woke up on the morning of September 27, 2010, life felt pretty great. A day earlier, the veteran Professional Golfers' Association (PGA) star had won the final event of the FedEx Cup play-offs, the tour championship in Atlanta. The victory earned him a $1.35 million check. His win also gave him enough points for first place in the FedEx play-offs—good for an additional $10 million. Not bad for a weekend's worth of work.

It certainly was a different feeling from the one Jim had experienced a month earlier. On August 25, he overslept and missed his pro-am tee time at the FedEx Cup's first tournament, The Barclays. Under PGA Tour rules, Jim's pro-am absence disqualified him from the tournament. *Oops!* But Jim didn't let that sleepy slipup stop him. He finished well enough in the next two tournaments to position himself for the overall play-off win in Atlanta.

What's the Score?

Like Jim's start at the 2010 FedEx Cup play-offs, we all make some pretty bad mistakes. If you have put your faith in Jesus, your sins are forgiven, but we all struggle with our sinful nature until we get to heaven. And sometimes, like Jim, we can commit some real whoppers. Have you ever done something so bad that you thought, *How can God ever forgive me for that one?*

This, however, is giving in to condemnation—a big word that simply means feeling blameworthy, like there's no hope because of what you've done. But that's not true! Jesus has taken the blame for our sins and nailed it to the cross. Because of Jesus' sacrifice, we can move on from our mistakes and not relive the past. We don't have to mope around or feel sorry for ourselves. We can work hard at obeying God, knowing that he has forgiven us and that one day a great reward awaits us!

) On the Ball

Write down all the sins you can remember committing this week. (Go ahead, even if it's a long list!) Now if you are a Christian, write "Forgiven!" next to each item, and thank Jesus for his amazing work on the cross.

+ _____

+ _____

+ _____

+ _____

) COACH'S COMMENT

Now there is no condemnation for those who belong to Christ Jesus. And because you belong to him, the power of the life-giving Spirit has freed you from the power of sin that leads to death. ROMANS 8:1-2

Imagine if you had to be perfect. Not mostly good. Not nearly great. But really and truly perfect. Blameless. Without blemish. In college football, that's what a team usually has to be to win the national championship. With one teeny-weeny loss, the dreams of a national championship are over. Even if a team goes undefeated, it may not make it to the championship game. In 2009, Alabama and Texas earned the opportunity to play in the Bowl Championship Series (BCS) title game. Both teams sported 13–0 records and had the highest rankings in the complicated BCS system.

Boise State finished the 2009 season with a perfect 14–0, but they never had a chance to win the national championship. In the wacky world of college football, which doesn't have play-offs, sometimes perfection doesn't guarantee you a shot at the BCS trophy. Just ask Cincinnati and Texas Christian University, who also finished the regular season unbeaten but were denied invitations to the BCS championship game.

What's the Score?
Often nothing less than perfection is required to reach college football's promised land. And sometimes not even perfection will get you there. That's a lot of pressure for teams to win games in September, October, and November.

Spiritually speaking, we are all in a similar predicament. To get to heaven and be in the presence of a holy God, we have to be perfect—without a single sin or blemish. *Uh-oh.* This is clearly a problem. Listen to what James 2:10 says: "The person who keeps all of the laws except one is as guilty as a person who has broken all of God's laws." We are all sinners and lawbreakers, so we have no hope of reaching God's standard. But wait—there is hope! In his mercy and grace, God knew we couldn't be perfect on our own. So he provided perfection for us through his own sinless Son, Jesus Christ. If we put our faith in Jesus, he will forgive all our sins and make us perfect in God's eyes. Clothed in Jesus' perfection, we will win the greatest trophy imaginable—eternal life with God in heaven!

) On the Ball
Read all of Romans 5 to understand more about how Jesus makes us perfect.

) COACH'S COMMENT
Most people would not be willing to die for an upright person, though someone might perhaps be willing to die for a person who is especially good. But God showed his great love for us by sending Christ to die for us while we were still sinners. ROMANS 5:7-8

Few women go from discussing carpets and curtains to jabs and uppercuts. But that's exactly what Eva Shain did. As a young adult, Eva worked as an interior decorator in New Jersey. But in the late 1960s, she reluctantly accompanied her husband, Frank, a boxing-ring announcer, to a fight at Madison Square Garden. She fell in love with the sport. Soon Eva began judging amateur bouts. The New York State Athletic Commission awarded a professional boxing judge license to Eva in 1975.

On September 29, 1977, she became the first woman to judge a heavyweight championship match when she worked the Muhammad Ali versus Earnie Shavers showdown at Madison Square Garden. Eva awarded Ali a unanimous-decision win after 15 rounds, which turned out to be the second-to-last victory of the great champion's career. Although that was her biggest fight, Eva remained an active judge until nine months before her death in 1999 at the age of 81. "It wasn't the idea of being a trailblazer," Eva once said of her second career. "It was something I wanted to do. It was a challenge."

⬚⬚ What's the Score?

Although she didn't plan to do so, Eva became a female pioneer—someone who accomplishes unprecedented feats. That's similar to Esther in the Bible.

Esther was a Jewish exile who lived in the Persian Empire in the fifth century BC, roughly 100 years after Babylonian King Nebuchadnezzar had conquered Judah and deported thousands of Jews. Like Eva, Esther's life took an unexpected turn. Thanks to her beauty, she went from being an unknown exile to being a queen of Persian King Xerxes. Later, she discovered a murderous plot by a Persian official named Haman to annihilate the Jews. But with God's power and the help of her cousin, Mordecai, Esther thwarted the conspiracy, saved the Jews, and kept alive God's promise of providing a coming Savior for all mankind through his chosen people.

Even today, some 2,500 years later, Jews still celebrate this great deliverance with the annual festival of Purim. As Esther's life proved, God has a unique plan for each of us. It might not always be what we think or hope for, but God's plan is always best. Since God is holy, all-knowing, and all-powerful, we can trust him and go wherever he leads.

⟩ On the Ball

Read the book of Esther. What are your favorite parts? How did Esther show courage and do what God wanted her to do? Write down some ways that you'd like to follow Esther's example:

+ _____

+ _____

+ _____

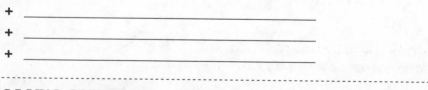

⟩ COACH'S COMMENT

Who knows if perhaps you were made queen for just such a time as this? ESTHER 4:14

He was the Sultan of Swat. The Colossus of Clout. The Great Bambino. Sportswriters showered him with nicknames. Hollywood made movies about him. He was the one and only Babe Ruth. In 1927, the New York Yankees' iconic slugger was at the height of his powers. He was the greatest hitter in baseball, and the Yankees were the sport's crème de la crème—the best of the best. On September 30, 1927, Babe did the unimaginable in a 4–2 win over the Washington Senators: he blasted his 60th home run of the season. Before that, no one other than Babe had ever hit more than 42 homers in a season. Babe's marvelous record stood another 34 years until another Yankee, Roger Maris, hit 61 in 1961.

For two decades, Babe seemed larger than life. The Hall of Famer enjoyed a dazzling career with 714 home runs, 2,213 RBIs, and a .342 batting average. And then—*poof!*— just like that, he was done. Because of age and failing health, his skills rapidly declined in the 1930s. By 1935, the Yankees released him. Babe signed with the Boston Braves but hit a sickly .181 in his first 28 games and retired two months into the season. He died in 1948 from complications with cancer. He was only 53.

⬜ What's the Score?

Babe Ruth's story is a sobering reminder of human weakness. Even the greatest athletes will eventually grow old and die. David describes humans as nothing more than "a breath" (Psalm 39:5) and "a passing shadow" (Psalm 144:4). Isaiah calls us withering grass and fading flowers (Isaiah 40:6-8).

This should provide a needed reality check to our sinful pride: we are not in charge of our lives. We are small and powerless without God. We can't even control how long we live. We rely on God for everything—even the air we breathe. David considered all these things in Psalm 39 and said, "And so, Lord, where do I put my hope? My only hope is in you" (verse 7). God is our hope too!

⟩ On the Ball

With a parent's permission, pick some grass and flowers from your yard. Store them without water in your house for a week, and see how much they wither. Let this activity remind you how much you rely on God for strength, health, and life.

⟩ COACH'S COMMENT

LORD, remind me how brief my time on earth will be. Remind me that my days are numbered—how fleeting my life is. You have made my life no longer than the width of my hand. My entire lifetime is just a moment to you; at best, each of us is but a breath. PSALM 39:4-5

A batter standing at home plate has less than half a second to react to a 90-mile-per-hour fastball. Sometimes that can make hitting in the major leagues a little scary. It certainly was a scary scene when Cincinnati Reds pitcher Micah Owings was struck in the head by a fastball during a 2009 game against the Atlanta Braves. Micah was batting with the bases loaded in the 12th inning when the ball hit his helmet.

"The pitch hit right around the hole in my helmet, and I immediately hit the ground," Micah wrote in his blog after the incident. "There was not a lot of pain because everything went numb right away. I remember looking up at the blue sky and being thankful, while thinking about how terrified my mother must have been. So I gave a thumbs-up."

Micah's parents were in the stadium watching the game. Micah suffered a perforated eardrum and needed five stitches. But his injuries could've been much worse. Cincinnati won the game because a runner came home when Micah was injured.

What's the Score?

Micah's baseball helmet was literally his "helmet of salvation." Scientists say a baseball traveling 90 miles per hour has one quarter of the kinetic energy of a bullet fired from a nine-millimeter handgun. That's a powerful impact!

While Micah's helmet may have saved his life, he knows that God saved his soul when he prayed for Jesus to be his Savior at age 10. Micah faithfully followed Jesus. He encouraged all kids to put on the full armor of God, including the helmet of salvation. Ephesians 6:17 says, "Put on salvation as your helmet." The Lord makes salvation free for the asking. By putting on the helmet, we're protected against Satan's schemes and can have supreme hope for our future in heaven. Plus, we can be confident that God's helmet will help us fend off the curveballs—and fastballs—that life throws our way.

) On the Ball

If you've never prayed to Jesus for salvation, you can do that now. Simply say, "Jesus, I know I haven't always acted perfectly. I believe you took the punishment for my sins on the cross so I could be forgiven. Thank you! I accept your gift of salvation and give my life to you. Amen."

If you just prayed that prayer, tell a parent or whoever gave you this book. When you strap on the helmet of salvation, you'll have no doubt about your future with God.

) COACH'S COMMENT

Put on salvation as your helmet, and take the sword of the Spirit, which is the word of God. EPHESIANS 6:17

Balancing on a surfboard to ride the waves is hard enough. Just imagine how difficult it is to stand up on a surfboard, holding a long paddle and rowing in rough ocean waters. For Danny Ching of Redondo Beach, California, standing on an 18-foot surfboard with a paddle in his hands looked as natural as riding a bike. Danny showed off his stand-up paddling skills on this day in 2010 at the Battle of the Paddle competition in Dana Point, California.

Danny defeated 159 other elite athletes in a five-mile, four-lap race. To make things more difficult, competitors had to paddle into the beach and run a 100-yard sprint between each lap. Danny took the lead early and never gave it up, winning the competition in 57 minutes and 45 seconds. Australian Jamie Mitchell stayed close to Danny most of the race, but he ended up losing by nearly two minutes.

What's the Score?

Danny said his plan to win the Battle of the Paddle was to take the lead from the start. He knew in a race with this many competitors that he didn't want to get caught in the pack. Danny had been training for a 32-mile ocean canoe race the following weekend, so his strength showed as he got to the front and stayed there the entire time.

As Christians, we shouldn't want to be in the pack either. God called many different individuals to lead in the Bible. After Moses, God chose Joshua to lead his people into the Promised Land. Joshua had trained to be a leader by watching Moses and trusting God. God's words to Joshua were straight to the point: "Be strong and courageous, for you are the one who will lead these people" (Joshua 1:6).

To be a leader, you have to show strength and courage. That's what Danny did to win the race. And that's what Joshua did in leading God's people into the land God promised them.

⟩ On the Ball

How do you show leadership? Write down a couple of ways:

Think about times when it's important to show leadership. Maybe it's when you're in a group and people are making bad choices. When you have a plan, it's easier to stand up and be a leader.

⟩ COACH'S COMMENT

Be strong and courageous, for you are the one who will lead these people to possess all the land I swore to their ancestors I would give them. JOSHUA 1:6

You've probably heard about the "shot heard 'round the world" as you've studied American history. In 1837 Ralph Waldo Emerson wrote the poem "Concord Hymn," in which he used the phrase "fired the shot heard 'round the world" to describe the opening gunshots that started the American Revolutionary War at the Battle of Lexington and Concord. But in sports that phrase has a whole different meaning. Longtime baseball fans think of just one thing when they hear "shot heard 'round the world": the home run Bobby Thomson hit on this day in 1951.

Bobby was an outfielder for the New York Giants (before the team moved to San Francisco). During August 1951, the Giants were more than 13 games out of first place. They won 37 of the next 44 games to tie the Brooklyn Dodgers for first place and to force a three-game play-off to see which team would advance to the World Series. The Giants won the first game, but then the Dodgers won the next one. In the deciding third game, Brooklyn held a 4–1 lead in the bottom of the ninth inning. Fans started leaving the stadium. However, the Giants got back-to-back singles and a double to make the score 4–2. With runners on second and third bases, Bobby drilled a home run over the left-field fence. Radio announcer Russ Hodges screamed, "The Giants win the pennant! The Giants win the pennant!" over and over again until he lost his voice.

What's the Score?
When reporters asked Bobby about his historic hit, the humble outfielder said, "It was just a home run." He didn't pound his chest. He didn't gloat. He didn't do or say anything to embarrass the Dodgers pitcher who had given up the home run.

As believers in Christ, we can learn a lot from Bobby's example. Jesus said, "Those who exalt themselves will be humbled, and those who humble themselves will be exalted" (Matthew 23:12). Bobby's heroic home run will always be remembered. But what may be more impressive is that his humble attitude allowed him to become lifelong friends with the Dodgers pitcher who allowed his famous hit. When we act humbly, God can lift us up to even greater heights.

) On the Ball
Have you ever earned a victory with a game-winning shot, a huge home run, or a magnificent goal? How did you act afterward? If you're fortunate enough to become a sports hero, remember to be humble.

) COACH'S COMMENT
Those who exalt themselves will be humbled, and those who humble themselves will be exalted. MATTHEW 23:12

Do you think the best computer-game players live in the United States? If so, you may want to think again. The World Cyber Games 2010 brought together the best online gamers at the Los Angeles Convention Center. More than 450 players from 58 countries battled it out for supremacy in 10 different games. An additional 400 international media people reported all the action.

The finals saw 32,000 spectators jam into the convention center and tens of millions of people watch online. In the end, South Korea came out on top at the world's largest computer and video game festival. Players from South Korea won three gold, two silver, and three bronze medals. Competitors from Brazil, the United Kingdom, and Germany took home one gold and one silver. The United States, Australia, Sweden, and Ukraine each claimed one gold medal. Not surprisingly, a German player won *FIFA 10*, while Alec Castillo of the United States took first in *Guitar Hero 5*.

⬜ What's the Score?

The World Cyber Games were a huge spectacle. But the event wasn't all about pressing buttons and moving joysticks. Samsung, a partner in the event, also used it for education. Samsung gave $120,000 worth of monitors to the Los Angeles County Education Foundation. These monitors were used in schools all over the state.

Samsung saw a need and gave to meet it. When King David was building God's Temple, he saw a need. He gave a lot of money and time to help build the Temple, and he asked his people to do the same. God's people knew they'd been blessed, so they gave generously. Read a list of their offerings in 1 Chronicles 29:6-8. The Israelites didn't hold back from God, and we should have that same attitude when we give to God's work.

⟩ On the Ball

Do you receive an allowance or get money for your birthday and Christmas? Do you pass along any of your money to church or other Christian organizations? Don't forget to give to God's work. And when you do, try to follow the Israelites' example by giving freely and wholeheartedly.

⟩ COACH'S COMMENT

The people rejoiced over the offerings, for they had given freely and wholeheartedly to the LORD, and King David was filled with joy. **1 CHRONICLES 29:9**

Billy Martin was certainly not the biggest name on the New York Yankees 1953 World Series team. Yogi Berra, Mickey Mantle, and Whitey Ford were more well known then and now. However, the five-foot-eleven-inch second baseman made the biggest impact against the Brooklyn Dodgers as the Yankees won their fifth-straight world championship.

In the first game of the series, Billy smacked a triple with the bases loaded and added three more hits in a 9–5 Yankee victory. He hit a home run in the Yankees' 4–2 victory in game two. After the Yankees lost the next two games, Billy had another home run in an 11–7 victory in game five. And on this day in 1953, Billy came to the plate in the ninth inning with runners on first and second. He promptly smacked a single to center field to win the World Series and set off a huge celebration in Yankee Stadium. Billy was named the most valuable player due to his 12 hits—a World Series record!

What's the Score?

Billy didn't impress opposing teams with his size or strength. But with his competitive spirit and will to win, the 160-pound baseball player struck fear in opponents. No matter what the situation, Billy faced it without fear. He seemed to rise to any challenge.

In the Bible, the Israelites faced a huge challenge. They had left Egypt to travel to God's Promised Land. However, when 12 spies went to look at the land, they came back with a frightening report. Sure, the land flowed with milk and honey, but there were giants in the land. Ten of the spies said the people were too big and the cities too strong to overcome. But Caleb and Joshua trusted God to come through on his promise. Caleb even shouted, "Let's go at once to take the land. . . . We can certainly conquer it!" (Numbers 13:30). Caleb showed courage in the face of a challenge. He knew God's people would win.

) On the Ball

The next time you face a huge challenge in your life, think about Caleb's words. You can read the whole story in Numbers 13. When challenges come your way, tackle them head-on with courage and without fear.

) COACH'S COMMENT

Caleb tried to quiet the people as they stood before Moses. "Let's go at once to take the land," he said. "We can certainly conquer it!" NUMBERS 13:30

It wasn't exactly David versus Goliath. At 29 years old and weighing nearly 300 pounds, super-heavyweight wrestler Rulon Gardner was much older, bigger, and stronger than young David in the Bible. However, when Rulon faced Russian Alexander Karelin in the 2000 Summer Olympics, people gave him about as much a chance of winning the gold as David had had to beat the giant. But in the finals of Greco-Roman wrestling at the Sydney Olympics, Rulon beat the unbeatable.

For 15 years, Alexander hadn't lost a match. The Russian wrestler was so dominant that nobody had even scored a single point against him in 10 years. But one point was all Rulon needed to win the gold and record one of the biggest upsets in sports history. In the first three minutes, neither wrestler could score. But in the second period, Rulon forced Alexander to lose his grip—which, according to Greco-Roman rules, earned him a point. The crowd gasped. Nobody could believe Rulon was ahead 1–0. But there was just one problem: more than five minutes were left in the match. Rulon countered every attack by Alexander, withstanding countless face slaps and grabs. Amid chants of "USA! USA!" the match ended with Rulon winning 1–0.

☐☐ What's the Score?

Rulon recorded an amazing victory. Alexander was so strong that he once had carried a refrigerator up seven flights of stairs—by himself! People feared the Russian. The only time these two had met before, Alexander had beaten Rulon 5–0, throwing Rulon on his face three different times. But at the 2000 Olympics, Rulon used his speed and strength to escape with a 1–0 victory.

Nobody thought Rulon would beat the mighty Russian—even he admitted that he didn't think he'd win. But Rulon did the impossible. God is in the business of doing the impossible. He helped David defeat Goliath. He parted the Red Sea. He created the universe out of nothing. He came to earth as a little baby. When you're facing seemingly insurmountable odds, remember that you serve a God who does the impossible.

⟩ On the Ball

Do you have a goal that you think you can't accomplish? Write it down:_____
_____. Pray for God to help you accomplish the impossible.
If it's his will, you can do the impossible.

⟩ COACH'S COMMENT

Nothing is impossible with God. **LUKE 1:37**

Totally tubular! That's the best way to describe the Association of Surfing Professionals (ASP) World Junior 2010 competition in Bali, Indonesia. The top junior riders were all assembled at Keramas Beach. While the rain and winds didn't make for great surfing weather, the waves cooperated by pumping out six-footers and all kinds of tubes.

Australian Jack Freestone caught one of the best tubes of the day to rocket out to a huge lead in the finals. Jack jumped up on his board and rode through a hollow tube as water roared all around him. He shot out the end, performed some stunning turns, and earned a 9.57 out of 10. Dale Staples of South Africa nearly pulled out the victory as he caught a tube in the closing moments of the 35-minute final. However, the barrel closed before Dale could escape, and he ended up wiping out.

　　 What's the Score?

Surfing can be a beautiful sport to watch. The sound of the ocean. The power of the waves. At just 18 years old, Jack was ranked as one of the best up-and-coming surfers in the ASP. He earned $10,000 by riding that perfect tube at Keramas. Dale took home half that amount for second place because his wave swallowed him up.

Waves can be a lot like sin. It looks inviting, but ends up being dangerous. Every sin starts with a temptation. Sometimes we give in to temptation only to be swallowed up. Have you ever been tempted to tell a "little white lie"? It may not seem like a big deal at first. But pretty soon you have to tell another lie to cover up for the first. Eventually, you can be caught in an ocean of lies.

When you find yourself tempted to make a bad decision, turn to God. The Bible says temptations in our lives come from our own evil desires—not from God (James 1:13-14). God is our rock in the middle of temptations. When we hold on to him, we won't get dragged away by the waves.

﹥ On the Ball

What's a recent temptation you've faced? How did you handle it? Did you fight the temptation or get swallowed by it? Tell God that you want to hold on to him when you're tempted.

﹥ COACH'S COMMENT

Remember, when you are being tempted, do not say, "God is tempting me." God is never tempted to do wrong, and he never tempts anyone else. Temptation comes from our own desires, which entice us and drag us away. JAMES 1:13-14

Dylan Galloway's touchdown didn't decide the outcome, but nobody at the high school football game will forget his play. Rivercrest was already ahead 47–0 when the Manila High School senior rolled onto the field on October 8, 2010. Yes, rolled. Dylan was born with cerebral palsy, which affects the part of the brain that controls motor skills, so he had spent most of his life in a wheelchair. But that didn't stop him from wanting to play football or score a touchdown. With time running out and Manila driving the ball to Rivercrest's four-yard line, coach Toby Doke sent Dylan onto the field. The coach had already worked out a plan with his quarterback and Rivercrest's coach.

Dylan took a handoff, followed his blockers around the left side of the field, and plowed into the end zone to make the score 47–6. Rivercrest players—part of the top-ranked team in Arkansas at the time—all signed a football that they gave to Dylan.

What's the Score?

Dylan's touchdown left a lasting impression on everybody who was at the game. It showed great sportsmanship on both teams. But it also showed that persistence pays off. Coach Doke told reporters after the game that Dylan had made known his wish to score a touch-down. "He had been after me all year in the hall, at lunchtime, and during the school day," the coach said, "and kept telling me he wanted to score a touchdown." The Manila High coach rewarded Dylan for his persistence, and God does the same for us.

In Luke 18, Jesus tells a story to his disciples about being persistent. In the story, a widow keeps bugging a bad judge to take care of her case. The judge doesn't want to do his job, but he finally gives in so the widow will stop bothering him. The point of the parable is that, if a corrupt judge can be persuaded by consistent requests, how much more likely will a kind and loving God answer our requests when we persistently pray to him?

⟩ On the Ball

Read the parable of the persistent widow in Luke 18:1-8. What details stand out to you? What are you tempted to give up praying about? Write it down and keep praying:

⟩ COACH'S COMMENT

One day Jesus told his disciples a story to show that they should always pray and never give up. LUKE 18:1

The Ford Ironman World Championship attracts only the finest athletes to compete in Kona, Hawaii. Rajesh Durbal fit that description. At the 2010 competition, Rajesh completed the 2.4-mile swim, the 112-mile bike ride, and the 26.2-mile marathon in just over 14 hours. He was the 1,460th person to cross the finish line (1,800 people competed). And, oh yeah, Rajesh was a triple amputee. He was born with a congenital deformity in his legs and right arm. When he was one, his legs were amputated. Later he had surgery to replace bones in his partial right arm.

But these physical difficulties never stopped Rajesh from competing in life. One of his elementary-school teachers wrote a book about Rajesh and his ability to do activities. In high school, he was called names. He didn't let that get him down. He focused his energies on skiing and track. He became a world-record holder in the 100-meter sprint. Rajesh started competing in shorter triathlons in 2009. But he loved a challenge and wanted to do one of the most difficult triathlons in the world—which he did when he completed the Hawaii Ironman.

⬜⬜ What's the Score?

Rajesh said he nearly drowned in the swim as other competitors swam over him. In the bike race, he had to hang on extra hard with his one good hand because the winds were so bad. Running may have been the hardest as his prosthetic legs would get going on downhill portions of the course, and he'd have a hard time slowing down. In spite of these dangers and physical obstacles, Rajesh never gave up. He poured ice down his back to cool off and just kept going.

We all have physical obstacles that we must overcome. Maybe we're not the fastest runner or strongest athlete. Perhaps we're considered too skinny or overweight. Whatever our limitations are, we'll probably never know what it would be like to grow up a triple amputee. God created us as he intended, and he doesn't make mistakes. No matter what we have to overcome, we can have confidence that God was in control when we were created, and he's in control now.

〉 On the Ball

What bothers you about your physical abilities or appearance? Thank God for making you exactly as you are. Then ask him for the power and patience to live with and/or to overcome your physical challenges.

〉 COACH'S COMMENT

You made all the delicate, inner parts of my body and knit me together in my mother's womb. Thank you for making me so wonderfully complex! Your workmanship is marvelous—how well I know it. PSALM 139:13-14

The Founders Cup is a kick! Kickball tournament, that is. Founders Cup XIII proved that competition in the World Adult Kickball Association (WAKA) was wackier and tighter than ever. For the first time in WAKA history, the championship match went into extra innings before Panik Attack pulled out a 6–2 victory against the Other Shot Callers. Panik Attack, from Virginia, took an early lead only to see the Other Shot Callers tie things at 2–2 in the fifth inning. When the game went into extra innings, Panik Attack tallied four runs in the sixth to win the title.

Okay, adults playing kickball may seem kind of silly. It's really more an elementary-school playground game than a serious sport, right? The WAKA competitors would probably agree. One of the teams was named Playground Posse. And that wasn't the only funny name. Meatballs, WAKAmole!, Your Mom, and the American Gladiators also vied for the championship.

⬚⬚ What's the Score?

Teams from around the United States gathered at Desert Breeze Park in Las Vegas, Nevada, to compete in the Founders Cup. Adults traveled from Florida, New York, Colorado, New Mexico, California, South Carolina, Missouri, Louisiana, and other states to show off their kickball abilities. And while some of the team names and outfits were a bit silly, everybody tried their hardest on the field in the three-day competition.

The book of Ecclesiastes reminds us to do well in whatever activity we're currently doing. Whether it's cleaning up our rooms, doing an art project, or playing kickball, we need to make a plan and do our best. When we put out our best effort, we can have more fun and end up with better results.

⟩ On the Ball

Is there something you do that seems kind of silly to you? Maybe it's writing in cursive or practicing passing drills in basketball. Instead of putting out less effort in those activities, do your best and try to do well.

⟩ COACH'S COMMENT

Whatever you do, do well. For when you go to the grave, there will be no work or planning or knowledge or wisdom. ECCLESIASTES 9:10

Have you ever played "knockout" with a basketball? No, that's not when you throw a basketball to a teammate who's not looking. That would be dangerous. In the game knockout, basketballs are given to the first two people in a long line. The first person attempts to shoot and make a free throw. If the first person misses and the second person sinks a shot before the first person makes a basket, the first person is out. No more playing for player No. 1. *Vamos.* You're outta here! If the first person makes the shot, he or she gives the ball to the next person in line. The game continues until there's only one player left. That person is the winner.

On this day in 2010, a group of students from George Washington University set a Guinness World Record for the largest game of knockout. The spirit program at George Washington University organized the 167 participants who showed up at the Smith Center to make history.

⬜⬜ What's the Score?

Freshman Drew Manville won the competition, which also included members of the men's and women's basketball teams at George Washington. Drew had hoped to just break into the Top 50, but his hot hand led him to victory.

The game knockout is known by many other monikers. Perhaps you've heard it called gotcha, killer, fireball, or lightning. No matter what you call it, the idea of knockout is to eliminate your opponent from the game. There is no second chance or forgiveness.

That's the exact opposite of the Christian life. When Jesus walked the earth, he and his disciples got into a conversation about forgiveness. Peter asked, "How often should I forgive someone who sins against me? Seven times?" (Matthew 18:21). Peter probably thought he was being generous in forgiving seven times. But Jesus said he should offer forgiveness 490 times—a limitless amount of forgiveness. We can never be "knocked out" of God's favor. When we pray and genuinely ask for forgiveness, God gives it to us. We need to have the same attitude toward people in our lives.

) On the Ball

Can you think of somebody you've "knocked out" of your life? Does God want you to forgive that person? If you have the chance, find that person and tell him or her that you forgive.

) COACH'S COMMENT

Peter came to him and asked, "Lord, how often should I forgive someone who sins against me? Seven times?" "No, not seven times," Jesus replied, "but seventy times seven!" MATTHEW 18:21-22

Josh Hamilton never knew being sprayed with soda pop would be this much fun. The Texas Rangers outfielder missed celebrating with teammates after the Rangers qualified for the 2010 play-offs. But the team leader was right in the middle of the celebration after Texas ousted Tampa Bay in the American League Division Series.

Josh, who had battled alcohol addiction, chose to stay away from the Rangers' first celebration because he figured the team would be spraying each other with champagne—which is a sports tradition. Josh didn't want to be around alcohol of any kind because it brought back too many bad memories. Alcohol and drugs had nearly ruined Josh's baseball career and marriage. But after Texas defeated Tampa Bay 5–1 in game five, teammates grabbed Josh and told him to put on some goggles. He was led into the clubhouse where teammates shouted, "Ginger ale!" and sprayed soda all over him.

What's the Score?

The Texas Rangers advanced all the way to the 2010 World Series because they were a close-knit group. By not bringing champagne into their celebration, Josh's teammates showed they respected him as a player and a person. Josh was open about his faith in Jesus Christ and his desire to live a clean life without alcohol or drugs. Josh honored God all the way through his amazing 2010 season. He hit 32 home runs, batted .359, and was named the American League Most Valuable Player.

By using ginger ale in their celebration, the Rangers lived out the Bible verse that says to "live in such a way that you will not cause another believer to stumble and fall" (Romans 14:13). Do you have a friend who struggles in a certain area of life? Maybe you have a buddy who's addicted to video games and tries to stay away from them. If you play video games around this person, you might cause him to stumble because the temptation is too great. As you live your life, be aware of your friends' weaknesses, and act in a way that builds them up—instead of causing them to fall.

⟩ On the Ball

God wants us to be a help, not a hindrance, to our friends. Are there any behaviors you need to change to help your friends live a life more dedicated to Christ?

⟩ COACH'S COMMENT

Each of us will give a personal account to God. So let's stop condemning each other. Decide instead to live in such a way that you will not cause another believer to stumble and fall. ROMANS 14:12-13

Kate Moore had some of the fastest thumbs in the world. The 15-year-old from Des Moines, Iowa, proved that fact at the 2009 LG US National Texting Championship. Kate defeated more than 250,000 competitors and 22 finalists to win $50,000. Surprisingly, she had received her first cell phone just eight months prior to the competition. In the finals Kate faced off against 14-year-old Morgan Dynda of Savannah, Georgia. Both girls had to type in three long phrases—including abbreviations, capitalization, and punctuation—without making any mistakes.

Each girl won one of the phrases to set up a tiebreaker. Kate won by mere seconds and had tears running down her face when she learned that she was the champion.

☐☐ What's the Score?

Kate was a texting machine. Heading into the competition, she averaged 14,000 texts a month. That's more than 450 every day! But she said she didn't just talk to friends electronically. She also enjoyed performing in school plays and hanging out with friends in person. She worked to get good grades, too.

A lot of kids prefer texting their friends instead of talking with them. Studies show the average teenager sends between 50 and 75 texts a day. Communicating with friends is important, but sometimes friends don't get your texts.

That's not the case with God. He always receives your messages. He always hears your prayers. One of the shortest verses in the Bible also contains some of the best advice. It says, "Never stop praying" (1 Thessalonians 5:17). God wants to hear from you. He wants you to tell him your every thought, need, and desire. He wants you to thank him for the good things he's given you. He wants you to admit the bad things you've done and ask for forgiveness. God desires for you to praise him for the mighty power he displays around the world. Your messages will always get through to God—and you don't even have to have fast thumbs.

⟩ On the Ball

How often do you pray to God? At every meal? Before every test? At the start of games? When you go to bed? God wants you to pray continually. Always keep talking to your best friend.

⟩ COACH'S COMMENT

Never stop praying. 1 THESSALONIANS 5:17

Respect your elders. That's good advice in life . . . and in surfing. At the 2010 Association of Surfing Professionals (ASP) World Tour event in Portugal, Kelly Slater proved that age doesn't determine success in surfing. The 38-year-old from Florida used his experience and skill to pull out a victory at the Rip Curl Pro Portugal. While the beach Supertubos sounds like it would have huge waves, the swells during the competition were less than stellar. The calm ocean conditions only churned up three-foot waves, but Kelly still managed huge tricks—including a 360 alley-oop on a nothing wave. The finals saw Kelly defeat Jordy Smith of South Africa by a score of 13.33 to 11.43.

The victory moved Kelly one step closer to his 10th ASP World Championship. Kelly claimed that championship later in the year. His 10 world championships were more than twice the number of Mark Richards from Australia, who had won four world titles in the late 1970s and early 1980s.

What's the Score?

Kelly was able to make something out of nothing to win the Rip Curl Pro Portugal. While younger surfers struggled to come up with big moves on tiny waves, Kelly was able to reach into his bag of tricks and still turn in top scores. Experience can be a huge asset in sports. Over the years Kelly had surfed in all kinds of conditions. He was born in Cocoa Beach, Florida, which was known as the small-wave capital of the East Coast. So he knew what to do on the tiny waves of Supertubos. Kelly may not have been the strongest surfer physically that day, but he was the best.

The Bible says "the gray hair of experience is the splendor of the old" (Proverbs 20:29). The smooth-scalped Kelly didn't have any hair at all, but he did have tons of experience. As you go through life and compete in sports, remember to respect your elders. You can learn a lot from the people who lived before you. Take time to talk with your grandparents and to learn from their experiences. Many young people rely only on their strength to get through. Older, wiser people have both strength and experience.

) On the Ball

Think of an older person in your life. Is there anything you could learn from him or her? The answer is *yes*! Write down a question you'd like to ask that person the next time you're together. It could be about sports, life, or faith in Jesus.

My question is _____

) COACH'S COMMENT

The glory of the young is their strength; the gray hair of experience is the splendor of the old. PROVERBS 20:29

Dale Earnhardt's last NASCAR victory may have been his best. This National Association for Stock Car Auto Racing (NASCAR) legend sat in 18th place with just five laps remaining at the Winston 500 on October 15, 2000. But nobody was ever better than Dale at driving the big 2.66-mile oval at Talladega.

For much of the 188-lap race, Dale had been battling with 25 other cars at the front of the pack. Twenty-one different drivers had led the race, and there were 49 lead changes. But when the checkered flag came down, it was Dale claiming the victory. After the race, Dale credited Kenny Wallace and Joe Nemechek for helping him get to the front. These three cars got in a tight bunch to help each other go faster. Dale zoomed through traffic and found himself in fourth place with two laps to go. Then in a bold move, Dale went to the outside and led Kenny and Joe to the front. For the final lap, Dale held off Kenny and Joe from passing him to earn his 76th victory.

What's the Score?

Dale Earnhardt was one of the biggest names in NASCAR—and for good reason. When many drivers would've given up hope, he drove hard to the end of every race. Dale's never-give-up attitude and amazing driving skills earned him the respect of fellow NASCAR racers. In the Winston 500, Dale used his experience and a little help from his friends to win the race. Even with the paint of his Number 3 car nearly rubbed off the right side and his bumper badly dinged from being hit from behind, Dale found a way to win his 10th race at the Talladega Speedway.

During the second-to-last lap, Dale could be seen motioning to Kenny to get on his bumper. Kenny did just that, and with Joe close behind, the trio went to the front. The Bible reminds us to do good things for other people. Without Kenny and Joe's help, Dale never would've won the race. Doing good doesn't always mean helping somebody win. You could help a friend with math homework or assist a sibling in cleaning her room. Always look for ways to help others.

) On the Ball

Take a moment to ask God to bring somebody to your mind who needs help. Write down that person's name: _____. What can you do for that person? Sharing with others and sacrificing to be helpful makes God happy.

) COACH'S COMMENT

Do not forget to do good and to share with others, for with such sacrifices God is pleased. HEBREWS 13:16 (NIV)

When Wayne Gretzky entered the National Hockey League (NHL) as a rookie in 1979, sportswriters said he was "too small, too wiry, and too slow to be a force." But in just 11 seasons, Wayne became the greatest scorer in hockey history. On this day in 1989, newspapers around the world printed the headline "The Great One Now the Greatest."

The night before, Wayne had led the Los Angeles Kings to a 5–4 overtime victory against the Edmonton Oilers. He entered the game with 1,849 points—just one point behind NHL all-time leading scorer Gordie Howe. Wayne picked up an assist on the game's first goal to tie Gordie's record. Then after sitting out much of the game with an injury, Wayne came onto the ice with three minutes left in the contest and the Kings trailing 4–3. With a minute remaining, Wayne beat everybody to a puck in front of the net and backhanded it in to tie the game and beat Gordie's record. In overtime, Wayne scored another goal to give his team the win.

⬜ **What's the Score?**

Wayne was called the "Great Gretzky" at a young age. Pretty soon everybody started calling him "The Great One." By the time he retired at the end of the 1998–1999 season, Wayne held or shared 61 NHL records. He finished his career with 894 goals and 1,963 assists for a total of 2,857 points.

There's no doubt that Wayne earned his nickname of "The Great One." However, there's only one truly "Great One," and that's God. God's name is above all other names. In the book of Ezekiel, the prophet writes that one day God will show all the nations how holy his great name is. The truth is, God is coming back. When Jesus returns, he will rule over all the heavens and earth. The Bible says that every knee will bow to Jesus when he comes back in his full glory. Now that's respect that the only "Great One" deserves.

⟩ **On the Ball**

What are some words that come to mind when you think about God? Write them down:

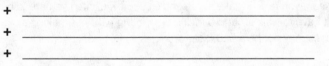

+ _____

+ _____

+ _____

You might have written *powerful*, *awesome*, or *mighty*. Praise God for the power he shows today and the power he'll display when he returns to earth.

- -

⟩ **COACH'S COMMENT**

I will show how holy my great name is—the name on which you brought shame among the nations. And when I reveal my holiness through you before their very eyes, says the Sovereign LORD, then the nations will know that I am the LORD. **EZEKIEL 36:23**

- -

What will you be remembered for? Freddy Schuman will be remembered as a great New York Yankees fan. For 22 years, people could count on Freddy to walk around Yankee Stadium banging a spoon against a frying pan to cheer on his favorite team. On this day in 2010, Freddy passed away at age 85.

Freddy became famous for his passion about the Yankees. People looked forward to hearing him walk around the ballpark banging on his pan. Plus, he always created encouraging signs on white poster board. At the top of each sign, he wrote, "Freddy 'Sez.'" That's what people called him: Freddy Sez. His comments were usually positive. One of his signs read, "Freddy 'Sez' Yankees have great come from behind ability." Another said, "Freddy 'Sez' Yankee Stadium gave birth to champions!"

⬜ What's the Score?

The New York Yankees gave Freddy plenty to cheer about. During his time at the stadium, the Yankees won five World Series championships—more than any other team in baseball. Plus, they were almost always in the play-offs.

The Yankees may be good, but we're on a better team: God's team. If Freddy could get excited and be committed to cheering on the Yankees, how should we be cheering for God, the ultimate victor? Would putting on face paint and cheering for Jesus be too much? Probably not. He deserves that kind of excitement and passion. The Bible says we are Christ's ambassadors. That means we represent him as members of his team. When people look at us, they should know we're committed to God. (And not because we're walking around in a "God Rules" jacket.) Maybe our joy makes us stand out. Perhaps it's our kindness that shows we're on God's team.

As you live your life, keep this question in mind: What will you be remembered for? Freddy was a great Yankees fan. Will you act like God's biggest fan?

❭ On the Ball

Can people tell what team you're on? Make sure people see how excited you are to be on God's team. You don't have to walk around banging on a frying pan, but making a sign to tell others about Jesus may not be a bad idea.

❭ COACH'S COMMENT

We are Christ's ambassadors; God is making his appeal through us. We speak for Christ when we plead, "Come back to God!" 2 CORINTHIANS 5:20

When siblings work together, they can accomplish amazing things—even a world record. In 2010, siblings Jason Chalmers and Tamlyn Locke set a Guinness World Record for greatest distance traveled on a scooter in 24 hours. That may not seem like much of a sport. After all, all they had to do was turn their wrists and hold down the accelerators. But when you consider the amount of endurance and concentration it took to go 735.5 miles in 24 hours, you have to agree these siblings displayed a lot of skill and ability.

The pair started off in Johannesburg, South Africa, and headed south on the N1, which is the national highway. With cars zooming past them, Jason and Tamlyn kept up speeds of around 45 miles per hour—the top speed for a scooter. Two vehicles traveled next to the siblings to keep them safe and to give them support and instructions. The vehicle in front filmed the journey. The vehicle behind cautioned other drivers about the slow-moving scooters. Jason and Tamlyn stopped every couple of hours to refuel the scooters and let the engines cool.

What's the Score?

Jason and Tamlyn never could have set a world record without their support team in the vehicles that drove ahead of and behind them. The people in these other cars watched over them, kept them safe, and gave them advice.

In our Christian lives, we have a support team that does the same thing for us—the Holy Spirit. When we pray to accept Jesus, God sends the Holy Spirit into our lives. Some people call him the Holy Ghost. But he's not spooky at all; he's actually really cool. God's Spirit can warn us about dangers coming from behind or decisions we're going to make that could affect our future. Do you ever feel that little nudge in your heart to do the right thing when you're about to make a poor decision? That nudge or "voice" whispering in your ear to follow God's Word comes from the Holy Spirit. The Spirit watches over us, keeps us safe, and gives us advice. In the Bible, Jesus said the Holy Spirit could also teach us about God and remind us of his teachings.

) On the Ball

Thank God for sending the Holy Spirit. Isn't it great to have such an amazing helper in your life? Listen for his voice inside today.

) COACH'S COMMENT

When the Father sends the Advocate as my representative—that is, the Holy Spirit— he will teach you everything and will remind you of everything I have told you. JOHN 14:26

When 250-pound athletes hit each other at speeds around 20 miles per hour, they can cause a lot of damage. The National Football League (NFL) makes rules to protect players from major injuries. Some of those rules state that a defender cannot lead with his helmet when making a tackle. Other rules guard against helmet-to-helmet contact or hitting a defenseless player who's vulnerable to a big collision. But football is such a fast-paced game that sometimes dangerous plays just happen.

On this day in 2010, the NFL gave fines that totaled $175,000 to three defensive players for dangerous hits. Pittsburgh Steelers linebacker James Harrison was fined $75,000, while New England Patriots safety Brandon Meriweather and Atlanta Falcons cornerback Dunta Robinson each got $50,000 fines. All of the hits resulted in injury. And Dunta's hit on Philadelphia Eagles wide receiver DeSean Jackson knocked both players out of the game.

What's the Score?

Some people said the fines were unjust because everybody knows football is dangerous. The players appealed their fines, but the NFL stood strong. NFL executive vice president of football operations Ray Anderson said, "We hope we are sending a message, emphatically, that going forward, hits to the head that are illegal . . . will be dealt with at a higher level." The NFL wanted its players to set an example for youth, high-school, and college teams by playing the right way.

Football is dangerous, but there are ways to make it safer. Life is similar. We face certain dangers, but there are ways to remain safe. The Bible says, "The wise are cautious and avoid danger; fools plunge ahead" (Proverbs 14:16). In football it's foolish to lead with your head in a tackle. In life, sometimes it's foolish to barrel ahead and take stupid risks. Think before you act. Stay away from people who act recklessly. Do your best to avoid dangerous situations. Showing wisdom in how you act is not wimpy—it's smart.

) On the Ball

Has anybody ever dared you to do something dangerous or something you know you shouldn't do? How did you respond? When dangerous situations arise be prepared to do the smart thing. Be wise and stay safe.

) COACH'S COMMENT

The wise are cautious and avoid danger; fools plunge ahead with reckless confidence.
PROVERBS 14:16

"Red Sox Rise from the Dead." Newspapers around the United States printed that headline on this day in 2004. The Boston Red Sox accomplished something that no other Major League Baseball team had ever done before—they'd come back from a 0–3 deficit to earn four straight victories and win a best-of-seven play-off series. Best of all, they'd done it against their rival New York Yankees.

The Yankees had dominated the first three games, winning by a combined score of 32–16. And it appeared as if New York would sweep Boston when it held a 4–3 lead going into the bottom of the ninth inning of game four. But Dave Roberts scored for Boston in the ninth, and then David Ortiz hit a home run in the 12th inning to win the game. Game five was equally as exciting as Boston scored two runs in the bottom of the eighth inning to tie the game 4–4. David again won the game—this time with an RBI single in the 14th inning. With the momentum behind them, the Red Sox outscored the Yankees 14–5 in the final two games to advance to the World Series.

What's the Score?

If there's one place you don't want to be, it's trailing 0–3 in a best-of-seven-game series. But that's where Boston was in 2004. The Red Sox were even three outs away from losing, but they came back to win it all.

Many stories of people rising from the dead appear in the Bible. We all know that Jesus rose from the dead after he died on the cross. During Jesus' ministry on earth, one of his best friends died. When Lazarus died, his sister told Jesus, "If only you had been here, my brother would not have died" (John 11:21). She knew Jesus could do miracles, and he was about to perform one of his greatest feats. Jesus replied to her, "Your brother will rise again" (John 11:23). Jesus went to Lazarus's tomb and asked for the stone to be rolled away. Lazarus had been dead four days, but Jesus yelled inside the tomb, "Lazarus, come out!" (John 11:43). Almost immediately, Lazarus walked out of the tomb.

⟩ On the Ball

Isn't it awesome that you serve a God who has power over death? As a Christian, you will never truly die. You will live forever with Jesus in heaven. Read about Jesus' raising Lazarus from the dead in John 11:1-44. Write down a couple of your favorite parts from this miracle:

⟩ COACH'S COMMENT

Jesus told her, "I am the resurrection and the life. Anyone who believes in me will live, even after dying. Everyone who lives in me and believes in me will never ever die."
JOHN 11:25-26

Everything in Mexico City is big. Amazing Aztec ruins. The largest bullfighting ring in the world. A gigantic population—some record books rank it as the third-largest city in the world, with over 20 million people. And chess. That's right, chess is huge in Mexico City. In fact in 2006, nearly 27,000 people gathered in El Zócalo, the city square, to play chess. The result was 13,446 games of chess being played at the same time at the same location, which set a Guinness World Record.

The gathering of chess players was so large that it could be seen from space. In addition to recreational players, several of the world's best players showed up to take part in the event.

⬜⬜ What's the Score?

To be a great chess player, experts say you must think at least three moves ahead. That means you have to imagine all the options that your opponent has and think how you would react to those moves. World chess champion Garry Kasparov said he usually thinks three to five moves ahead during a match. However, if the situation arises, Garry said he can think 12 to 14 moves ahead. Garry, a chess grand master, was at the Mexico City event.

Planning ahead is key to success in chess and in life. Of course, you can't always predict what's going to happen in life. Things happen that are outside of your control. Unexpected things always seem to pop up. In chess, the pieces can only move in certain ways. In life, many more variables exist. You can't always plan to have success.

The Bible says that, if you want to succeed, you should commit your actions to the Lord (Proverbs 16:3). When you honor God with your words, actions, and plans, he can help you be a success.

⟩ On the Ball

Do you always commit your actions to the Lord? How can you commit what you do to him? Write down some ideas:

When you make your plans, plan first to have your actions always honor God.

⟩ COACH'S COMMENT

Commit your actions to the LORD, and your plans will succeed. PROVERBS 16:3

Scientists say the tongue is one of the strongest muscles in the human body. Your heart probably works more as it pumps blood to keep you alive. But your tongue almost never stops working. It flaps around when you talk. It directs food and water down your throat when you eat or drink. It even works when you're asleep to keep you from choking on saliva. *Ewww.* Your tongue may be pretty strong, but Thomas Blackthorne's tongue was known for being the strongest.

In 2008, Thomas set the world record for amount of weight lifted by the tongue as he pulled up more than 27½ pounds. To perform this amazing feat, Thomas put a hook through his tongue and attached it to a huge weight on the ground. Then he slowly raised his head until the weight lifted off the ground. By lifting that much weight with his tongue, Thomas broke his own Guinness World Record.

☐☐ What's the Score?

To be fair, Thomas's tongue didn't do a whole lot of the lifting. He mainly used his back and leg muscles to get the weight off the ground. But his tongue did hold the massive weight without ripping. *Yuck!*

The Bible talks a lot about the power of the tongue. God isn't impressed with how much weight you can lift with your tongue or how strong it is. He cares about how you use your tongue. Proverbs 18:21 says, "The tongue has the power of life and death" (NIV). That's a lot of power! That verse doesn't mean your tongue can literally kill (although cruel words can wound deeply). It does mean that the words you say are important. By using kind words and by being friendly, you can draw a lot of friends to yourself and help them find new life in Jesus Christ. But if your words are mean, you'll have a difficult time.

) On the Ball

What would your friends say about you? Are your words kind, or do they bite with cruelty? The way people look at you is greatly determined by your words, so use the power of your tongue carefully.

> COACH'S COMMENT

The tongue has the power of life and death. PROVERBS 18:21 (NIV)

Have you ever ridden in a pumpkin boat? No, not a pumpkin-colored boat—an actual pumpkin. That may sound silly, but thousands of people gather every year in Tualatin, Oregon, to take part in the Giant Pumpkin Regatta.

At the 2010 competition, Jay Collins impressed the spectators with his hollowed-out 1,042-pound pumpkin that had an engine attached to it. Jay looked relaxed sitting in his pumpkin and revving the electric motor. But Jay didn't win the race that was created for paddlers in gigantic gourds. The seventh annual West Coast Giant Pumpkin Regatta came down to two of its fiercest teams—the Tualatin Valley Fire and Rescue and the Portland District US Army Corps of Engineers. These two groups battled for vegetable boat domination year after year. In 2010, it was decided the winner would be the team that got all of its participants across the finish line first. Although it was a firefighting team that crossed the line first, a firefighter also paddled the last pumpkin to finish, so the engineers claimed the victory.

What's the Score?

Pumpkins can be good for a lot of things. They make nice decorations, a yummy pie, or an awesome boat. In 2010, the Tualatin Valley Fire and Rescue workers proved the old adage that a team is only as strong as its weakest player. When a firefighting team won the race, it looked like the firefighters would take home the victory. But the engineers all finished closely together to gain the overall victory.

As Christians we need to look for ways to help the weaker people around us. This is true in our lives and on the sporting field. Instead of getting frustrated by a teammate who doesn't have the same skill level as you, look for ways to encourage him or her to get better. The Bible says to "encourage those who are timid. Take tender care of those who are weak. Be patient with everyone" (1 Thessalonians 5:14). By helping our weaker teammates, we make our teams stronger. And when we give assistance to the weaker people in our lives, we make our communities better places to live.

) On the Ball

Have you ever been frustrated by a weak teammate? What did you do? Maybe you were the weakest player on a team. Try to always be patient with your teammates, and help them to play better.

) COACH'S COMMENT

Brothers and sisters, we urge you to warn those who are lazy. Encourage those who are timid. Take tender care of those who are weak. Be patient with everyone.
1 THESSALONIANS 5:14

The 1992 World Series had people from multiple countries on the edges of their seats. In 1992, the Toronto Blue Jays defeated the Atlanta Braves in six games to win the first baseball world championship for a team in Canada. Four of the six games were decided by one run, and the final game went to extra innings—which added to the excitement.

Atlanta won the first game, thanks to a great pitching performance from Tom Glavine. But the underdog Blue Jays claimed game two following Ed Sprague's pinch-hit, two-run home run in the ninth inning. Game three was tied 2–2 in the ninth before Candy Maldonado singled in the winning run. Toronto made it three straight victories by claiming a 2–1 decision in game four. After Atlanta won the fifth game, the series went back to Georgia. However, it wasn't a happy homecoming. With the game tied 2–2 in the 11th inning, 41-year-old Blue Jays outfielder Dave Winfield stepped to the plate and hammered a pitch down the left field line to score two runs. The game ended 4–3, and Toronto had won the World Series.

What's the Score?

The victory set off a huge celebration in Canada and around the world. The Blue Jays were truly an international team. The squad featured a player from Puerto Rico, a Jamaican, three players from the Dominican Republic, and no Canadians. Toronto showed that a team of players from around the world could be the best in baseball. Today, players from nearly 20 countries can be found playing on Major League Baseball teams.

As popular as baseball is, it doesn't compare to the Christian faith. Christianity is the most popular religion in the world. Nearly 2.2 billion people follow the teachings of Jesus Christ. As believers in Christ, we're stronger when we join together with our talents—just like the Blue Jays did. The Bible says that God doesn't show favoritism (Acts 10:34). He died for all people. Anybody who prays to accept Jesus becomes part of God's team. And that's a pretty strong team!

On the Ball

God accepts people from all nations who pray to him and do what is right. But some nations treat Christians badly—even burning their houses or throwing them in jail. Pray for people in other nations who get persecuted for their faith in Christ.

COACH'S COMMENT

Peter replied, "I see very clearly that God shows no favoritism. In every nation he accepts those who fear him and do what is right." ACTS 10:34-35

From 63 yards away, the uprights on an NFL goalpost look pretty skinny. That's what Denver Broncos kicker Jason Elam thought before his 63-yard field goal attempt on this day in 1998. Of course, NFL uprights are always 18-feet-6-inches apart. That's plenty of room to kick a ball through. But from 63 yards, wind and a number of other factors make it a nearly impossible kick. Only one kicker—Tom Dempsey—had ever made one from that distance.

Denver led Jacksonville 24–10 with four seconds remaining in the first half. Originally, Jason ran onto the field to attempt a 58-yarder. But Denver coach Mike Shanahan decided to take a five-yard delay-of-game penalty so Jason could go for his record-tying kick. As Jason impacted the ball, he nearly slipped from the force of his kick. The low, line-drive kick tumbled through the air. Jason started running toward the end zone after the ball. As the ball split the uprights with plenty of room to spare, Jason thrust his arms into the air. He had just tied the NFL record for longest field goal ever made!

⬜ What's the Score?

Jason said he could always crush a football with his foot. He didn't start playing football until his sophomore year of high school and immediately discovered he had a strong leg. It was just a gift God had given him. Jason grew up in a Christian home. He knew about God, but he didn't really have any direction in his life. Once Jason started reading his Bible and following God, the direction of his life started going straight.

The Bible says every good gift comes from God. God gave Jason the ability to kick a football. When Jason got the direction of his life going toward God, God gave him a platform to tell others about Jesus. Don't forget, too, that God doesn't change. We may wander, but he'll always be fixed in place waiting for us to follow him. He's even more consistent than the width of football uprights. He "does not change like shifting shadows" (James 1:17, NIV). That means we can count on him no matter what.

⟩ On the Ball

What direction is your life going? If you're wandering aimlessly right now, make a plan. What's one God-given gift you have? How can you use it for Jesus Christ?

⟩ COACH'S COMMENT

Every good and perfect gift is from above, coming down from the Father of the heavenly lights, who does not change like shifting shadows. JAMES 1:17 (NIV)

Yelling at a referee is never a good idea. Coaches tell their young players not to complain about a call. But on this day in 2010, a player in an adult British soccer league did more than complain about a bad call—he drove his car onto the soccer field and *at* the referee!

When 28-year-old Joseph Rimmer thought he was fouled in the game's 60th minute, he shouted at the referee to give him a free kick. Instead the ref said to play on. Joseph didn't continue playing; he just started screaming at the referee. The ref quickly awarded the other team a free kick. And when the referee was about to give Joseph a red card, he left the field, climbed into his Range Rover, and drove the car onto the field. As players ran off the field, Joseph drove in circles and threatened the referee. After a few minutes of chaos, the game was canceled and Joseph was arrested.

☐☐ What's the Score?

Joseph was not only disqualified from playing in the league, but he also had his driver's license taken away for a year. At James's trial, a judge in England sentenced him to 24 weeks in prison.

Sports can bring out the best and the worst in a person. It brought out the worst in Joseph. He let his anger rule his actions. Joseph could have let his perceived injustice go after he was fouled. Instead he screamed, threatened the referee, and acted like a fool. The Bible says to control your temper. When you get angry, it's easy for that anger to escalate. You would probably never jump on your bike and ride it at the referee, but when you complain about the referee, you lose your focus on the game. When you're playing sports, concentrate on your game—not on what the referee is doing.

⟩ On the Ball

Showing your anger on the playing field makes you look like a fool. Treat your opponents and the referee with respect. Then you'll be able to play your best.

⟩ COACH'S COMMENT

Control your temper, for anger labels you a fool. ECCLESIASTES 7:9

Emmitt Smith could dance. He proved that when he won the mirror-ball trophy on *Dancing with the Stars* in 2006. But long before Emmitt danced on TV, he danced through holes and around tacklers on the football field. In fact, the Dallas Cowboys running back finished his career as the best running back in NFL history. That's not bad for a player that NFL scouts thought was too small and too slow to make a big impact in the league.

On this day in 2002, the five-foot-nine-inch running back became the NFL's all-time leading rusher, breaking Walter Payton's record. Emmitt entered the game against the Seattle Seahawks needing 93 yards to tie Walter's mark of 16,726 rushing yards. With 10 minutes left in the game, he was only 13 yards away from the record. Emmitt gained three yards on a first-down carry. Then on a second down, he took a handoff, slashed off the left tackle, got a huge block from fullback Robert Thomas, broke a tackle, and rambled for 11 yards. The record was his! The crowd at Texas Stadium gave Emmitt a five-minute standing ovation as he hugged his mother and kissed his wife and children on the sidelines.

🏈 What's the Score?

Emmitt retired from football in 2004 with a total of 18,355 rushing yards. He was the only running back to rush for more than 1,000 yards in 11 straight seasons. His 164 rushing touchdowns were also an all-time record. For a running back who people thought was small, Emmitt proved his toughness and durability. He got the most out of his God-given talents. Emmitt ran low to the ground, had great balance, and could burst through small holes that the offensive line opened up. Even though he wasn't as big as a lot of other running backs, Emmitt missed only four starts in his 14-year career.

If Emmitt picked a Bible verse to describe his NFL career, he might choose Psalm 140:4, where David asks the Lord to keep him safe and to protect him from violent people who want to trip him up. The Lord kept Emmitt safe and gave him great balance, so he didn't trip.

) On the Ball

Do you have a Bible verse that describes your life? Some people call it a "life verse" that describes how you want to live. What is your life verse? Write it down:

If you don't have a life verse, pick one for yourself.

) COACH'S COMMENT

Keep me safe, LORD, from the hands of the wicked; protect me from the violent, who devise ways to trip my feet. PSALM 140:4 (NIV)

Fans don't have to go to stadiums to enjoy the live action of sports these days. Cable TV, special sports networks, even cell phones allow fans to watch the action almost anywhere. But it wasn't always this way. Before the 1920s, sports fans had to read what happened to their team the next day in the newspaper. Or maybe they could find out the score on the radio when the game was over. But on October 28, 1922, sports fans received a treat when the first-ever around-the-country broadcast of a college football game was aired. The game pitted the Princeton Tigers against the University of Chicago Maroons. The game was played in Chicago, but fans along the East Coast gathered around radios to hear the action.

Chicago built an 18–7 lead heading into the fourth quarter. But a defensive touchdown and Harry Crum's second score of the game gave the Tigers a 21–18 victory. Princeton clinched the game when it stopped Chicago just one foot away from the end zone as time ran out.

What's the Score?

It's so easy to get information today. But a hundred years ago, news traveled slowly. That made this game a really big deal. A *New York Times* reporter wrote that the town of Princeton, New Jersey, was filled with people "cheering madly one minute, groaning hoarsely the next." Technology changed the way people enjoyed sports. Now they could hear how their favorite team was doing, even when the team was playing out of town.

Technology has also changed how Christians can tell others about Jesus Christ. After Jesus rose from the dead, he told his disciples to "go into all the world and preach the Good News to everyone" (Mark 16:15). That meant Jesus' followers had to travel on foot or by boat to tell about God's life-changing message. Today, we don't have to be face to face to tell others about Jesus. You can use the Internet, text messages, phone, podcast, or any number of other ways to share God's Good News. Of course, face to face still works, too.

) On the Ball

What do you think would be the best way to tell others about Jesus? Why? Write down your ideas and try them out:

) COACH'S COMMENT

He told them, "Go into all the world and preach the Good News to everyone." MARK 16:15

Sports cards collectors make millions of dollars every year selling baseball cards. In 2007, a near-mint-condition Honus Wagner card from the early 1900s sold for $2.8 million. That's a lot of money for ink and cardboard! More recently in 2010, a Honus Wagner baseball card was donated to the School Sisters of Notre Dame in Baltimore, Maryland. The nuns decided to sell the card—which wasn't in the best shape—and donate the money to ministries in 35 countries around the world.

Honus was one of the best players in the history of the game. The Pittsburgh Pirates shortstop was one of the first five inductees into the Baseball Hall of Fame. Dallas-based Heritage Auctions sold the card for $220,000 to a doctor in Philadelphia who has been collecting sports memorabilia for 30 years.

What's the Score?

When the brother of a nun died in 2010, he left the Honus Wagner card to the School Sisters of Notre Dame. They found the card in a safe-deposit box with a note that said, "Although damaged, the value of this baseball card should increase exponentially throughout the 21st century." Instead of giving the valuable baseball card to family, the owner donated it to charity. And when the nuns sold it for about a quarter of a million dollars, they were able to help people around the world.

In the Old Testament, God commanded landowners not to harvest the grain on the edges of their fields (Leviticus 23:22). This grain was left so needy people could easily pick it up and have something to eat. God wanted his people to provide for the poor.

The same is true today. God wants his followers to be generous.

) On the Ball

Do you have anything that you could give to the less fortunate in your community? Maybe you have some toys you don't play with or clothes you've outgrown. With a parent's help, go through your room and find some things that you could give away.

) COACH'S COMMENT

When you harvest the crops of your land, do not harvest the grain along the edges of your fields, and do not pick up what the harvesters drop. Leave it for the poor and the foreigners living among you. I am the LORD your God. LEVITICUS 23:22

Knowing the rules is important. At the 2010 Mission Hills Star Trophy tournament in China, not knowing the rules cost professional golfer Ryuji Imada 26 penalty strokes! Ryuji, who plays in the Professional Golfers' Association (PGA) in the United States, wasn't aware of the rules in China. During the soft and wet conditions on the Blackstone course, Ryuji's ball kept getting muddy. According to PGA rules, Ryuji would've been allowed to pick up his ball, clean it off, and place it one club length away from its original position. But rules in many places in Europe and Asia insist that players put their ball just one scorecard away from its original spot.

Ryuji learned about the rule at the end of his round and immediately informed tournament officials. Ryuji estimated that he broke the rule 13 times and was assessed a two-stroke penalty for each instance. That meant 26 strokes were added to his scorecard.

What's the Score?

By not knowing and following the rules, Ryuji had no chance of winning the tournament. After the tournament he admitted to feeling stupid for not having read the rule book before playing his round.

As followers of Christ, we're given a rule book to follow in our lives—the Bible. Just like it was Ryuji's responsibility to read and know the book, it's our duty to know God's commands. Not knowing the rule was no excuse; Ryuji was still given a 26-stroke penalty. God expects us to know his rules. But knowing the rules takes effort. You have to read and memorize God's Word in order to know what he wants you to do. In the book of Timothy, the apostle Paul writes that athletes cannot win the prize unless they follow the rules (2 Timothy 2:5). Ryuji learned that the hard way. Hopefully, you won't have to.

) On the Ball

How well do you know God's rule book? Do you read it every day? Every week? Every month? Make a plan to learn your Bible better. Then you'll be able to win a prize as God's athlete.

> **COACH'S COMMENT**
Athletes cannot win the prize unless they follow the rules. 2 TIMOTHY 2:5

Nothing is scarier than a face carved into a turnip. Okay, not really. But the tradition of carving jack-o'-lanterns dates back hundreds of years to Ireland when people carved faces into turnips. Those veggie faces were placed outside of doors to ward off evil spirits. More recently people have turned to pumpkin carving this time of year. And nobody could carve more pumpkins faster than Stephen Clarke.

In 2008, Stephen carved one ton of pumpkins—that's 2,000 pounds of orange gourds—in just three hours, 33 minutes, and 49 seconds. During his record-setting performance in Atlantic City, New Jersey, Stephen carved a face on a pumpkin (complete with eyes, ears, nose, mouth, and eyebrows) in just 24.03 seconds! Both of these times are world records.

What's the Score?

Stephen carved all kinds of faces in pumpkins during his world-record run. Smiley faces. Silly faces. Weird faces. Angry faces. Some people enjoy carving the likenesses of cartoon characters, political figures, or athletes into pumpkins. Today, people carve pumpkins for fun—not to fight off evil spirits.

Besides, only God has control over spirits. In the beginning of Christ's ministry, he went into a town to preach. While he was in the synagogue teaching the people, a man possessed by an evil spirit began shouting, "I know who you are—the Holy One of God!" (Mark 1:24). Jesus told the man to be quiet and ordered the evil spirit to leave the man. Immediately the spirit left him. All the people were amazed by Jesus' power. "Even evil spirits obey his orders!" the people said (Mark 1:27).

Pumpkins have no power over evil spirits. Jesus does. Jesus has power over everything on earth and in heaven. There's nothing in your life that Jesus can't help you overcome. Whenever you're scared, confused, or don't know what to do, pray to him and ask for him to give you his power.

) On the Ball

Jesus cast out numerous evil spirits during his time on earth. Read about a couple of these instances in Mark 1:21-27 and Mark 5:1-13. Praise Jesus for his power.

) COACH'S COMMENT

Amazement gripped the audience, and they began to discuss what had happened. "What sort of new teaching is this?" they asked excitedly. "It has such authority! Even evil spirits obey his orders!" The news about Jesus spread quickly throughout the entire region of Galilee. MARK 1:27-28

Sometimes a strong team makes up for the lack of a superstar. It happened November 1, 2010, when the San Francisco Giants won their first World Series championship since moving to the City by the Bay in 1958.

Oh, the Giants had come close to claiming baseball's greatest prize in 1962 and in 1989. They should have won it in 2002 when all-time home-run king Barry Bonds led the team. Barry played like a superstar, and the Giants were only six outs away from victory. In the eighth inning of game six, the Giants were up 5–3, but the miraculous Anaheim Angels snatched a comeback victory. The Angels won the series the next night.

But the 2010 Giants were a team without superstars. Sure, they had the two-time Cy Young Award–winning pitcher Tim Lincecum. But no one had expected the Giants to come close to making it to the World Series, much less win it. Their underdog cast buried its egos and worked hard to find little ways to defeat the Texas Rangers in five games. A 3–1 victory on this day delivered a championship that even the big-name Giants of history couldn't claim.

What's the Score?

There will always be superstars, but it takes a team to win a championship. When everybody contributes, it makes victory even more satisfying and puts the credit where it should be—on the hard work of the whole group.

God wanted to teach his people a similar lesson in ancient Israel by choosing Gideon to lead his people. Gideon was no superstar. He gathered the biggest army he could. That sounds like a good idea when you're going to fight a war, right? God said, "Nope, too many fighters." God wanted a small band of underdogs to gain the victory, which would ultimately show his power. God told Gideon to fight in a really weird way—by blowing horns and smashing clay pots! Read about the battle in Judges 7. But it worked. Israel triumphed. God got the credit. And the people turned their hearts back to him. That's God's kind of championship!

) On the Ball

Are you a superstar? It could be in the classroom instead of on a sports field. How can you stay humble, help your teammates reach their potential, and give the credit to God? Write down some ideas:

) COACH'S COMMENT

The LORD said to Gideon, "You have too many warriors with you. If I let all of you fight the Midianites, the Israelites will boast to me that they saved themselves by their own strength." JUDGES 7:2

A bad attitude can derail a great player. It seems that's what happened to Randy Moss. The Minnesota Vikings fired the Pro Bowl wide receiver after he had played only four games for them in the 2010 season. The surprise move came after Randy criticized coaches in a postgame press conference. Some reports suggested Randy had asked the Vikings owner to fire the head coach. The receiver had also openly insulted caterers who served a team meal after practice.

Anyone can make mistakes, but Randy already had a long history of attitude and legal problems reaching back to his high school days. When he entered the NFL in 1997, *Sports Illustrated* called him "the most gifted player in college football" but also noted, "Moss is a stud, but attitude a dud." His talents were impressive on the field. He set the record for most touchdown catches in a season: 23 in 2007. But when things weren't going Randy's way—playing for a losing team, not getting enough catches, or not earning as much money as he wanted—selfishness shone through in his actions and words.

What's the Score?

The most talented player in the world can hurt a team with a bad attitude, selfish demands, or negative complaints. You might have seen it firsthand on a team or in your class. Nobody wants to play with a ball hog, and people get tired of hanging around a person who's always complaining or putting others down. Proverbs 12:18 reminds us that "some people make cutting remarks, but the words of the wise bring healing."

The Bible teaches that God cares a lot about the words and actions that express our attitudes. He looks more at the motivations behind our actions than at our stats or accomplishments. Our words should lift up others, not tear them down. Our words and actions should show respect, fairness, humility, love, and all the other traits of God's spirit—on the field and off. That's when we show we're truly wise.

) On the Ball

Give yourself an attitude check. Ask a coach, teacher, and parent if there's anything you can do to improve your play, studies, or attitude. Give their advice a try even if it's hard to do at first.

) COACH'S COMMENT

Some people make cutting remarks, but the words of the wise bring healing.
PROVERBS 12:18

Ryan Hall qualified for the 2008 Beijing Summer Olympics by shattering the US Olympic marathon trials record—and it was only the second marathon he had ever run! Ryan's accomplishment set the running world buzzing. It had been years since any American was a real threat to win a world-class marathon. Ryan didn't win Olympic gold like he'd hoped, but he finished a respectable 10th.

Disappointing? Yes, but Ryan knew there was much more to his running than winning. "Running is my way to really worship the Lord," he said. "I believe the Lord can do something amazing, but I want to have my heart in a place where I'm content with whatever the outcome will be."

Running was also the platform Ryan and his wife, Sara, used to serve the poor and encourage others to do the same. The couple partnered with World Vision and Invisible Children to help recreational runners raise money to bring clean water and medical treatment to Africa and to serve the poor in the United States.

☐☐ What's the Score?

God cares a lot about poor people and those who get pushed to the bottom of the world's social order. It's easy for us to think a homeless person is being lazy or that poor people should just get a job. It's also easy for us to want new clothes and cool electronics from fancy shopping malls—and easy not to think about poor people in other countries who made those items.

Jesus told a story in Matthew 25 about blessing and cursing people based on how they helped him when he was hungry, thirsty, alone, naked, sick, and in prison. Everyone asked with surprise, "When did we see you like that?" Jesus' answer cut straight to the point. He said whatever you do for the lowliest people, you do for him. The good news is, with a little attention, we can find lots of ways to help others—and show our love for Jesus at the same time.

⟩ On the Ball

Look around and find a way to help some people with big needs. Maybe you can run a race and raise money for orphans or to provide clean water. Maybe you can pack snacks or basic necessities into bags for homeless people. List three ideas here:

1. _____

2. _____

3. _____

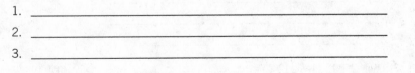

⟩ COACH'S COMMENT

The King will say, "I tell you the truth, when you did it to one of the least of these my brothers and sisters, you were doing it to me!" MATTHEW 25:40

In soccer, you're supposed to use your head to hit the ball—not another player. But in the final match of the 2006 World Cup, French superstar Zinedine Zidane let his anger get the best of him.

Zizou, as his fans called him, was one of the best soccer players in the world. He had led France to the World Cup finals against Italy. But with the score tied 1–1 late in extra time, he suddenly turned and head butted Italian defender Marco Materazzi in the chest. Marco had insulted Zinedine's mother, and Zizou reacted with anger. The powerful blow sent the Italian sprawling. Zizou was red carded and ejected from the game. France ended up losing on penalty kicks while their captain sat in the locker room.

Fast-forward four years. Zinedine had said he would never forgive Marco for insulting his mother. Then the two accidentally met in an Italian hotel lobby while visiting a coach who had instructed both players. Rumors swirled after the meeting. Marco confirmed that the two had talked but wouldn't reveal what was said. "Let's say I did most of the talking and when at the end he held out his hand, I shook it firmly until he looked me properly in the eye," Marco told Mediaset TV.

⏸ What's the Score?

The infamous head butt was Zizou's last act as a professional player, and it left a stain on his stellar career. He had already announced he would retire right after the 2006 World Cup. Did the Frenchman finally forgive his sworn enemy in that hotel? Did he let go of any bitterness in his heart? We may never know.

But we do know that God calls us to forgive even our worst enemies. Colossians 3:13 says to "make allowance for each other's faults, and forgive anyone who offends you." That's hard to do sometimes. People can hurt us badly—with words or weapons, on purpose or accidentally, once or over and over. Sometimes we need help from parents or other grown-up Christians to deal with our pain and to help us start to forgive. But we start with this: all of our worst, meanest, most rotten, and most hurtful sins killed Jesus—yet he forgave us. If Jesus can do that, he can help us learn to forgive other people who hurt us.

⟩ On the Ball

Choose to forgive. List some people who have hurt you.

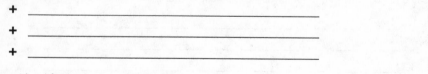

+ _____

+ _____

+ _____

Say out loud for each name, "I forgive _____. God, help me to really mean it and to show it."

- -

⟩ COACH'S COMMENT

Make allowance for each other's faults, and forgive anyone who offends you. Remember, the Lord forgave you, so you must forgive others. COLOSSIANS 3:13

- -

Sarah Glidden hears a lot of deer jokes. Are you going to compete in blaze orange? Will you go hunting with me? You're a real deer magnet! When are they going to put those deer-crossing signs on the course?

Sarah doesn't mind. She can laugh about the whole event—the one when a deer ran into her during a 2010 Wisconsin cross-country sectional meet. The high school sophomore was only about a hundred meters from the finish line when a deer bolted out of the woods, onto the racecourse, and smacked her. The startled runner could feel fur against her legs and a hoof against her shin. She was spun around but not badly hurt. However, she did lose valuable seconds.

The only chance at reaching the state meet was to finish in the top five. Sarah was already trailing the leaders, and she ended up finishing 18th. Did the deer encounter cost her a shot at state? It's hard to say, but Sarah kept a positive attitude anyway, talking with reporters and joking with friends.

What's the Score?

Sometimes life's problems blindside us. We can be cruising along just fine when *Thwack!* trouble hits our lives, kind of like a deer on a racecourse. Maybe it's a mean comment from a good friend, a bad grade, or the illness or death of a loved one. Sadly, we all experience bad or painful experiences as we live in this world.

The good news is that Jesus promised to be with us through every tough and awful situation we face. He promised his peace to help and comfort us—no matter how bad the problem. Jesus said, "Here on earth you will have many trials and sorrows. But take heart, because I have overcome the world" (John 16:33). He overcame our world and all the worst it can offer. One day, with his help, we will overcome too!

) On the Ball

What's your biggest problem right now? Talk to God about it. Ask what you can learn from it and how you can overcome it.

) COACH'S COMMENT

I have told you all this so that you may have peace in me. Here on earth you will have many trials and sorrows. But take heart, because I have overcome the world. JOHN 16:33

Most young athletes dream of winning a world championship. Holding a trophy over-head—just once—would be an incredible feeling. And then there's Kelly Slater. The pro surfer claimed his 10th world title on November 6, 2010! That's more championships than Michael Jordan or Lance Armstrong ever won. Following the victory, Kelly held the record for the youngest and oldest person to win an Association of Surfing Professionals (ASP) world championship. He claimed his first as a 20-year-old in 1992 and his 10th when he was 38. And he won more world ASP contests than anyone else.

That's impressive enough, but think about this: surfing advanced quite a bit in the 20 years after Kelly turned pro in 1990. You've seen crazy skateboarding and snowboarding tricks, right? Surfing is similar. Wave riders constantly create harder and higher tricks—finding new intense ways to ride the waves. Kelly helped to launch a new style of surfing when he turned pro as an 18-year-old—and he kept his progressive edge for more than 20 years.

What's the Score?

It takes a lot of commitment to stay at the top of a sport for two decades. It also takes a lot of love for what you do. Kelly Slater loves surfing, but in 1999 he unexpectedly retired after winning the ASP championship five years in a row. After resting and recharging his batteries, Kelly returned to competition in 2001 and claimed titles in 2005, 2006, 2008, and 2010.

Even a game or activity you love can get tiring sometimes. That's part of the reason God tells us to take a break with a Sabbath rest. The fourth commandment in Exodus 20:8-11 talks about setting apart a special day to honor God and rest. God even rested for a day after creating the universe (Genesis 2:2-3). He knows we need a spiritual rest so we can worship him and renew our spiritual batteries. Taking a day off each week helps us keep our priorities straight so we can get back to honoring God in whatever game or activity we love to do.

) On the Ball

Take a break. It doesn't have to be Sunday, but it's a good choice if your family already worships at church that day. Get any homework or sports and music practice done ahead of time so you can relax with your family and God.

) COACH'S COMMENT

On the seventh day God had finished his work of creation, so he rested from all his work. And God blessed the seventh day and declared it holy, because it was the day when he rested from all his work of creation. GENESIS 2:2-3

Have you ever dreamed of running a marathon? It's a great accomplishment to run for more than 26 miles. What would you do when you crossed the finish line? Collapse? Dive into the nearest pool? Drink a big milkshake and then sleep for three weeks? How about run another marathon—for the next 50 days straight?

That might sound crazy, but that's exactly what Dean Karnazes did in 2006. The professional ultramarathoner called it the Endurance 50—50 marathons on 50 consecutive days in all 50 states! He started in St. Louis and finished at the New York City Marathon in November. Oh, and then he ran back to where he started—St. Louis, a mere extra 1,300 miles. Dean's 50-marathon feat was seriously superhuman. But he was no stranger to difficult challenges. He ran a 135-mile ultramarathon across Death Valley in 120-degree heat, a marathon to the South Pole in negative-40-degree temperatures, and a 350-mile race. Plus, he won numerous 100-mile endurance races, including the world's toughest Badwater Ultramarathon.

⬜ What's the Score?

Dean ran because he loved it. And he enjoyed inspiring other people to get off the couch and go farther than they ever thought they could. When people hear about Dean's achievements, they usually think two things: (1) *He's crazy,* and (2) *Hey, maybe I could do something amazing.* Dean endured a lot of pain to train his body to run great distances. And he showed the world it's possible to achieve a goal when everything screams, "Give up, *now!*"

If a normal human can obliterate expectations like that, just think about what God is able to do. Paul wrote in Ephesians that God is able to amaze us. He's able to use his power in us to accomplish "infinitely more than we might ask or think" (Ephesians 3:20). Ponder that. But you really can't, because it's more than you can think of! He wants to blow right past your expectations. Do some dreaming with God. Then trust him as he leads you step by step to reach your goals.

⟩ On the Ball

Ask God for a big dream. You won't accomplish it overnight, but take the first step of trusting him.

⟩ COACH'S COMMENT

All glory to God, who is able, through his mighty power at work within us, to accomplish infinitely more than we might ask or think. EPHESIANS 3:20

Tom Dempsey was born with no toes on his right foot and with partial fingers on his right hand. That's not exactly how a lot of future NFL players start off in life. But the New Orleans Saints kicker made professional football history on this day in 1970 by booting a 63-yard field goal to beat the Detroit Lions with two seconds left in the game.

"The Kick," as it's still called, made Tom famous, but most people know little about the rest of his career. Tom played 10 years in the NFL and went to the Pro Bowl his rookie season. In college he was actually an all-conference defensive end and started kicking when his coach asked every player to try a kickoff. Tom boomed the ball. In high school he was on the wrestling and track teams, too. Kids had made fun of his hand and foot when he was young, but Tom didn't let the disability slow him down. After his football career was over, he even spoke to school groups about overcoming life's obstacles. One moment made Tom famous, but it was a million small moments that shaped his life.

⬜⬜ What's the Score?

What will your greatest moment be? You might never have one big moment of fame—but you will have a lifetime of daily successes and failures that will shape who you are.

The Bible teaches us to be consistent and committed to God in every moment. Tom Dempsey didn't even realize how long his famous kick was at the time. He found out it was a record breaker after the game. He was simply doing what he always did to try to help his team win—making the best of a small moment. The apostle Paul wrote his letter to Titus to encourage the church leader to stay consistent in all the little things. That's the kind of effort that builds integrity. Do your best to show consistent strength with your life. That's the kind of faithfulness that makes God happy.

⟩ On the Ball

Do today well. Focus on the little things of living out God's Word and loving the people around you. Jot down some ideas of little things that can add up to something big:

⟩ COACH'S COMMENT

You yourself must be an example to them by doing good works of every kind. Let everything you do reflect the integrity and seriousness of your teaching. TITUS 2:7

It was a classic trick play. Down 6–0 late in the third quarter of the championship game, the Driscoll Middle School Defenders of Corpus Christi, Texas, turned to their trick "Penalty Play." They had just drawn the Wynn Seale defense offsides. The Defenders came back to the line of scrimmage and reset for the next play. Eighth-grade quarterback Jason Garza looked to the sidelines like he was confused. Then the center handed the ball over his shoulder to Jason as he walked through the puzzled defenders. The Driscoll offensive line remained crouched at the line. The defensive line stood and watched Jason with total confusion.

Jason walked about five yards untouched—then bolted. That's when the defense finally came unfrozen. One cornerback sprinted after Jason and stayed on his heels. But he couldn't catch the wily quarterback. Jason was gone for a 67-yard touchdown.

What's the Score?

So was it a fair play? The snap was legal, even though it didn't come through the center's legs, and the touchdown stood. There's nothing in the rules against what Driscoll did, but it was definitely deceptive.

That's the way evil can be in our lives—sneaky and subtle. The devil is always looking for a trick play to beat us with, so we need to keep our guard up. We know we'll face temptation, so we must be prepared on how to handle it ahead of time. What will you say when someone asks for answers on a test? What will you do when someone offers you drugs? How about when a friend asks you to lie for her? What's your plan for telling a friend no thanks because that kind of movie, music, or video game makes God unhappy? Make your own game plan, and you won't get caught standing around like a tackling dummy.

) On the Ball

List temptations you know you'll face sooner or later. Start with the questions above to get you started. Then write your game plan for beating each one.

+ _____

+ _____

+ _____

+ _____

) COACH'S COMMENT

We are familiar with [Satan's] evil schemes. 2 CORINTHIANS 2:11

Do you ever go for a walk, maybe with your dog or with your family? Ever thought about going for a walk from Boston to San Francisco—and back? That's Andrew Skurka's kind of walk—at least the distance is. But he preferred to venture in wild places, not big cities. In November 2007, the 26-year-old hiker finished a route he called the Great Western Loop: a 6,875-mile circle around the western United States that took him through five major mountain ranges, 12 national parks, and 75 wilderness areas. It took him 208 days.

Andrew had done lots of epic-distance hikes. He had covered all the American long routes, including the Appalachian and Pacific Crest Trails. He had also walked across Iceland and had gone from the Atlantic Ocean in Quebec, Canada, to the Pacific Ocean in Washington state. *Phew!* Are you tired yet? Maybe you're wondering how Andrew always knew which direction to go. Sometimes he walked on trails, but other times he found himself on off-trail routes. Normally, Andrew used maps and a compass. Sometimes he turned to a GPS unit.

⬜⬜ What's the Score?

You've probably heard people say that life is a journey. It's true. Each day we face new challenges. We learn and grow. As Christians our goal is to follow God in all of life's adventures.

But sometimes we come to a place where we wonder which way to go. We want to follow God's will and make decisions that please him—but which way is that? It can be confusing, and we wish God would just speak to us in a big, booming voice. That's not usually how God communicates with people, but he has promised to guide us. Proverbs 3:6 says, "Seek his will in all you do, and he will show you which path to take." We can discover God's direction when we pray and listen for him to guide us with his Word. Plus, advice from wise Christians like our parents, teachers, and pastors will help us find God's will. We can have confidence that God will guide and go with us no matter where his adventures lead.

⟩ On the Ball

Talk to God about a hard decision you're facing. Ask your parents for advice, and look in the Bible for any principles that might guide your situation.

⟩ COACH'S COMMENT

Trust in the LORD with all your heart; do not depend on your own understanding. Seek his will in all you do, and he will show you which path to take. PROVERBS 3:5-6

Sports are cool. Comics are cool. What if you put them together? Supercool. Make that superhero cool. That's what the National Hockey League did. They partnered with Stan Lee, the famous comic artist who created Spider-Man, to create the Guardian Project. Stan and his team of artists dreamed up 30 new superheroes, one based on each pro hockey team.

The NHL revealed all the heroes' identities during the month of January, leading up to the 2010 All-Star game. Each Guardian had superpowers—often relating to his team's name. The Guardian for the Pittsburgh Penguins was unveiled first. The Penguin was an inventor who had penguin wings attached to his arms that allowed him to maneuver quickly in the water. The Flame, from Calgary, loved to snow ski and could generate flames in his bare hands and throw fireballs at his enemies. The Bruin from Boston was a gigantic, well-educated bear. All the Guardians worked together to fight evil, but there were some tensions between real-life rivals. Wondering how the Guardians handle a stick? Not necessarily very well. They're fans of their hockey teams, but their adventures take place in a world outside the arena.

□□ What's the Score?

Stan Lee would get body checked out of the rink in the NHL, but players like Sidney Crosby and Alex Ovechkin would be stuck scribbling stick figures (get it? *stick* figures) if they tried to be comic artists. Together they created cool new characters and stories.

God gives different gifts to different people. Some are great musicians or students or athletes or artists. When it came time to build God's Tabernacle and later his Temple in the Old Testament, leaders such as Moses and Solomon called on their best artists and craftsmen to do the work. The book of Exodus notes that "the LORD has given them special skills as engravers, designers, embroiderers in blue, purple, and scarlet thread on fine linen cloth, and weavers" (35:35). Artists throughout history inspire us with new ways of imagining or seeing things. And artists who follow God can reflect God's beauty and creativity in fresh, new ways. If you're good at art, give your creations all you've got for God. If art's not your thing, use whatever you like to do to glorify God.

⟩ On the Ball

Create something cool as a way to praise God. Draw, paint, sculpt, or build. Express yourself to your creative Creator.

⟩ COACH'S COMMENT

The LORD has given them special skills as engravers, designers, embroiderers in blue, purple, and scarlet thread on fine linen cloth, and weavers. They excel as craftsmen and as designers. EXODUS 35:35

Rachel Jennings really wanted to beat Duke University in field hockey. Sure, it would help Virginia's seeding in the ACC tournament. But even more, she wanted to beat her sister Tara, a Duke midfielder. Rachel was undefeated when facing Tara and their other triplet, Erin, a midfielder at Princeton.

Yep, you read that right: three sisters—triplets—all playing field hockey at different Division I field-hockey schools. And yes, they had a serious case of sibling rivalry, at least on the field. They said it's what drove them to be the best players they could be. The girls played together in high school, and all three were heavily recruited. Michigan State offered all of them full scholarships when they were just sophomores. But Rachel, Tara, and Erin wanted to go to different schools. They'd shared a room long enough.

Off the field, the Jennings sisters were good friends who kept in close touch. On the field, they pushed each other hard. For the record, Virginia beat Duke at the end of the 2010 regular season to keep Rachel's unbeaten streak against her sisters alive.

☐☐ What's the Score?

Sibling rivalry can be a problem. It can tear up a relationship. But competition and shared goals can also drive us to be better. A sibling or friend who's willing to push us in the right direction can make us the best we can be. That's what the Bible means when it talks about iron sharpening iron.

We need each other. We're stronger together. Sometimes there might be friction, so it's important to make sure love is the foundation of our relationships. We can push each other to be our best through encouragement, but other times we may have to deliver a difficult message. Maybe we'll have to tell a friend he or she is being selfish or needs to try harder when things get tough. A little friction doesn't have to be a bad thing—it can also make us sharper.

⟩ On the Ball

Set a goal with a friend, and plan how to achieve it. Create a team. Earn a good grade. Win a contest. Read a book of the Bible. Come up with your own ideas.

⟩ COACH'S COMMENT

As iron sharpens iron, so a friend sharpens a friend. **PROVERBS 27:17**

How many cartwheels can you do? Have you ever tried? Could you do 1,321 in a row? That's how many Abhinandan Sadalge did in November 2010 to set a new world record for most consecutive cartwheels. It took him nearly 38 minutes. Try doing cartwheels for five minutes straight. That's a long time to be spinning in circles. Are you getting dizzy just thinking about it?

The nine-year-old boy from Belgaum, India, didn't simply decide on the spur of the moment to do more than a thousand cartwheels in a row. Abhinandan's karate teachers had discovered his knack for cartwheels and helped him train for his record-breaking feat. Or should we call it a hands and feat? *Ha!*

▢▢ What's the Score?

Any great accomplishment takes practice and training. There has to be some natural ability involved, but that's not enough. Abhinandan is good at cartwheels, but so are lots of kids. It took him hours of disciplined practice and training to be able to do more than anyone else in the world.

Proper training provides the foundation for positive results. That's true in sports, music, school, hobbies, and work. It's also true in our spiritual lives. Our love for Jesus grows naturally in our hearts, but we have to train our heads and hands to learn God's ways. When we display discipline in our training, it builds habits that help us live for him. Thankfully, we're not in it alone in our training. We have God's Spirit to help us and to give us strength. We also have the motivation that our reward will last way longer than any medal, grade, honor, or award—even longer than any world record. Don't believe it? Just check out 1 Corinthians 9:25.

⟩ On the Ball

Set two goals, one for an earthly accomplishment and one for something in your spiritual life.

Goal: Training Steps:

_____   _____

_____   _____

⟩ COACH'S COMMENT

All athletes are disciplined in their training. They do it to win a prize that will fade away, but we do it for an eternal prize. 1 CORINTHIANS 9:25

The weather was bad. The plane was too low. On the night of November 14, 1970, a DC-9 airplane hit a hilltop, crashed, and exploded. The passengers were the Marshall University Thundering Herd football team, coaches, and booster-club members flying home after a game against East Carolina University. All 75 people on board were killed. It was the worst air tragedy in American sports history. Marshall and the entire state of West Virginia mourned the loss.

Jack Lengyel was hired to be the new coach and rebuild the football program that had been completely wiped out. His team was made up of a few returning players who hadn't made the trip, the former freshman team, and walk-on players. It took a long time for the school and community to grieve. But the new football coach gave them hope. By the 1990s, Marshall had become the winningest football team of the decade. The tragedy has never been forgotten, and the rebirth of Marshall—the team and the school—is still an inspiration.

⬜⬜ What's the Score?

Most tragedies are hard to understand. They make us ask God why. Most of the time there are no good answers except that our world is broken by sin. It breaks God's heart even more than ours to see the terrible things that happen. One day he will make every-thing right again. Until then, victims of tragedies need lots of help from God and from other people to heal.

God can and does bring hope. We have his promise that he can use our worst pain and suffering and turn it into something good—maybe even better than before. The apostle Paul, who went through a lot of suffering, wrote, "We know that in all things God works for the good of those who love him" (Romans 8:28, NIV). Maybe we'll be stronger than we were. Maybe we can help other people facing similar hard times. Or maybe we can find a solution or cure to keep others from suffering like we did. That's hard to imag-ine in the middle of pain, but God can give hope for a brand-new future.

⟩ On the Ball

Do you know someone who is hurting? Let that person know you care by writing an encouraging note, offering to talk, or just saying, "I'm sorry about what happened." Pray for God's goodness to show through.

⟩ COACH'S COMMENT

We know that in all things God works for the good of those who love him, who have been called according to his purpose. ROMANS 8:28 (NIV)

What do you get when you combine nearly 5 million dominoes, 90 workers, and two months of hard work? Answer: a world record! In 2009, 90 builders gathered in the Netherlands to help at the 11th Domino Day. Robin Paul Weijers, better known as "Mr. Domino," had worked all year to design different patterns and techniques that would creatively knock down 4,491,863 blocks. Over the course of two months, the helpers carefully set up each domino until everything was just perfect.

Sometimes the workers, who came from 14 different European countries, used tweezers and rulers to place each block in the right position. Once everything was ready, a miniature globe ran down a ramp to knock down the first domino at 11 p.m. That single falling domino set off a chain reaction that toppled all 4,491,863 blocks. As the dominoes fell, they unveiled different images from around the world, including the Statue of Liberty, the Parthenon, Mount Rushmore, and other famous landmarks. While it took more than 60 days to set up, all the dominoes fell in about one and a half hours!

What's the Score?

The old record of 4,345,027 falling dominos was set in 2008 at the same event by Mr. Domino. Watching that many blocks fall was amazing, especially as some of them set off bursts of fire or revealed hidden images. But sometimes the "domino effect" isn't a good thing.

Have you ever told a lie and then had to tell another one to cover up the truth? The writer of Proverbs 30 knew the dangers of lying. That's why he asked God to "help me never to tell a lie." Lying can cause a chain reaction. Before you know it, you've done so many wrong things that you can't count them all. God knew one bad decision would lead to another. That's why he commands us to always tell the truth and to follow his rule book. But remember, when you mess up you don't have to set off a chain reaction. You can ask God for forgiveness and stop yourself from being crushed by 5 million falling dominoes.

) On the Ball

Can you remember a time you didn't tell the truth? Ask God for forgiveness. Then find the person you lied to and admit what you did.

) COACH'S COMMENT

O God, I beg two favors from you; let me have them before I die. First, help me never to tell a lie. Second, give me neither poverty nor riches! **PROVERBS 30:7-8**

Oklahoma Sooners fans knew their team's victory over rival Texas was big, but nobody knew how big it would turn out to be. Following a 19–14 victory over Texas during the 1953 season, the Sooners wouldn't lose for the rest of the season. Oklahoma didn't lose the next season. Or the next season. Or the next!

Oklahoma University (OU) rolled off another seven wins in 1957, but then Notre Dame came to Norman, Oklahoma, with an iron defense. Neither team scored until the fourth quarter, when the Fighting Irish marched 80 yards to score a touchdown with less than four minutes left. The Sooners couldn't answer. On November 16, 1957, Oklahoma lost for the first time in nearly four years. The Oklahoma crowd stood and applauded Notre Dame at the end of the game to show their sportsmanship. The unbeaten streak had lasted 47 games—the longest in college football history. During that time the Sooners won two national championships—in 1955 and 1956.

What's the Score?

Everybody loses sometimes. Even the Sooners found that out . . . eventually. Have you ever heard the saying "You win some and you lose some"? It's the way life is. And that's a good thing. Winning *and* losing can give us chances to learn important lessons.

Ecclesiastes tells us there is a time for everything. We experience both good times and bad times, including being born and dying, laughing and crying, and peace and war. No matter what's going on, God is always with us. We can thank him in good times and in bad times. He never changes, and he will never leave us. He's the streak that will never end, even when our lives are showing more defeats than victories.

) On the Ball

Ask God what he wants to show you when you lose or are having a bad day. God is more concerned with improving your character than with the number of victories you can amass.

> COACH'S COMMENT

For everything there is a season, a time for every activity under heaven. ECCLESIASTES 3:1

Looking at the players on the 2010 Michigan Wolverines men's basketball team, you may wonder, *Was this a college roster or an NBA team?* It's easy to be confused by the names Horford, Hardaway, and Dumars.

Three of the Wolverines were the sons of former NBA players, and one, Josh Bartelstein, was the son of a pro sports agent. Jon Horford's dad, Tito, had played for the Milwaukee Bucks in the late 1980s, and his brother Al played in the NBA for the Atlanta Hawks. Tim Hardaway Jr.'s dad played 13 years in the pros until 2003. And Jordan Dumars's father, Joe, won NBA championships with the Detroit Pistons in 1989 and 1990 and was the president of the Pistons operations when his son started college. You could say the 2010 Wolverines had a ball growing up. Get it? They got to attend NBA games and hang out around professional athletes. But each of them realized his name didn't mean anything until he proved what he could do on the court.

What's the Score?

All three of these famous fathers said they didn't push their sons into basketball. Instead they were ready to support their sons in whatever activities they chose. But Michigan's Horford, Dumars, Hardaway Jr., and Bartelstein learned from their fathers. They paid attention. They listened to their dads' tips and advice, and they put into practice the same kind of work ethic their fathers had used to reach the highest levels of basketball.

What can you learn from your dad or mom? The Bible tells us not only to obey our parents (Ephesians 6:1), but also to listen to them (Proverbs 23:22). That's because God knows we need their guidance and wisdom to learn how to do well in life. Watch and listen to the ways your mom and dad work, play, and treat other people. Every dad and mom has his or her strengths and weaknesses. Nobody is perfect. They'll make mistakes, and sometimes we can learn even from watching those. But your parents have experienced a lot of things and know the challenges life brings—even if they've never played pro sports. You can gain lots of skill and wisdom right there in your very own home.

) On the Ball

Watch Mom and Dad. List three things they're good at that you'd like to be able to do too. Ask them for their advice; then write down their secrets.

1. _____

2. _____

3. _____

) COACH'S COMMENT

Listen to your father, who gave you life, and don't despise your mother when she is old.
PROVERBS 23:22

Many start exercising to lose weight. Miki Gorman started running to gain weight. She weighed only 87 pounds! Miki thought exercise would make her hungrier so that she would eat more and put on a few pounds. That was in 1968, before many women took part in running. Female marathon runners were even more rare. At the 1967 Boston Marathon, a race official even tried to physically pull a woman runner off the course—just for being female.

Miki ran her first marathon in 1973, when she was 38. Later that year, she set an unofficial world record! She went on to become the first and only woman to win the New York and Boston Marathons twice (Boston in 1974 and 1977 and New York in 1976 and 1977). Miki thought mental discipline was a big part of her running success. She had learned to be mentally tough growing up very poor in Japan after World War II. Even with her name in the record books, Miki views her greatest accomplishment as building a successful life in the United States after having left Japan with only $10 in her pocket.

What's the Score?

Hard work pays off. That doesn't mean you'll always win, but there is always something to gain from giving your best effort. You might learn something that pays off right away. Or you might look back later in life, like Miki, and see how discipline and hard work made you stronger.

It's easy to slack off or to think there's no point to what you're learning in school. Don't give in to that kind of thinking. The Bible tells us we reap what we sow (Galatians 6:7-8). In other words, we get out of life what we put in. That's true spiritually and physically. How's your work ethic? Are you ready to roll up your sleeves and sweat? Work hard in whatever you do, and watch the good results happen (Proverbs 12:14).

) On the Ball

Get a job. Be creative and find ways to earn extra money around your house or neighborhood. Working hard is good.

) COACH'S COMMENT

Wise words bring many benefits, and hard work brings rewards. PROVERBS 12:14

There's one cupcake left. You and your little brother want it. Who gets it? Maybe your mom will decide, or maybe you and your brother will play Rock, Paper, Scissors. It's a universal game. Everybody plays it. If only world leaders would adopt this game, we could avoid wars. Just kidding. But this game is so simple—it's genius!

You know how it works. You count to three and put out your hand. A flat hand is paper. A fist means rock. Two fingers are scissors. Paper covers rock. Rock breaks scissors. Scissors cut paper. Simple, right? Wrong. At the Rock, Paper, Scissors (RPS) annual world championships, this contest gets serious. Teams come up with strategies, team names, and uniforms—okay, they're more like costumes. Plus, there are special RPS terminologies. Three rocks in a row are called "The Avalanche." When scissors, paper, and scissors are played in consecutive order, it's "Paper Dolls." Want to know how to win? Guys like to play lots of rock, so play paper on the first throw. Or try to get your opponent not to play rock while you play scissors—if she plays paper, you win; if she plays scissors, it's a tie.

🎲 What's the Score?

There's probably more to Rock, Paper, Scissors than you thought, but there's still a lot of chance involved too. Thankfully, we don't have to rely on chance to face our battles in life. We can bring them to God. He has promised to fight for us. He has won the ultimate war even when we lose some daily battles.

God reminded his people in 2 Chronicles 20 that he fights for them. When three different armies ganged up on Israel, God said, "Hey, I've got this battle taken care of." So Israel went marching to the battle singing and praising God—and God wiped out their enemies before they even got there. What a great way to face our struggles and problems . . . much better than Rock, Paper, Scissors!

⟩ On the Ball

Turn your attention off your problems or people who have hurt you, and praise God instead. Sing, write a poem, or make a list of all the ways he's helped and cared for you.

⟩ COACH'S COMMENT

He said, "Listen, all you people of Judah and Jerusalem! Listen, King Jehoshaphat! This is what the LORD says: Do not be afraid! Don't be discouraged by this mighty army, for the battle is not yours, but God's." **2 CHRONICLES 20:15**

The goal wasn't a thing of beauty, but it was beautiful for Colorado Rapids fans. Trailing FC Dallas 1–0 in the 2010 Major League Soccer (MLS) Cup finals, the Rapids' Jamie Smith broke free on the left wing and played a beautiful rolling pass toward the near goalpost. Colorado forward Conor Casey slid for the ball, but so did Dallas goalkeeper Kevin Hartman and defender Jair Benitez. All three players ended up in a jumble on the ground. The ball bounced free, and Conor spun around on his backside to somehow get a foot on the ball and send it into the goal.

Colorado, a team that nobody thought would be in the 2010 MLS finals, ended up winning the game 2–1 in extra time. The Rapids had earned the seventh (out of eight) play-off slot and had been the underdogs all the way through the postseason. The final against Dallas wasn't a pretty game, but the scrappy Rapids fought hard to claim their first championship in the league's 15-year history. Even when they'd been knocked down—Casey literally—the Rapids refused to give up.

What's the Score?

Life has a way of knocking us around. We might be tempted to quit or to stop trying so hard. But don't give up! God is always with us and working to protect us, even if we can't see it at the moment. In the apostle Paul's letter to the Corinthians, he tells people in the early church to be encouraged when they suffer. At first that may seem like strange advice, but the truth is that suffering reminds us of God's great strength. When we go through difficult times, Jesus has a chance to shine through us and our problems.

What disappointments have knocked you down recently? Don't give up! Thank God for a chance to learn and to try again. Ask for his strength. Then get back up and keep kicking.

) On the Ball

Draw a picture of your problem or trouble. Then draw another picture of God taking care of it.

) COACH'S COMMENT

We are pressed on every side by troubles, but we are not crushed. We are perplexed, but not driven to despair. We are hunted down, but never abandoned by God. We get knocked down, but we are not destroyed. Through suffering, our bodies continue to share in the death of Jesus so that the life of Jesus may also be seen in our bodies.
2 CORINTHIANS 4:8-10

Drivers in NASCAR gain all the fame and become household names, but it's the pit crews behind the drivers that make them great—or not. Without the pit crew's mechanical wizardry to keep the cars running their best, the drivers might as well be steering go-karts. Just ask Jimmie Johnson. The driver of the No. 48 car came into the 2010 season-ending Ford 400 at Homestead-Miami Speedway, trailing Denny Hamlin in the overall NASCAR Sprint Cup Series points race. Jimmie had won four straight NASCAR titles, but only twice in history had the leader lost his lead in the final race. It looked like J.J.'s streak might be over.

Jimmie's team struggled early in the race, botching one pit stop. But crew chief Chad Knaus came through when it mattered most. Calling for a crucial adjustment, the fine-tuned No. 48 allowed Jimmie to move from 11th place to second in the final 69 laps. By claiming second, Jimmie earned enough points to achieve his record-breaking fifth-straight Sprint Cup championship. Denny took 14th in the race and settled for second overall.

☐☐ What's the Score?

Jimmie's fifth-straight Sprint Cup championship was a victory for the whole team. The Bible says we need others to help us be successful living for God. Ecclesiastes 4:12 gives us a great word picture. Have you ever looked closely at a rope? Instead of one solo strand, it's actually several cords braided together. The rope is way stronger when all the bands are wrapped together.

People are the same way. We all need at least one close friend we can trust to give us solid advice and encouragement. It's called accountability, and it means walking together toward the same goal of living for God. A friend we're accountable to is someone we can be totally honest with. In other words, we can freely talk about our hopes, dreams, struggles, failures, and successes. Friends like that won't laugh at us; they'll encourage us to keep going for God. An accountability partner keeps us fine tuned—just like a NASCAR crew chief.

〉 On the Ball

Who has your back? List your most trustworthy friends, and talk to them privately about pursuing God together. You might set a goal of memorizing some Bible verses or reading parts of the Bible together.

Friends:

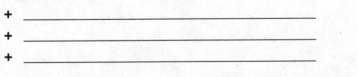

+ _____

+ _____

+ _____

〉 COACH'S COMMENT

A person standing alone can be attacked and defeated, but two can stand back-to-back and conquer. Three are even better, for a triple-braided cord is not easily broken.
ECCLESIASTES 4:12

Many professional athletes make so much money, they're rolling in dough. Members of the US Pizza Team (USPT) just roll the dough. They can make a delicious meal and put on a good show by throwing and spinning pizza dough. You might have seen them in the 2010 Macy's Thanksgiving Day Parade. The 30 or so members of the team have traveled to international pizza competitions too. Pizza competitions—who knew?

If you haven't seen the USPT, these pizza spinners combine acrobatics, break dancing, juggling, and gymnastics. They can spin multiple pizzas at once or roll them across their shoulders or behind their backs. Feeling inspired to toss around some dough—or just plain hungry? Research shows the average American consumes 23 pounds of pizza every year. Just remember the US Pizza Team members were trained professionals. Don't try their tricks at home, especially if your pizza is already cooked.

What's the Score?

Pizza spinning all comes down to a basic move: the Whip. That's when you hold the dough flat like a Frisbee and toss it in a figure-eight motion. Without this move, you have no hope of joining the US Pizza Team. It's like learning to read, or to throw and catch, or to play scales and chords. It's the foundation.

Jesus told us the core move to be a Christian is to love God with all our heart, soul, mind, and strength (Mark 12:30). Every other spiritual fundamental is based off this move. Loving God leads us to loving other people. It makes us want to obey him, learn about him, spend time with him, get involved in what he cares about, avoid temptation, and help other people. Want to build a stronger spiritual life? Start by loving God with everything you've got.

) On the Ball

Spend some time hanging out with God. Go for a walk and pray. Read a chapter in the Bible. Write a praise song. Or eat some pizza and talk with him.

) COACH'S COMMENT

Jesus replied, "The most important commandment is this: 'Listen, O Israel! The LORD our God is the one and only LORD. And you must love the LORD your God with all your heart, all your soul, all your mind, and all your strength.'" MARK 12:29-30

Surfers have a special way of honoring their friends and family members who die. It's called a paddle out. The surfers paddle past the breaking waves into calmer water where they form a circle as they sit on their surfboards. Sometimes they hold hands while they share stories or pray. They might even scatter ashes of their loved one into the ocean.

In November 2010, thousands paddled surfboards, outrigger canoes, and other boats into the waters off Kauai, Hawaii, to honor Andy Irons. Even more stayed on the beach after a memorial service. Andy was a great surfer and a three-time world champion. He was only 32 when he died unexpectedly. Andy will be remembered as a fierce competitor who also had a big, giving heart. His paddle out was a reminder that many people will miss him, especially family and friends who lost him so suddenly.

⬜⬜ What's the Score?

Has someone you loved died? It really hurts, especially if that person's death came tragically or unexpectedly. We feel comforted when the person who died was a Christian, because we know he or she is with Jesus in heaven. It helps to know he or she is free of any pain and enjoying eternal life. But it still hurts because we miss our friend or relative.

Death wasn't part of God's original plan. It didn't exist in the Garden of Eden. It's the worst effect of sin. Thankfully, Jesus overcame death and gave us a way to eternal life in him. For now we hope for that life to come. In the book of Isaiah, God promises to one day get rid of death once and for all (Isaiah 25:8). When Jesus sets up his new heaven and new earth, there won't be any more sadness, crying, loss, separation, or death. There won't be any more need for paddle outs either.

⟩ On the Ball

Lots of times it takes help and support from other people to deal with the death of a loved one. Talk with somebody if you're facing that kind of loss. If not, pray for someone you know who is.

⟩ COACH'S COMMENT

He will swallow up death forever. The Lord and King will wipe away the tears from everyone's face. He will remove the shame of his people from the whole earth. The Lord has spoken. ISAIAH 25:8 (NIrV)

When can praying earn you a penalty? Never, right? Wrong. In the Washington Class 2A state semifinal football game, Tumwater High School running back Ronnie Hastie received a 15-yard unsportsmanlike conduct penalty for giving glory to God. The flag came from out of the blue—and actually hit the junior running back as he knelt in the end zone.

After running for a 23-yard touchdown, Ronnie did what he had done 17 times before in the 2010 season: he knelt, bowed his head, and then pointed a finger to the sky. It's his way of giving glory to God, not himself, he told reporters afterward. He'd never been penalized for it before. But this time, the referee told him he couldn't draw attention to himself. Ironically, the penalty received national attention. Fortunately, the penalty didn't hurt his team. Ronnie's Thunderbirds defeated East Valley 63–27 to advance to the state championship. Tumwater claimed the state championship the following week with a 34–14 victory over Archbishop Murphy High School.

⬜ What's the Score?

Did Ronnie do anything wrong? No. The reason for the rule was to crack down on players doing end-zone celebrations or dances or choreographed moves. But Ronnie wasn't trying to draw attention to himself. He wanted to honor God. Many people raised a big outcry in the weeks following the game. Ronnie didn't make a big deal of it, even though the whole situation caught him by surprise. The high school junior didn't want to hurt his team, so he said he would just kneel and thank God on the sideline after scoring future touchdowns.

In the early days of the church, Peter and some other apostles were arrested and dragged before the priests. Why? For preaching about Jesus—just like Jesus had told them to do. When they were faced with punishment and maybe even death, they told the priests they wouldn't stop telling others about Jesus. Obeying God was more important than obeying men (Acts 5:29). Jesus taught us to respect authorities, so we should—until that means we would have to disobey God. When there's a conflict, God should always come first.

⟩ On the Ball

How do you give credit to God when you accomplish something good? Make a plan to thank God and respect other people when you score, get a good grade, or win a contest or prize.

⟩ COACH'S COMMENT

Peter and the apostles replied, "We must obey God rather than any human authority."
ACTS 5:29

Who doesn't love to battle it out with a cardboard tube? That brown roller at the center of wrapping paper makes a great sword. Kids are usually the masters when it comes to cardboard warfare. The Cardboard Tube Fighting League wanted to make sure adults didn't outgrow the fun either.

The league started in San Francisco when Robert Easley reinterpreted the US Constitution's right to bear arms to include cardboard tubes. There's an official chapter in Australia, too. Official league rules state, "No stabbing, no blocking with arms, and no body slamming." The last person with an unbroken tube wins the duel. The Cardboard Tube Fighting League holds contests where anyone can fight in mass battles. Some tournaments feature one-on-one duels. Many competitors wear fancy costumes or cardboard armor—samurai-style looks awesome! Robert wanted to make cardboard dueling an official Olympic sport. Can you imagine winning a gold medal for your cardboard-tube skills?

▢▢ What's the Score?

Cardboard fighting is fun, but did you know you're also part of a great battle? It's the ultimate battle between good and evil—between God and Satan. The Bible describes God as a warrior (Exodus 15:3) and says he trains us for battle (Psalm 144:1). Paul gives us the imagery of our spiritual armor and tells us that we fight against spiritual forces (Ephesians 6:11-18). We're not fighting other people; we're fighting God's enemies.

What does that look like for us? Most importantly, it means remembering we have an enemy. We have to keep our guard up against temptation and anything that will pull our hearts away from God. And we must look to God for our training so he can shape us with his Word. Cardboard tubes may be fun, but they won't do a lot of good against the devil.

⟩ On the Ball

Fight God's way. Pray about any problems you're facing. Talk to him about any people you're having trouble with. Ask him to help you stay strong.

⟩ COACH'S COMMENT

Praise the LORD, who is my rock. He trains my hands for war and gives my fingers skill for battle. PSALM 144:1

The game looked hopeless for Auburn fans. The Tigers trailed 24–0 midway through the second quarter in the 2010 Iron Bowl. That's what the annual football game between Auburn and Alabama is called. These universities first played each other in 1893, and many people think it's the biggest rivalry in college football.

Early on, the 2010 game went all Alabama's way. The Crimson Tide scored three touchdowns in the first quarter and added a field goal in the second. Auburn was supposed to be the favorite. The Tigers were undefeated and ranked second in the nation, thanks to their Heisman Trophy–winning quarterback, Cam Newton. But the Tigers faced their biggest deficit of the season and were playing in Alabama's home stadium, where the Tide hadn't lost in 20 games!

Auburn's coaches and quarterback steadied their team. Cam threw a touchdown pass before halftime. Then on the first drive of the second half, Cam connected with Terrell Zachery for a 70-yard score. Momentum swung Auburn's way. With 11:55 left in the fourth quarter, Cam completed his third touchdown pass to put Auburn on top for good. The Tigers won the game 28–27. Auburn fans called it the greatest Iron Bowl ever. The Tigers never gave up, and their determination paid off with an incredible victory that kept them marching toward a national championship.

🏈 What's the Score?

It's easy to give up when you're way behind. You can feel the defeat seeping in, and everything inside says you should quit. Maybe your math grade is so low that you don't think you'll ever pull it up. Maybe you've hurt a friend's feelings so deeply it seems like you'll never be friends again.

When you start to feel that way, don't give up! Don't get tired of doing good. Paul tells us we'll eventually see some results from our efforts. "Let's not get tired of doing what is good. At just the right time we will reap a harvest of blessing if we don't give up" (Galatians 6:9). God will reward our obedience. We may not see our reward until heaven, but other times we'll see results sooner. Even when we're struggling, God sees how we're trying. Ask for his strength, and then keep going!

) On the Ball

Are you tempted to give up on something? Don't quit. Talk to your parents, and ask for help. Pray to God for his strength to keep going.

) COACH'S COMMENT

Let's not get tired of doing what is good. At just the right time we will reap a harvest of blessing if we don't give up. GALATIANS 6:9

When your parents ask you to sweep the kitchen—do it! They may be training you to become an Olympic curler. Unless you live in Canada or close to it, the sport of curling probably looks a little strange. It's kind of like shuffleboard on ice. One player slides a smooth granite stone down a sheet of ice toward a big, flat bull's-eye. Sweepers with special brooms wildly brush the ice in front of the stone to keep the stone moving smoothly and in the right path.

Some curlers from the Coaldale Curling Club in Alberta, Canada, wanted to bring attention to their sport in 2010, so they set a world record. Team Rough Cookie took on Technical Foul in the longest curling match in history: 57 straight hours. That's almost two and half days and nights of nonstop curling! Each team had five teens, including one sub. Each player got a five-minute break every hour and a two-hour nap every eight hours—but the bed had to stay on the ice.

Once the curlers had broken the old record of 54 hours, the focus became more about winning. Rough Cookie beat Technical Foul 178–172. The teams raised $8,000 for renovations to their curling club and claimed the world record!

☐☐ What's the Score?

Think you could play any game for almost three straight days? You would definitely have to be passionate about the sport. Rough Cookie and Technical Foul showed a lot of endurance and patience—two traits God wants us to show in our spiritual lives.

Sometimes it takes awhile to hear God's answers to our prayers. He wants us to learn through the process. Colossians 1:11 says, "We also pray that you will be strengthened with all his glorious power so you will have all the endurance and patience you need." Sometimes we have to keep showing Christ's love to people around us. Sometimes we can feel tired because people make fun of us for not going along with activities that don't please God. But just like these Canadian curlers, we can set a strong example that gains respect. When we show endurance and patience, other people see our commitment and want to get involved—with God!

⟩ On the Ball

Ask your parents or friends to pray for you to have endurance and patience in your spiritual life.

⟩ COACH'S COMMENT

We also pray that you will be strengthened with all his glorious power so you will have all the endurance and patience you need. COLOSSIANS 1:11

Would you keep playing your instrument or sport if you knew it could cost your life? That's a real question that women on Afghanistan's national soccer team had to answer. When the Taliban was in power, women and girls were not allowed to play sports in Afghanistan. The United States drove the Taliban out of power in 2001, but many of those cultural feelings toward women remained.

That didn't stop some women from playing soccer. Some of those players, such as Khatol Shahzad Amarkhel, received death threats. Friends warned 19-year-old Sajay Sahar to quit, but she wouldn't. She saw playing soccer as a form of protest and a challenge to the Taliban. The team practiced every other day, but they had to travel to other countries to play games. Team captain Zahra Mahmoodi wanted to show all Afghan girls that they could play sports.

☐☐ What's the Score?

Showing courage doesn't mean you're not afraid. It means you do the right thing even when you *are* afraid. God's message to his people and their new leader, Joshua, was to take courage when they were on the verge of finally going into the land God had promised them. God also gave them a promise: "God is with you wherever you go" (Joshua 1:9).

Does that message make you feel bold and brave? It should. When you have God on your side, you couldn't have a better "teammate," because God is bigger than any challenge or enemy we'll face. He can see the big picture when we can't. He can turn our bad into good. Afghan women played soccer for freedom. Their love for the game drove them through danger and fear. Our love for God can drive us through any fear and obstacle we face, too!

) On the Ball

What's your biggest fear? Draw a picture of God helping you beat it with his courage.

) COACH'S COMMENT

This is my command—be strong and courageous! Do not be afraid or discouraged. For the LORD your God is with you wherever you go. JOSHUA 1:9

You know you've been coaching for a while when the US Congress passes a resolution to honor you—for 400 wins! Joe Paterno had been coaching Penn State's football team for so long that his name was nearly synonymous with the Nittany Lions. He started coaching at Penn State in 1966 and was still going strong in 2010.

How unheard of is it to last more than four decades coaching college football, especially at one school? Well, from 1966 through 2010, there were 874 head-coaching changes in the top ranks of college football. That's more than six coaching changes per school! But Joe's success made him an icon. He ranked at or near the top of all-time wins, winning percentage, and postseason victories.

But when the Nittany Lions struggled in the early 2000s, many fans complained that Joe was too old to keep coaching. Even in his eighties, Joe never wavered, and Penn State stuck by him. He still held a deep passion for the game and for helping his young players. He certainly brought more wisdom and experience to the game than anyone else around.

What's the Score?

How old are your grandparents? Sometimes it's easy to look at old people like they're out of touch. But we can learn a lot from the senior citizens in our families, churches, and communities. Sure, some may move a little slower than you and not be up with the current technology. But their brains and hearts are filled with amazing experiences and lessons learned about God, life, careers, people, and much more.

Don't miss out on your opportunities to learn from the world's wisest. Job 12:12 tells us that "wisdom belongs to the aged, and understanding to the old." Visit your grandparents and your friends' grandparents. Get to know different seniors at church. Invite them to your class or middle-school group. Reach out to those in your neighborhood with a plate of cookies, or offer to help them with some yard work for free.

) On the Ball

Hang out with some older people, and let their wisdom rub off on you. List some old people you know and how you can help them and connect with them. You'll be surprised by what you learn.

1. _____
2. _____
3. _____

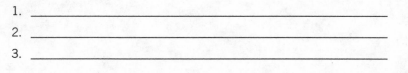

) COACH'S COMMENT

Wisdom belongs to the aged, and understanding to the old. JOB 12:12

Børge Ousland had a love for ice and snow. In November 1996, the Norwegian polar explorer started out to cross Antarctica alone with no support or resupply. *In a super-heated snowcat, right?* you might think. *Or at least on a snowmobile.* Nope, on foot, with cross-country skis. For 64 days, Børge towed a sled with his supplies through temperatures down to negative 68°F. He passed the South Pole and reached the far side of Antarctica 1,768 miles later. Sounds like a once-in-a-lifetime accomplishment. Not for the man *National Geographic Adventure* has called "arguably the most accomplished polar explorer alive!"

Børge's other accomplishments included being the first human to ski alone to each of the earth's poles, the first to reach the North Pole in winter, and the first to cross the Arctic alone. The guy just couldn't get enough of wintry, long-distance adventures. After a 2007 journey crossing the Arctic islands of Russia's Franz Josef Land, Børge sailed back to southern Norway—and then rode his bike the remaining 775 miles home to Oslo!

What's the Score?

Don't you love snow days? It's fun to get a day off school, but can you imagine 64 snow days in a row—without a cozy fireplace? Just a wintry, white wonderland. When you think about it, snow is so cool. It falls silently. It's cold, pure, and beautiful as it blankets the earth.

That's probably why God used it to paint a picture of his forgiveness. God says he washes away our sins to make us as white as snow (Isaiah 1:18). That's pure white, clean, and fresh. All our ugly sin is washed away by beautiful forgiveness. The next time you get a snow day, look out your window or roll over from making a snow angel and remember God's amazing forgiveness. Thank him for washing you as white as the snow!

) On the Ball

Confess your sins to God and feel great knowing he forgives you and cleans your heart. If there's snow outside, go build a snowman to celebrate!

) COACH'S COMMENT

"Come now, let's settle this," says the LORD. "Though your sins are like scarlet, I will make them as white as snow. Though they are red like crimson, I will make them as white as wool." ISAIAH 1:18

Indianapolis Colts star quarterback Peyton Manning is a master of calling the right play at the right time. Most NFL teams called a play in the huddle, lined up, and ran it. When Peyton was on the field, the Colts rarely huddled at all. Instead Peyton looked at the defense and shouted out some signals that only his team could understand. Then the Colts would line up, and Peyton would bark out different commands. Suddenly, everybody would shift to a new play.

In football terms, Peyton was calling an "audible." That's when a quarterback changes a play based on how he sees the defense lining up. If you've ever watched a Colts game, you've probably seen Peyton's animated hand flaps, exaggerated foot stomps, and other wild body motions. Peyton was always watching the opposing team's safeties and middle linebackers to try to determine where the defense's weaknesses were going to be. Then he would change the Colts' play accordingly. In just 40 seconds, Peyton could change a play several times based on the defense's alignment.

What's the Score?

Peyton changed the Colts' plays all the time, and it served him well. Heading into the 2011 season, Peyton already held many NFL passing records and had led Indianapolis to a victory in Super Bowl XLI. He will go down in history as one of the greatest quarterbacks ever, thanks in part to his ability to change plays on short notice.

Change was good for the Colts, but Christians should be thankful we serve a God who never changes. God's unchanging nature is one of his most important characteristics explained in Scripture. Think about it: What if God could change? What if he could improve, or change for the better? That would mean he wasn't the best possible God in the first place. And even more alarming, it would mean he could possibly change for the worse.

Thankfully, we don't have to worry about those questions because God never changes (Malachi 3:6). He never makes a bad choice and then has to do something over. His character is consistent. He is always the same holy God, who is all-powerful, all-knowing, perfectly loving, and just. The greatest NFL quarterbacks might change, but God never does!

) On the Ball

Drop some "change" in your pocket—some pennies, nickels, and dimes. Then reach in and pull out a coin. Look at the number of cents represented by the coin, and think of that number of ways that God doesn't change. For instance, if you pull out a penny, think of one way God doesn't change; if it's a nickel, think of five ways.

) COACH'S COMMENT

I am the LORD, and I do not change.   MALACHI 3:6

Michael Vick entered the 2010 NFL season as one of the most hated people in sports. He finished the year as one of the most respected. Playing quarterback for the Philadelphia Eagles, Michael made defenders look silly as they tried to catch him. At first, fans weren't sure how to react. Several years earlier, Michael had served a 19-month prison term for his involvement in illegal dogfighting. Many people felt the 2001 first overall draft pick should never be allowed to play football again. Because of his terrible crimes, they said he didn't deserve a second chance.

Philadelphia signed Michael in 2009, but he hardly played. When the Eagles' starting quarterback got injured at the beginning of the 2010 season, Michael stepped in and showed his past greatness. In fact, maybe he played even better than he ever had before. Shortly after Michael led Philadelphia to consecutive wins against Washington and New York, *Sports Illustrated* ran a cover story on him with the headline, "Is It OK to Cheer?"

What's the Score?

Regardless of what people thought of him, Michael was grateful for a second chance. Jonah was thankful for a second chance too. You remember Jonah, right? God instructed the Old Testament prophet to tell the wicked people of Nineveh to repent and follow God. But Jonah said no and sailed in the opposite direction to Tarshish. Bad idea. God caused a great storm. When the crew realized Jonah was the cause of their problems, they threw him overboard. Things looked pretty bad for Jonah until he cried out to the Lord in his great trouble, and God answered him (Jonah 2:2). God miraculously saved Jonah by sending a great fish to swallow him and spit him onto dry land three days later. Grateful for his second chance, Jonah preached to the Ninevites, who repented.

We're more like Jonah than we care to admit. Maybe we haven't tried to board a ship to Tarshish, but we've all said no to God. That's called sin. Just like Jonah learned, going against God's commands is not very smart. God has every right to punish us for our sins. But in his mercy, he provided us a second chance through his Son, Jesus Christ. And finding forgiveness in Jesus is way better than traveling around in a smelly fish.

) On the Ball

The next time you beat someone in a game, give that person a second chance. Remember what God has done for you.

) COACH'S COMMENT

He said, "I cried out to the LORD in my great trouble, and he answered me." JONAH 2:2

When **penguins r*efuse*** to live somewhere, you know it's cold.

Every winter since 2006, a small group of brave souls have journeyed south—way, way south!—to compete in the Antarctic Ice Marathon, a 26.2-mile footrace in one of the coldest, driest, most unforgiving environments on earth. The competitors come to this icy wasteland for a challenge that you can't get running in famous metropolitan races like the New York City or Boston marathons. At a remote location only a few hundred miles from the South Pole, temperatures frequently dip below zero. Katabatic winds swirl through the area at a steady 20 miles per hour. And at an altitude of 3,000 feet above sea level, it is difficult to breathe.

The severe conditions make the race much more about endurance than speed. Jason Wolfe, the 2010 Antarctic Ice Marathon winner, finished in four hours, 46 minutes, and 50 seconds. For perspective, Ethiopia's Gebre Gebrmariam won the 2010 New York City Marathon in less than half that time (2:08.14).

What's the Score?

Extreme marathoners get a kick out of traveling to a place as remote and forbidding as Antarctica to run a race. While the apostle Paul never visited the South Pole, he traveled to the corners of the known world in the first century to spread the gospel of Jesus Christ. In Paul's day, the borders of the Roman Empire were considered the boundaries of the civilized world, stretching from what is now Great Britain and Spain to Palestine and Egypt. Inspired by Jesus' command in Matthew 28:16-20 to preach Christianity everywhere, Paul traveled to far-off places like Corinth, Philippi, Crete, Malta, and Rome.

Jesus' command, known as "the great commission," still applies to Christians today. If you have trusted in Jesus, you are called to share the Good News of salvation through Christ with others just like Paul did (Ephesians 3:8). God might call you one day to be a missionary to faraway lands. But you don't have to get a passport to tell someone about Jesus. There are plenty of opportunities nearby. Whom do you know that needs to hear the gospel? A close friend? A neighbor or a classmate? A family member? Chances are, you don't need to go far to share your faith.

) On the Ball

Choose one person you know to share the gospel with this week.

) COACH'S COMMENT

Although I am less than the least of all the Lord's people, this grace was given me: to preach to the Gentiles the boundless riches of Christ. **EPHESIANS 3:8 (NIV)**

This tweet was not so sweet. During the 2010 NFL season, Bills wide receiver Steve Johnson had a chance to upset the highly favored Pittsburgh Steelers with a game-winning catch. The Bills and the Steelers were tied at 16–16 in overtime when Bills quarterback Ryan Fitzpatrick lofted a beautiful 40-yard pass to Steve and into the end zone. But unexplainably Steve dropped it. On their next possession, the Steelers won the game on a field goal. After the game, Steve posted this message on his Twitter account: "I PRAISE YOU 24/7!!!!!! AND THIS HOW YOU DO ME!!!!! YOU EXPECT ME TO LEARN FROM THIS??? HOW???!!! ILL NEVER FORGET THIS!! EVER!!! THX THO . . ."

Steve's tweet presumably directed blame for the loss at God. Steve seemed to be saying, "God, why is this happening to me? Is this your best plan? Don't I deserve better?"

⏸ What's the Score?

Steve's pattern of thinking was a familiar one. Humans have been asking those questions since the world began. When things don't go as we had hoped, we often ask, "Why, God?"

Seven hundred years before Christ came to earth, Habakkuk asked the same thing. Habakkuk was an Old Testament prophet who predicted the Babylonian invasions of Judah as divine punishment for Judah's flagrant idolatry against God. But Habakkuk didn't understand why God would punish Judah using a nation more wicked than itself. He questioned God's wisdom and goodness.

But here's a better question: Who are we to question God?

God is the holy creator of all things and the perfect author of goodness. We, on the other hand, are human. Anything good that we receive is a gift of God's mercy. God's definition of goodness is far different from ours. He often uses difficult situations in our lives—even those that are painful—to produce ultimate good. He can do this because he is all-knowing and all-powerful. We often can't see God's good purposes because we have a very limited understanding. Habakkuk eventually realized this. The last three verses of his Old Testament book show his change of heart. He went from questioning God's goodness to trusting and praising God, even if he didn't fully understand what God was doing.

⟩ On the Ball

Read the book of Habakkuk and see how Habakkuk eventually learned not to question God's goodness. When things don't go as you had hoped, follow Habakkuk's example.

⟩ COACH'S COMMENT

Even though the flocks die in the fields, and the cattle barns are empty, yet I will rejoice in the LORD! I will be joyful in the God of my salvation! HABAKKUK 3:17-18

Timber! All Canadian trees beware—it's lumberjacking season in the Great White North! A lumberjack, in case you didn't know, is a person who cuts down trees. Think axes, saws, and heavy flannel shirts. December is the heart of the Canadian Intercollegiate Lumberjacking Association (CILA) season. CILA events are contested between October and February each year among six Canadian colleges and universities—Algonquin, McGill, Nova Scotia Agricultural, Sir Sandford Fleming, New Brunswick, and Maritime College of Forest Technology. Who else but America's husky northern neighbors would create a competitive sport that involves chain saws, axes, and log stacking?

The rules of CILA competition are relatively simple: try to score more points than the other team, and don't chop off your hand. Just kidding. Actually, CILA events are a little more complex than that. Participants compete in Chain Saw, Underhand Chop, Pole Climb, Log Decking, Ax Throw, and Super Swede Saw. If you feel more manly just reading about this sport, consider that lumberjacking isn't just for men. The CILA hosts women's competitions, too. (I wonder if they're called lumberjills.)

What's the Score?

Believe it or not, Jesus used the imagery of lumberjacking to teach us an important lesson about life. In Luke 3:9, Jesus said God's judgment is like a sharp ax and that people are like trees. If a tree produces good fruit, it is safe. But any bad, fruitless tree will be cut down and destroyed. In other words, we all have a choice to make. We can be healthy trees that produce the good, pleasing fruit of obedience, thanks to a heart that is changed by Jesus. The fruit of a healthy tree can be found in Galatians 5:22-23. God will bless these trees. Or we can choose to be bad trees, withered by sin and a lack of faith. Fruitless trees are worthless.

Just like a farmer wouldn't keep an apple tree that doesn't produce apples, God will cut down, or separate from himself, all those who aren't connected to him and don't produce the kind of fruit that comes as a result of being saved through his grace. With this in mind, the choice is obvious. Be a good, fruit-bearing tree for the Lord!

) On the Ball

Ask your parents to help you plant and care for a tree as a reminder that God wants you to be a healthy, fruitful Christian.

) COACH'S COMMENT

Even now the ax of God's judgment is poised, ready to sever the roots of the trees. Yes, every tree that does not produce good fruit will be chopped down and thrown into the fire. LUKE 3:9

"C'mon guys, let's go out there and be *really* mediocre!" When was the last time you heard a professional athlete yell that in the pregame huddle? Never. No athlete, regardless of the sport, wants to be average, either in his or her personal performance or as a team.

But certain professional leagues have play-off systems that sometimes reward mediocrity. Take the NBA and NHL, for instance. Sixteen of the 30 teams in each league qualify for the play-offs each year. That's more than half! In 2008, the Atlanta Hawks backed into the NBA play-offs with a 37–45 record. A year later, the Detroit Pistons did the same after a 39–43 regular season. Talk about average! In the NHL, the Edmonton Oilers reached the Stanley Cup play-offs with a losing record five times between 1980 and 1999. The NFL is a little more demanding when it comes to the play-offs, allowing only 12 of 32 teams to make the postseason play. But play-off mediocrity happens there, too. In 2010, the Seattle Seahawks hosted a play-off game after winning the NFC West Division with a 7–9 record.

What's the Score?

Being average might work for certain professional sports leagues, but it doesn't work in the Christian life. God calls his children to the highest possible standard: holiness. The word *holy* means "set apart." In all creation, only God is truly holy. He is set apart by his infinite perfection in righteousness, justice, wisdom, and power. On the other hand, we are mediocre at best. Some people make as many bad decisions as they do good ones.

In Leviticus, God gave the Israelites (and us) a shocking command: "Be holy because I, the LORD, am holy." If it seems like an impossible request, it is—at least for us. There's nothing we can do to achieve holiness on our own. But God provided a way for us to reach his perfect standard—by sending his perfect Son, Jesus Christ, to die for our sins. When we place our faith in Jesus, God credits Jesus' righteousness to us and considers us holy too. God doesn't accept anything less than holiness. But he *does* accept the sacrifice of his holy Son on our behalf. Incredible!

) On the Ball

Using a Bible concordance, do a study on the word *holy* by looking up Scripture passages where it is mentioned. Write down your favorite verse here:

) COACH'S COMMENT

You must be holy because I, the LORD, am holy. I have set you apart from all other people to be my very own. LEVITICUS 20:26

Star players often receive the star treatment. They receive special privileges because of their tremendous skills. But when Washington Redskins coach Mike Shanahan suspended star defensive lineman Albert Haynesworth, he called it "an easy decision." On this day in 2010, Mike suspended Albert without pay for the last four games of the season, citing conduct detrimental to the team. Albert was separated from the organization that hired him to be a star.

Almost from the moment he signed a record $100 million contract in February 2009, Albert was immersed in controversy. In the 22 months he spent with the Redskins before the suspension, he skipped off-season workouts, failed several preseason conditioning tests, was sent home from practice for disciplinary reasons, and complained about his role on the team. Finally, two days after Albert had missed a practice before a game against the New York Giants, the Redskins suspended him.

What's the Score?

Teams suspend or cut troublesome players only as a last resort. Sadly, there comes a time after giving people many chances to repent when God has to separate himself from the wicked and condemn them forever to a place called hell. Hell isn't mentioned much these days. It's not a fun subject to talk about. But hell is a real place, and it's important that we know about it.

Hell is a terrible place that the Bible calls "the lake of fire" (Revelation 20:14-15) and a place of "outer darkness" and "weeping and gnashing of teeth" (Matthew 8:12). What's worse, hell is where unbelievers will be separated from God—forever cut off from his love and fellowship (2 Thessalonians 1:9).

Some people don't believe in hell. "How can a just, loving God send people to such a place?" they ask. But we all deserve to be separated from God, because God's holy justice requires punishment for sin. The fact that God allows anyone into heaven is a wonderful display of mercy and love. Christians don't need to fear hell because God promises heaven to his children. But hell's reality should cause us to be even more grateful that God offers salvation through Christ.

) On the Ball

As terrible as hell will be, heaven will be amazingly wonderful. Draw a picture of what you think it'll be like. Tell a non-Christian friend about Jesus. It could be a life-saving moment for that person.

) COACH'S COMMENT

He will come with his mighty angels, in flaming fire, bringing judgment on those who don't know God and on those who refuse to obey the Good News of our Lord Jesus. They will be punished with eternal destruction, forever separated from the Lord and from his glorious power. 2 THESSALONIANS 1:7-9

Lending a hand is easy. Lending a kidney? Not so much. But that's exactly what Washington Nationals hitting coach Rick Eckstein did. Rick comes from a family with a history of kidney failure. Four of his immediate family members—his father, two sisters, and a brother—all needed kidney transplants at one time or another. Near the end of the 2010 Major League Baseball season, Rick started feeling a heavy burden for his brother, Ken, who had received his first kidney transplant in 1991 and needed to replace the 19-year-old organ quickly.

Rick decided to donate one of his kidneys to Ken. This was no small decision. Not only was he giving up an organ, but he was also potentially affecting his career. As a highly dedicated hitting coach, Rick had learned how to swing like each hitter on the team so he could better teach his players. Any complications from surgery might have hindered that ability. No matter. Because of his deep love for his brother, Rick endured a success-ful five-and-a-half-hour transplant surgery with Ken on this day in 2010. As he was being wheeled into his recovery room, Rick gave Ken a thumbs-up.

⬜ What's the Score?

Rick Eckstein's decision to help his brother was an incredible example of Philippians 2:3: "Be humble, thinking of others as better than yourselves." And while not all of us are called to donate organs, we all must obey the biblical command to consider others better than ourselves.

A simpler way to say it is, "Put others first." This is at the heart of the gospel mes-sage. When we place our faith in Jesus, we are committing our lives to the ultimate model of putting others first.

After all, Jesus humbled himself by coming to earth and dying for all of humanity's sins. If that's not putting others first, nothing is! To put others first, we must stop thinking of ourselves so highly and actively look for ways to serve others. If Jesus considered us better than himself (even though we're far from it!), certainly we can do the same to others.

⟩ On the Ball

Read Philippians 2:1-11 to better understand Christ's example of considering others better than yourself. Then list three ways you can do that today:

1. _____
2. _____
3. _____

- -

⟩ COACH'S COMMENT

Don't be selfish; don't try to impress others. Be humble, thinking of others as better than yourselves. PHILIPPIANS 2:3

- -

Whoosh! Pete Sampras's running forehands used to disappear past opponents like cupcakes at a birthday party. One moment you saw it. The next it was gone. But early in December 2010, it was Pete's championship trophies that vanished in a headline-making case of thievery. In a 15-year Hall of Fame career, Pete had won 64 total tournaments, including a then-record 14 Grand Slam titles. That's a lot of hardware! But most of Pete's collection of trophies and other memorabilia was swiped from a public storage facility in West Los Angeles, California.

Thirteen of his major championship trophies remained safe in other locations, but his 1994 Australian Open trophy and all his other awards were gone. The haul also included an Olympic ring and his awards for being ranked No. 1 in the world for six straight years, winning five season-ending ATP World Tour titles, and playing on two Davis Cup–winning teams. "Losing this stuff," Pete told reporters, "is like having the history of my tennis life taken away."

What's the Score?

Sadly, Pete learned a real-life lesson of something Jesus talked about in the Bible. In Matthew 6, Jesus warned a large group of followers not to chase after earthly possessions. We would do well to heed Jesus' words too.

We love stuff. Toys, video games, musical devices, sports equipment, clothes, money—you name it. We love cool new gadgets and the latest fads. It's part of our sinful nature to crave more and more. But all earthly possessions will eventually fade away. They'll break, deteriorate, get lost, become outdated or, like Pete's trophies, get stolen. Think about it: in a few years, your favorite video game, toy, or electronic device will probably be broken, lost, or replaced by the next hot item. Why run after things like that? Rather, Jesus said, we should store up heavenly treasures that will last forever. These are the eternal blessings that Christians will receive after they die for obeying God and serving others here on earth. Let's go after those treasures instead!

) On the Ball

Give away some of your possessions to those less fortunate than you. Surprise a needy friend or neighbor. Or drop off a package at a thrift store such as the Salvation Army or Goodwill.

) COACH'S COMMENT

Don't store up treasures here on earth, where moths eat them and rust destroys them, and where thieves break in and steal. Store your treasures in heaven, where moths and rust cannot destroy, and thieves do not break in and steal. Wherever your treasure is, there the desires of your heart will also be. MATTHEW 6:19-21

Rules never seemed so exciting . . . or expensive. On this day in 2010, David Booth, a billionaire from Texas, purchased basketball's original set of rules for $4.3 million at an auction in New York City. The two-page, mostly typewritten document fetched the largest sum ever paid for sports memorabilia.

Dr. James Naismith, basketball's inventor, wrote the "Founding Rules of Basketball" in 1891 in Springfield, Massachusetts, so students at a local YMCA school could enjoy an indoor sport in the winter. He certainly never dreamed basketball would become as popular as it is today. All of the dunking, three-point shooting, high-flying excitement began because of a humble set of rules in 1891.

What's the Score?

Let's admit it: we don't like rules. Oh sure, rules are good for keeping the peace in sports, traffic safety, and government. But honestly, nobody likes being told what to do. So it's not surprising that many people stay away from the Pentateuch. The Penta-what? The Pentateuch is the old Greek name for the first five books of the Bible—Genesis, Exodus, Leviticus, Numbers, and Deuteronomy. Many Christians might read Genesis but then skip the last four because they contain seemingly outdated Jewish rules. *How,* we ask, *are all these rules about eating, washing, religious festivals, offerings, and priestly duties relevant to us today?*

Very much, actually. First, the Old Testament is just as much Holy Scripture as the New Testament. While we are not bound to certain Old Testament rules today (like priestly garments, animal sacrifices, etc.), plenty of the Pentateuch still applies—such as the Ten Commandments and the call to love God wholeheartedly. But most importantly, Old Testament law revealed to ancient Israel how desperately we fall short of God's holy standard. As Romans 3:20 tells us, "Through the law we become conscious of our sin" (NIV). Old Testament law provides us a greater awareness of how rebellious we are and how merciful God is. God knew we couldn't follow his law perfectly. So he provided a sinless Savior, his Son, Jesus Christ, to fulfill the law for us (Matthew 5:17). The entire Old Testament points to Jesus and his sacrificial death. Where the law failed, Christ succeeded!

) On the Ball

To better understand how Old Testament law applies to us today, study Galatians 2–5 and Romans 2:12-16.

) COACH'S COMMENT

No one will be declared righteous in God's sight by the works of the law; rather, through the law we become conscious of our sin. ROMANS 3:20 (NIV)

You probably won't see one of these teams vying for a national championship, but when Army and Navy play football, it's one of the most compelling rivalries in all of sports. It's a game that pits America's future warriors against each other, fighting for touchdowns before fighting for our freedom. The rivalry started in 1890 and has been contested annually since 1930.

Navy has dominated the rivalry lately. The Midshipmen's 31–17 win in 2010 was their ninth straight over the Black Knights and gave them a 55–49–7 edge all-time in the series. Part of what makes the games so compelling is the military history and patriotic sacrifice among its participants. Most of the players on each team enter active military duty once they graduate. In fact, 10 days before the 2010 game, Navy's 24 seniors received their service assignments. Many were assigned to the war in Afghanistan or other dangerous parts of the world. "You know this is it for them," Navy coach Ken Niumatalolo told the *Washington Post* shortly before the 2010 Army-Navy game. "They'll be in harm's way. It's really an emotional time in the locker room after the game." These athletes are true warriors!

What's the Score?

In Zephaniah 3, the Bible describes God as a mighty warrior. Zephaniah was an Old Testament prophet who lived in Judah during the reign of Josiah in the late seventh century BC. Zephaniah prophesied future judgment for Judah because they worshiped idols instead of the one true God. At the end of the book, Zephaniah promises that God will fight for his people and restore them. He calls God a "Mighty Warrior who saves" (Zephaniah 3:17, NIV).

Thanks to its impressive soldiers like those in the annual Army-Navy game, the United States has one of the world's strongest militaries. But no power in the universe is stronger than God. He created and controls all things. He wins every battle. One day, he will once and for all destroy his greatest enemy, Satan. This same warrior God is one we can have a personal relationship with. God loves us and wants to help us fight against sin. He is the Mighty Warrior indeed!

⟩ On the Ball

Do you have a family member or know someone who serves in the military? Today, take time to write that person a thank you note. You may also want to send a care package and let that person know you're praying for him or her.

⟩ COACH'S COMMENT

The LORD your God is with you, the Mighty Warrior who saves. He will take great delight in you; in his love he will no longer rebuke you, but will rejoice over you with singing.
ZEPHANIAH 3:17 (NIV)

Imagine if you had to watch sports without saying a word. That wouldn't be much fun, would it? How would you celebrate a great play or yell at the referees for a bad call? Admit it: you've yelled—or, at the very least, complained—at a referee's call while watching a game on TV. Maybe you've even done it while attending a game in person. It doesn't matter what sport—we've all done it.

Some people get really creative at what they yell at a referee. Simply booing isn't enough for these folks. See if any of these examples sound familiar:

- "Hey, ref, if you had one more eye, you'd be a Cyclops!"
- "Hey, ref, how much is the other team paying you?"
- "My grandmother sees better than you!"

And so on . . .

What's the Score?

Yep, we can get pretty creative (and unkind) when we are convinced a referee has blown a call. Why do we act this way? Do we really think that we know better than referees, even though they are highly trained professionals who typically make the call a few feet from the play? If you think about it that way, it sounds kind of silly.

But pride makes us act silly. We often think we know more than we do. Compared to God, or to referees, our knowledge is extremely limited. We don't even know what will happen to us one minute from now. God is omniscient, or all-knowing. First John 3:20 says, "He knows everything." He never learns or forgets. He never scratches his head while trying to remember something. His knowledge never changes. This is a critically important truth for us to understand. If we believe our knowledge is superior to God's, or at least is sufficient without him in certain situations, we could easily argue that we don't need God. But that would be a terrible error that would harm our lives in countless ways.

The more we understand that God is all-knowing, the better off we will be. It will help us worship him and trust him. It will help us persevere through difficult trials. It will give us hope for the present and the future. And it might even help us forgive referees.

On the Ball

Next time you're at the library, try to count how many books there are. Then consider this: all the knowledge in those books is only a small fraction of what God knows.

COACH'S COMMENT

He knows everything. 1 JOHN 3:20

For Matt Capps, this day in 2009 was a really bad day. The former Pittsburgh Pirates closer had endured the worst season of his young career, going 4–8 with an unsightly 5.80 earned-run average. So that December, the Pirates cut him. More than anything, Matt wanted to talk to his father, Mike. But that wasn't possible. Two months earlier, Mike Capps had fallen off a ladder in his garage, gone into a coma, and died. Mike's death was a devastating blow to Matt—much more so than being cut from a team. Mike had been Matt's best friend and mentor for many years. They used to talk almost every day on the phone, especially after Matt had had a bad game. On nights Matt pitched, he would call his father around 1 a.m. to discuss his performance and receive helpful tips.

Sometimes Mike would give soothing words of encouragement. Other times he would offer constructive criticism. But either way, the conversations meant a great deal to Matt. In 2010, with the memory of his father fresh in his mind, Matt earned his first All-Star Game appearance, combining for a 2.47 ERA and 42 saves with the Minnesota Twins.

☐☐ What's the Score?

One of Matt Capps's greatest joys in life was talking to his father every day. We should have the same attitude with our heavenly Father. Prayer is a great privilege. Do you treat it that way? Many Christians don't. They think it's too hard, or they don't know what to say. Knowing this, Jesus gave us a model to follow in Matthew 6:9-13, which is known as the Lord's Prayer.

Open your Bible and read this prayer. You'll notice that Jesus encourages us first to praise God and to ask for our desires to match his (verses 9-10). We are to ask God to provide for our daily needs (verse 11) and to help us obey him, avoid sin, and show love to others (verses 12-13). Notice that selfish requests like "Please give me more video games" or "Please let my team win" are absent from the Lord's Prayer. While it's okay to make our requests known to God, our prayers should be focused on his will, not ours. The Bible has much more to say about prayer, but learning some of the basics from the Lord's Prayer is a great way to start.

) On the Ball

Memorize the Lord's Prayer in Matthew 6:9-13.

> COACH'S COMMENT

Pray like this: Our Father in heaven, may your name be kept holy. MATTHEW 6:9

Jason Campbell just couldn't seem to catch a break. In 2005, Jason's NFL career seemed destined for greatness. After having led Auburn University to a 13-0 record a season earlier, Jason was drafted in the first round by the Washington Redskins and was named their quarterback of the future. But he never really caught on in DC, which wasn't entirely his fault. The Redskins changed offensive systems almost every year that Jason was in Washington, and he rarely had a strong offensive line to protect him. In the Redskins' last play-off season, Jason was sidelined with an injury when the team's record was 6-7 and watched as backup Todd Collins led the team to three straight wins and a play-off berth in 2007.

Finally, after five frustrating seasons, the Redskins traded Jason to Oakland. It seemed like a fresh start. But midway through the second game of the 2010 season, the Raiders benched Jason in favor of Bruce Gradkowski.

What's the Score?

While Jason didn't always perform like a first-round draft pick, the problems he faced were often out of his control. Yet throughout his career, he has never complained or given up. Jason, who became a Christian when he was in junior high, realizes that difficulties are meant for our good.

The Bible teaches that trials—or difficult situations—are actually good because they show us who we are. They are like an X-ray, examining everything that's going on inside us. Trials test our faith, reveal what we're trusting in, and show us where we need to grow. In fact, God often allows us to go through different types of trials. This is not unkind of him. It actually shows that he loves us, because trials help us pinpoint where our hearts and minds are sinful and need to be adjusted. The next time you endure a trial, do the unexpected: thank God for it!

) On the Ball

Make a list of trials you've gone through in life and what God has taught you through them.

Trial	What I Learned
_____	_____
_____	_____
_____	_____
_____	_____

) COACH'S COMMENT

Dear brothers and sisters, when troubles come your way, consider it an opportunity for great joy. For you know that when your faith is tested, your endurance has a chance to grow. So let it grow, for when your endurance is fully developed, you will be perfect and complete, needing nothing. JAMES 1:2-4

At age 11, Adrian Moore was a scrawny sixth grader in Arkansas. He was still three years away from being able to legally get his learner's permit in his home state and seven years away from being allowed to vote. But man, the kid sure could dunk!

In 2010, Adrian became an Internet sensation for his ability to rattle rims as a six-foot-two-inch middle schooler. That fall, Middle School Elite ranked him as the No. 6 player in the country. Rumors circulated that Baylor University in Texas had already taken note of his talent. Many of Adrian's mad skillz (when you can dunk at 11, your abilities graduate from "skills" to "skillz") can be found online. One of the best highlights is a dunk where Adrian launched into the air for a one-handed jam, like a young Michael Jordan. At age 11, the sky truly seemed to be the limit for Moore.

░░ What's the Score?

Adrian's basketball talent got him a lot of notice at a young age. But that's nothing compared to King Josiah of the Bible. Sure, Josiah might not have dunked (basketball was about 2,500 years from being invented), but like Adrian, he was way ahead of his time. Josiah was one of Judah's greatest kings, ruling in Palestine for 31 years. But check this out: he became king at age eight!

Josiah took over as king under terrible circumstances. His father, Amon, and grandfather Manasseh were two of the worst kings in Judah's history, having plunged the nation into idolatry and wickedness. Two years into Amon's reign, his servants murdered him and replaced him with Josiah. To make matters worse, Egypt, Assyria, and Babylonia were all jockeying for Middle Eastern control. With this moral and political chaos going on, Josiah spent his time as king trying to return Judah to worshiping the one true God. He repaired God's Temple, destroyed the country's idols, reinstituted the Passover celebration, and told the people to obey God. Josiah proved that age matters little to God. What's important is following God with all your heart. The Bible sums up Josiah's life by saying, "He did not turn away from doing what was right" (2 Kings 22:2). Whether you are an eight-year-old king, an 11-year-old basketball prodigy, or just a normal kid, God wants you to follow him, no matter what.

) On the Ball

Read about Josiah's amazing life in 2 Kings 22–23 and 2 Chronicles 34–35. Write down some parts of his life that impress you most:

) COACH'S COMMENT

[Josiah] did what was pleasing in the LORD's sight and followed the example of his ancestor David. He did not turn away from doing what was right. **2 KINGS 22:2**

Like a lot of kids, Jay Fleming loved sports. His favorites were baseball, basketball, and swimming. Nothing particularly unique about that, right? But on December 16, 2010, Jay found out he had won a national home-video contest on ESPN. So why all the attention? Because Jay only has one arm.

Jay, a resident of Hendersonville, Tennessee, was 10 years old when he won the contest. He lost his left arm in a boating accident at age six, but that didn't stop him from playing sports. Remarkably, Jay helped his youth baseball team win a championship, and the home video that won an ESPN contest showed him winning his 25-meter butterfly heat against two-armed competitors in a 2010 Nashville city swim meet. After national viewers voted Jay's video as the winner, ESPN called him at his local elementary school for a live interview on *SportsCenter*. "He never gives up," Jay's mother told Nashville's WSMV-Channel 4. "He is very determined. To see him go out there with these other swimmers who have an advantage, he swims his best, and has won a lot of competitions. I'm just really proud."

⛀ What's the Score?

Considering his circumstances, it would have been understandable if Jay had avoided sports. But he didn't use his disability as an excuse. While most of us will never experience anything as difficult as Jay has, we all go through trials in life. As passages like James 1:2-4 and 1 Peter 1:6-7 tell us, trials are meant for our good and God's glory. That still doesn't make them easy or enjoyable.

So how do we endure trials? The answer is found in Philippians 4:13: "I can do everything through Christ, who gives me strength." No matter what challenge you are going through, the strength to persevere and overcome does not originate inside you. By recognizing where your strength comes from and relying on that power, you can overcome any trial. The strength to persevere through difficulties comes from the eternal Son of God who created the world, sacrificed himself for your sins, rose from the dead, and now reigns in heaven with all majesty and glory.

⟩ On the Ball

Have you prayed recently about a trial you are going through? Take a moment right now to pray for Christ's strength, knowing he will be faithful to answer your request.

⟩ COACH'S COMMENT

I can do everything through Christ, who gives me strength. **PHILIPPIANS 4:13**

When Scott Hamilton won the gold medal at the 1984 Winter Olympics in Sarajevo, he became one of the most famous male figure skaters in US history. But who knows what his life would have been like if he hadn't been adopted? Ernest and Dorothy Hamilton, two schoolteachers from Bowling Green, Ohio, adopted Scott when he was six weeks old. After he put on ice skates at age nine, it quickly became evident that he was a rising star.

Scott eventually won numerous national and world championships. In 1990, he was inducted into the World Figure Skating and US Olympic Halls of Fame. Following his competitive skating days, Scott has enjoyed a wide-ranging career. In the 1980s and 1990s, he went on 15 national tours with *Stars on Ice*. He also produced other ice shows, TV specials, and an off-Broadway production. Scott is often seen on TV, giving his insights on various figure-skating competitions. He has even authored several books. Would any of this have happened if two loving parents hadn't adopted Scott? We'll never know.

What's the Score?

Did you know that all Christians are adopted? It's true! When you put your faith in Jesus, you are not only forgiven of your sins, but God also adopts you as his child! John 1, Romans 8, Galatians 4, Ephesians 1, and 1 John 3 all talk about this wonderful act. By adopting us, God reveals a lot about his loving character.

God doesn't want to merely forgive us of our sins—although that in itself is amazing! He also wants to train us to become more like him as our loving heavenly Father. By adopting true believers, God gives us the full rights and privileges of sons and daughters—his love, his blessings, and his Spirit. Rather than being a distant God, he is intimately near to us. Our adoption as children of God has future benefits too. All believers will spend eternity with him in heaven, where we will see his face. Amazing!

) On the Ball

Talk with your parents about "adopting" a child in a third-world country through a charitable organization such as Compassion or World Vision. You can help another child to know a loving heavenly Father by providing money, food, and Bibles; writing letters; and praying for him or her.

) COACH'S COMMENT

He predestined us for adoption to sonship through Jesus Christ, in accordance with his pleasure and will. EPHESIANS 1:5 (NIV)

Home plate is nice. So is the finish line when you're running. But football's end zone might be the greatest final destination in all American sports. End zones have produced some memorable moments. In the 1982 NFC championship game, San Francisco quarterback Joe Montana seemingly threw a ball out of the end zone before Dwight Clark made an amazing leaping grab that's simply remembered as "The Catch." Then there was the heartbreaking final play of Super Bowl XXXIV when Tennessee Titans receiver Kevin Dyson came up one yard short of the end zone.

College football has provided its share of memorable end-zone moments too. In the 2007 Fiesta Bowl, Boise State shocked Oklahoma 43–42 in overtime. The Broncos used a trick-play two-point conversion called the Statue of Liberty to beat the mighty Sooners. Moments after Boise State's Ian Johnson ran into the end zone, he found his girlfriend, a Broncos cheerleader, and asked her to marry him. She said yes! The end zone never felt so good.

⏸ What's the Score?

The end zone is where every football player strives to go. But spiritually speaking, there's an infinitely greater final destination we should all aspire to: heaven. Heaven is a real place. It's where God dwells in indescribable holiness, majesty, and power. In his love, God has offered eternal life in heaven to all followers of his Son, Jesus Christ. In fact, after his death and resurrection, Jesus returned to heaven to prepare it for all Christians (John 14:2-3).

While much of heaven will be a secret until we get there, God gives us a sneak peak in the book of Revelation. Check out chapters 21 and 22—human words can scarcely describe heaven's glory. To be in God's presence for eternity is beyond all comprehension. Sadly, heaven is not for everyone. The Bible is clear that only the righteous—those who accept Jesus' gift of salvation and who live for him—will enter heaven. Good works can't get you there. Neither can simply going to church or being raised by Christian parents. Heaven is reserved for those who turn from their sins and put their faith in Jesus Christ. Even though we will die one day, our souls will live forever—either in heaven or hell. Choose heaven, the greatest destination!

〉 On the Ball

Read Revelation 21–22 to learn more about heaven. Write down some of the most amazing parts:

If you're not sure where you will go when you die, talk to your parents, your youth pastor, or another trusted adult.

〉 COACH'S COMMENT

Nothing evil will be allowed to enter, nor anyone who practices shameful idolatry and dishonesty—but only those whose names are written in the Lamb's Book of Life.

REVELATION 21:27

"I can't do it" was not a familiar phrase to Anthony Robles during his college wrestling career. With an upper body that looked chiseled out of granite, superb technical skills, and a never-say-never spirit, Anthony put together an impressive four years at Arizona State University. That's saying a lot, considering the amazing history of the Sun Devils' program. But here's the most amazing thing about Anthony's supremacy on the mat: he had only one leg.

Anthony was born without a right leg. But he never used his physical limitation as an excuse. By high school, he was one of the top wrestlers in the country, winning two Arizona state titles and the 2006 High School Senior Nationals. On this day in 2010, Anthony, the third-ranked 125-pounder in the nation at the time, earned his 100th collegiate victory. He dominated his foes at the Reno Tournament of Champions in Nevada by a cumulative 73–3 score and reeled off five straight wins. Career win 100 was just another accolade in Anthony's vast trophy case, which already included two straight All-American awards and Pac-10 championships.

What's the Score?

While Anthony almost always appeared powerful and in control on the mat, there certainly were times when he felt weak. At some point, he must have struggled with his physical limitations as he learned to live with one leg. But even if our bodies are fully formed, we all feel weak at times. It's a natural human condition. Here's the good news: God specializes in helping the weak. Isaiah 40:29 says, "He gives power to the weak and strength to the powerless."

Are you feeling physically or mentally weak right now? God can give you strength. Are you feeling spiritually weak? God can give you the faith needed to follow him. Isn't it incredible that the all-powerful God of the universe cares about weak mortals like us? God loves showing his power through our weaknesses. It brings him glory and strengthens our faith. So when you feel weak or powerless, take heart. God wants to help!

) On the Ball

Push yourself to your physical limit by seeing how many push-ups and sit-ups you can do. When your muscles start to wear down, be reminded that God empowers the weak.

) COACH'S COMMENT

He gives power to the weak and strength to the powerless.   ISAIAH 40:29

Broadway shows have nothing over the theatrics created before professional sporting events. Before Miami Heat basketball games during the 2010–2011 season, a video of a flaming gold basketball lit screens inside the stadium. Music blared, and fireworks blasted as players' names were read. And there was no way that the game could start until LeBron James smacked his hands together, causing a cloud of white powder to billow into the air.

The Baltimore Ravens featured a gigantic bird with flashing eyes in its pregame spectacle. Ten-foot-high columns spewed flames and smoke into the air. Fireworks exploded in the sky. As music blared, players began appearing from the smoky tunnel. Finally, No. 52 emerged as the last player out. With eye black covering his face like war paint, Ray Lewis roared onto the field doing his famous pregame dance.

What's the Score?

Fans love to cheer when their favorite athletes enter the arena. They rise to their feet as the announcer shouts the players' names. But if you think that's an impressive show, you should check out the Bible's description of what will happen when Jesus returns to earth. A day is coming when Jesus will come back to take all Christians to heaven and begin God's final judgment. The Bible often refers to this as "the day of the Lord." It's a date in the future—known only to God himself—when the current heaven and earth will be destroyed and a new heavenly Kingdom will be created to last forever.

Joel 2:31 says "the sun will become dark, and the moon will turn blood red" on this day. Although it sounds scary, followers of Christ don't have to fear this coming judgment. After the frightening words of Joel 2:30-31, verse 32 provides this reassuring promise: "Everyone who calls on the name of the LORD will be saved." God's future judgment will be on the wicked, not on the righteous. Anyone who has put his or her faith in Jesus as Lord and Savior can look forward to, not dread, his second coming—and the amazing display of God's power that will announce it.

On the Ball

Learn more about the "day of the Lord" and the end times in general by reading Matthew 24, Mark 13, and the entire book of Revelation. Write down any questions you have about these Scriptures to ask a pastor or a parent.

COACH'S COMMENT

I will cause wonders in the heavens and on the earth—blood and fire and columns of smoke. The sun will become dark, and the moon will turn blood red before that great and terrible day of the LORD arrives. JOEL 2:30-31

No team is unbeatable. But for several years, the University of Connecticut women's basketball team sure seemed unstoppable. On December 21, 2010, UConn won its 89th straight game with a 93–62 blowout of Florida State, giving the Huskies the all-time record for consecutive wins at the college level—men or women. Legendary coach John Wooden and his UCLA men's program had held the previous record of 88 games between 1971 and 1974 while they were in the middle of an unmatched streak of seven straight national championships. UCLA's 88-game mark was thought by many college basketball insiders to be a virtually unbreakable record.

But coach Geno Auriemma's Huskies were a rare breed (no dog pun intended). UConn's last loss before the streak started was on April 6, 2008, in the NCAA Tournament semifinals against Stanford. During their record-breaking span, the Huskies steamrolled opponents. Only twice during that time did they beat an opponent by less than 10 points. UConn finally lost two games later against Stanford, ending its streak at 90 games, but that didn't tarnish the Huskies' amazing accomplishment.

☐☐ What's the Score?

No team can win that many consecutive games without a sharp focus on its goal. It's no different in the Christian life. To be most effective in God's Kingdom, we have to know what our goals are. This leads to the question, What *is* the main goal for all Christians? It's simple: to glorify God. That's what we were created to do.

We glorify God by obeying him and by using the special abilities God has given us to bring him praise. We were created to worship and glorify God. So ask yourself, *What is my game plan to glorify God?* Too many Christians are on cruise control. Are you just coasting through life with no real direction or goal? Are things like TV, video games, friends, or other earthly concerns more important to you than God is? It's time to get focused like those UConn Huskies. Find out where God has gifted you, and use those skills for his glory.

⟩ On the Ball

Create an acrostic with the word *focus* or *goal* to list some specific ways you can glorify God with your gifts. (An acrostic is where a word's letters are used to form a list of other words.) Here's an example using the word *goal*:

Go help elderly neighbor with yard work.
Opt to memorize Scripture.
Ask God to make me more like Jesus.
Listen to and obey parents.

⟩ COACH'S COMMENT

Bring all who claim me as their God, for I have made them for my glory. It was I who created them. ISAIAH 43:7

So you want to be an NFL star? How much do you like to read?

That's right—being in the NFL requires a ton of reading. No, you won't be reading Dr. Seuss or *Moby Dick*. And you probably won't pick up too much Shakespeare. But NFL players must read and memorize huge playbooks.

The NFL playbook is the lifeblood of every team. It includes every play that the offense and defense will run. Some playbooks are relatively small. Others are enormous. The playbook of Al Saunders, a longtime NFL offensive coach, was rumored to exceed 800 pages. To a normal person, an NFL playbook looks like a bunch of random phrases and diagrams of *X*s and *O*s. But to professional football players, it makes sense. Still, many rookies take several years to feel comfortable with a team's playbook, and most players never truly master it. Veteran NFL center Matt Birk told ESPN.com in 2007, "This is my tenth year in the league, and I still take my playbook home [to study it]."

What's the Score?

No matter how talented a player may be, he'll never succeed without knowing his play-book. Likewise, no Christian will succeed without knowing God's playbook: the Bible. Reading the Bible helps us grow spiritually and navigate through life. It is filled with wisdom unlike any other book on earth. But calling the Bible our "life playbook" doesn't do it justice. The Bible isn't just a book of rules or suggestions. It is the living, active Word of God. It is God speaking directly to us!

Reading the Bible is not optional for Christians. We are commanded to consistently soak up its contents. We should read God's Word every day and memorize what it says. Here are some of the benefits of knowing Scripture:

1. It is God's main source of revelation (Romans 16:25-26).
2. It makes us "wise for salvation" (2 Timothy 3:15).
3. It is the ultimate standard of truth (John 17:17).
4. It convicts us of sin (Romans 7:7).
5. It guides our paths (Psalm 119:105).
6. It trains us in righteousness (2 Timothy 3:16).
7. It will prosper us (Joshua 1:8).

And that's just for starters. Reading God's Word has countless benefits. Trust in Christ, know your Bible, and be a winner in life!

) On the Ball

Start a plan to read the entire Bible in one year.

) COACH'S COMMENT

Keep this Book of the Law always on your lips; meditate on it day and night, so that you may be careful to do everything written in it. Then you will be prosperous and successful. JOSHUA 1:8 (NIV)

A boy going blind helped the USC football team to truly see. In the fall of 2009, Jake Olson, a big University of Southern California football fan, received some terrible news: he was about to go completely blind. When Jake was one year old, cancerous tumors in both of his eyes forced doctors to remove his left eye. They saved his right one with chemotherapy and radiation. But when Jake turned 12, the cancer in his right eye returned a ninth time and couldn't be treated.

Jake's last wish before sight-ending surgery was to attend a USC football game. When former USC coach Pete Carroll heard about Jake, he invited him to practice. The team quickly fell in love with the skinny 12-year-old, who became an unofficial team mascot. He got to hang out with players in the locker room, give pep talks, and even walk down the steps of Los Angeles Memorial Coliseum with the team before a home game. After a successful surgery, Jake returned to USC, to the delight of the Trojans. Since then, he has stayed in touch with various USC players and Pete, who became the Seattle Seahawks' head coach in 2010. "Jake just reminded me that life is fragile," Trojans quarterback Matt Barkley told ESPN.com in December 2010. "To take advantage of every opportunity you get, whether it's twelve games, thirteen games, whether it's your life—you never know when it's going to be gone."

What's the Score?

Jake taught Matt and his USC teammates a valuable life lesson: life is short and unpredictable. We need to understand this too. We are not guaranteed good health or a certain number of years on earth. We could be gone tomorrow or live until we're 100 years old. Only God knows the number of our days.

Rather than frighten us, this thought should humble us and help us think more clearly. Since we have a limited amount of time on earth, we should fill those days with activities that glorify God. In Psalm 90, Moses pondered the greatness of God and the shortness of human life. He came away asking God for wisdom to live in a manner pleasing to the Lord. May we do the same!

> On the Ball

Write out three life goals you'd like to accomplish for God's glory. Put the paper in a place you can remember. Pray that God would help you achieve those goals, if they're his will.

> COACH'S COMMENT

Teach us to realize the brevity of life, so that we may grow in wisdom. PSALM 90:12

What's all this nonsense about Santa Claus being unathletic, overweight, and only willing to travel in first-class reindeer sleighs? Bah! Humbug! Every Christmas Eve, Santa and some of his holiday buddies (who all look curiously like people in costumes) put on a chilly water show at the National Harbor Marina in Prince George's County, Maryland.

The 2010 event, which marked the show's 25th anniversary, was performed in mid-30-degree weather and 34-degree water. Hope good ol' St. Nick wore his wet suit. With chattering teeth, Santa water-skied for the crowd while reindeer rode kneeboards, elves performed flips on hydrofoils, and a mischievous Grinch zigzagged on a jet ski. Frosty the Snowman even made an appearance in a slow-moving dinghy. The whole event makes you wonder if Santa & Co. is preparing to enter the annual Water Ski World Championships in the summer. Well, everybody but Frosty. Rumor has it he can't stand the heat.

What's the Score?

It's impossible to get through Christmas without being bombarded by TV specials, songs, mall sightings—and even winter water-skiing shows—that feature Santa Claus. But often lost in all the modern Christmas mythology is a story so improbable and incredible that it makes a silly tale about a jolly, white-bearded man on a one-night, worldwide toy-distribution mission seem believable. In fact, Jesus Christ coming to earth is the most amazing story in history.

Did God really become man? Yes, he did! Some 2,000 years ago, Jesus came to earth in human form to save us from our sins. Think for a moment how astounding this is. John 1 tells us that Jesus—God the Son—has existed for all time and was active in creation with God the Father and the Holy Spirit. Then at the Father's appointed time, the Son came to earth as a baby. His birth was not by normal human conception, but an indescribable miracle. As Matthew 1:23 says, he took the name Immanuel, which means "God is with us." Fully God and fully man, Jesus lived a perfect, sinless life and died a sinner's death so that we might receive eternal life by trusting in him. Then he rose from the dead and returned to heaven, where he is preparing an eternal home for all believers. That's an amazing story, and it's the one Christmas story you can believe in!

On the Ball
Read the account of Jesus' birth in Matthew 1:18–2:23.

COACH'S COMMENT
Look! The virgin will conceive a child! She will give birth to a son, and they will call him Immanuel, which means "God is with us." MATTHEW 1:23

The NBA wishes you a very merry Christmas. Now would you please put down your gifts and tune in to all the league's games today? Playing games on Christmas has become a hot topic in the NBA, which has increased the number of contests from two to five in recent years. Several prominent coaches, including the Los Angeles Lakers' Phil Jackson and the Orlando Magic's Stan Van Gundy, have spoken out against December 25 games. "It's like Christian holidays don't mean anything to them anymore," Phil told reporters before the Lakers hosted Miami on Christmas Day 2010. Stan resorted to sarcasm to make his point: "The NBA is Christmas, to me anyway," he joked. "It's what it's all about."

The reason the NBA plays games on Christmas is simple: money. Tickets for the Lakers-Heat Christmas game in 2010 averaged a whopping $556 each, according to a Fox Sports report. The report also said that the league's December 25 games averaged 7 million TV viewers between 2001 and 2009. That means huge TV contracts and advertising revenue for the NBA. "The league has been good to all of us in terms of what we get out of all these TV contracts and everything, so it would be a little disingenuous to complain too much," Stan told reporters in December 2009. "But if I had my way, we would take a five-day break at Christmas."

⬜⬜ What's the Score?

The fact is, money drives all professional sports. But money shouldn't drive us. Money is not wrong in and of itself. But the love of money is. The Bible is very clear on this. First Timothy 6:10 says, "The love of money is a root of all kinds of evil" (NIV).

Loving money is not only wrong; it's foolish. Money and possessions fade away. When we die, we can't take a single earthly treasure with us. We are to love God, not money or the stuff it can buy. God graciously provides us with what we need to meet our daily needs. We should never let money replace God as the object of our worship.

〉 On the Ball

We can determine what we love the most by considering how much time we spend on it. Keep a daily log of how much time you spend in prayer and God's Word compared to the following:

1. Video games
2. Watching TV/movies
3. Hanging out with friends
4. Playing sports
5. Doing other hobbies

〉 COACH'S COMMENT

The love of money is a root of all kinds of evil. Some people, eager for money, have wandered from the faith and pierced themselves with many griefs. 1 TIMOTHY 6:10 (NIV)

Surf's up. Actually, surf is way, way up! Every winter since 1986, dozens of surfers meet at Waimea Bay in northern Oahu for a big-wave surfing contest in Hawaii called the "Quiksilver in Memory of Eddie Aikau." Big-wave surfing is not for the faint of heart. It differs from traditional surfing because big-wave surfers tackle waves 20 feet or higher. It's a thrill ride—literally. At the 2009 "Eddie" tournament, 26-year-old Greg Long of California won first place for his masterful surfing of waves up to 50 feet high!

Still, that's child's play compare d to what some of the world's most daring surfers try. In January 2008, a group of surfers raced 105 miles off Southern California to catch what was believed at the time to be the largest waves ever ridden—storm-produced swells estimated at nearly 85 feet. That's higher than an eight-story building! To catch waves that big, surfers must be towed by jet ski to the wave's breaking point, where they release the towline and drop into the wave. While big-wave surfing provides an incomparable adrenaline rush, it can also be deadly. Wipeouts can send a surfer dozens of feet below the surface, where he or she can drown or be slammed into the ocean floor. In December 2007, California surfer Peter Davi died while riding 40-foot waves at Pebble Beach, California. Similar big-wave surfing deaths have occurred at other locations in California and Hawaii over the years. Hang ten if you must, but hang on for dear life!

⬜ What's the Score?

The ocean is an incredibly powerful part of nature. But guess what? The ocean, as awesome and devastating as it can be, is completely under God's control.

As the almighty Creator of the universe, God governs the waves, the wind, and all forces of nature. He is in charge of rain, thunder, and lightning. He rules over tsunamis, hurricanes, tornadoes, and earthquakes. He tells the mountains how high they can reach and the seas how far they can stretch. He tells the sun when to rise and set. He keeps the stars in their places and the planets in orbit. He is an awesome God who rules over all creation!

〉 On the Ball

Look into the sky on a clear night, consider God's awesome power in ruling the universe, and give him praise!

〉 COACH'S COMMENT

You rule the oceans. You subdue their storm-tossed waves. PSALM 89:9

"The Greatest." It's a title that, by its very nature, can be given only to one athlete. In boxing circles, it is often bestowed upon Muhammad Ali. From the time he rocketed to fame as a light heavyweight gold medalist at the 1960 Olympics until his last fight in 1981, Muhammad cemented his status as a boxing legend and a cultural icon. He finished his career with a 56-5 record, including 37 knockouts. Eleven different times he ended the year as the heavyweight world champion.

His epic battles with the likes of George Foreman, Joe Frazier, Sonny Liston, Ken Norton, and Floyd Patterson are some of the most famous prizefights ever. If Ali isn't the greatest, he is certainly on the short list as one of the greatest boxers of all time.

☐☐ What's the Score?

As fans, we love to debate who the greatest athletes of all time are, whatever the sport. Depending on whom you talk to, Ali might get competition in boxing for the title of "The Greatest" from Sugar Ray Robinson, Joe Louis, or Rocky Marciano.

But there is one name that is far greater than any athlete, celebrity, or king. And there's no competition! His name is Jesus Christ. He is the Son of God, who was with the Father at the time of creation, came to earth in human form, lived a sinless life, died on the cross as a substitute for our sins, and rose from the dead to confirm his deity and saving power. Some people may argue that Jesus isn't the greatest, but in the end they're going to lose that argument. Philippians 2:10-11 says, "At the name of Jesus every knee should bow, in heaven and on earth and under the earth, and every tongue confess that Jesus Christ is Lord, to the glory of God the Father." Notice that it doesn't say that *some* knees will bow. One day everybody will bow and acknowledge that Jesus is Lord. And there's no arguing that!

⟩ On the Ball

What are some of Jesus' characteristics that make him "the greatest"? Get a piece of paper and write down a short list. Then hang that list in your bathroom to remind yourself to give honor to God.

⟩ COACH'S COMMENT

God elevated him to the place of highest honor and gave him the name above all other names, that at the name of Jesus every knee should bow, in heaven and on earth and under the earth, and every tongue confess that Jesus Christ is Lord, to the glory of God the Father. PHILIPPIANS 2:9-11

Duke University men's basketball coach Mike Krzyzewski wasn't just miffed or annoyed. He was, in his own words, "really angry." On this day in 2010, Mike didn't like what he saw from his team in practice. The Blue Devils were about to hit the road to face the University of North Carolina–Greensboro, and Mike wasn't happy with how his players were adjusting to the loss of injured point guard Kyrie Irving. Maybe the Blue Devils were a little overconfident. At the time, they were the defending national champions with an 11-0 record and a No. 1 ranking. Or maybe they were distracted by the fact that Mike was about to become the second-winningest coach in NCAA history.

No matter. Mike lit into his players, telling them they were soft, spoiled, and unprepared for the rigors of the upcoming Atlantic Coast Conference portion of their schedule. "That's why I got angry," Mike later told a reporter. "I've been blessed with the ability to get angry. Anger is good when you use it to make something better."

⬜⬜ What's the Score?

Mike's coaching abilities are unquestioned. His success speaks for itself. The Bible wouldn't say getting angry is something you're blessed with. In fact, the Bible consistently tells us to avoid anger. Proverbs 27:4 says that "anger is cruel." Ecclesiastes 7:9 says, "Anger labels you a fool." Ephesians 4:31 and Colossians 3:8 command us to get rid of anger. James 1:20 tells us, "Human anger does not produce the righteousness God desires." And Psalm 37:8 clearly says, "Stop being angry!"

Occasionally, situations might arise in which anger isn't a sin. If a bully hits your little sibling, then anger is understandable. But even in these situations, Ephesians 4:26 reminds us, "Don't sin by letting anger control you." Instead of showing anger, we should show patience and love to others. After all, isn't that what God has done for us? The Bible is filled with references to God's anger, but his is a righteous anger because God is holy. That's good news for us, because sin angers God. But rather than punish us in anger, he showed us love and compassion by sending his Son, Jesus Christ.

⟩ On the Ball

To avoid sinning in your anger, try pausing, taking a deep breath, and thinking before you speak or act.

⟩ COACH'S COMMENT

Stop being angry! Turn from your rage! Do not lose your temper—it only leads to harm.
PSALM 37:8

Go ahead and blink. Don't worry—you won't miss a thing. The annual Rickshaw Challenge isn't the world's slowest race, but it's close. The Rickshaw Challenge is a series of four annual automobile races in India using—you guessed it—rickshaws. If you don't know what an auto rickshaw is, picture a goofy-looking, three-wheeled, motorized bicycle that includes covered seating for three people. Add a seven-horsepower lawnmower engine, and you've got a pretty good idea. These vehicles can cruise at 35 miles per hour and top out at 50. It's not exactly NASCAR.

Anyone with a need for (not-so-much) speed can enter any of four separate Rickshaw Challenge races. They are held along various courses in India at different times of the year. The 2010–2011 Classic Run, for instance, was a 10-day trek starting on December 29 that stretched 590 miles from Chennai to Poovar. Auto rickshaws are not the world's safest vehicles. The Rickshaw Challenge website admits that they are "not well-regarded in safety crash tests." But fear not, rickshaw drivers! The race's website also gives us this good news: "Because auto rickshaws have low maximum speeds, they're not likely to get into major crashes."

What's the Score?

So maybe your heart isn't set on entering the next Rickshaw Challenge. After all, who likes slow? Have you ever wondered why God often doesn't answer prayers right away? Or why God fails to judge wicked people more quickly? Or why Jesus hasn't returned yet? If we're not careful, we can start thinking God is slow or distant or that he has forgotten us.

But he is none of those things. The Lord's timing is not like ours. He is the eternal God of the universe, without beginning or end. While a month or a year may seem like an eternity to us, it's a microscopic speck on God's timeline. As 2 Peter 3:8 says, "A day is like a thousand years to the Lord, and a thousand years is like a day." This truth calls for faith, patience, and persistence on our part. Keep praying. Keep trusting God. His timing isn't slow; it's perfect. He will do what's best for you . . . in his time.

) On the Ball

Keep a prayer journal to track when God answers your prayers. Some answers might come the same day. Others might take years. But God's timing is always right.

) COACH'S COMMENT

You must not forget this one thing, dear friends: A day is like a thousand years to the Lord, and a thousand years is like a day. The Lord isn't really being slow about his promise, as some people think. No, he is being patient for your sake. **2 PETER 3:8-9**

Imagine being Noah's son trying to build a boat. Intimidating, huh? Big shoes to fill? That's probably how Marcus Jordan felt when he picked up a basketball. But on this day in 2010, Marcus, a six-foot-three-inch sophomore guard at the University of Central Florida, enjoyed perhaps the finest performance of his young college career. He scored 22 of his game-high 26 points in the second half to lead the Knights to a 68–62 comeback win over a strong Princeton team, earning UCF Holiday Classic MVP honors in the process.

Marcus, as you might have guessed, is the son of NBA Hall of Famer Michael Jordan, who is considered by many to be the greatest basketball player ever. So what do you do when your father is a former five-time NBA MVP with six NBA championship rings and a face that is recognized across the globe? For one, you have to put up with a lot of heckling. Opposing fans taunted Marcus in virtually every road game, unfavorably comparing him with his dad whenever he missed a shot. But Marcus certainly held his own at UCF. As one of the team's leading scorers, he helped the Knights crack the top-25 national rankings for the first time ever in December 2010. Not bad for a kid with a famous father.

⛹ What's the Score?

Fair or not, Marcus Jordan will always be compared to his world-famous father. It's human nature. We love to compare people to others. But King David knew better than to compare the one true God to the silly, little gods that were being worshiped in his day. In David's lifetime, ancient Israel was surrounded by pagan nations that worshiped false gods. David knew all these other deities were nothing compared to God. That's why he wrote in Psalm 86:8, "Among the gods there is none like you, Lord; no deeds can compare with yours" (NIV).

The God of the Bible cannot be compared to anything in this universe. He holds all knowledge and power. Nothing exists apart from him. No other religion or god provides true forgiveness of sins, like God did through his Son. There's no need to compare God to other gods, because there's no comparison!

⟩ On the Ball

List five reasons why the God of the Bible is greater than any man-made god:

1. _____
2. _____
3. _____
4. _____
5. _____

⟩ COACH'S COMMENT

Among the gods there is none like you, Lord; no deeds can compare with yours.

PSALM 86:8 (NIV)

New Year's Eve is a time for joy and celebration. But in the sports world, there was nothing to be happy about on this day in 1972. That was the night the great Roberto Clemente died. Roberto, a native of Puerto Rico, was one of baseball's all-time best. In an 18-year Hall of Fame career, the Pittsburgh Pirates' strong-armed outfielder batted .317 with 3,000 hits, 245 home runs, and 1,305 RBIs. He was a 12-time All-Star who won four National League batting titles, 12 Gold Glove Awards, the 1966 National League MVP, and the 1971 World Series MVP. He also led the previously hapless Pirates to four play-off appearances and two World Series titles (1960 and 1971).

But on that New Year's Eve night in 1972, Roberto died tragically in a plane crash while attempting to bring relief supplies to earthquake victims in Nicaragua. He was only 38 years old.

☐☐ What's the Score?

Why did Roberto die, especially when he was trying to do good for others? Tragedies like this often cause us to ask tough questions about life. We wonder, *Why does God let bad things happen to good people?* Left to our own limited understanding, we can blame God and question his goodness and love. But this is backward reasoning. It assumes that God owes us something when, actually, he doesn't. A better question to ask is this: Why does God allow anything good to happen to us at all?

When God created the world, he made everything good. Bad things like death, evil, tragedy, sickness, and sorrow entered the world because of sin when Adam and Eve disobeyed God's command. The Bible says sin deserves death (Romans 6:23). As sinful beings, we don't deserve anything good. The fact that *anything* good happens to us is a gift from a loving God. He even uses trials and tragedies for the good of true believers, although he doesn't always explain why they happen. Job understood this when he said, "Should we accept only good things from the hand of God and never anything bad?" (Job 2:10). Instead of questioning God's goodness, we should be thankful that he hasn't given us what we really deserve. Incredibly, he blesses us with life, family, and friends, and offers us what we *don't* deserve—salvation from sins through his Son, Jesus Christ. He is a good God indeed!

⟩ On the Ball

When difficulty comes, say a prayer of thanksgiving to God, even if you don't understand why it's happening.

⟩ COACH'S COMMENT

Job replied, "You talk like a foolish woman. Should we accept only good things from the hand of God and never anything bad?" JOB 2:10
